STABILITY IN THE FINANCIAL SYSTEM

THE JEROME LEVY ECONOMICS INSTITUTE SERIES

General Editor: Dimitri B. Papadimitriou, Levy Institute Professor of Economics, Bard College, Annandale-on-Hudson, New York

Ghislain Deleplace and Edward J. Nell (*editors*)
MONEY IN MOTION

Geoffrey Harcourt, Alessandro Roncaglia and Robin Rowley (*editors*)
INCOME AND EMPLOYMENT THEORY AND PRACTICE

Dimitri B. Papadimitriou (*editor*)
ASPECTS OF DISTRIBUTION OF WEALTH AND INCOME
STABILITY IN THE FINANCIAL SYSTEM

Dimitri B. Papadimitriou and Edward N. Wolff (*editors*)
POVERTY AND PROSPERITY IN THE USA IN THE LATE TWENTIETH CENTURY

Stability in the Financial System

Edited by

Dimitri B. Papadimitriou
Levy Institute Professor of Economics
Bard College
Annandale-on-Hudson
New York

First published in Great Britain 1996 by
MACMILLAN PRESS LTD
Houndmills, Basingstoke, Hampshire RG21 6XS
and London
Companies and representatives
throughout the world

A catalogue record for this book is available
from the British Library.

ISBN 0–333–61506–9

First published in the United States of America 1996 by
ST. MARTIN'S PRESS, INC.,
Scholarly and Reference Division,
175 Fifth Avenue,
New York, N.Y. 10010

ISBN 0–312–15935–8

Library of Congress Cataloging-in-Publication Data
Stability in the financial system / edited by Dimitri B.
Papadimitriou.
p. cm. — (The Jerome Levy Economics Institute series)
"First published in Great Britain 1996 by Macmillan Press Ltd"—T.p.
verso.
Includes bibliographical references and index.
ISBN 0–312–15935–8
1. Finance—United States. 2. Financial institutions—United
States. 3. Banks and banking—United States. 4. Banks and banking–
–United States—State supervision. I. Papadimitriou, Dimitri B.
II. Series.
HG181.5792 1996
332.1'0973—dc20 96–10557
CIP

---

10 9 8 7 6 5 4 3 2 1
05 04 03 02 01 00 99 98 97 96

Printed in Great Britain by
Ipswich Book Co Ltd, Ipswich, Suffolk

Contents

List of Figures

List of Tables

The Jerome Levy Economics Institute of Bard College

Founded in 1986, The Jerome Levy Economics Institute of Bard College is an autonomous, independently endowed research organization. It is nonpartisan, open to the examination of diverse points of view, and dedicated to public service.

The Institute believes in the potential of economics to improve the human condition. Its purpose is to generate viable, effective public policy responses to important economic problems. It is concerned with issues that profoundly affect the quality of life in the United States, in other highly industrialized nations, and in countries with developing economies.

The Institute's present research agenda includes such issues as financial instability, poverty and problems associated with the distribution of income and wealth. Other research interests include the issues of public and private investment and their relationship to productivity, competitiveness, and the prospects for growth and employment. In all its endeavors, the Institute places heavy emphasis on the values of personal freedom and justice. The opinions and policy proposals expressed in this volume are those of the authors and do not necessarily represent those of the Institute's Board of Governors or Board of Advisors.

Acknowledgements

I would like to thank the Board of Governors of the Jerome Levy Economics Institute of Bard College for sponsoring the on-going research project on the *Reconstitution of the Financial Structure*. As part of this project, a number of distinguished scholars visit the Institute and participate at conferences and seminars of profound importance to the policy aspects of this project. I am indebted in many ways to all of them, and the contributors of the essays included in this volume for their cooperation and readiness in carrying out revisions. I want to thank Hyman P. Minsky for the direction of this project, his constant encouragement, support and friendship. Deborah C. Treadway, my assistant, provided invaluable research and other assistance in preparing this manuscript. Finally, sincere thanks are due to Tim Farmiloe and Giovanna Davitti, my publishing editors, and to Keith Povey for his editorial assistance.

DIMITRI B. PAPADIMITRIOU

Notes on the Contributors

James R. Barth, PhD, Ohio State University; Lowder Eminent Scholar in Finance at Auburn University. He was the Chief Economist of the Office of Thrift Supervision and prior to that the Chief Economist of the Federal Home Loan Bank Board. Dr Barth has also been a Professor of Economics at George Washington University, Visiting Scholar at the US Congressional Budget Office, Visiting Scholar at the Federal Reserve Bank of Atlanta and Associate Director of the Economics Program at the National Science Foundation. He has published more than 100 articles in professional journals and books, is the author of *The Great Savings and Loan Debacle* published by the American Enterprise Institute, co-editor of *The Reform of Federal Deposit Insurance: Disciplining the Government and Protecting the Taxpayers* published by HarperBusiness in 1992 and co-author of *The Future of American Banking* published by M. E. Sharpe in 1992.

R. Dan Brumbaugh, Jr., PhD, George Washington University. Dr Brumbaugh is the author of *The Collapse of Federally Insured Depositories: The Savings and Loans as Precursor* (Garland, 1993) and *Thrifts Under Siege: Restoring Order to American Banking* (Harper & Row, 1988). He is co-editor (with James R. Barth) of *The Reform of Deposit Insurance: Disciplining the Government and Protecting Taxpayers* (Harper/Collins Business, 1992) and co-author (with James R. Barth and Robert E. Litan) of *The Future of American Banking* (M. E. Sharpe, Inc., 1992). Dr Brumbaugh has served as a consultant to financial service firms and industries, to the House of Representatives Subcommittee on Financial Institutions, and most recently to the National Commission on Financial Institutions Reform, Recovery and Enforcement. He was Visiting Scholar, the Federal Home Loan Bank Board, was the Deputy Chief Economist at the Bank Board and was President and Chief Executive Officer of Independence Savings and Loan headquartered in Vallejo, California.

Gerard Caprio, Jr., PhD, University of Michigan. Dr Caprio pursues research and contributes to World Bank operations on financial sector issues in developing and reforming socialist economies. His volume (with I. Atiyas and J. Hanson), *Financial Reform: Theory and Experience* draws lessons for financial reform from a wide range of case studies as well as various analytical pieces. An earlier volume (with Patrick Honohan), *Monetary Policy Instruments for Developing Countries*, serves as a handbook for central bankers interested in moving away from direct controls to more indirect methods of monetary policy implementation. Prior to joining the Bank, Dr Caprio was Vice President and head of the global economics unit at J.P. Morgan where, among other duties, he wrote articles for *World Financial Markets*, Morgan's flagship periodical. He also worked as an economist in the International Finance Division of the Board of Governors of the Federal Reserve System.

Gary A. Dymski, PhD, University of Massachusetts–Amherst; Assistant Professor of Economics, University of California–Riverside. He was a research fellow in Economic Studies at the Brookings Institution and taught at the University of Southern California. Dr Dymski has written extensively on banking and monetary macroeconomics. He has two co-edited volumes, *New Directions in Monetary Macroeconomics: Essays in the Tradition of Hyman P. Minsky* (University of Michigan Press) with Robert Pollin, and *Transforming the US Financial Systems: An Equitable and Efficient Structure for the 21st Century* (M. E. Sharpe, Inc.), co-edited with Gerry Epstein and Robert Pollin. Dr Dymski is presently writing a book on banking, race and development in Los Angeles.

Catherine England, PhD, Texas A & M; President of England Economics, an Alexandria, Virginia consulting firm specializing in regulatory analysis with an emphasis in the area of financial institutions. She is also an adjunct faculty member at both The American and Georgetown Universities. Dr England was previously with the Cato Institute as Director of Regulatory Studies and Senior Editor of *Regulation* magazine. She is the editor of two books, *The Financial Services Revolution: Policy Directions for the Future* (co-edited with Thomas Huertas) and *Governing Banking's Future: Markets vs. Regulation*. She is the author of numerous articles in both popular and professional publications.

Mark D. Flood, PhD, University of North Carolina at Chapel Hill; Economist at the Federal Reserve Bank of St Louis. He won the St Louis Federal Reserve's annual award for 'Best *Review* Article' in 1991. His research interests include financial markets and institutions, and bank market structure and regulatory policy.

Gillian Garcia began her career as an Assistant Professor in the School of Business at the University of California–Berkeley. From there she became a consultant and senior economist at the Federal Reserve Bank of Chicago and then director of a new group of finance specialists and economists studying problems in the financial sector at the US General Accounting Office. She currently manages the oversight of banks, thrifts, credit unions and their regulators for the Senate Banking Committee and has worked on the FIRREA and FDICIA legislation. Dr Garcia is a Distinguished Professorial Lecturer in the Business School of Georgetown, has published articles in the area of money, banking and the financial markets and is the co-author of four books, two on financial legislation. Her latest book is: *The Federal Reserve: Lender of Last Resort.*

R. Alton Gilbert, PhD, Texas A & M. He joined the Research Department of the Federal Reserve Bank of St Louis as an Economist in 1970, was promoted to Senior Economist in 1976, to Research Officer in 1982, to Assistant Vice President in 1984, and Vice President in 1993.

George G. Kaufman, PhD, University of Iowa; Professor, Loyola University of Chicago and consultant to the Federal Reserve Bank of Chicago. He has also taught at the University of Southern California, Stanford University, and the University of California–Berkeley, and was a visiting scholar at the Federal Reserve Bank of San Francisco and the Office of the Comptroller of the Currency. He has published extensively in the *American Economic Review*, *Journal of Finance*, *Journal of Financial and Quantitative Analysis*, and other professional journals. Professor Kaufman is also the author of numerous books, including *The U.S. Financial System: Money, Markets, and Institutions* (fifth edition, Prentice-Hall, 1992); *Perspectives on Safe and Sound Banking: Past. Present, and Future* (MIT Press, 1986) (co-author); *Restructuring the American Financial System* (Kluwer, 1990) (editor); and the annual *Research in Financial Services* (JAI Press) (editor). He is presently co-editor of the *Journal of Financial Services Research* and is on the editorial boards of a number of major professional journals, including the *Journal of Money, Credit and Banking, Journal of Financial Research and Contemporary Policy Issues*.

Randall S. Kroszner, PhD, Harvard University; Assistant Professor of Business Economics at the University of Chicago's Graduate School of Business where he teaches money and banking and international financial institutions and markets. His research interests include financial regulation, comparative financial history, and monetary economics. His articles have appeared in scholarly journals, including the *Journal of Political*

Economy and the *Journal of Money, Credit, and Banking*, policy journals, including The Public Interest and the Cato Journal, and numerous books, including the *New Palgrave Dictionary of Money and Finance*. Professor Kroszner was an economist on the President's Council of Economic Advisers during 1987–88 and a visiting scholar at the Securities and Exchange Commission in 1992.

Donald J. Mathieson, PhD, Stanford University; Chief, Developing Countries Studies Division, Research Department of the International Monetary Fund. He has taught at Columbia and has previously served as an Advisor and Chief of the Capital Markets and Financial Studies Division of the Research Department. He has published in the areas of international finance, development finance and monetary theory and policy.

Hyman P. Minsky, PhD, Harvard University; Distinguished Scholar at The Jerome Levy Economics Institute of Bard College, and Professor of Economics Emeritus at Washington University–St Louis. Professor Minsky is the author of *John Maynard Keynes, Can 'It' Happen Again*, and *Stabilizing an Unstable Economy*.

Larry R. Mote, Fulbright Scholar at the University of Cologne before doing graduate work in economics at Cornell University. He is an Economic Adviser and Vice President at the Federal Reserve Bank of Chicago. His responsibilities include supervision of the Research Department's bank merger and bank holding company casework, writing on bank regulatory topics for the Reserve Bank's bimonthly review and other publications, commenting on proposed regulatory changes. In 1991 he took a leave of absence from the Bank to serve as a visiting scholar with the Congressional Budget Office, where he helped to prepare testimony on the Treasury's proposals for deposit insurance reform. His current research interests include the effects on bank risk of entry into bank securities activities, the local impact of bank failures, the impact of deregulation on the profitability of depository institutions, and the problems of measuring the performance of bank regulatory agencies.

Richard W. Nelson, PhD, Yale University; Vice President at Wells Fargo Bank. He has also served as Chief Economist of the Federal Home Loan Bank of San Francisco, where he directed research on S&L issues, served on the Bank's Credit Committee, participated in the financial management of the Bank and marketing of its credit products, and produced the Bank's

Cost of Funds Index. Previously, Dr Nelson headed banking and financial research groups at Chemical Bank and at the Federal Reserve Bank of New York. He has served as a lecturer at the Haas School of Business at the University of California, Berkeley, and as Professor of Finance and Economics at the State University of New York, Binghamton. He is a member of the Blue Chip Financial Forecast Panel.

Dimitri B. Papadimitriou, PhD, Graduate Faculty, New School for Social Research; Executive Vice President and Levy Institute Professor of Economics, Bard College and Executive Director of the Jerome Levy Economics Institute and the Bard Center. Visiting Scholar, Center for Economic Planning and Research (Athens, Greece); Wye Fellow, Aspen Institute. Dr Papadimitriou is the editor of *Profits, Deficits, and Instability* (Macmillan and St Martin's Press, 1992); *Aspects of Distribution of Income and Wealth* (Macmillan, 1994); with Steven Fazzari, *Financial Conditions and Macroeconomic Performance: Essays in Honor of Hyman P. Minsky* (M.E. Sharpe, 1992); and with Edward N. Wolff, *Poverty and Prosperity in America at the Close of the Twentieth Century* (Macmillan and St Martin's Press, 1993).

Ronnie J. Phillips, Resident Scholar at The Jerome Levy Economics Institute of Bard College and Professor of Economics at Colorado State University in Fort Collins. He received his PhD at the University of Texas at Austin and previously taught at Texas A&M University. He has published articles in the *Southern Economic Journal*, the *Journal of International Economics*, and other professional journals as well as book chapters. His most recent articles are: 'Persistence of the Veblenian "Old Japan": Organizational Efficiency as a Wellspring of Competitiveness', in *Revista Internazionale di Scienze Economiche e Commerciali*, forthcoming (co-authored with Terutomo Ozawa) and 'How Regulation Turned a Winner into a Loser', *American Banker*, 28 October 1992.

Bernard Shull, PhD, University of Wisconsin; Professor in the Department of Economics at Hunter College, a member of the Graduate Faculty of the City University of New York, and a Special Consultant to National Economic Research Associates, Inc. He has also taught in the Departments of Finance and Economics at the Wharton School, University of Pennsylvania, at the University of Wisconsin–Milwaukee, and the University of Illinois. Prior to teaching at Hunter College, Professor Shull held various positions with the Federal Reserve Board, including Associate Advisor to the Board of Governors, Chief of the Banking

Markets Section and Research Director for the Federal Reserve's Reappraisal of the Discount Mechanism. He was also a Senior Economist in the Office of the Comptroller of the Currency, and Economist at the Federal Reserve Bank of Philadelphia. Recent publications include: 'How Should Bank Regulatory Agencies Be Organized', *Contemporary Policy Issues*, (January 1993) and 'Risk-taking by Thrift Institutions: A Framework for Empirical Investigation' (with D. Golbe), *Contemporary Policy Issues*, (July 1991). Forthcoming publications include 'Banking and Commerce in the United States', *Journal of Banking and Finance*, and 'Savings Institutions and Credit Unions', *Encyclopedia of New York*, and 'Interest Rate Risk and Capital Adequacy' (with Gerald Haanweck).

Kenneth Spong, MA, University of Chicago; Federal Reserve Bank of Kansas City. He is in the Policy and Special Projects Department, engaged in research in various topics relating to the regulation, supervision, and performance of banks and other financial institutions. His research work includes the performance of banks acquired on an interstate basis, banking consolidation and competition, relationship between examiner loan classifications and subsequent loan performance, problem bank characteristics and resolutions, and banking reform issues – deposit insurance, broader powers, and narrow banking. He has also published a book on the basics of banking regulation, which is entitled *Banking Regulation: ILS Purposes. Implementation, and Effects*.

Lawrence H. Summers, PhD., Harvard University; Undersecretary for International Economics, US Treasury, formerly Vice President and Chief Economist, The World Bank. Dr Summers is the Nathaniel Ropes Professor of Political Economy, Harvard University. Professor Summers has published widely in most economic journals.

Richard Sylla, PhD, Harvard University; Henry Kaufman Professor of the History of Financial Institutions and Markets and Professor of Economics at the Stern School of Business of New York University. He is also a Research Associate of the National Bureau of Economic Research. He is the author of *The American Capital Market, 1846–1914* (1975), co-author of *The Evolution of the American Economy* (1993; first edition 1980) and co-editor of *Patterns of European Industrialization – The Nineteenth Century* (1991), and of journal articles, essays, and reviews in economics and economic history. He is a former editor of *The Journal of Economic History* and served as a consultant to such firms as Citibank and Chase Manhattan Bank.

David C. Wheelock, Assistant Professor in the Department of Economics at the University of Texas at Austin, and is presently a visiting scholar at the Federal Reserve Bank of St Louis. Dr Wheelock's research interests are the history of Federal Reserve policy making, bank regulation, and deposit insurance. His recent publications include *The Strategy and Consistency of Federal Reserve Monetary Policy, 1924–1933* (Cambridge University Press, 1991), 'Deposit Insurance and Bank Failures: New Evidence from the 1920's', *Economic Inquiry* (July 1992), and 'Regulation and Bank Failures: New Evidence from the Agricultural Collapse of the 1920's', *The Journal of Economic History* (December 1992).

L. Randall Wray, PhD, Washington University–St Louis; Research Associate, The Jerome Levy Economics Institute and Associate Professor of Economics, University of Denver. Dr Wray's numerous publications include *Money and Credit in Capitalist Economies: The Endogenous Money Approach*, 'Minsky's Financial Instability Hypothesis and Endogeneity of Money', in *Financial Conditions and Macroeconomic Performance: Essays in Honor of Hyman P. Minsky* (edited by Steven Fazzari and Dimitri B. Papadimitriou), and articles in many economic journals.

1 Stability in the US Financial System

Dimitri B. Papadimitriou

1.1 HISTORICAL PERSPECTIVES

The essays in this volume attempt to fulfill a three-fold purpose: first, to review and analyze the success of the legislative package of the 1930s, including the Emergency Banking Act of 1933, the Banking Act of 1935 and other related legislation, which in combination produced the longest period of financial stability in the history of the United States, lasting 50 years or so, until the 1980s. An understanding of the events that led to those reforms may provide a parallel to the pressing issues presently facing the banking and financial system in the US.

Second, to examine the reforms that have been implemented during the last decade and to answer the question of why, in recent years, we have had so many banking and financial market disruptions. We know that the answers vary, and include: overextension of the safety net because of the 'too big to fail' doctrine that provides *de facto* full insurance on deposits; lack of market discipline; and, pressure from the investor community for larger profits. While there is a lot of truth in all these observations, the answer, as will be indicated later, lies elsewhere.

And third, to explore the development and implementation of a set of new policy proposals which would reform and modernize the US financial system, and alter the supervisory arrangements associated with the operation of that system. The new organizational framework will insure the financing of the capital development of our economy and the safety of a payments system.

Policy proposals are not always politically 'digestible', especially if they are not for the near term. In response to a remark addressed to him in February 1933, regarding the great anxiety that bank closings were causing many millions of innocent depositors, Rexford Tugwell, the future Assistant Secretary of Agriculture in the Roosevelt Administration proposed, 'let them [banks] bust – then we'll get things on a sound basis'. Was this a proper policy response? I think not. I hope not.

The existing set of banking regulations is essentially obsolete. It was instituted in the 1930s on three premises: first, that banks have a unique role in the financial markets; second, that the federal government has a responsibility to safeguard the soundness of the financial structure by regulating and supervising banks; and third, that domestic financial markets are insulated from the turbulent international markets (Sellon 1988). When financial crises both on the national level – thrift industry problems – and international – Less Developed Countries (LDC) debt – occur, the concern and motivation for reform is heightened. Furthermore, the increasing role of nonbank institutions – including pension funds, mutual funds and insurance companies – and the ensuing competitive pressure they exert on traditional banks, along with the global nature of financial markets and the introduction of esoteric and in some cases exotic types of financial instruments, generically named derivatives, are not reflected in the existing regulatory framework. Financial reform, therefore, first and foremost must be consistent with and sensitive to the new and evolving high-tech financial marketplace. Banking regulation should, then, seek to foster two critical structural objectives: (1) ensure the long-term stability of the financial system, and (2) promote the financing of the capital development of the economy. In addressing these two objectives, reform must necessarily deal with the issues of linkage and transparency between banks, nonbank banks and non-financial firms, competitive market structures, and the safety and soundness of the payments system.

The banking crisis of the 1930s as a decisive episode in the history of the American economy has been interpreted both as significant (Litan, 1987) and exaggerated (White, 1984). It is, however, considered a turning point, even though the explanations for its root causes vary. One such explanation couples the incompetence of banks' management with the public lack of confidence in banks, as factors causing an illiquidity, mostly of a localized nature, rather than an insolvency crisis (Friedman and Schwartz, 1963). Another attributes banks' weakened ability to withstand regional economic difficulties to excessive regulatory constraints (White, 1984). Yet a third points to an inherent system instability that carried into the Depression years. President Franklin D. Roosevelt declared a 'bank holiday' to stave off the collapse of the US financial system. The legislation that followed these unenviable times gave birth to the federal deposit insurance which provided depositors safety for their deposits, and soundness and stability in the banking structure. The deposit insurance came with a revised set of compliance regulations to ensure the protection of the federal insurance agencies from excessive risks undertaken by banks. There were other legislative provisions included in the Banking Act of 1933; that is, Regulation Q on interest rates, Glass–Steagall restrictions relating to investment banking activities for banks and bank holding companies, and McFadden Act restrictions on interstate banking, which were designed to avail credit fairly and equitably, and to control the economic and political power of banks. Richard Sylla, in the next chapter, reviews the financial reforms of the 1930s extensively, and contrasts them with those of earlier periods of the US economic history. Sylla uses this rich background to draw a number of parallels that suggest where and how the present system should and could be reformed. David Wheelock in his commentary to Sylla's chapter, casts his agreement and, reinforcing Sylla's view of the successes and failures of the New Deal reforms, offers his own interpretation. At the end, he argues that reforms can be successful once ideological and political interests are put aside. Randall Kroszner, also commenting on Sylla's chapter, echoes Wheelock's observations of the need to distinguish the various perspectives which influence the political process leading to regulatory reform: 'ideological preference', 'public', and 'private interest'. Kroszner, concentrating on a specific 1930s legislation (the Glass–Steagall Act), cautions that strict reliance on the 'public interest' perspective might not necessarily yield good legislative results.

As was mentioned earlier, one of the most significant pieces of the 1930s banking legislation was federal deposit insurance. Deposit guarantees, on the federal level, were opposed by many in the 1930s, including initially President Roosevelt, and by the bankers' lobby up to the very end, as Mark Flood points out in Chapter 3. It was not surprising, therefore, that so many attempts prior to the 1930s to institute a federal *insurance* or government *guaranty* on deposits had 'failed in Congress – more than 150 times in the preceding 50 years'. The opposition, Flood suggests in his painstaking documentation, was not for the obvious reasons of moral hazard and 'actuarial infeasibility', but rather because of required regulatory changes relating to bank chartering and monitoring applied in conjunction with the system's duality of both federal and state involvement. In the rush to ascribe the recent Savings and Loan (S&L) debacle of the 1990s to the flaws of deposit insurance – excessive risks because of *de facto* federal guaranty of deposits in any amount – we may be ignoring other causes for the system's breakdown. Nelson (Chapter 4), while partly agreeing with Flood (Chapter 3), advances the proposition that inadequate supervision, especially in appraising risk, deregulation policies, the interfering effects of political interests on banks, and economic and financial instability causing interest-rates volatility contributed to the system's ineffectiveness, and cannot be pushed aside.

Federal deposit insurance was not the only legislative option to restore the public's confidence in the banking system of the 1930s. Ronnie Phillips (Chapter 5) chronicles with extraordinary detail the efforts of a group of economists at the University of Chicago to have their plan of monetary reform, advocating the abandonment of fractional reserves in favor of 100 per cent reserves, considered by the Roosevelt Administration and Congress. The plan, known as 'The Chicago Plan' might have averted the calamity of the recent S&L bail-outs, as Phillips points out, but may not have been successful in alleviating the credit crunch of the time. The plan's role, however, in shaping the New Deal banking legislation (1933–5) was unquestionably important then, as are now the current reform proposals for 'core' or 'narrow' banking.

1.2 ISSUES OF FINANCIAL REFORM

Economic or political reforms do not just happen. Empirical evidence shows that reforms, indeed all kinds of reforms, follow a crisis. This, as we saw, was the case in the 1930s that resulted in the enactment of wide-ranging and far-reaching legislation, as is also the case in the recent flurry to reform that started in 1989, with the passage of the Financial Institutions Reform, Recovery and Enforcement Act (FIRREA). To be sure, there have been other legislative enactments in the 1970s and 1980s – that is, the 1970 Amendment to the Bank Holding Company Act of 1956, the Community Reinvestment Act of 1978 (CRA), and the Depository Institutions Deregulation and Monetary Control Act of 1980 (DIDMCA) – that have had major effects in the organization and operation of financial services firms in the United States. It has been observed, nevertheless, that a very long time elapses before legislation is enacted. There seem to be two kinds of time lags: one that may be called *recognition* lag, the other *process* lag. The recognition lag usually follows a political or economic crisis, or a serious event of some magnitude, causing a consensus on the need to rectify the crisis or event by beginning a process of change (reform). The process lag is the time period required for the legislative process to go through the traditional steps for the change to be enacted. Even though these time lags are universally observed, the key point is that their duration is much longer in the United States than in other industrialized countries. Firsthand observation of these processes for two countries, the US and the UK respectively, reveals significant differences which are illustrative of this, and instructive as well, especially when the process time lags in the US have been and may, in the future, become detrimental to the stability of the financial system. This view, however, by no means should be taken to mean that 'fast track' legislative action is necessarily better. Rather, it is important to emphasize the significant role of special interests, and the costs entailed during extended periods of inaction, as the example of the 1990s long-lived S&L bail-outs testifies. The differences in implementing legislation are carefully explored in Gillian Garcia's essay on *The Political Economy of Financial Reform in the US and the UK*, which is the subject matter of Chapter 6.

An important issue of financial reform that has commanded the attention of academicians and lawmakers alike, focuses on the organizational structure of government supervision and regulation. If one accepts the 'bad bankers' theory (Minsky, 1993), and the ensuing malfunction of the financial system, then the system's supervisory and regulating functions take center-stage in any serious effort of reform. The 1970s phenomenon of the large number of bank failures was attributed not only to the inept management and corrupt practices of bankers, but also to the systemic failure of the regulatory and supervisory structure. The financial system is, however, vulnerable to unanticipated monetary surprises and exogenous shocks which can occur even during periods of prosperity (Minsky, 1957, 1971), which will make the banks 'fragile' and the entire financial system unstable. As Bernard Shull argues in Chapter 7, there are certain limitations in the present organization of the federal bank regulatory agencies to effectively fulfill the functions that include the protection of depositors and insurance funds, the security of the payments mechanism, and the control of the money supply. Building on the good beginnings of FIRREA and FDICIA, Shull's proposal for a consolidated federal regulatory agency might provide the answer for greater efficiency, improved policy planning and better accountability. In his analysis of the current state of regulatory reform, George Kaufman (Chapter 8) partly echoes Shull, but as one of the drafters of FDICIA, Kaufman insists that the importance of this legislation is more far-reaching than has been recognized. FDICIA, he contends, basically removes the perverse incentives of bankers for excessive risks, provided that regulators apply its provisions uniformly, both in the spirit and letter of the Act, and that Congress and the Administration see to it that they do so.

Finally, Chapter 9 evaluates seven proposals of banking reform advanced in the mid-1980s that relate to a specific form of 'universal banking'. Alton Gilbert calculates statistical outcomes of particular aspects of a universal banking-like structure. His tests attempt to determine, among other propositions, (1) whether a bank holding company that owns banks and nonbanks would unduly expose the bank subsidiary or affiliate to excessive risk, if the nonbank subsidiary or affiliate fails, and (2) whether the banking subsidiary or affiliate can conduct nonbanking activities without compromising in the diversification of risk by conducting nonbanking activities. His conclusions infer that 'banks are not necessarily safer' if the nonbanking business is carried by separate subsidiaries, and, in addition, the loss of deposit insurance funds may be lower if deposits were to finance nonbanking activities by banking subsidiaries. Moreover, he shows that 'shareholders of a holding company generally do not benefit by having the bank subsidiary lend at a subsidized rate to the nonbank subsidiary'.

1.3 POLICY OPTIONS

Views on financial reform and policy proposals that have been advanced during the last few years vary. All have been in response to the actions taken by the Administration and Congress to put forth a meaningful legislative agenda to address the reforms needed in reconfiguring the deposit insurance, the overlapping regulatory and supervisory authority of the Federal Reserve, the Comptroller of the Currency and the FDIC, and the organization and capitalization of the financial services industry. In assessing reform alternatives, England (Chapter 10) and Barth and Brumbaugh (Chapter 11) take into consideration the objectives of bank regulation and market competition. The fundamental goal of bank regulation is the maintenance of confidence and stability in the financial system, while the goal of market competition contributes to the mission of an efficient allocation of resources. Given, however, the substantial changes over several decades in the market for financial services offered by both bank and nonbank firms, 'regulation should facilitate the prompt resolution of firms whose performance leads to financial distress' (Chapter 11).

Catherine England (Chapter 10), reviews a number of proposals that attempt to reconstitute the structure of deposit insurance by redefining its role. In her overview, she assesses proposals that 'range from eliminating federal guarantees' altogether 'to expanding them to include all bank and S&L deposits'. In particular, 'narrow banks' (a topic widely explored by Kenneth Spong, in Chapter 12), 'limited' or 'roll[ed] back' deposit guarantees, and modified payouts of deposits in the instances of FDIC bailouts are carefully considered but not necessarily wholeheartedly endorsed, since each proposal involves some degree of system instability. The chapter concludes with a thoughtful commentary by Larry Mote, who, while agreeing with England's evaluation of these proposals, suggests that his experience as a regulator leads him to place greater reliance on proposals that strengthen market discipline rather than regulatory discipline.

Barth and Brumbaugh (Chapter 11), on the other hand, argue that bank regulation must be consistent with the dynamic trends in the financial services industry, which demonstrate increasing inter-industry competition manifest, by and large, via technological advancement in information technology. Moreover, the evolving nature of markets that leads from 'direct holdings of stocks and bonds and holdings in depositories and life insurance companies to indirect holdings of stocks and bonds through pension funds and mutual funds' imposes additional burdens on the regulatory framework. Barth and Brumbaugh also evaluate a number of reform alternatives and conclude that a new financial structure must meet the following tests: first, be adaptable to the continuous evolution of the financial marketplace; second, protect the payments and credit mechanisms; and third, promote competition within the financial services industry. Gary Dymski, in his commentary to Chapter 11, agrees with Barth and Brumbaugh on many points, but raises important questions on the dysfunctional aspects of the present-day financial system that are missing from the authors' analysis and their recommended remedies for its reform. Dymski's criticism relates to the inefficiency of credit market outcomes, especially those affecting lower-income and inner-city neighborhoods. Any reform, Dymski urges, must take into account not only the private, but also the *social* functions of the financial system. He points to the successful experiments of certain banking initiatives, for example, South Shore Bank in Chicago, aimed at restoring the much needed financial intermediation of underserved communities. Reform proposals, therefore, need to address community development banking, the subject of Chapter 13, and reinforce community reinvestment responsibilities of banks.

The most extensively studied approach to banking reform involves the functional separation of the depository and lending activities of banks. The policy prescription underlying this approach is the institution of 'narrow banks' (Litan, 1987), banks maintaining 100 per cent required reserves, banks with 'deposited currency' (Tobin, 1988) or 'collateralized money' (Pollock, 1992). Narrow banking, a term coined by Robert Litan (1987), has been widely supported because, as Ronnie Phillips (1993) suggests, it meets the safety and soundness of the payments system and the goals of banking regulation, and offers an alternative structure that can adjust to market forces and technological innovation. These characteristics, it will be recalled, coincide with the three tests outlined by Barth and Brumbaugh in Chapter 11, and are explored in much detail by Kenneth Spong in Chapter 12. According to Spong and other proponents of narrow banking, the separation of monetary and financial services functions of banks would eliminate or reduce deposit insurance and enhance the stability within the banking system.

The existing financial structure, as was pointed out by Gary Dymski's commentary to Chapter 11, is particularly weak in servicing small and start-up businesses, as well as certain consumer groups. This weakness has been exacerbated because of a decrease in the number of independent financing alternatives and the rise in the size distribution of financing sources, which have increased the financial system's bias toward larger transactions. Community development banking as outlined in the proposal developed by Minsky, Papadimitriou, Phillips and Wray in Chapter 13, is premised on the notion that a critical function of the financial system is not adequately performed by the existing institutions for well-defined segments of the US population: low-income citizens, inner-city minorities, and entrepreneurs who seek modest financing for small businesses. The authors argue that the primary function of any financial system is to advance the capital development of the economy by increasing its real productive capacity and wealth-producing ability. Thus, the financial structure must be fashioned to provide a broad range of financial services to various segments of the economy, including consumers, small and large businesses, retailers, developers, and all levels of government. It should not restrict access and force certain segments of the population to resort to the fringe banking of check-cashing outlets and pawnshops.

The book ends with the essay by Gerard Caprio and Lawrence Summers (Chapter 14) contrasting various types of financial structures, including those with heavy government intervention and those based on market-oriented incentives. Even though the authors demonstrate that market-oriented financial systems would perform better than those with government involvement, they by no means embrace the notions of *laissez-faire* and perfectly competitive markets. They accept the need for a limited government intervention, especially for developing countries and transitional socialist economies (TSEs), to ensure the soundness and stability of the system. Donald Mathieson in his commentary to the chapter, while in general agreement with the authors, raises important issues confronting the developing economies and the TSEs as well. These include the inflexibility of their financial systems, the lack of efficiency in their banks' portfolios, and the frequent domestic and external shocks that are sizable compared to their GDPs.

The chapters in this volume detail many of the innovative and dramatic changes that have taken place in the financial services sector over the last two decades that have led to the enactment of several 'narrow' and 'reactive' pieces of federal legislation. The views of many academicians and lawmakers, however, are that more legislative enactment is necessary.

We have witnessed an era of rapid technological change, particularly the wholesale introduction of information technologies which has precipitated increased competition, and rendered obsolete the longstanding established 'habitat' among players in the financial services industry. The findings of the National Commission on Financial Institution Reform, Recovery and Enforcement reaffirm the need for new banking regulation. Regulation that is consistent with the diversified nature of the firms operating in the rapidly changing environment of financial markets, would strengthen the financial system and avoid another S&L crisis. Although the common perception faults greed as the principal cause of the S&L crisis, the Commission determined that only 10 to 15 per cent of total losses were attributable to greed. Rather, the existing structure and organization of deposit insurance which provided S&L operators with added incentive for excessive risk-taking, along with a problematic asset structure exacerbated by deregulation, precipitated the S&L disaster.

The Commission's recommendations echo many of the findings and proposals to be found in the various chapters of this book. In essence, actions such as unifying chartering and regulatory control and forming institutions in which deposits are safe (100 per cent 'reserved' or invested in highly liquid and high-rated short-term securities) as organizations separate from those carrying uninsured deposits (that is, finance companies), would facilitate the creation of an industry that can adapt to market forces, reduce risk, increase profitability and eliminate taxpayer bail outs. As we reflect on more than 60 years after the Banking Crisis of 1933, we cannot but agree that the problems confronting us now are not that dissimilar: the competence of the regulator and banker, the sophistication of tomorrow's markets and financial innovation, and the assumption that these cannot be regulated by yesterday's regulations.

References

Friedman, Milton and Anna J. Schwartz (1963) *A Monetary History of the United States 1867–1960* (Princeton: Princeton University Press).

Litan, Robert E. (1987) *What Should Banks Do?* (Washington, DC: The Brookings Institution).

Minsky, Hyman P. (1957) 'Central Banking and Money Market Changes', *Quarterly Journal of Economics* (May) LXXI, 2.

Minsky, Hyman P. (1971) 'Financial Instability Revisited', *Reappraisal of the Federal Reserve Discount Mechanism* (Washington, DC: Federal Reserve Board) 3, 95–136.

Minsky, Hyman P. (1993) 'Introduction', *Public Policy Brief*, The Jerome Levy Economics Institute, No. 5.

Phillips, Ronnie (1993) 'The "Chicago Plan" and New Deal Banking Reform,' The Jerome Levy Economics Institute, Working Paper No. 76 (June) and Chapter 5, this volume.

Pollock, Alex (1992) 'Collateralized Money: An Idea Whose Time Has Come Again', *Challenge* (September/October).

Sellon Jr., Gordon H. (1988) 'Restructuring the Financial System: Summary of the Bank's Symposium', *Economic Review*, Federal Reserve Bank of Kansas City (January).

Tobin, James (1988) 'The Case for Preserving Regulatory Distinctions', in 'Restructuring the Financial System', *Economic Review*, Federal Reserve Bank of Kansas City (January).

White, Eugene N. (1984) 'A Reinterpretation of the Banking Crisis of 1930', *Journal of Economic History* (March) XLIV, 1.

Part I

Historical Perspectives

2 The 1930s Financial Reforms in Historical Perspective

Richard Sylla

In 1993, we mark the 60th anniversary of what arguably was the most comprehensive program of financial reform in US history. It began with Franklin D. Roosevelt's inauguration as president, reached peak momentum during the first 100 days of legislative activity of FDR's New Deal, and continued at a more moderate pace through the remainder of the 1930s, ending with the Investment Company Act of 1940.

This chapter interprets the financial reforms of the 1930s in the larger perspective of more than two centuries of US economic and financial history. In sections 2.1 and 2.2, I review the financial crisis of early 1933, and the key reforms that were responses to it respectively. Then, in section 2.3, I consider the only earlier instance of comprehensive financial reform in US history, that of 1789–92, while in section 2.4, I compare its content and fate with those of the New Deal reforms. Although some of the New Deal reforms, like the ones much earlier, unraveled, others were successful and persisted for decades. The two cases of comprehensive financial reform in the United States were the products of major financial crises. Some now argue that the multitude of financial problems that arose in the 1980s, the legacy of which perhaps continues in the sluggish economy of the early 1990s, constitutes still another major crisis. Talk of financial reform is again in the policy agenda. But the current crisis in US finance, if such it be, seems to me to be of a much lower order than the crises of the 1780s and the 1930s. In the last section, I conclude that the possibilities for another comprehensive financial reform package comparable to the two earlier ones in our history are, at present, minimal.

2.1 EARLY 1933: A LOOK BACK

The month before FDR's inauguration on 4 March 1933, may have been the darkest in US financial history. Four weeks earlier, on 4 February, Louisiana declared a bank holiday, and on 14 February the banking system of Michigan collapsed. The climax to three and one-half years of market crashes, waves of bank failures, and unprecedented economic depression was underway.

On 15 February, Ferdinand Pecora, the recently appointed counsel to the subcommittee of the Senate Banking and Currency Committee that was investigating stock exchange practices, began questioning witnesses regarding the collapse of Samuel Insull's financial empire. One of the witnesses, Harold Stuart, the head of the investment banking house of Halsey Stuart, Insull's principal bankers, admitted that his firm bought radio time and hired a University of Chicago professor to read scripts on the principles of sound investment that, in fact, were written not by the 'Old Counsellor', the professor's radio name, but by Halsey Stuart. Further, Halsey Stuart had led a client to sell other securities and invest in an Insull company without revealing that he (Halsey Stuart) held a large stock interest in it, and that Halsey Stuart partners served as officers of the company. The American public was shocked by revelations of what were taken to be conflicts of interest and attempts of fiduciaries to make things seem to be different from what they actually were.

The following week, on 21 February, Pecora began questioning Charles Mitchell, head of the National City Bank and its securities affiliate the National City Company, uncovering what were taken by the public to be even greater abuses by the country's leading financiers and financial institutions not paying taxes, huge salaries and bonuses, stock manipulations, selling securities with inadequate or misleading information provided to the buying clients, other conflicts of interest, and so on. The National City revelations, involving as they did one of the nation's pre-eminent financial institutions, again shocked the public, and, this time, they reverberated in high places. A week later, on 28 February, Mitchell resigned his National City position, supposedly after being told by a close friend, who was also in the FDR camp, that the president-elect thought it advisable for Mitchell to do so.

While these events were unfolding, the banking situation took a nasty turn. Bank failures and bank holidays were accompanied by calls of Democratic leaders for abandoning the gold standard and inflating the money supply, with reports that the president-elect shared these views. The result was a run on gold. Up to that point in the Great Depression, as in earlier US banking panics since the Civil War, bank depositors rushed to convert their deposits to currency. By February 1933, even currency became suspect. In the run on gold, the stock of the yellow metal in the Treasury and Federal Reserve banks fell 17 per cent during the two and one-half weeks between 15 February and inauguration day. More states declared bank holidays. In the early morning hours of 4 March, inauguration day, Governor Lehman of New York, on the urging of New York banks that were having massive withdrawals of funds by US and foreign banks, issued a proclamation closing the banks of the Empire State. When FDR proclaimed the bank holiday two days later, most of the nation's banks had already closed their doors.

Recounting the events of that pre-inaugural month, 60 years ago, serves to remind us that all the pillars of the US financial system were then collapsing. A monetary system based on gold and the gold standard was no longer tenable. A banking system that destroyed money and confidence by shutting its doors to its customers was not really a banking system at all. Capital markets and institutions that misled their clients, hid pertinent information from them, and were headed by seemingly unprincipled persons who abused fiduciary trust could not survive. It is worth remembering the integrated, across-the-board nature of the financial collapse of the early 1930s. It provided the backdrop for the reforms of the New Deal era that followed. And it demonstrated the interrelatedness of finance. Financial reform in the 1930s involved not merely individual measures such as changing the monetary base, insuring bank deposits, divorcing investment banking from commercial banking, allowing greater latitude for branch banking, or having capital markets and institutions disclose pertinent information to their clients. Rather, it embodied a comprehensive approach involving all of these measures.

2.2 THE NEW DEAL REFORMS

What were the major New Deal financial reforms? In the interest of pointing out their comprehensive nature involving money, banking, and the capital markets, I provide the following list of Measures and their Effects:

- 6 Mar 1933 Executive Order
  Banks closed for Bank Holiday and prohibited from paying out specie.
- 9 Mar 1933 Emergency Banking Act
  Authority granted to nationalize gold holdings; bank holiday extended but way paved for reopenings; banks authorized to issue preferred stock for recapitalization; collateral for Federal Reserve Bank advances broadened.
- 10 Mar 1933 Executive Order
  Prohibition of gold exports; end of gold standard.

- 27 May 1933 Securities Act
Registration of new offerings of securities with FTC (later, with SEC) and disclosure by prospectus of sufficient information from registration statement to allow prospective investors to judge value of offering.

- 5 June 1933 Joint Resolution of Congress
Abrogation of gold clauses in contracts.

- 16 June 1933 Banking Act of 1933
Deposit insurance instituted through new FDIC; (Glass–Steagall) interest on demand deposits prohibited and interest on time deposits regulated; commercial and investment banking separated; national banks allowed to branch consistent with state law; Federal Open Market Committee created with one member from each Federal district.

- 30–31 Jan 1934 Gold Reserve Act
Dollar devaluation authorized; dollar devalued next day to 59 per cent of former gold value; US adopted gold exchange standard internationally and paper standard domestically.

- 6 June 1934 Securities Exchange Act
SEC established; registration and disclosure requirements of Securities Act applied to all listed securities; listed corporations to file annual financial reports and quarterly earnings statements; exchange procedures and manipulative practices banned; margin requirements on brokers' loans under Fed's supervision.

- 23 Aug 1935 Banking Act of 1935
Fed renamed and reorganized with greater centralization of powers; Federal Open Market Committee changed to 7 Governors plus 5 voting Reserve Bank presidents; Board of Governors given power to vary reserve requirements within limits and to approve discount rate changes; regulation of deposit interest rates extended.

- 26 Aug 1935 Public Utility Holding Company Act
Limited a utility holding company to control of a Company Act single, integrated system; more stringent SEC regulation.

- 25 June 1938 Maloney Act
Led to National Association of Security Dealers and SEC regulation of the over-the-counter market.

- 10 Nov 1940 Investment Company Act
Extended SEC registration and disclosure requirements to investment companies.

It is evident from the list that the reforms were comprehensive, applying to money, banking, the central bank, and the capital markets. Half of the dozen items in the list came during the first '100 days' of New Deal legislation. Eight of the twelve came during the term of the 73rd Congress.

There were numerous other executive orders, resolutions and acts related to financial reform, but the ones listed here are, I think, the main ones that changed the US financial system in ways that lasted for decades. Indeed, a good number of the New Deal reforms are still in effect today, six decades after they were instituted. But others have been eroded by subsequent events or, as in the case of the gold exchange standard, have been abandoned.

Today, some students of American finance argue that comprehensive financial reform is again necessary, to correct the defects that have been found with the New Deal measures and others that have arisen. Other analysts contend that the reforms of the 1930s were flawed from the start and should now be scrapped. The New Deal reforms eventually did lead to a number of financial problems, but they also accomplished much that was good. Critics of the New Deal reforms should make an attempt to consider what the financial condition of the United States was on 4 March 1933. They could recall, for example, the 1936 words of Joseph P. Kennedy, the Wall Street figure who became the first chairman of the SEC: 'I am not ashamed to record that in those days I felt and said I would be willing to part with half of what I had if I could be sure of keeping, under law and order, the other half.' I will return to the issue of evaluating the New Deal reforms later, but I want first to provide some historical perspective by examining the nature and consequences of what I consider to be the only other example of comprehensive financial reform in the nation's history. It provides interesting parallels as well as contrasts with the 1930s reforms.

2.3 THE 1780s AND 1790s: A LOOK FARTHER BACK

In teaching US economic and financial history, I like to stress the point that the Constitution of 1787, revered by Americans as coming almost from on high, was actually a document that directly addressed the critical economic problems of its time. The Revolutionary War had flooded the fledgling nation with paper money, prompting hyperinflation, and created a huge and unorganized debt overhang at both the national and state levels. The national government, under the Articles of Confederation, had no taxing power, relying instead on requisitions of funds from the states.

In the depressed economic conditions of the 1780s, the states were reluctant to pay their shares of national expenses, and the national government, therefore, was sometimes unable to pay the interest on its debt, much less debts themselves when they became due.

The states were not much better off in this regard, although they did have taxing powers. But when a state, such as Massachusetts, raised taxes to pay state war debts in the midst of depressed economic conditions, the result was a taxpayers' revolt in the form of an armed insurrection, Shays' rebellion in 1786. The depression of the 1780s led to state measures that raised questions about how united were the United States: tariffs on imports from other states to relieve the depression and export unemployment – and, of course, to retaliation by other states – as well as state paper-money issues with legal-tender clauses to relieve debtors and exploit creditors and citizens of other states.

The Constitution directly addressed this crisis of the 1780s. The new federal government was given taxing and borrowing powers and responsibility for its old debts. It received, as well, the power to coin money and regulate its value. And it was given the power to oversee and regulate commerce between the states. At the same time, the Constitution prohibited the states from issuing paper money, from making anything other than gold or silver legal tender, from passing laws that impaired the obligation of contracts, and from interfering with interstate commerce. When the new federal government took office in 1789, however, these constitutional provisions were little more than words on a sheet of paper. They pointed to some directions that US economic institutions *should* take, leaving open the issue of how the country would get there.

Implementation of the constitutional mandate in the area of financial reform came quickly, like the New Deal reforms, during the first administration of President Washington. Unlike the New Deal reforms, the financial reform program of 1789–92 was largely the work of one person, Alexander Hamilton. When Hamilton became the nation's first Secretary of the Treasury in September 1789 – after drafting the bill that established the Treasury Department – the Tariff Act of July 1789 was in place to furnish revenue for the new government. That was the crucial underpinning of the debt funding scheme Hamilton then worked out and reported to Congress in January 1790. This first report on public credit also called for additional revenue from excise taxes on distilled spirits, which became the new government's first internal tax in 1791. After much debate over Hamilton's plan to have the federal government assume the debts of the states, resolved by the famous compromise that moved the national capital first from New York to Philadelphia and then to the new federal city on the Potomac in 1800, Congress adopted Hamilton's debt plan in July 1790.

In the first report, Hamilton hinted that he would soon recommend establishment of a national bank, which he did in a second report on public credit in December 1790. The Bank of the United States was to be a mixed enterprise, owned partly by the government and partly by private investors, and serving both parties. Its public functions included augmenting the nation's money supply with banknotes (only a handful of small, local banks were then in existence); lending to the government when necessary; receiving, holding, and transferring public funds, and – cleverly – supporting the new public debt which in Hamilton's plan could be used by private investors to purchase stock in the bank. After considerable controversy regarding the bank's constitutionality, the president signed the act of Congress embodying Hamilton's bank proposal in February 1791, and the Bank of the United States began to be organized.

While the bank bill was being considered, Hamilton, in late January 1791, furnished Congress with a report on establishing a mint. Following ideas suggested by Thomas Jefferson to the old Confederation government, Hamilton defined the dollar, the unit of account, in terms of both gold and silver (bimetallism), and proposed a variety of coins based on the decimal system, unique at the time. The Coinage Act of 1792 embodied Hamilton's proposals, and the mint opened in Philadelphia in 1794.

As they were implemented, Hamilton's financial reforms effectively launched – as he intended – the development of a US capital market, which had hardly existed before 1790. Old evidences of public debt – national and state – were exchanged for some $70 million dollars of Federal bonds, payable – principal and interest – in specie and, as noted, subscribable for stock in the Bank of the United States. Even before Bank stock, $10 million in total, was issued, an active market in 'scrip', the rights to buy it, developed. Speculation in these new federal security issues, along with that in other, smaller private and public securities, led to a crash, Wall Street's first, in early 1792. The crash, in turn, led to the Buttonwood Agreement, forerunner of the New York Stock Exchange, in May 1792, as brokers formed a private club to trade securities after New York State, in an early regulatory response to a crash, banned public auctions of securities in an 'Act to Prevent the Pernicious Practice of Stock-Jobbing'. By that time the crash was over and securities trading continued to develop, on Wall Street and elsewhere, apace with the expansion of the US economy.

With these changes in the monetary system, in banking and central banking arrangements, and in the capital markets, the comprehensive financial reforms of 1789–92 were every bit as dramatic as the reforms of 1933–5. The main difference in the two reform scenarios, it seems, is that in the former period the Wall Street crash came at the end, while in the latter it came at the beginning.

The fate of Hamilton's reforms is instructive. Some lasted for a long time; others were eroded and eventually disappeared. The US Treasury Department and national debt, which Hamilton put into place, are still there, and now furnish the materials for the largest financial market in history. Bimetallism was flawed conceptually and never worked very well in practice, but the specie-based dollar lasted, with occasional interruptions, to the 1930s. The unpopular internal tax system was undermined by Jefferson when he became president, to the embarrassment of his successor, Madison, when war came in 1812 and cut imports and customs revenues. But it was in time rebuilt. And the growing economic influence and political power of state-chartered banks – they mushroomed as a result of the Hamiltonian reforms – paradoxically caused the federal charters of Hamilton's Bank and its successor, the Second Bank, to fail of renewal when they expired 20 years after going into effect in 1791 and 1816. The powers and privileges of these central banks were resented by many state bankers. The attack of the Jacksonians on the Second Bank, the 'Bank War' of 1829–36, was especially bitter. Congress eventually remedied the loss of a Bank of the United States when it founded a politically less vulnerable central bank in 1913. Wall Street survived its first crash to have many more, and to become a power in its own right, even if reined in during the 1930s.

Hamilton, by effectively organizing the basic elements of financial infrastructure in the first years of the nation's existence, cast a long shadow over its subsequent economic history. Even when he failed in his own time to persuade Congress to follow him, as with his Report on Manufactures calling for protective tariffs and subsidies to infant manufacturing enterprises, his program eventually was adopted. One can see his arguments in today's debates on strategic trade, industrial policy, and so on. I suspect that of all of the founding fathers he would be the one least surprised and most pleased, if he could come back now and witness what Americans have done with their economy and society in two centuries.

2.4 FATE OF THE 1930s REFORMS

With a historical basis for a comparative study, let us turn to the fate of the 1930s reforms. The monetary reform – a fiat paper standard at home and a gold bullion standard internationally – proved in time to have conceptual and practical flaws similar to those of bimetallism. With the implementation of the Bretton Woods system after World War II, the dollar became international money, convertible into gold if it found its way into a foreign central bank that wanted to convert it. When the United States flooded the world with dollars in the 1950s and 1960s, some foreign central banks decided to convert. The United States soon realized that it did not have enough gold to meet these demands, and it dropped the Bretton Woods system in 1971. Under bimetallism one of the two metals served as money, and the other became a commodity fluctuating in price. Under the fiat paper and gold system of the 1930s, one of the two served as money and the other – eventually – became a commodity fluctuating in price. In each case the item that the market decided was the less valuable of the two options ended up serving as money.

The New Deal's banking reforms in the short run seemed to do the most good, but in the longer run appear to have done the most harm, at least as far as US commercial banking is concerned. Deposit insurance initially was not favored by FDR or by Senator Glass, whose alternative to it was wider branch banking, but whose main interest was in getting commercial banks out of the securities business. Congressman Steagall favored deposit insurance, the preferred measure of the small-town bankers who loathed branch banking and feared competition from big, money-center banks. The Banking Act of 1933 was a compromise. Glass got the separation of commercial and investment banking as well as a slight relaxation of restrictions on branch banking, while Steagall got deposit insurance as the main prop for commercial banks. The banning of interest on demand deposits and the setting of maximum interest on time deposits is said by some to have been a sop to bankers, whose interests costs would be reduced as an offset to the increased costs represented by deposit insurance premiums.

Deposit insurance ended banking panics. For that reason alone, many consider it a signal reform contributing to economic stability. But the interest-rate, entry, and other regulatory controls that accompanied it, while reducing bank failures, eventually victimized the commercial banking industry when rising market interest rates and financial innovation, in such forms as money-market funds and cash-management accounts, undermined the cozy banking cartels put in place by the New Deal reforms. When banks tried to stem their losses of profits and market share in financial services by entering new (really, old) lines of business, they ran afoul of the Glass–Steagall separation. They also took risks that increased failures and in time depleted deposit insurance funds. Because of the New Deal measures, US commercial banking is in decline both at home and in the world.

Before the 1980s, deposit insurance was viewed as the greatest and most successful of the New Deal reforms. Few are of that opinion today. A better candidate now would be the capital-market reforms – registration, disclosure, the SEC, and so on. Why? By placing the capital markets on a higher informational and regulatory plane, these reforms increased public confidence and participation in them, led to the rise of intermediated investment by institutions such as pension and mutual funds, and produced markets of great depth and innovativeness, sometimes to the discomfort of other parts of the financial system. It was the reverse of what happened with banking reform. Initially, the capital markets were demoralized by the New Deal reforms, but in the longer run they benefited greatly from them. A century and a half apart, two national leaders from New York, Hamilton and FDR, pursued reforms that rebounded to the long-term benefit of Wall Street.

The fate of the central banking component of the two great comprehensive financial reform programs in US history was quite different. The two federal Banks of the United States went by the boards in 1811 and 1836. In contrast, the Federal Reserve System has remained almost untouched by Congress since the Banking Act of 1935. There is a paradox here. The two Banks of the United States for the most part served the country well before they were done in by politics. On the other hand, the Fed, we now know, contributed in a major way to the debacle of the Great Depression, and many would argue that it was at least the proximate cause of the great inflation of 1965 to 1981 that did so much to undermine the US financial system during and after that era. (An alternative *was* possible; compare how the Fed behaved during the late 1960s and 1970s with how the Bundesbank in Germany has been holding the line against inflation under similar pressures in recent years.) For good or ill or both, the Fed is the financial component that has been least changed since the 1930s reforms increased and centralized its powers. Given the record, that is certainly interesting. Will the central bank continue to remain untouched while the other components of the financial system around it are tossed and tumbled by the winds of economic change?

2.5 CONCLUDING OBSERVATIONS

A balanced account of the New Deal financial reforms is emerging. There were successes and failures. The monetary and banking reforms were flawed, and the flaws becoming apparent by the 1960s. Deposit insurance ended banking panics, but how much of the 'socialization of risk' that it represents can the nation afford? The central banking reform has remained relatively untouched since 1935, but the issues of the constitutional basis of central banking, of who controls the central bank, and of what are its goals and the proper means of reaching them are still widely discussed and very much open.

The capital-market reforms of the 1930s have been the most successful component of the New Deal package. But even here the success has been less than complete, and it is of more than parochial interest to consider why that is the case. The Glass–Steagall separation of commercial and investment banking, although somewhat relaxed, is still in effect despite studies that have found little hard evidence of the alleged shortcomings and abuses that provided the rationale for it in 1933. The Glass–Steagall separation is best explained, I think, as a manifestation of an ideological predisposition that has been present throughout the entire sweep of US financial history, one that comes down against any concentration of financial resources and favors fragmenting financial institutions and markets by legal restrictions and regulations.

This ideology of financial fragmentation was behind the slaying of the two Banks of the United States, behind the 'states'-rights' approach to banking that persists in the dual banking system, behind the pro-unit-, anti-branch-banking movements, and behind the original, decentralized Fed in its first two decades. It was a key element of the New Deal reforms: the Glass–Steagall separation, the preference for deposit insurance over liberalized branch banking, the Public Utility Holding Company Act, and the Investment Company Act. The last of these placed portfolio restrictions on investment companies; a mutual fund, for example, was precluded from putting more than 5 per cent of its assets into the securities of any one issuer or from purchasing more than 10 per cent of any one company's securities. While the former provision might be justified on diversification grounds, the latter was clearly intended to prevent finance from controlling non-financial business. The ideology continues in portfolio restrictions on insurance companies and pension funds (ERISA) as well as in the multiple layers of financial regulation both within and among the federal and state governments.

Fear of concentrated financial power is a staple of US history, and is supplemented, of course, by the perceived self-interest of particular financial institutions and markets. Perhaps it made political and economic sense when finance was more secretive and less open than it is now, and when financial institutions were the representatives of a wealthy minority instead of the masses of bank and insurance customers, securities investors, and pension-fund accumulators that they now represent. But is it still justified?

An evaluation of the New Deal reforms and their contributions to US financial stability and efficiency after 1933 should take into account the larger context of the United States in the world economy. Some degree of the reforms' success was not inherent in the reform legislation so much as it was the result of the unique position of economic strength that the US enjoyed in the world of the 1940s, 1950s and 1960s. The war of 1939–45 damaged the economies of every other large nation but strengthened that of the United States. In the mid-1940s, the United States, with 6 per cent of world population, produced about half of total world output. In this situation, it was easy for Americans to attribute some measure of their good fortune to preceding economic reforms. Two decades of economic growth, with price stability after 1945, served to reinforce the argument. But that way of arguing gave more credit than was justified to the reforms and less than was due to larger historical circumstances of an unusual nature. As the other nations recovered and returned to more normal economic relationships with the United States, and as the United States itself went on an inflationary binge, the flaws of many of the New Deal financial reforms became apparent in the credit crunches of the 1960s and 1970s, in the collapse of the Bretton Woods international monetary system, and in the debts, deficits and defaults of the 1980s.

These events lead some to think that comprehensive financial reform is once again necessary. If so, is it possible? A student of US financial history would not be sanguine on this question. If history is a guide, comprehensive reform appears to require a major crisis. It does not appear that the financial disturbances of the 1970s and 1980s merit such a label. One piece of evidence supporting this contention is what happened after the US Treasury called for comprehensive reform in its report of early 1991, *Modernizing the Financial System*. What happened was essentially nothing. After reaching Congress, the Treasury proposals were chewed up and spit out of the legislative mill. And it appears that the United States, in 1993, has fewer major financial problems than it did during 1989–91. It will take more of a financial crisis than we now have – one on the order of the crises of the 1780s and 1930s – before another round of comprehensive reform will take place in the United States.

References

Benston, George J. (1990) *The Separation of Commercial and Investment Banking* (New York: Oxford University Press).

Carosso, Vincent P. (1970) *Investment Banking in America* (Cambridge: Harvard University Press).

Cleveland, Harold van B. and Thomas Huertas (1985) *Citibank, 1812–1970* (Cambridge: Harvard University Press).

Degen, Robert A. (1987) *The American Monetary System* (Lexington: Lexington Books).

Friedman, Milton and Anna J. Schwartz (1963) *A Monetary History of the United States, 1867–1960* (Princeton: Princeton University Press).

Kroszner, Randall S. and Raghuram G. Rajan (1992) 'Is Glass–Steagall Justified? A Study of U.S. Experience with Universal Banking before 1933', Working Paper, University of Chicago Business School.

Nussbaum, Arthur (1957) *A History of the Dollar* (New York: Columbia University Press).

Phillips, Ronnie J. (1993) 'The Chicago Plan and New Deal Banking Reform', Chapter 5, this volume.

Ratner, Sidney, James H. Soltow and Richard Sylla (1993) *The Evolution of the American Economy* (New York: Basic Books).

Sobel, Robert (1965) *The Big Board* (New York: Free Press).

Studenski, Paul and Herman Krooss (1963) *Financial History of the United States* (New York: McGraw-Hill).

Sylla, Richard (1992) 'William Duer and the Stock Market Crash of 1792', *Friends of Financial History*, **46**, 26–9.

US Treasury (1991) *Modernizing the Financial System* (February).

Comments

DAVID C. WHEELOCK

Professor Sylla provides a thoughtful perspective on the reasons for and significance of New Deal financial reforms, and an evaluation of their apparent success and future prospects. The scope of New Deal legislation is rivaled only by the financial development of the years immediately following ratification of the Federal Constitution, which Sylla uses to demonstrate that major financial reforms come only after severe crises. The reforms of 1789–92 were in response to a fiscal crisis: those of the New Deal in response to a financial crisis. Piecemeal adjustments, and some significant changes, such as the National Bank Act of 1863 and the Federal Reserve Act of 1913, occurred over intervening years, but none was as sweeping. Because I find Sylla's interpretation of New Deal reforms generally persuasive, my comments will develop further some of the points he raises, as well as offer my own perspective on the success or failure of particular reforms.

Sylla argues that critics of New Deal reforms should consider the state of the financial system on 4 March 1933. Given the near total collapse of financial markets and institutions, the New Deal reforms, though radical, do not seem unreasonable. The enactment of deposit insurance, for example, does not seem an immodest response to the 7000 bank failures of 1930 to 1933. Nor does the forced separation of commercial and investment banking, given the allegations of widespread abuses of fiduciary responsibility by banks with security affiliates. Similarly, the reorganization of the Federal Reserve System and the partial abandonment of the gold standard were substantial changes, but again seem modest in light of the banking crises and 30 per cent decline in the price level from 1930 to 1933.

Sixty years of experience, plus volumes of research, suggest, however, that many of the premises upon which New Deal reforms were based are suspect. The high number of bank and savings and loan failures in the last dozen years, and the resulting losses to the deposit insurance funds, has naturally focused a great deal of attention on one New Deal reform in particular – federal deposit insurance. As Sylla points out, until recently, deposit insurance was regarded as perhaps the most successful of the New Deal changes. Even free market economists, such as Milton Friedman and Anna Schwartz, concluded that deposit insurance was a vital reform:

> Federal insurance of bank deposits was the most important structural change in the banking system to result from the 1933 panic, and, indeed in our view, the structural change most conducive to monetary stability since state bank note issues were taxed out of existence immediately after the Civil War... Federal deposit insurance, to 1960 at least, has succeeded in achieving what had been a major objective of banking reform for at least a century, namely, the prevention of banking panics.[1]

The high cost of deposit insurance was revealed in the 1980s, when a mix of deregulation, inadequate supervision and politics permitted banks and S&Ls to exploit the incentive for excess risk-taking created by deposit insurance. The resulting failures produced insurance fund liabilities in the hundreds of billions of dollars.

The ugly side of deposit insurance did not appear until the 1980s, in part because other New Deal banking reforms discouraged excessive risk-taking and prevented risk-prone institutions from growing rapidly. Legal barriers to entry, for example, protected bank charter values and, thus, discouraged risk-taking, whereas deposit interest-rate ceilings limited the opportunity for banks to grow rapidly. Congress, apparently, understood in 1933 the need to constrain the risk-taking of institutions with insured liabilities (Flood, 1992). The combination of increased deposit insurance coverage and less regulation and supervision that was adopted in the early 1980s was a significant, and unfortunate, departure from New Deal policy.

The experience of the 1980s has also raised new questions about the necessity of deposit insurance for preventing banking panics. Some proponents of free banking suggest that an entirely unregulated banking system would not suffer from panics (Dowd, 1993). More economists would argue that the Federal Reserve could have offset banking panics during the Great Depression. If the Fed had fully accommodated the demand for liquidity from 1930 to 1933, the circumstances that led Congress to enact deposit insurance might not have arisen. The operations of clearinghouses to increase liquidity in response to extraordinary demands in the nineteenth century suggests that lower-cost alternatives to deposit insurance might exist. If deposit insurance is to remain, mutual guarantee insurance, like that of the state systems of Indiana, Ohio and Iowa in the antebellum era, might be a better alternative to the present system.

Another central feature of the Banking Act of 1933 is the separation of commercial and investment banking. Banks were forced to give up their securities affiliates because of alleged conflicts of interest and other abuses, and because observers believed that investment in high-risk securities had caused many banks to fail. As with deposit insurance, some researchers have questioned the premises underlying this reform. The alleged abuses of banks operating securities affiliates appear to have been mostly smoke, and little fire, and the failure rate of banks operating securities affiliates was lower than that of other banks during the Depression (Benston, 1990; White, 1986).

Yet, another significant New Deal change, the reorganization of the Federal Reserve System to centralize policy-making authority in Washington also appears to have been justified on a suspect premise. Marriner Eccles, whom President Roosevelt appointed to head the Federal Reserve Board in 1934, argued strongly for placing all control over monetary policy within the Federal Reserve Board. Eccles believed that the Fed's anemic response to the Depression was due to the control of open-market policy by the district Reserve Banks, and that they tended to act in the interest of commercial banks rather than in the public interest. Eccles' view that monetary policy would have been substantially more responsive during the Depression had the Federal Reserve Board been in complete control is doubtful, however. Though most of the regional Reserve Banks had argued for what were, in effect, contractionary policies, so did most members of the Federal Reserve Board. Real bills doctrine – loans limited for productive purposes – views of various forms permeated the Fed, and there is no evidence that the Fed would have pursued a significantly more expansionary policy before 1933 if policy had been decided upon only by the Board in Washington (Wheelock, 1991). Eccles' premises about the loyalties of Reserve Bank presidents and whether the interests of commercial banks differed from those of the public as a whole are also debatable.

Although a faulty underlying premise does not necessarily imply that a particular reform should be undone, those which seem unsupported by historical evidence should be reexamined. It may be worthwhile, for example, to repeal New Deal prohibitions on securities-related activities by banks to enable them to compete better with foreign banks. A lesson of the 1980s is that any changes need to be thought through carefully, however.

In examining the success of New Deal reforms, Professor Sylla makes an important distinction between immediate success and success over the long-run. Deposit insurance and other New Deal banking reforms, for example, were of great immediate benefit in restoring public confidence in the banking system at a crucial time. Though costly in recent years, these reforms may well have been the best medicine possible in 1933. Other reforms imposed a large burden when first introduced but generated lasting benefits. Sylla notes that New Deal capital-market reforms initially 'demoralized' financial markets, but have had lasting benefits. Professor Sylla makes a persuasive case that capital-market reforms, such as the registration of new securities, disclosure requirements and adequate supervision, have been the most successful of all New Deal financial and monetary reforms. These changes increased the flow of accurate information to investors and enhanced public confidence and participation. They created the conditions under which the US capital market could flourish and innovate, while New Deal banking reforms, by contrast, did to the banking industry what some have claimed the ICC did to railroads.

What are the prospects for significant changes in the regulation of financial markets and intermediaries in the future? Professor Sylla's view that major changes will not occur unless there is a serious crisis seems correct. Sylla contends that 'ideology' favoring a fragmented financial system and institutions explains why the Glass–Steagall separation of commercial and investment banking remains in place today, as well as the predisposition, historically, to oppose universal banking, branch banking, and other forms of concentration. I would add that the political clout of particular interests helps to maintain this ideology in the face of economic evidence against it. Securities and insurance firms have, thus, lobbied successfully against expanded powers for banks, while small banks have been able to hold off interstate branching.

I believe Sylla is also right when he mentions that the financial problems of the 1980s were insufficient to produce reforms of the scale of the New Deal changes. Because of the bank and S&L mess, we have had regulatory changes around the edges of problems. For example, new capital requirements will somewhat lessen the incentive for banks to take excessive risks, and early closure policies should limit insurance system losses. The US may also be forced to modify some of its banking laws in response to further gains by foreign banks. The most significant of President Bush's administration banking reform proposals, such as the removal of barriers to interstate branching and bank underwriting of securities, and the ownership of banks by firms in other industries, have gone nowhere, however.

In 1991 and 1992, banking industry reforms were at the top of Congress' banking and monetary policy agenda. In 1993–4, it appears that much of the focus will be on the Federal Reserve System. The recent recession and a perception that the Federal Reserve was not sufficiently responsive may result in some changes in the Fed's structure. It remains to be seen, however, whether dissatisfaction with the Fed's performance has been great enough to lead to radical changes in the System.

Though I have attempted to embellish or extend some of Professor Sylla's arguments in my comments, his Chapter provides a very solid base upon which to build.

Note

1. Friedman and Schwartz (1963) pp. 434–40.

References

Benston, George J. (1990) *The Separation of Commercial and Investment Banking* (Oxford: Oxford University Press).

Dowd, Kevin (1993) 'Deposit Insurance: A Skeptical View', *Review* (Federal Reserve Bank of St Louis).

Flood, Mark D. (1992) 'The Great Deposit Insurance Debate', *Review* (Federal Reserve Bank of St Louis) 51–77 and Chapter 3, this volume.

Friedman, Milton and Anna J. Schwartz (1963) *A Monetary History of the United States, 1867–1960* (Princeton: Princeton University Press).

Wheelock, David C. (1991) *The Strategy and Consistency of Federal Reserve Monetary Policy, 1924–1933* (Cambridge: Cambridge University Press).

White, Eugene N. (1986) 'Before the Glass–Steagall Act: An Analysis of the Investment Banking Activities of National Banks', *Explorations in Economic History*, **23**, 33–55.

RANDALL S. KROSZNER

An investigation of past reforms and how they came to be enacted is extremely important for understanding current policy and how it can be reformed. Professor Sylla's chapter provides a concise overview and evaluation of the major financial reforms enacted in the New Deal. In addition, the chapter examines the fundamental financial restructuring that occurred almost a century and a half ago in the early years of the United States. By juxtaposing these financial reform episodes, Sylla draws important insights about the process of financial reform. My comments will focus upon elaborating one of these insights.

A significant lesson that Professor Sylla draws from his examination of US financial history is: 'Comprehensive reform appears to require a major crisis'. Starting at the beginning, Sylla reminds us that the US Constitution and Alexander Hamilton's subsequent reforms involved an attempt to address the economic crisis of the 1780s. Obviously, the New Deal reforms occurred in the context of crisis. In addition, other major US financial reforms – albeit not as wideranging as those of the 1780s and 1930s – were precipitated by crises. The dual banking system, for example, originated in 1863 as the Union tried to enhance the demand for the debt it was issuing to financing the Civil War; the founding of the Federal Reserve System came in response to the Panic of 1907.

While there undoubtedly is a relationship between crisis and reform, we understand little about why the reforms take the particular forms that they do. Certainly, in a time of financial upheaval, politicians felt an imperative to react and 'do something'. This standard political response to a crisis does not tell us what types of actions they will undertake and whether those reforms will be fundamental and longlasting or simply temporary. The hyperinflation and debt overhang problems plaguing the young United States have been repeated in many countries at various times, but there have been many different regulatory responses. During the Great Depression, financial reform followed a great variety of paths across countries.

In the US, the New Deal financial reforms were of the fundamental and longlasting variety. The Banking Act of 1933 (Glass–Steagall), for example, radically transformed the structure of the US financial services industry. During the 1920s, commercial banks increasingly entered the securities business. The US appeared to be moving toward a Germanstyle universal banking system. The Glass–Steagall Act formally arrested this development by requiring complete separation of investment banking from commercial banking.

There are different approaches to understanding government regulatory choices. The traditional perspective is the 'public interest' approach. In this view, the political process reacts to problems discovered in the markets. After identifying the sources of these troubles, the government then attempts to develop regulation that will help to improve the economic welfare of the nation, addressing the market 'failures'. The alternative 'private interest' perspective argues that regulation emerges from a competition among interest groups to influence the government to enact regulations that help one group at the expense of another. Thus, the influence of various groups in the battle for redistribution is the primary determinant of regulatory policy. Another alternative, which is the one Professor Sylla apparently favors, is that ideological preferences of the political actors (and their constituents) for fragmentation of financial power hold the key (Roe, 1990).

Two major categories of 'public interest' rationales were advanced for the separation of investment banking and commercial banking in the 1930s. These arguments are still made today. First, direct commercial bank involvement in investment banking could increase the riskiness of banks and, thereby, the whole financial system. Second, commercial banks that were also underwriting securities could be subject to conflict of interest that could give the banks an incentive to mislead investors and, thereby, ultimately undermine confidence in the financial markets and the banks.

Prior to the passage of the Glass–Steagall Act, however, there was no study investigating the consequences of the combination of commercial and investment banking. The Senate hearing held by Carter Glass in 1931 and 1932 contained some examples of supposed 'abuses'. Only a handful of the 'revelatory' anecdotes of the Pecora hearings (1933–4) relating to commercial bank involvement in the securities business occurred prior to the passage of the legislation.

Subsequent research has found very little evidence from the 1920s and 1930s to support the separation. George Benston (1990) has investigated the specific cases examined in the 1930s hearings and found that, upon closer scrutiny, few provide evidence for the rationales. Eugene White (1986) found that before Glass–Steagall, commercial banks actively involved in the securities markets tended to have higher capital ratios and more stable earnings than otherwise similar commercial banks that did not participate in the securities markets. Raghuram Rajan and I (1994) have found no support for the hypothesis that potential conflicts of interest lead commercial banks to take advantage of investors.

Since the public interest rationales appear to have had little systematic evidence in their favor, we must turn to another perspective to try to discover why this important regulatory change was undertaken and why it has had such longevity. To answer this question would require an investigation of a wideranging scope, but it would be extremely important for understanding what financial reforms are feasible today. I am hopeful that the combination of economists, historians, practioners, and policy-makers can begin to make headway on this problem which Professor Sylla's stimulating chapter raises.

References

Benston, George (1990) *The Separation of Commercial and Investment Banking* (Oxford: Oxford University Press).

Kindleberger, Charles (1984) *A Financial History of Western Europe* (London: George Allen & Unwin).

Kroszner, Randall and Raghuram Rajan (1994) 'Is the Glass–Steagall Act Justified? A Study of the U.S. Experience with Universal Banking Before 1933', *American Economic Review* (December) **84**, 810–32.

Macey, Jonathan and Geoffrey Miller (1992) *Banking Law and Regulation* (Boston: Little, Brown & Co.).

Peltzman, Sam (1976) 'Toward a More General Theory of Regulation', *Journal of Law and Economics* (August) **19**.

Roe, Mark (1990) 'Political and Legal Constraints on Ownership and Control of Public Corporations', *Journal of Financial Economics* (September) **27**, 7–42.

Stigler, George (1971) 'The Theory of Economic Regulation', *Bell Journal of Economics and Management Science* (Spring) **2**.

White, Eugene (1986) 'Before the Glass–Steagall Act: An Analysis of the Investment Banking Activities of National Banks', *Explorations in Economic History*, **23**, 33–55.

3 The Great Deposit Insurance Debate

Mark D. Flood*

> In the stress of the recent banking crisis ... there was a very definite appeal from bankers for the United States Government itself to insure all bank deposits so that no depositor anywhere in the country need have any fear as to the loss of his account. Such a guarantee as that would indeed have put a premium on bad banking. Such a guarantee as that would have made the Government pay substantially all losses which had been accumulated, whether by misfortune, by unwise judgment, or by sheer recklessness, and it might well have brought an intolerable burden upon the Federal Treasury.
>
> (Sen. Robert Bulkley (D-OH), Address to the US Chamber of Commerce, 4 May, 1933)[1]

> The only danger is that having learned the lesson, we may forget it. Human nature is such a funny thing. We learn something today, it is impressed upon us, and in a few short years we seem to forget all about it and go along and make the same mistakes over again.
>
> (Francis M. Law, 1934, p. 41)

The ongoing proliferation of bank and thrift failures is the foremost current issue for financial regulators. Failures of federally insured banks and thrifts numbered in the thousands during the 1980s. The problem is especially important for public policy, because of the potential liability of the federal taxpayer. For example, by 1989, the Federal Savings and Loan Insurance Corporation (FSLIC) was so deeply overextended – on the order of $200 billion – that only the US Treasury could fund its shortfall. The significance of insurance is seen elsewhere as well: economists are quick to point to flat-rate deposit insurance as a factor in causing the high failure rates. Flat-rate deposit insurance is said to create a moral hazard: if no one charges bankers a higher rate for assuming risk, then bankers will exploit the risk-return trade-off to invest in a riskier portfolio.

Why, then, do we have taxpayer-backed, flat-rate deposit insurance?[2] A simple answer would be that the legislators who adopted federal deposit insurance in 1933 did not understand the economic incentives involved.

This simple answer seems wrong, however. It has been pointed out that certain observers articulated the problems with deposit insurance quite clearly in 1933. In this view, the fault lies with the policymakers of 1933, who failed to heed those warnings.

This fails to answer why policymakers would ignore these arguments. Moreover, it does not explain why it should have taken almost 50 years for the flaws in deposit insurance to take effect. This chapter examines the deposit insurance debate of 1933, first to see precisely what the issues and arguments were at the time and, secondarily, to see how those issues were treated in the legislation. Briefly, I conclude that the legislators of 1933 both understood the difficulties with deposit insurance and incorporated in the legislation numerous provisions designed to mitigate those problems.

The Banking Act of 1933 separated commercial and investment banking, limited bank securities activities, expanded the branching privileges of Federal Reserve member banks, authorized federal regulators to remove the officers and directors of member banks, regulated the payment of interest on deposits, and increased minimum capital requirements for new national banks, among numerous lesser provisions. It also established a temporary deposit insurance plan lasting from 1 January to 1 July 1934, and a permanent plan that was to have started on 1 July 1934.[3] Although this chapter focuses on deposit insurance, it is important to bear in mind that both the deposit insurance provisions of the bill and the debate that surrounded them each had a larger context. The various provisions of the Banking Act of 1933 constituted an interdependent package.

The deposit guaranty provisions of the bill were initially opposed by President Roosevelt, Carter Glass (Senate sponsor of the bill and Congress's elder statesman on banking issues), Treasury Secretary Woodin, the American Bankers Association (ABA), and the Association of Reserve City Bankers, among others.[4] Despite this opposition, on 13 June 1933, the bill passed virtually unanimously in the Senate, with six dissents in the House, and was signed into law by the President on 16 June.[5] Not surprisingly then, the public debate preceding and surrounding the adoption of federal deposit insurance was active and far-reaching.

This chapter is organized around the major themes of the debate: the actuarial questions concerning the effects of deposit insurance, the philosophical and practical questions of fairness to depositors and of depositor protection as an expedient means to financial stability, and the political and legal questions surrounding bank chartering and supervision. Much of the debate was motivated by economic and political self-interest and was structured rhetorically in terms of morality and justice. Considerable

Table 3.1 A chronology

10 Jan 1933	Sen. Huey Long's filibuster of the Glass legislation begins
21 Jan 1933	Senate filibuster ends
30 Jan 1933	Hitler becomes Chancellor of Germany
20 Feb 1933	Prohibition repealed
4 Mar 1933	Franklin D. Roosevelt is inaugurated 72nd Congress 2nd session ends Senate of the 73rd Congress convenes in special session
6 Mar 1933	Pres. Roosevelt declares a nation-wide bank holiday, lasting nine days
9 Mar 1933	Congress convenes in extraordinary session (first session of the 73rd Congress) The Emergency Banking Act is introduced, passed and signed into law
15 May 1933	Carter Glass introduces S. 1631
17 May 1933	Henry Steagall introduces H. R. 5661
19 May 1933	Arthur Vandenberg introduces an amendment to the Glass bill
23 May 1933	House passes Steagall bill
26 May 1933	Senate passes Glass–Vandenberg bill
27 May 1933	The Securities Act of 1933 signed
12 June 1933	World Monetary and Economic Conference opens in London
13 June 1933	Conference committee submits a conference report on the Banking Act to Congress Banking Act of 1933 is approved by Congress
16 June 1933	Pres. Roosevelt signs the Banking Act of 1933 First session of the 73rd Congress adjourns
4 Sept 1933	ABA Convention begins in Chicago (ends 7 Sept 1933)
17 Sept 1933	ABA President Frank Sisson dies
1 Jan 1934	Federal Deposit Insurance Corporation is chartered Temporary deposit insurance begins

attention is paid here to rhetorical detail.[6] A chronology to the debate is given in Table 3.1.

As much as possible, I have attempted to report the debate in its own terms – liberal use is made of quotations and epigraphs – rather than risk misconstruing the meaning through inaccurate paraphrase.

3.1 BACKGROUND TO THE DEBATE

The banking debate in 1933 covered not only deposit insurance and the separation of commercial and investment banking, but the full catalogue of financial matters: the gold standard, inflation, monetary policy and the contraction of bank credit, interstate branching, the relative merits of federal and state charters, holding company regulation, and so on. By 1933, nearly anything to do with banks or banking was an important political issue.

3.1.1 The Great Contraction

> The people know that the Federal Reserve octopus loaned ... to the gamblers of this Nation in 1928 some sixty billion dollars of credit money – bank money – hot air ... and then when the crisis came in the last 3 months of 1929, cut that credit money – bank money – hot air – down to thirteen billion.
>
> No nation, no industry, can survive such an expansion and contraction of money and credit. Give to me the power to double the money at will, and then give me the power to cut it square in two at will, and I can keep you in bondage.[7]

It is reasonable to begin a recollection of the debate over deposit insurance with the price collapse on the New York Stock Exchange of 29 October 1929. The stock market crash was popularly recognized as the start of the Great Depression. The remainder of the Hoover administration's tenure witnessed historic declines in national economic activity. By the beginning of 1933, industrial production and nominal GNP had both been cut in half; unemployment had topped 24 per cent. Bank failure rates, which had already been high throughout the 1920s, had increased fourfold, while both money supply and velocity had plummeted. The price level fell accordingly.

For contemporary economic commentators, the stock market crash was more than a marker between historical eras. For many, there was a causal relationship between the stock market's collapse and subsequent real economic activity. In most cases, this causality was more elaborate than *post hoc ergo propter hoc*. A prescient Paul Warburg, for example, warned in March 1929:

> If orgies of unrestrained speculation are permitted to spread too far, however, the ultimate collapse is certain not only to affect the speculators themselves, but also to bring about a general depression involving the entire country.[8]

The logic was that stock market speculation 'absorbs so much of the nation's credit supply that it threatens to cripple the country's regular business'.[9] A more radical theory was advanced by the 'liquidationists', who held sway in influential circles of government and the academy.[10] For them, the cyclical contraction was a good thing: it reflected the liquidation of unsuccessful investments that crept in during the boom years, thus freeing economic resources for a more efficient redeployment elsewhere.

3.1.2 Crisis and Unlimited Possibility

> We are confused. We grasp, as at straws, for the significance of events and of proposed government action. Never before in our lives have we had such great need for someone to interpret underlying movements for our guidance.[11]

By 1933, the correlation between economic activity and bank credit was lost on no one. During the interregnum between Hoover's electoral loss in November 1932 and Roosevelt's inauguration in March 1933, what had been a debilitating banking malaise became a desperate crisis. Starting with Michigan, on Valentine's Day, whole states began to declare official bank holidays; elsewhere, individual banks in scores were suspending withdrawals. By inauguration day, 4 March, most states had declared a holiday.[12] Even much earlier, bank failures had left whole towns without normal payment services, relegating them to barter.[13]

Theories of the connection between bank failures, monetary contraction and the more general macroeconomic torpidity were widespread and varied. Roosevelt, in his inaugural address, suggested that the set of people who correctly understood the nation's economic problems did not overlap with the set of people who had held the reins:

> Their efforts have been cast in the pattern of an outworn tradition. Faced by failure of credit they have proposed only the lending of more money. Stripped of the lure of profit by which to induce our people to follow their false leadership, they have resorted to exhortations, pleading tearfully for restored confidence. They know only the rules of a generation of self-seekers. They have no vision, and when there is no vision the people perish.[14]

To some extent, such a suggestion was accurate; Treasury Secretary Mellon and the liquidationists had initially refused even to admit that there was a problem.

Some proposed that complex intrigues were at work to sap the nation's wealth. Rep. Lemke (see the quote referenced by endnote 7), for example, advanced a monetarist thesis that both the boom of 1929 and the Depression were the intentional result of Federal Reserve policy. More conspiratorial still was Rep. McFadden's belief, advanced on the House floor, that 'money Jews' lay behind the banking crisis.[15] Rep. Weideman, offering the metaphor that 'the most dangerous beasts in the jungle make the softest approach', claimed that 'international money lenders' had duped the Congress into creating a system for skimming bank gold reserves into a central pool 'to feed the maw of international speculation'.[16]

Alarm generated by the crisis, and frustration at the lack of a remedy, combined to expand the political horizons. Radical solutions were suggested. Informed by the political experiments underway elsewhere, relatively sober proposals were submitted to scrap the inefficient bureaucracies of representative democracy in favor of a fascist dictatorship or state socialism.[17] More popular was a flirtation with government by 'technocracy', a small panel or cabinet of experts to replace the congressional and executive branches. Relative to alternatives such as these, federal deposit insurance – which had failed in Congress more than 150 times in the preceding 50 years – was a remarkably moderate option.[18]

3.1.3 Moral Overtones to the Debate

> The money changers have fled from their high seats in the temple of our civilization. We may now restore that temple to the ancient truths. The measure of the restoration lies in the extent to which we apply social values more noble than mere monetary profit.[19]

Both proponents and opponents of the deposit guaranty features of the Banking Act took the rhetorical high ground in arguing their point. Indeed, recourse to morality in public debate was widespread. The 'noble experiment' with the prohibition of liquor was still an issue in the 1932 election.[20] Oratory was laden with biblical imagery. Sen. Vandenberg (R-MI) referred to 'B.C. days – which is to say, Before the Crash ...'[21] A. C. Robinson saw fit to lecture subscribers to the *ABA Journal* on the 'Moral Values of Thrift', advising bankers of the need for 'an unshakeable conviction of these ideals [truth and morality] and their ultimate triumph. "If thou faint in the day of adversity, thy strength is small"'.[22]

For many, the Depression represented an atonement for the excesses of the bull market. By all accounts, 1929 was characterized by stock market speculation.[23] As the extent of the avarice became clear with hindsight, the notion of economic depression as punishment for economic transgression took hold:

> We are passing through chastening experiences, as severe for the banker as for anyone else, many of the illusions have disappeared and the

trappings of a meretricious prosperity have been stripped from most persons.[24]

The notion of recession as a necessary purgative unfortunately extended to policymakers as well. Mellon's advice to Hoover exposes the pious foundations to the liquidationist view of the Depression:

> It will purge the rottenness out of the system. High costs of living and high living will come down. People will work harder, live a more moral life. Values will be adjusted, and enterprising people will pick up the wrecks from less competent people.[25]

This fluency with righteousness revealed itself on all sides of the deposit insurance debate. Both proponents and detractors of the deposit guaranty provisions of the Banking Act argued that their position was ultimately a matter of simple justice, which dare not be denied. The bankers declared that well-managed banks should not be forced to subsidize poorly-run banks. Supporters of the legislation maintained that depositors should not have to bear the losses accruing to their bankers' mistakes. Those who felt that deposit insurance was a ploy to destroy the dual banking system painted a picture of the unit bank as the pillar of the national economy, untainted by corruption. The remainder of this chapter is organized around these three loosely defined constituencies.

3.2 ACTUARIAL DIFFICULTIES

Opposition to deposit insurance can be roughly organized into two classes: objections on technical actuarial grounds, and objections to its anticipated impact on bank structure. The core constituency in the former category consisted of the money-center banks, with ABA President Francis Sisson, himself a Wall Street banker, taking the lead.[26] The economic motivation for their opposition was the belief that insurance meant a net transfer from big banks, where the bulk of deposits lay, to state-chartered unit banks, where they expected the bulk of the losses.

3.2.1 Insurance and Guaranties

> In the law as written the guaranty plan is referred to not as a guaranty of bank deposits, but as an insurance plan. There is nothing in this plan that entitles it to be classed as insurance.[27]

> I think you gentlemen are all wrong to call this a guarantee of deposits. There is not a thing in the bill that talks about guarantee. It is an insurance of deposits.[28]

The actuarial correctness of the term 'deposit insurance' as a description of the proposed legislation was a point of contention. The alternative label, offered by opponents, was 'deposit guaranty'. One's choice of terms usually revealed where one stood on the issue, and the semantic controversy became a microcosm of the actuarial issues involved.[29] By labeling the various schemes as plans to 'guaranty' deposits, opponents were able to associate the plans immediately with the infelicitous recent experience with state deposit guaranty schemes (discussed in the next subsection). The natural response for supporters was to insist on a different label.

Both proponents and opponents devoted energy to identifying the desirable 'insurance principle,' which then either accurately described or failed to describe the proposed legislation.[30] Like blind men describing an elephant, however, few agreed on a definition for the insurance principle. This was so, despite Rep. Steagall's claim that the principle of insurance was 'the most universally accepted principle known to the business life of the world'.[31]

Deposit insurance was clearly similar in many respects to other types of insurance, which had been in widespread use in the United States for decades. Even the most ardent detractor recognized some resemblance:

> The general argument employed to promote the guaranty plan began with the premises that property can be insured and bank deposits are property. It travelled to the broad assumptions that the principle of the distribution of risk through insurance could be applied to bank deposits.[32]

The salient principles here, espoused repeatedly by supporters of the legislation, were the diversification of risk and the diffusion of losses. In this respect, a national plan would differ from the state plans, which had 'violated the primary insurance tenet that risks must be decentralized and sufficiently spread so as to avoid concentrated losses'.[33]

For others, the distinction between government and private backing defined the difference between insurance and guaranty. Both Sen. Glass and Rep. Steagall were adamant that coverage be provided privately, not by the government:

> This is not a Government guaranty of deposits ... The Government is only involved in an initial subscription to the capital of a corporation that we think will pay a dividend to the Government on its investment. It is not a Government guaranty.[34]

> I do not mean to be understood as favoring Government guaranty of bank deposits. I do not. I have never favored such a plan ... Bankers should insure their own deposits.[35]

The argument against government backing was outlined by Sen. Bulkley.[36]

An insurance feature included in both the Steagall and Glass bills and in Sen. Vandenberg's temporary insurance amendment to the Glass bill was a provision for depositor co-insurance.[37] The Glass and Steagall bills called for a progressive depositor copayment schedule: the first $10 000 would be covered in full, the next $40 000 would be covered at 75 per cent, and only 50 per cent of amounts over $50 000 would be covered; the Vandenberg amendment set a single coverage ceiling at $2500. Some proponents saw no need for such mitigating features. Rep. Dingell (D-MI), for example, offered bankers no quarter; his idea was 'to guarantee every dollar put in by the depositor from now on and to make the banker and the borrower pay the cost'.[38] For Sen. Vandenberg, on the other hand, co-insurance was crucial; he complained angrily when Treasury Secretary Woodin proposed 'not a limited insurance such as is included in the amendment which the Senate adopted, but a complete 100 per cent guarantee'.[39]

Opponents in the banking industry were unimpressed by such arguments. Although all of the proposals achieved a spreading of losses and many had other familiar features of insurance, such as co-insurance or provision for a large reserve fund, they still were not 'insurance'.[40] Francis Sisson was obstinate: 'Detailed and technical differences in this bill as compared with former guaranty schemes do not differentiate it in essential principle from them.'[41] For all their trouble, crafters of the legislation had failed to meet the bankers' standard for insurance, the principle of selected risks:

> Insurance involves an old and tried principle. The essence of insurance is the payment *by the insured* of premiums in *actuarial relation to the risk involved*. Under the terms of the permanent plan, however, the costs or premiums are not charged according to the risk.[42]

Roosevelt made a similar connection. In his first presidential press conference, he asserted:

> I can tell you as to guaranteeing bank deposits my own views, and I think those of the old Administration. The general underlying thought behind the use of the word 'guarantee' with respect to bank deposits is that you guarantee bad banks as well as good banks. The minute the Government starts to do that the Government runs into a probable loss.[43]

Although he associates the 'guaranty' terminology with government backing, its defining characteristic is clearly the absence of selected risks.

Despite the attention given to selected risks in the debate, no significant attempt appears to have been made to include a risk-based premium in legislation. Emerson, for one, thought such an arrangement could work.[44] The ABA, on the other hand, thought it impossible:

> The apparently unsurmountable actuarial difficulty in the guaranty plan appears to be the impossibility of placing it on the basis of selected risks;

the risks involved were 'wholly unpredictable', and banks were subject to 'internal deterioration' when their deposits were guaranteed.[45]

3.2.2 History and Geography

> As to the history of the guaranty plan, a wave of guaranty of state bank deposits laws swept over the seven contiguous western states of Oklahoma, Kansas, Texas, Nebraska, Mississippi, South Dakota and North Dakota and the Pacific Coast state of Washington in the period 1908–17 ... The laws establishing it were repealed or allowed to become inoperative as one after another of the plans became financially insolvent and was recognized as serving to make banking matters worse.[46]

As in the case of branch banking, nation-wide diversification of insurance risks would secure banking against any eventuality except such a national calamity as would destroy the Government itself.[47]

The 'guaranty' terminology connoted the defunct state deposit guaranty plans, a specter that terrorized the bankers. The mere mention of deposit guaranties could induce a banker to show 'every sign of incipient apoplexy'.[48] At the same time, the unvarying failure of the state plans provided a trove of evidence for foes of the federal scheme.[49] Release of the ABA report coincided with the introduction of the Glass and Steagall bills in Congress. It found perverse delight in the failure of all eight of the state plans:

> Eight large scale tests, by practical working experience, of the guaranty of bank deposits plan as a means for strengthening banking conditions and safeguarding the public interest are a matter of record. Each one of these attempts failed of its purpose.
>
> Taken separately, special circumstances such as technical defects in the plan or faulty administration might be held accountable for the breakdown in any given instance, leaving it an open question as to whether the idea might not be successful under different circumstances. Taken as a composite whole, however, the failures of the various plans not only confirm one another in their defects, but each one also supplies added special features that were tested and found wanting.[50]

This unbroken string of failures demanded an explanation from supporters of federal legislation. Proponents chose to distinguish clearly the new plan from the state schemes: 'there is no logical relationship between these old *State* Guarantees and this new *Federal* Insurance; no analogy; no parallel; and no reason to confuse the mortality of the former with the vitality of the latter'.[51]

To make this case, supporters emphasized foremost the much broader geographic – and therefore industrial – diversification of a federal insurance fund. 'The fact that bank-deposit-guaranty projects have failed in local, restricted areas only proves one of the fundamental principles of insurance, that is, that there must exist wide and general distribution and diversification.'[52] In particular, the old plans were said to have suffered from a 'one-crop' problem, that is, their application in states overwhelmingly dependent upon agriculture:

> There is a vast difference between what can be accomplished by a small number of banks in one State dependent upon a single crop and what can be successfully accomplished by the banking system of this great Nation that holds the financial leadership of the world in its hands.[53]

On this point, at least, the bankers were forced to concede.[54]

The bankers revealed the geographic breadth of the federal plan to be a two-edged sword, however, and used it to fight back. They exploited the well-known fact that bank failures throughout the 1920s had occurred disproportionately among small, rural banks (see Table 3.2).[55]

Table 3.2 Estimated assessments and losses by geographic division

Geographic division	*Per cent of assessments in each division to total assessment*	*Per cent of losses in each division during 1921–31 to total losses*
New England	7.6	3.7
Middle Atlantic	44.0	20.0
North Central	18.6	21.9
Southern Mountain	3.5	5.8
Southeastern	2.8	13.7
Southwestern	4.3	7.0
Western Grain	8.0	20.7
Rocky Mountain	1.8	4.5
Pacific Coast	9.4	2.7
United States	100.0%	100.0%

Source: Association of Reserve City Bankers (1933).

This information was used to argue that, with insurance premia assessed against deposits, the burden of funding federal deposit insurance – had it existed during the 1920s – would have been borne in large measure by the money center banks of the Northeast, where much of the industry's deposit base lay. The benefits of insurance, however – the payments to cover losses in failed banks – would have gone south and west.

3.2.3 Subsidy and Discipline

> For it is to be remembered that the weak banks get the same insurance as the strong ones, and, unlike the situation in other kinds of insurance, the bad risk pays no more for its insurance than the good one. This means competition among banks in slackness in the granting of loans. The bank with the loose credit policy gets the business and the bank with the careful, cautious credit policy loses it. The slack banker dances and the conservative banker pays the fiddler. If the conservative banker protests, the slack one invites him to go to a warmer climate. Soon all are dancing and the fiddler, if paid at all, must collect from the depositors or from the taxpayers.[56]

For those who opposed deposit insurance on actuarial grounds, such technicalities were merely manifestations of a more fundamental issue. As a matter of principle, deposit insurance was held to be unjust. It involved the forced subsidization of poorly managed banks by well managed institutions; it subsidized the 'bad' banker at the expense of the 'good'. This moral point provided substantial emotional force. Opponents concluded that only good bank management could ultimately assure safe and sound banking.

Their argument, founded in actuarial theory and the experience of the state plans, proceeded in two steps. First, by protecting depositors against loss, a deposit guaranty would destroy discipline; insured depositors would take no interest in the quality of their bank's management. Recalling the state plans, the guaranty had created 'a sense of false security and lack of discrimination as between good and bad banking'.[57] In many minds, this dichotomy between good and bad bankers was the central issue.[58] *Bankers Magazine* editorialized that 'the surest reliance of good banking is to be found in the men who manage the banks rather than in the laws governing their operations'.[59] In 1931, ABA President Rome Stephenson contended that a large element in the internal conditions of the banks that failed was bad management and that a predominant element in the internal conditions of the bank that remained sound in the face of the same external conditions was good management.[60] What was needed was to teach 'the conception of scientific banking'.[61]

The second step in the logic of opposition was an objection to the subsidy implicit in a guaranty. In the tones of a prudish parent, the ABA complained that the beneficiaries of state systems had been the 'bankers with easier standards', who gained competitive advantages over those with 'sounder but less attractive methods'.[62] The subsidy was especially problematic among those banks 'which have little chance of ultimate success'.[63]

> A bank which does not earn a fair average rate of return over a period of years not only is unable to build up reserves against bad times, but, in order to improve profits, is under constant temptation to take risks which in the end are likely to lead to failure.
>
> The tendency of a guaranty plan will be to nurture these unprofitable units and keep them going temporarily in the knowledge that upon failure the losses can be shifted to other banks.[64]

Thus, the subsidy was seen to extend beyond the simple protection of unsound institutions from the competitive pressures of vigilant depositors. Given their contention that, 'no provision is made for building up a reserve fund', losses charged to the insurer by failing banks would have to be recouped after the fact from the survivors.[65] Such a system would necessarily entail transfers of wealth from surviving to failed banks.

There was no consensus in Congress on the importance of discipline; some members pointed out that life insurance was no incentive for suicide.[66] The framers of the Glass and Steagall bills, however, recognized the validity of the bankers' objections and addressed the issue directly. Both bills, as well as the temporary insurance amendment in the Senate, were careful to limit coverage. Sen. Vandenberg stated explicitly the rationale for coverage ceilings:

> the *State* Guarantees involved complete protection for *all* banking resources ... *Federal* Insurance, on the other hand, leaves the individual bank and banker so seriously responsible for such a preponderance of their resources that there is no appreciable immunity at all.[67]

Sen. Glass noted a second source of discipline inherent in the plan. Because the banks insured each other, deposit insurance would 'lead to the severest espionage upon the rotten banks of this country that we have ever had'.[68]

Under both the temporary and permanent plans, the small depositor was to be covered in full, in recognition of his inability to monitor bank management adequately:

> At present the depositor is at the mercy of his fellow depositors, over whom he has no control, and of the management of the bank, about which he is not usually in a position to be well informed. The depositor takes the risks, and the banks take the profits.[69]

A survey conducted by the Comptroller of the Currency and the Federal Reserve in May 1933 revealed that the ceiling of $2500 under the temporary plan would fully cover 96.5 per cent of depositors and 23.7 per cent of total deposits in member banks.[70]

3.3 PROTECTING DEPOSITS

While most industry opponents fought the deposit insurance plan on actuarial grounds, supporters argued that deposits *per se* required protection to stabilize the medium of exchange and promote a renewed expansion of bank credit. More significantly, proponents responded with an argument of powerful simplicity: the losses to innocent depositors in a bank failure were a plain injustice. Given the status of banks in the political climate of 1933, this was a charge that the bankers ultimately could not counter.

3.3.1 The Agglomeration of Deposits for Speculation

> The use of banking funds for speculation became a stench in the nostrils of the people.[71]

There was a strong sense that the banking industry in the 1920s had functioned as an elaborate network to collect savings at the local level and funnel them into lending on securities speculation:

> Another cause for many banking collapses was the domination of smaller banks by their large metropolitan correspondents, which drained funds from the country districts for speculative purposes and loaded up the small bank with worthless securities.[72]

Indeed, this was a primary motivation for those sections of the Banking Act requiring a separation of commercial and investment banking. Similar arguments were brought against proposals for nationwide branch, chain and group banking.[73]

A sensitivity to such a possibility was doubtless nurtured by the popularity of Ponzi schemes in the 1920s, including the infamous Florida land swindles.[74] With such analogies in mind, banks came to be seen as:

> ... merely fueling departments in enterprises run not by bankers concerned with operating banks but by promoters whose object was to exploit the credit resources of the bank ...
>
> The primary evil in our banks for many years has been the incessant efforts of promoters to get control of the funds which flow into the banks. The bank is the depository of the community's funds and as such is the basis of the available credit of the community. The promoter-banker needs nothing so much as access to these credit pools.[75]

Such accusations were inevitably tinged with at least a hint of the conspiratorial.[76]

In keeping with this theme, the issues were framed for popular consumption as a morality play in which the naive depositor is pitted against the sophisticated banker. The depositor tucks away the hard-earned wages of his honest labor, only to be systematically duped by the cunning intrigues of the banker. At the extreme, some politicians played the religious card face up: 'We discovered that what we believed to be a bank system was in fact a respectable racket and so many connected with it only cheap, petty loan sharks and Shylocks'.[77] In the end, a providential government was seen to intercede on behalf of the depositor, and deposit insurance was trumpeted as 'the shadow of a great rock in a weary land'.[78]

The notion of the small depositor as an innocent victim had immense popular appeal. McCutcheon's 1931 political cartoon celebrating the blamelessness of the depositor in a failed bank won the Pulitzer Prize. Such popularity, of course, was plainly evident to politicians, who responded by introducing deposit insurance legislation in Congress. Rep. Steagall is reported to have told House Speaker Garner in April 1932, 'You know, this fellow Hoover is going to wake up one day soon and come in here with a message recommending guarantee of bank deposits, and as sure as he does, he'll be re-elected'.[79]

For obvious reasons, bank failures concentrated the attention of large numbers of voters, and Congressmen were anxious to associate themselves with the legislation. Sen. Vandenberg, up for re-election in 1934, was always careful to call his temporary insurance amendment to the Banking Act of 1933 'The Vandenberg Amendment'. Rep. Dingell announced: 'guaranty of bank deposits is my baby in Michigan'.[80] A petition circulated in the House in June 1933 to postpone adjournment indefinitely until a deposit insurance bill was made law.[81] Figure 3.1 reveals that the number of guaranty bills introduced in Congress correlated neatly with the number of bank failures.

Theatrics aside, the central point for proponents of the legislation remained, and it was difficult to refute: 'The main point is always this – *the depositor owns the money*. If he puts it in for safe-keeping it should be safely kept'.[82] Indeed, opponents conceded directly that depositor losses in bank failure were unjust.[83] Instead, they tried to redirect the debate to the question of 'whether the guaranty plan will in fact cure the defects in our banking system and give depositors the safety which they seek and to which they are entitled'.[84] On this latter question, the bankers remained obstinately negative; they favored 'reform methods for banking that really strengthen banking', and therefore opposed deposit guaranties.[85]

3.3.2 The Stabilization of the Medium of Exchange

> We think of the busy bee and the ant as tireless, but they are loafers compared with the activity of a busy dollar.[86]

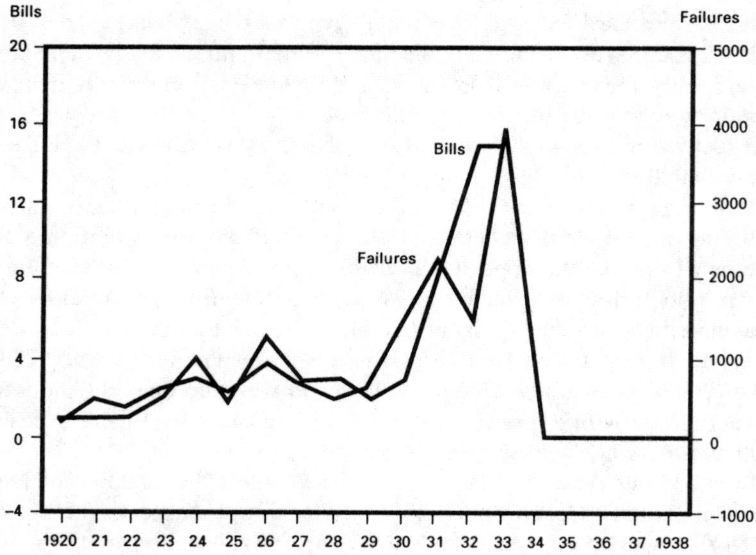

Figure 3.1 The cause of deposit insurance

> We got the guarantee of bank notes after having had wildcat banking in connection with State bank notes and after having had people injured who held notes of the State banks …
>
> It is much more important in principle to guarantee bank deposits, because the real circulating medium of the country is bank deposits.[87]

Although, as a strictly political matter, depositor protection was the central motivation responsible for the progress of deposit insurance in Congress, other forces were at issue. Chief among these was the role of banking in the real economy. Regarding bank failures, it was recognized that causality ran two ways: just as the general drop in real incomes had caused loan defaults and thus widespread bank failures, bank failures and the concomitant restriction of bank services had caused real incomes to fall. The latter effect was seen to operate both directly and indirectly.

Bank suspensions and failures could trap depositors' wealth for a period of months or even years until the bank either reopened or its bankruptcy was resolved. The direct result was reduced consumption and investment spending by the affected depositors. In the extreme case, when a town's lone bank failed, even the simplest forms of exchange could be hopelessly encumbered:

> [The unacceptability of failure] would perhaps not be so if they were grocery stores or butcher shops, where failure would be disastrous to only a few people at most; but bank failures paralyze the economic life of whole communities, not only through the loss of money accumulations but by the destruction of the deposit currency which is the principal medium of exchange in all business activity.[88]

Under such circumstances, some affected regions instituted scrip currencies, wooden coinage or systematic barter arrangements, the most elaborate of which was the Emergency Exchange Association in New York, headed by Leland Olds.[89]

A depositor's natural response to these possibilities was to withdraw his funds before failure occurred. Both bank runs and the hoarding of currency received considerable attention.[90] Withdrawals for the purpose of safeguarding one's wealth were deemed unpatriotic; legislation was even proposed to outlaw the practice. Banks had a natural response to the threat of runs: 'Credit was tightened in the desire to remain as liquid as possible to meet the emergencies of runs'.[91] Bankers maintained large cash reserves rather than lend:

> It is estimated that banks now have available billions of dollars of collateral for use in extending loans, but the plain fact is that for more than 3 years bankers have given little thought to anything except to keep their banks in liquid condition ... The fear that grips the minds and hearts of bankers, keeping ever before them the nightmare of bank runs, makes it impossible for them to extend the credits that are indispensable to trade and commerce.[92]

This analysis is confirmed by the facts. The aggregate excess reserves of Federal Reserve member banks, for example, had ballooned from $42 million in October 1929 to a peak of $584 million in January 1933, even though the number of member banks had fallen from 8616 to 6816 over roughly the same period.[93] Thus, bank failures were seen to have an indirect effect on output, as both depositors and bankers in solvent institutions prepared for the possibility of runs and failures.

In the final analysis, depositor protection and stabilization of the medium of exchange were recognized as opposite sides of the same coin:

> We may talk about percentage of gold back of our currency, we may discuss technical provisions of legislation ... The public does not understand these technical discussions, but from one end of this land to the

> other the people understand what we mean by guaranty of bank deposits; and they demand of you and me that we provide a banking system worthy of this great Nation and banks in which citizens may place the fruits of their toil and know that a deposit slip in return for their hard earnings will be as safe as a Government bond. [Applause]
>
> They know that banks cannot serve the public until confidence is restored, until the public is willing to take money now in hiding and return it to the banks as a basis for the expansion of bank credit. This is indispensable to the support of business and the successful financing of the Treasury. It will bring increased earnings, higher incomes, and make it possible to balance the Government's Budget without resort to vicious and vexatious methods of taxation.[94]

As such, they should be considered inseparable; it is clear that supporters of the legislation intended it to achieve both ends. Attempts to rank the two issues according to their relative importance are likely to be inconclusive.[95]

3.3.3 The Chastening of Wall Street

> One banker in my state attempted to marry a white woman and they lynched him.[96]

The opposition to federal deposit guaranties emanated largely from the nation's bankers. This fact was a crushing liability to their cause in the political climate of 1933. The introduction of the Glass and Steagall bills came on the heels of the banking panic and, not entirely coincidentally, amid the daily revelations of self-dealing and other cupidities from the Pecora hearings.[97] The banker had become a pariah.

Roosevelt fired the opening volley for his administration in his inaugural address:

> Plenty is at our doorstep, but a generous use of it languishes in the very sight of the supply. Primarily this is because the rulers of the exchange of mankind's goods have failed, through their own stubbornness and their own incompetence, have admitted their failure, and abdicated. Practices of the unscrupulous money changers stand indicted in the court of public opinion, rejected by the hearts and minds of men.[98]

He went on to demand safeguards against the 'evils of the old order': strict supervision of banking, an end to speculation with 'other people's money', and provision for an adequate but sound currency.[99]

Others were happy to follow this lead. It was commonplace to hold the bankers, and particularly their 'speculative orgy' of 1929, responsible for the nation's woes:

> You brought this country to the greatest panic in human history! ... There never was such an economic failure in the history of mankind as your outfit has brought upon us at this time, and it is due to this same speculation that you are defending here more than any other one thing.[100]

> But these affiliates, I repeat, were the most unscrupulous contributors, next to the debauch of the New York Stock Exchange, to the financial catastrophe which visited this country and was mainly responsible for the depression under which we have been suffering since.[101]

In the previous year, Huey Long had announced his intent to campaign for Roosevelt under the slogan: 'Rid the country of the millionaires'.[102] A popular ditty mocked:

> Mellon pulled the whistle,
> Hoover rang the bell,
> Wall Street gave the signal,
> And the country went to hell.[103]

In short, the bankers were vilified.

Although some felt such indiscriminate abuse was slanderous, they fought against the tide.[104] One of the casualties of the anti-banker sentiment was the bankers' battle against deposit insurance. Some in Congress announced that the bankers' opinions should be openly ignored:

> I believe that the myopic banker as an adviser should receive about as much consideration at the hands of the House as a braying jackass on the prairies of Missouri. They proved by their inability to maintain their own business that they have absolutely no right to advise the House as to what course we should follow.[105]

The bankers, while they acknowledged the merit of individual aspects of the deposit insurance proposals, obstinately refused to countenance any of the schemes as a realistic reform. Even as the legislation was signed into law, Francis Sisson called a crusade, rallying ABA members to fight 'to the last ditch against the guaranty provisions' of the bill.[106] That the bankers' concerns were not ignored entirely resulted largely from the presence in government of opponents of deposit guaranties who were more politically astute than the bankers themselves. Sen. Glass, for example, compromised his principles in a bid for some control over the legislation, explaining that it was 'better to deal with the problem in a cautious and a conservative way than to have ourselves run over in a stampede'.[107] Roosevelt held out until the very end, thus forcing Congress to concede in delaying implementation of the temporary plan until January 1934.

3.4 BANK MARKET STRUCTURE

The ramifications of deposit insurance were recognized as far-reaching. In many ways, the central and most contentious battle concerned neither actuarial feasibility nor the desirability of protecting deposits, but the regulatory issues of bank chartering and supervision. Because of the fundamental legal issues involved, it was here that the economic and political aspects of the debate became most fully intertwined. This was a fight with the weight of a long tradition behind it, and arguments were often self-consciously historical.

3.4.1 Regulatory Competition and Lax Supervision

> Bank examinations to be effective must be made by experienced men, free from political influence ... We will never have proper banking supervision, national or state, until it is taken entirely away from political influence.[108]

Much of the blame for high rates of bank failure throughout the 1920s was placed upon competition between state and federal authorities. Because banks could choose the less costly of federal and state charters – and the associated regulations – state and federal regulators were forced into a 'competition in laxity' if they were to sustain the realm of their bureaucratic influence.[109] For example, as a prelude to recommending broader powers for national banks, Comptroller Pole emphasized that:

> If Congress therefore would protect itself from the loss of its present banking instrumentality, it must make it to the advantage of capital to seek the national rather than a [state] trust company charter ...

> ... it is within the power of Congress to turn the advantage in favor of the national banks and thereby make it to the interest of all banks to operate under the national charter.[110]

In the eyes of opponents of deposit insurance, an especially important manifestation of the competition in laxity was the 'promiscuous granting of bank charters'.[111] The immediate result of loose chartering was a condition called 'over-banking', or:

> ...a host of weak, unreliable banks that crowd one another out of existence by being too numerously organized in places where there is no support for the multifarious institutions that have been established there.[112]

This 'indiscreet indulgence of charter applicants' was held responsible for the vast numbers of bank failures throughout the previous decade:[113]

> There are too many banks in the United States. The areas of greatest density of banks per capita coincide with the areas where failures are proportionately highest.[114]

The function of a deposit guaranty under such circumstances would be to exacerbate the problem by mitigating one source of public scrutiny: inspection by depositors. Opponents confirmed their contention by reference to the ill-fated state guaranty schemes:

> In practice the guaranty of deposits plan generally tended to induce an unsound expansion in the number of banks ... This was clearly connected with the indiscriminate popular confidence created toward the banks under the guaranty.[115]

> It is to be feared that the adoption of deposit guaranty laws may have somewhat retarded the inevitably slow and unsensational process of strengthening the banking system by strict regulation, vigilant public opinion and strict requirements.[116]

The Association of Reserve City Bankers went further, predicting that managers of the insurance fund would be slow to close troubled institutions.[117] In addition to regulatory competition, some saw political influence as a secondary force debilitating the supervisory process:

> We never will have such supervision under political regulation and examination; we will never have any supervision worthy of the name that does not have real authority and heavy responsibility tied to it.[118]

Only a few supporters of insurance addressed directly the plan's implications for the regulatory process, which they presented as a counterweight to incentives for bad banking under a guaranty. Rome Stephenson felt that the additional regulatory powers in the Banking Act differentiated the FDIC markedly from the state plans:

> Right there is the crux of the debate: Will banks under the federal plan be permitted the abuses which were tolerated in every one of the states where guaranty was tried? If so, then failure is inevitable. If not, success is practically certain ... let me assert unequivocally that the men who drew up the federal plan profited by the mistakes of the state guaranty failures and avoided them ... None of the state laws had teeth in them. The federal law has teeth like a man-eating shark, and already has done some highly effective biting.[119]

Carter Glass, railing that 'the Comptroller's office has not done its duty – its sworn duty – and has permitted this great number of banks to engage in irregular and illicit practices', argued that mutual responsibility inherent in the insurance plan implied mutual supervision: if the strong banker 'knows that he has got to bear a part of the burden of my irregular banking, he is going to report me to the Comptroller of the Currency and is going to insist that his examiners come there and do their duty'.[120]

3.4.2 The Dual Banking Question

> The fact is, of course, that the deposit insurance scheme would not have been permitted by the conservative leaders in Congress if its organization could not have been so shaped as to further their idea of a unified system of banking in the country under the Reserve System. On the other hand, the more radical elements, in response to popular demand for some sort of protection for bank depositors, could not have built a nationwide guaranty system upon any other foundation than the Reserve organization.[121]

Questions about the effect of insurance on the quality of chartering and supervision were sideshows to the main event, however. At the heart of the debate lay a decades-old controversy over the dual banking system.

Given its far-reaching nature, the proposed legislation was universally regarded as a prime opportunity for fundamental changes in banking policy.

Comptroller Pole had campaigned vigorously throughout his four-year tenure for some form of interstate branching for national banks. He drew a strong distinction between the small, state-chartered, rural unit bank – the 'country' bank – and the large, nationally chartered institution. While he pretended to maintain great respect for the small unit bank as the 'single type of institution which has contributed the most to … the foundation of our national development', he was fighting to have them replaced by branch networks of national banks.[122] He justified this split sentiment by arguing that irreversible social changes – telephone, radio, and especially the automobile – had forever obviated the rural isolation that had made the unit bank competitively viable. Accompanied by a long parade of statistics, he emphasized the high failure rate of small, state-chartered banks during the 1920s.[123] The country bank, he said, could not survive in competition with large metropolitan institutions, which had more professional management and were inevitably better diversified.

Comptroller Pole was not alone in this crusade. The McFadden Act had already broadened the branching powers of national banks; in 1930, the House Banking Committee arranged new hearings into the possibility of national or regional branch banking.[124] The unsuccessful Glass bill of 1932 included limited provisions for statewide branching by national banks. *Business Week* staked out the extreme position, announcing that 'what we really need is just one big bank with 20 000 branches'.[125] Supporters of branch banking took heart in the Canadian experience:

> Canada has branch banking, and Canada has not had any bank failures during the depression. Is this a matter of cause and effect?
> 'It is', declare the advocates of branch banking in the United States.[126]

Such highly concentrated branch networks were offered as an alternative to deposit insurance as a means for the geographic diffusion of loan losses and the diversification of credit risks.[127]

Comptroller Pole, of course, felt branching to be the better option:

> Any attempt to maintain the present country bank system by force of legislation in the nature of guaranty of deposits or the like, would be economically unsound and would not accomplish the purpose intended.[128]

Deposit guaranties had long been advocated as a way of diversifying risk for the unit bank without a fundamental change in the ownership structure of the banking industry.[129] The various histories of Populism, 'Bryanism', the Panic of 1907 and the Pujo hearings all contained elements of a deep popular mistrust of money center banks. The publicity of the Pecora hearings in 1933 clearly did not assuage this mistrust. It was not pure coincidence that the western agricultural states – the heart of the Grange and Populist movements – had been the ones to enact state deposit guaranties. In this context, then, it is ironic that, in 1933, federal deposit insurance should most often have been viewed as a lethal threat to the country bank. That it was such a threat testifies to the influence and legislative skill of Carter Glass.

Sen. Glass, who had shepherded the Federal Reserve Act through the House in 1913, was protective of his handiwork:

> I took occasion to tell the Secretary of the Treasury the other day that if they pursue present policies much longer they will literally wreck the Federal Reserve System; that Woodrow Wilson in history will enjoy the distinction of having set up a banking system that fought the war for us and saved the Nation in the post-war period, and if they keep on making a doormat of it this Congress will enjoy the distinction of having wrecked it.[130]

His primary concern in the banking legislation of 1933 was to buttress that system. Thus, the Glass bill required all FDIC member banks to join the Federal Reserve System, ostensibly to give the Fed the legal right to examine FDIC members (the Fed was to be a prominent shareholder in the FDIC).[131] Because an uninsured country bank facing insured competitors was not considered viable, and because Fed membership would require at least $25 000 minimum capital, deposit insurance represented the end for the small, state non-member banks.[132] Deposit insurance would force a consolidation of banking within the Federal Reserve System.

It is instructive to note that Glass had abandoned an earlier scheme that would have forced the same consolidation within the Fed: unification of banking in the National Banking System. Comptroller Pole had sought to accomplish the same thing indirectly, by providing national banks with an undeniable competitive advantage in the form of interstate branching privileges. In 1932, Glass had requested of Gov. Meyer of the Federal Reserve a constitutional method of unifying banking:

Meyer: 'Do you want to bring about unified banking?'
Glass: 'Why, undoubtedly, yes'.
Meyer: 'I shall be glad to help you'.
Glass: 'I think the curse of the banking business in this country is the dual system'.
Meyer: 'Then the Board is entirely in sympathy with the Committee on the subject'.[133]

The result was a legal opinion prepared by the General Counsel of the Federal Reserve Board on the constitutionality of such unification in the absence of a constitutional amendment.[134] While Board Counsel confirmed that such a constitutional means existed, Sen. Gore introduced a constitutional amendment.[135] Constitutionality was crucial, because champions of the rural unit bank were certain to raise the powerful specter of states' rights in opposition:

> The fight regarding the American Dual System of Banking is a clear-cut issue between those who believe in the sovereignty of our states and home rule, and those who are in favor of a 'unification of our banking system' into one Washington bureau.[136]

Indeed, the political sensitivity of the states' rights issue was sufficient to force Sen. Glass to abandon such a direct assault on the state banks before it could earnestly begin.[137]

Arrayed against Sen. Glass in the battle for unification within the Fed was a coalition led by Henry Steagall in the House and Huey Long in the Senate.[138] Sen. Long had crippled Glass's banking bill in the previous Congress with a ten-day filibuster; as champion of the common man, he had objected to an envisioned concentration of power implicit in the bill's branching provisions.[139] This coalition indeed viewed deposit insurance as a means of survival for the small bank:

> If there is one purpose more than another which is inherent in the amendment which is now at stake in this conference, it is the purpose to protect the smaller banking institutions, and to make the reopening of closed banks possible as speedily and as safely as it can be done.[140]

The final legislation was a two-stage compromise between Sen. Glass's push for unification and the Steagall–Long coalition's desire to preserve the dual banking system. In the first stage, Glass agreed to support a deposit guaranty in exchange for provisions for significantly expanded Federal Reserve authority:

> With these provisions, dependent upon them in fact, the Senate bill drafters were willing to accept the new Steagall bill for the insurance or guaranty of bank deposits in Federal Reserve member banks – but in member banks only.[141]

In the second stage, the dual banking supporters obtained several concessions, most notably: immediate insurance coverage for non-member banks under the temporary plan, and grandfathering of small state banks under the new minimum capital standards for Fed membership. Non-member banks would still have to apply for Federal Reserve membership by 1 July 1936 at the latest. With these changes, Sen. Long supported the bill, which then passed the Senate without objection.[142] A summary of the legislation is shown in Table 3.3.

3.5 CONCLUSIONS

> Prophesying the future of Federal Deposit Insurance is at the same time both difficult and simple. It is difficult because the subject cannot be treated independently, that is, without relation to banking structure, banking practice, political and economic trends and human emotions. It is easy, on the other hand, because ... any man's guess is as good as that of another.[143]

It is obvious from an examination of the record that the debate surrounding the adoption of federal deposit insurance was both wide-ranging and well informed. The banking crisis in March 1933, coming at the depths of the Great Depression and breaking on inauguration day, had focused attention with unique intensity on all aspects of public policy toward banks. While some contended that the urgency accompanying the crisis injected haste into the proceedings, it also ensured that all major interests were roused to offer their views and argue their cases.

It has been suggested that the framers of the Banking Act of 1933 failed to consider the warnings about the potential dangers of government-sponsored deposit insurance.[144] It is significant, then, that an examination of the historical record clearly shows that bill's chief patrons were aware of the failure of the state schemes, the actuarial arguments against deposit guaranties, and the various chartering issues involved. Moreover, they took

Table 3.3 The four that passed

	Banking Act of 1933 (temporary plan)	*Banking Act of 1933 (permanent plan)*	*Act of 1934 extending temporary deposit insurance*	*Banking Act of 1935*
Period of Operation	From 1 Jan 1934 to 1 July 1934, or earlier if the President so proclaims	From 1 July 1934 (or earlier if Pres. proclaims). – Never operational –	From 1 July 1934 to 1 July 1935 (extended to 31 Aug 1935 in June of 1935)	From 23 August 1935 onward
Coverage	All deposits covered in full up to $2500	100% coverage up to $10 000 75% on the next $40 000 50% of all over $50 000	All deposits covered in full up to $5000	All deposits covered in full up to $5000
Membership	All Fed member banks required to join. Non-members allowed in with state certification and approval of the corporation	All Fed member banks required to join. Non-members allowed in from 1 July 1934 to 1 July 1936 (with state and FDIC approval); Fed membership required by 1 July 1936	All Fed member banks required to join. Non-members allowed in until 1 July 1937 (with state and FDIC approval); Fed membership required by 1 July 1937	All Fed member banks required to join. Non-members allowed in with FDIC approval. Non-members with 1941 avg. deposits over $1 mill. must join by 1 July 1942

Table 3.3 Continued

	Banking Act of 1933 (temporary plan)	*Banking Act of 1933 (permanent plan)*	*Act of 1934 extending temporary deposit insurance*	*Banking Act of 1935*
Assessments on insured banks	0.5% of insured deposits, one half paid in cash, the other half subject to call. One more such assessment as needed. Surplus as of 1 July 1934 to be refunded	0.5% of total deposits, half in cash, half subject to call. Extra assessments of 0.25% of total deposits, as needed and without upper limit	Same as under the temporary plan of the Banking Act of 1933, except the surplus is to be measured and refunded as of 1 July 1935	Annual assessment of 1/12 of 1% of avg. total deposits, payablle in two instalments
FDIC's Capital	Provided according to the assessment schedule	$150 mill. on call from Treasury (to pay 6% div.) + one-half the surplus of Fed Res. banks (ca. $139 mill.) for $100 par, no-div., non-voting stock + 0.5% of deposits of FDIC banks ($150–200 mill.) for $100 par, 6% div., non-voting stock	Provided according to the assessment schedule	Same as under the permanent plan of 1933, except: all stock is nopar, nodiv., non-voting; insured banks do not buy FDIC stock; and Fed Res. bank surpluses are measured as of 1 Jan 1935, rather than 1 Jan 1933
Control	Board of three: the Comptroller and two Presidential appointees	Same	Same	Same

these issues into account when crafting the bill. In the end, even the Association of Reserve City Bankers was able to recommend the temporary insurance plan:

> It appears to this Commission that if guaranty is retained after 1 July 1934 [the date for implementation of the permanent plan], this temporary plan, in some modified form, would meet every emergency need, and eliminate many of the dangers in the permanent plan.[145]

Under the temporary plan, coverage ceilings were conservative, the insurance corporation was emphatically segregated from the federal taxpayer, chartering standards for national banks were raised, and supervisory authority was broadly increased. These characteristics were retained under the permanent plan of the Banking Act of 1935. As such, deposit insurance, as construed in the Banking Acts of 1933 and 1935, succeeded in simultaneously protecting the small depositor and leaving the banker answerable to both supervisors and large depositors for the quality of his management.

At the same time, the deposit insurance provisions of the Banking Act of 1933 were used as leverage to consolidate the industry within the Federal Reserve, although the Banking Act of 1935 significantly weakened the requirements for Fed membership of insured banks. A piecemeal dismantling of other provisions of the original legislation has also occurred in the intervening decades: coverage ceilings have risen steadily, even after accounting for inflation and before considering brokered deposits or too-big-to-fail policies; the full taxing authority of the US Treasury has, *de facto*, been inserted behind the deposit insurance corporations; and deregulation has subjected both banks and thrifts to increasingly harsher competition – and, in some cases, relaxed regulatory scrutiny – without simultaneously making bankers responsible to depositors for the riskiness of bank assets.[146] It is perhaps with this more recent negation of individual elements of a complex and interdependent package of bank reforms that we should seek the proximate cause of our recent deposit insurance troubles, rather than with policy flaws in the Banking Act of 1933 itself.

Notes

* This essay was delivered at a conference of The Jerome Levy Economics Institute in 1993 and previously published in the *Review* (Federal Reserve Bank of St Louis, 1992)

1. Quoted by Sen. Murphy (D-IA) in *Congressional Record* (1933), p. 3008.

2. The Federal Deposit Insurance Corporation (FDIC) has recently announced a move toward risk-adjustment of its insurance premia.
3. The Act is often called the Glass–Steagall Act. It is referred to here as the Banking Act of 1933 to avoid confusion with the separate Glass–Steagall Act of 1932. Significantly, it also has the longer official title: 'An Act to provide for the safer and more effective use of the assets of banks, to regulate interbank control, to prevent the undue diversion of funds into speculative operations, and for other purposes'. The temporary plan was later extended, and the permanent plan delayed, for one year (to 1 July 1935) by the Act of 16 June 1934. The Banking Act of 1935 substantially emended the permanent plan to resemble closely the temporary plan. See Table 3.3, 'The four that passed' for further details of the various plans.
4. The Federal Reserve did not adopt an official position, although there is some evidence of opposition: 'Deposit guaranty by mutual insurance is not part of the Presidential program, nor is it favored by Federal Reserve authorities', 'Permanent Bank Reform' (1933); see also Kennedy (1973), pp. 217–18. Comptroller O'Connor favored deposit insurance; former Comptroller Pole opposed it.
5. The Senate did not record a vote, although even Sen. Huey Long (D-LA), who had been a flamboyant detractor, rose to speak in favor of the bill. Cummings (1933) claims that the Senate vote was unanimous. The House dissenters included Reps. McFadden (R-PA), McGugin (R-KS), Beck (R-PA) and Kvale (Farmer/Labor-MN). See 'Congress Passes and President Roosevelt Signs Glass–Steagall Bank Bill as Agreed on in Conference' (1933), p. 4192. Rep. McGugin's request for a division revealed 191 ayes and 6 noes; a quorum of 237 was reported present; *Congressional Record* (1933), p. 5898.
6. Most of what remains of the debate is formalized oratory: prepared speeches, Congressional debate, letters to the editor, etc. Because the debate was a cacophony of voices, rather than an orderly dialogue, no attempt has been made to present the arguments in chronological order. A time line of the significant events of 1933 is provided in Table 3.1, 'a chronology'. In terms of the written record, academic economists entered the debate late, for the most part after the Banking Act of 1933 had already been signed into law. See H. Preston (1933), Westerfield (1933), Willis (1934), Willis and Chapman (1934), Taggart and Jennings (1934), Fox (1936) and Jones (1938). Phillips (1993) reports that Frank Knight and several colleagues at the University of Chicago advocated federal guaranty of deposits as part of comprehensive bank reforms proposed during the banking crisis in March 1933. Willis had been an advisor to Carter Glass since the debate over the Federal Reserve Act in 1912. Guy Emerson, who published in the *Quarterly Journal of Economics*, was not an academician, but an officer at Bankers Trust Co. and the 1930 president of the Association of Reserve City Bankers; Emerson (1934) is largely a paraphrase of Association of Reserve City Bankers (1933), which he co-authored.
7. Rep. Lemke (R-ND), *Congressional Record* (1933), p. 3908.
8. Warburg (1929), p. 569.
9. Warburg (1929), p. 571.
10. De Long (1990) provides a valuable review of the liquidationist perspective. The liquidationists included Secretary of the Treasury Andrew Mellon,

as well as the economists Friedrich von Hayek, Lionel Robbins, Seymour Harris and Joseph Schumpeter. More recent economic analyses have discounted the role of the crash in causing the Depression, emphasizing instead other forces, both monetary and non-monetary; see Wheelock (1992a) and the references therein.

11. Love (1932), p. 25.
12. Before deposit insurance, banks in financial trouble were generally treated like any other business. Closure might be declared by supervisors or the directors of the bank. One option was then to seek protection from depositors and other creditors by declaring bankruptcy and accepting a court-appointed receivership. In the case of a temporary liquidity problem, a bank might instead suspend withdrawals or close to the public until the problem could be resolved. In practice, the terms 'failure' and 'suspension' were often used interchangeably. In the period 1921–32, roughly 85 per cent of failed banks – holding 76 per cent of the deposits in failed banks – were state banks (including mutual savings banks and private banks). See Bremer (1935), especially footnote 1 and pp. 41–9. See Federal Reserve Board (1934a), Colt and Keith (1933) or Friedman and Schwartz (1963) for a chronology of the banking crisis and the bank holidays. In a sense, Roosevelt had stage-managed the crisis. By refusing to participate with the outgoing administration over the banking situation, he projected the image of making a clean break with the past. At the same time, however, the resulting uncertainty surrounding his policy toward banking and the gold standard helped to provoke the crisis. See Kennedy (1973), pp. 135–55, or Burns (1974), pp. 31–51.
13. See 'What'll We Use for Money?' (1933).
14. Roosevelt (1938), p. 12.
15. McFadden lost his House seat over the incident. Scandalized by his comments, the Republican and Democratic parties, both of which had endorsed him in 1932, repudiated him in the 1934 elections. See Martin (1990) p. 249, and Rep. McFadden (R-PA), *Congressional Record* (1933), pp. 6225–7.
16. Rep. Weideman (D-MI), *Congressional Record* (1933), pp. 3921–2. Weideman, in a conspiracy theory shared by the radio priest, Fr. Coughlin [see Chernow (1990), pp. 381–2], also claimed that the Great War had been orchestrated by international financiers, noting that: 'Six months after the Federal Reserve Act was passed the war began'.
17. See, for example, Ogg (1932), Calverton (1933) and Schlesinger (1960). Indeed, for many, the New Deal was state socialism. One must bear in mind that 1933 predated most of the failures and atrocities of the various European dictatorships. Although the collectivization of Soviet agriculture was largely complete, Stalin's great political purges did not begin until the mid-1930s. Mussolini was still widely respected as the man who had brought order and unity to Italy; the invasion of Abyssinia was not until 1935. In Germany, Hitler was only beginning to wrest control from the notoriously ineffectual Weimar republic; he became Chancellor in late January 1933, and the Nazis burned the Reichstag four weeks later.
18. See FDIC (1951) and Paton (1932); Paton also cites H.R. 7806, introduced by Rep. Cable (R-OH) on January 15, 1932 and later revised as H.R. 10201. H.R. 7806 is omitted from the FDIC (1951) digest.

19. Roosevelt (1938), p. 12.
20. Prohibition was widely recognized as having failed by this time; see Kent (1932), p. 261. The Eighteenth Amendment was repealed in 1933.
21. Vandenberg (1933), p. 39.
22. Robinson (1931), p. 209.
23. 'Orgy of speculation' was the catch phrase that captured the popular sentiment. For example, 'Our Orgy of Speculation' (1929), p. 907, quotes Chancellor of the Exchequer Philip Snowden: 'There has been a perfect orgy of speculation in New York during the last twelve months'.
24. Robinson (1931), p. 209.
25. Hoover, quoted in De Long (1990), p. 5. *Bankers Magazine* offered it as a modern paradox, 'that depressions are sent by heaven for the chastening of mankind'. See 'Modern Paradoxes' (1933). The liquidationists drew a sardonic retort from Keynes, who identified it as sanctimony masquerading as economics: 'It would, they feel, be a victory for the mammon of unrighteousness if so much prosperity was not subsequently balanced by universal bankruptcy'. See Keynes (1973), p. 349. Mellon's advice also offers an example of a common tendency to anthropomorphize the economy, in this case as a system to be purged. For a more extreme example, see Taussig (1932), who draws an elaborate analogy between physicians and economists.
26. The Economic Policy Commission of the ABA (1933a) dissected the failure of the various state insurance schemes. The Association of Reserve City Bankers (1933) published a monograph late in the debate outlining the actuarial objections to deposit insurance.
27. Association of Reserve City Bankers (1933), p. 27.
28. C. F. Dabelstein, in ABA (1933b), p. 58. For similar remarks, see Rep. Beedy (R-ME), *Congressional Record* (1933), p. 3911; Sen. Glass (D-VA), *ibid.*, p. 3726–7; and Donald Despain, quoted by Sen. Schall (R-MN), *ibid.*, p. 4632.
29. The FDIC (1951), p. 69, provides a clear distinction between insurance and guaranty. By their definition, a guaranty is a promise from the US government to pay off depositors in a failed bank; insurance is paid from an independent private fund. There was no agreed definition for insurance or guaranty in 1933, however, although the explicit acknowledgement that 'no clear distinction (between the terms "guaranty" and "insurance") has been made', was rare; see Rep. Bacon (R-NY), *Congressional Record* (1933), p. 3959. W. B. Hughes also attempted to extricate the 'inexcusable mixture of the two terms ... Guarantee is where you make the good bank pay for the poor one. Insurance is where you make those who get the benefit pay for it'. See ABA (1933b) p. 59. I use the two terms interchangeably in this chapter.
30. In fact there were numerous conflicting legislative proposals afoot. That of Henry Steagall, who chaired the House Banking Committee, was taken most seriously; it eventually became law. See FDIC (1951) and Paton (1932).
31. *Congressional Record* (1933), p. 3836.
32. ABA (1933a), p. 7.
33. Sen. Vandenberg, *Congressional Record* (1933), p. 4239.
34. Sen. Glass, *Congressional Record* (1933), p. 3729. See also endnote 28.

35. Rep. Steagall, *Congressional Record* (1933), p. 3838.
36. See the quote referenced by endnote 1. Similar concerns were voiced by Jamison (1933), p. 451: 'The great urgency for balancing the national budget precludes even the thought of piling another subsidy on the shoulders of the already overburdened taxpayers'.

    These sentiments are especially noteworthy in light of recent attempts to paint the insurance schemes as having taxpayer backing from the start. For example, Title IX of the Competitive Equality Banking Act of 1987 states that Congress 'should *reaffirm* that deposits up to the statutorily prescribed amount in federally insured depository institutions are backed by the full faith and credit of the United States;' (emphasis added).
37. Co-insurance is the insurance practice of involving the insured party in some portion of the risk. Common techniques of co-insurance are coverage ceilings, deductibles and copayment percentages. The aim of such provisions is to mitigate the problem of moral hazard or the tendency of people to behave more riskily when insured.
38. *Congressional Record* (1933), p. 489. More thoughtful commentators realized that the incidence of the cost could not be contained. Rep. Kloeb (D-OH), *ibid.*, p. 489, challenged Rep. Dingell immediately: 'Assuming that an assessment is made upon the bankers, how are we going to prevent that from sifting down to the depositors?' Similarly, Jamison (1933), p. 454, explained that, 'while the banks would remit the premiums', they would also adjust their interest rates, so that, 'in the end the banks' customers would pay the premiums'.
39. Quoted in 'Congress Passes and President Roosevelt Signs Glass–Steagall Bank Bill as Agreed on in Conference' (1933), p. 4193. The proposal itself is surprising, given Woodin's strong objections to deposit insurance. Many others shared Vandenberg's view; see, for example, Sen. Glass, *Congressional Record* (1933), p. 3728; Sen. Bulkley (quoted by Sen. Murphy), *ibid.*, p. 3007.
40. There was disagreement about the reserve fund even after the legislation had been signed. The Association of Reserve City Bankers (1933), p. 28, asserted baldly that 'no provision is made for building up a reserve fund as would be the case under a true insurance plan', while Sen. Vandenberg (1933), p. 39, contended that the plan was 'capitalized with truly prodigal reserves' (any irony in his use of the adjective 'prodigal' is doubtless unintended). The discrepancy lies in the fact that, unlike Vandenberg, the Association of Reserve City Bankers did not treat the FDIC's capital as an insurance reserve fund.
41. Sisson (1933b), p. 31.
42. Association of Reserve City Bankers (1933), p. 27, (emphasis in the original). 'Selecting risks' refers to the practice of differentiating insured parties according to risk, and charging insurance premia according to those risk classes. For example, 17-year-old men on average pose a greater risk to auto insurers than do 30-year-old men; therefore, 17-year-olds usually pay higher auto insurance premia.
43. Roosevelt (1938), p. 37.
44. Emerson (1934), p. 244, states, 'To put such a provision [assessments levied according to risk] into effect would require the classification of the

banks of the country according to various standards: geographical location, size, type, and character of banking policy. The last would present administrative difficulties, but these would not be insuperable'. *Bankers Magazine* had also thought it feasible: 'Presumably, an insurance company could be formed ... which by carefully selecting its risks, might operate successfully'. See 'Protecting Bank Depositors' (1931), p. 435.

45. ABA (1933a), pp. 42–3. Similarly, Jamison (1933), p. 454, argued that selection of risks in this context would present 'complications that can not be easily overcome'.
46. ABA (1933a), p. 7. The seven states listed are not, in fact, contiguous.
47. Rep. Bacon, *Congressional Record* (1933), p. 3959.
48. Stephenson (1934), p. 35. There is a hint of truth in Stephenson's hyperbole. Francis Sisson died of heart failure within a fortnight of the ABA convention of September 1933 – which had included excoriating harangues [see Bell (1934)] delivered by Jesse Jones of the Reconstruction Finance Corporation and soon-to-be FDIC board member J. F. T. O'Connor; see 'Death of Francis H. Sisson, Vice-President Guaranty Trust Co. of New York and Former President American Bankers Association' (1933), and O'Connor (1933). In a tribute at the next convention, Sisson's ABA colleagues offered that his death was 'a tragic demonstration of devotion to duty even to the extent of exceeding the physical power of endurance ... He was a martyr to his work in your behalf'. Nahm (1934), p. 30.
49. Several groups dissected the state plans in the course of the debate; see American Savings, Building and Loan Institute (1933), ABA (1933a), Blocker (1929), Boeckel (1932), and the Association of Reserve City Bankers (1933). Reference was also made to an earlier essay by Robb (1921). There are also numerous retrospective accounts of the state guaranty plans, including Calomiris (1989 and 1990), Wheelock (1992b and 1992c), and Wheelock and Kumbhaker (1991); the most comprehensive, however, is Warburton (1959), parts of which appear in FDIC (1953 and 1957). The original legislation is collected in Federal Reserve Board (1925a and 1925b).
50. ABA (1933a), p. 7.
51. Vandenberg (1933), p. 39, (emphasis in the original).
52. Donald Despain, quoted by Sen. Schall, *Congressional Record* (1933), pp. 4631–2. Virtually identical arguments are offered by Vandenberg (1933), p. 39, and Rep. Bacon, *Congressional Record* (1933), p. 3959.
53. Rep. Steagall, *Congressional Record* (1933), p. 3838.
54. For example, the Association of Reserve City Bankers (1933), pp. 31–2, acknowledged that, 'It is suggested ... that a single crop failure could shake the stability of all the banks in a State. On a national scale the plan would operate upon a broader base. This is true'.
55. The table is reproduced from Association of Reserve City Bankers (1933), p. 26. See Bremer (1935) and Upham and Lamke (1934) for analyses of failures in the 1920s.
56. E. W. Kemmerer of Princeton University, speaking to the Savings Bank Association of Massachusetts on 14 September 1933, and quoted in Association of Reserve City Bankers (1933), pp. 40–1. Kemmerer was the economic advisor to the commission that produced the latter. Similar thoughts were offered by Jamison (1933), p. 451: 'Government guaranty of

bank deposits can be but one of two things – an outright subsidy ... or a plan of insurance'. Bradford (1933), p. 538, added: 'Such subsidization of weak banks by the Government, however, carried out on the basis of taxpayers' money, is so monstrous as to be almost unthinkable'.

57. ABA (1933a), p. 13.
58. There were many cartoons, at the time, depicting an insurer's characterization of the bad banker.
59. 'Federal Guaranty of Bank Deposits' (1932), p. 381.
60. Stephenson (1931), p. 592.
61. *Ibid.*, p. 592.
62. ABA (1933a), p. 25. More specifically, 'greater numbers than ever of undercapitalized, ill-situated banks, as well as of persons wholly unfitted as to training, character or methods to be allowed to conduct banks, were able to command public trust and patronage and to attract large deposits to their institutions through high interest rates and trading on faith in the guaranty plan'. ABA (1933a), p. 17.
63. Association of Reserve City Bankers (1933), p. 29.
64. *Ibid.*, pp. 19–20.
65. *Ibid.*, p. 28.
66. See, for example, Rep. Luce (R-MA), *Congressional Record* (1933), p. 3918. Sens. King (D-UT) and Glass briefly debated the role of immortality in the context of this analogy; *Congressional Record* (1933), p. 3728.
67. Vandenberg (1933), p. 39, (emphasis in the original).
68. Sen. Glass, *Congressional Record* (1933), p. 3728.
69. Rep. Bacon, *Congressional Record* (1933), p. 3959.
70. See Federal Reserve Board (1933c), p. 414. The point to be made was that even the temporary plan succeeded in fully covering the vast majority of depositors. The survey, of course, took place before depositors had an incentive to split larger deposits into multiple accounts to achieve full deposit insurance coverage.
71. Rep. Luce, *Congressional Record* (1933), p. 3914.
72. Rep. Bacon, *Congressional Record* (1933), p. 3952. Comptroller Pole was instrumental in dichotomizing the industry into 'two definite types of banking, namely, that carried on by the small country bank and that of the large city bank'. See 'Comptroller Pole's Views on Rural Unit Banking' (1930), p. 468.
73. Group banking and chain banking are essentially variants of the modern bank holding company form of organization. Group banking presumed some degree of standardization among the subsidiary banks in the holding company, while chain banks were operated as largely independent franchises within the holding company.
74. A Ponzi scheme is a fraudulent investment plan, such as a chain letter, in which returns to existing investors are paid directly from the deposits of new investors, with the director of the scheme skimming the difference. Some of the Ponzi schemes had been run by Charles Ponzi himself. After several jail terms and a stint on the lam, Ponzi was finally deported to his native Italy in 1934. This was not his first one-way ticket. In 1903, his family had bought him a one-way ticket to Boston on the *S. S. Vancouver* in a successful bid to get rid of him. See Grodsky (1990).

75. Flynn (1934), pp. 394–6.
76. Rep. Steagall, for example, avowed that a 'campaign was turned on urging bankers everywhere to ... employ their facilities in investment banking, in speculation, in stock gambling, and in aid of wild and reckless international high finance'. *Congressional Record* (1933), p. 3835. The Seventy-first Congress had formed a Senate Banking and Currency Subcommittee to investigate the extent to which the Federal Reserve and National Banking systems had been co-opted to 'finance the carrying of speculative securities'. Sen. Bulkley, quoted by Sen. Murphy, *Congressional Record* (1933), p. 3006. See also footnotes 15 and 16 and the related text.
77. Rep. Dingell, *Congressional Record* (1933), p. 3906.
78. Rep. Hill (D-AL), *Congressional Record* (1933), p. 5899. Hill's pronouncement was met with a round of applause in the House.
79. Timmons (1948), p. 179. Garner responded, 'You're right as rain, Henry, so get to work in a hurry. Report out a deposit insurance bill and we'll shove it through'. The result was H. R. 11362, which passed the House on 27 May 1932.
80. Rep. Dingell, *Congressional Record* (1933), p. 3906. It is noteworthy that both Sen. Vandenberg and Rep. Dingell were from Michigan, where, on 14 February 1933, William A. Comstock had become the first governor to declare a state banking holiday during the crisis; see Colt and Keith (1933), pp. 6–8. In light of the temporary insurance amendment, any dispassionate observer would have to regard deposit insurance as Vandenberg's baby in Michigan.
81. See Preston (1933), p. 589, and Rep. McLeod (R-MI), *Congressional Record* (1933), p. 5825.
82. Ford (1933), p. 9, (emphasis in the original). Similarly, Sen. Vandenberg stated: 'The savings of America must be made safe', *Congressional Record* (1933), p. 4428. The question of legal title to deposited funds was somewhat more subtle than Ford's quote suggests; see, for example, Amberg (1935), pp. 49–51.
83. Amberg (1935), p. 51, felt that the struggle and fear of a bank run *per se* were bad, and that 'a great social purpose would be served if the occasion of such fear could be removed'.
84. Association of Reserve City Bankers (1933), p. 2.
85. Sisson (1933a), p. 563. He added: 'There can be no question that the people of the United States should have a banking structure based on conditions rendering the banks immune from failure'.
86. Donald Despain, quoted by Rep. Schall, *Congressional Record* (1933), p. 4631.
87. Fisher (1932), p. 143.
88. Greer (1933b), p. 538.
89. See 'What'll We Use for Money?' (1933).
90. See Ives (1931) for colorful accounts of depositor runs and the various responses of bankers. Rep. Bacon, *Congressional Record* (1933), p. 3959, estimated hoarding at $1.5 billion in January 1933. The extent of hoarding was also roughly gauged by tracking deposits in the US Postal Savings system. Such deposits roughly quadrupled in the two years ending 30 June 1933 [see O'Connor (1933), p. 23]. Friedman and Schwartz (1963), p. 173,

state that such deposits remained a 'minor factor' in spite of their growth. The system was established by the Postal Savings Bill of 1910 and was intended primarily for the savings of new immigrants. Deposits were guarantied in full. Vice-President-elect Garner reportedly told Roosevelt, 'You'll have to have it (deposit insurance), Cap'n, or get more clerks in the Postal Savings banks'. See Timmons (1948), p. 179.

91. Rep. Bacon, *Congressional Record* (1933), p. 3959.
92. Rep. Steagall, *Congressional Record* (1933), p. 3840.
93. Federal Reserve Board (1943), pp. 72–4, 371.
94. Rep. Steagall, *Congressional Record* (1933), p. 3840.
95. Golembe (1960) has argued that, among the motives for deposit insurance, depositor protection was secondary to protection of the circulating medium. Others have gone further, arguing that protection of depositors was a rationalization created after the fact. The issue raised by Golembe is certainly plausible; Rep. Bacon, for example, appears to have ranked them this way [*Congressional Record* (1933), p. 3959]. On the other hand, it is noteworthy that Sen. Glass in 1933 abandoned his earlier plan for a liquidation fund, which would have prevented the freezing of funds in suspended banks while still not protecting depositors from loss. The latter notion of depositor protection as an ex-post or revisionist justification is clearly false, however.
96. This was a popular quip that made the rounds in 1933. In this instance, it is attributed to Carter Glass; see Kennedy (1973), p. 133; Bell (1934), pp. 262–3, also cites it. The joke is startling in its insensitivity. Examples of bankers of the day indulging in overtly racist humor are also available; see, for example, Dyer (1933), pp. 91 and 94, and Amberg (1935), p. 49.
97. The hearings were organized in January 1933 by the Senate Committee on Banking and Currency, and were run by the Committee's counsel, Ferdinand Pecora; see Pecora (1939). The dust jacket relates that, in one instance, a journalist 'begged Mr. Pecora not to break so many front-page stories daily because it was physically impossible to cover them all'. See Benston (1990) for a thorough, revisionist view of the hearings.
98. Roosevelt (1938), pp. 11–12.
99. Roosevelt (1938), p. 13. His reference to 'other people's money' was a nod to Justice Brandeis's book of the same title, a reprint of his articles on the money trust that appeared in *Harper's Weekly* in 1913–14. Those who hold that all the great thoughts have long since been had will be pleased to learn that Kane's (1991) reference to the 'Sorcerer's Apprentice' segment of Walt Disney's *Fantasia* as a metaphor for bank regulation was anticipated by Brandeis. Lacking Mickey Mouse's rendition, however, Brandeis was forced to use the German original, Goethe's *Der Zauberlehrling*; see Brandeis (1933), p. vii.
100. Sen. Brookhart (R-IA) speaking to a New York Stock Exchange official at a Senate committee hearing in 1932; quoted by Danielian (1933), p. 496.
101. Sen. Glass, *Congressional Record* (1933), p. 3726. Glass is referring to the proposed separation of investment affiliates from Federal Reserve member banks.
102. Kent (1932), p. 260.
103. Kennedy (1973), p. 26.

104. See, for example, Bell (1934). Sisson (1933b), p. 30, offered that the treatment of bankers as 'demons of darkness' and as an 'unseen mythical power for evil which spreads its baneful influence over [human beings]' merely satisfied an emotional need for a scapegoat.
105. Rep. Dingell, *Congressional Record* (1933), p. 3906.
106. Sisson's telegram is quoted in Pecora (1939), pp. 294–5.
107. Sen. Glass, *Congressional Record* (1933), p. 5862.
108. Andrew (1934b), p. 93.
109. Daiger (1933), p. 563, attributes coinage of the phrase 'competition in laxity' to Eugene Meyer in 1923 testimony to the House Banking and Currency Committee. The phrase attained some popularity; it was also used, for example, by Wyatt (1933), p. 186, and Awalt (1933), p. 4.
110. Pole (1929), p. 23.
111. Association of Reserve City Bankers (1933), p. 30.
112. H. Parker Willis, quoted in Lawrence (1930), p. 105.
113. Lawrence (1930), p. 104. Lawrence took this priggish tone one step further, admonishing that 'A little birth control of banks on the part of the states which now suffer most from bank failures might have had a wholesome effect on the rate of mortality'; *ibid.*, p. 84.
114. Westerfield (1931), p. 17; the 'multiplicity of banks' was first on his list of the six causes of bank failures since 1920. Andrew (1934b), p. 93, concurred that 'Everyone agrees that one of the main causes of our banking trouble was too many banks.' See also Bremer (1935). Awalt (1933), p. 4, attributes the boom in charters to 'lax State laws' and the 1900 reduction in the minimum capitalization for national banks from $50 000 to $25 000.
115. ABA (1933a), p. 42. Mississippi was held up as the exception that proved the rule: 'The banking authorities in Mississippi had full discretion in the matter of granting new charters and used it liberally in refusing permission for unneeded banks or to unqualified promoters to open new institutions'; *ibid.*, p. 22. The result was seen to be less over-banking and fewer failures relative to Oklahoma and Nebraska.
116. A *Saturday Evening Post* editorial of 9 August 1924, quoted in Association of Reserve City Bankers (1933), p. 42.
117. See the quote referenced by note 64.
118. Donald Despain, quoted by Sen. Schall, *Congressional Record* (1933), p. 4632.
119. Stephenson (1934), p. 46. In addition to authorizing the supervisory power of the FDIC, the Banking Act of 1933: increased the punitive authority of the Federal Reserve for member banks financing securities 'speculation', prohibited insider lending for member banks, authorized federal regulators to remove the officers and directors of member banks for illegality or unsound banking practice, and required deposit-taking private banks to submit to supervision by the Comptroller's office.
120. Sen. Glass, *Congressional Record* (1933), p. 3728.
121. Anderson (1933c), p. 17.
122. Pole (1929), p. 24.
123. See Pole (1930a, 1931, 1932a and 1932b), 'The Need of a New Banking Policy' (1929) and 'Comptroller Pole's Views on Rural Unit Banking' (1930).

124. US Congress, House of Representatives, Committee on Banking and Currency (1930).
125. 'The Ideal Bank' (1933), p. 16.
126. Greer (1933a), p. 722. See also Lawrence (1930), and Rep. Bacon, *Congressional Record* (1933), pp. 3949–50.
127. For example, Rep. Bacon, *Congressional Record* (1933), p. 3961, noted that 'deposit guaranty is undoubtedly a guaranty of reckless banking ... Safety for the depositor can best be achieved by a unified branch banking system'.
128. Pole (1930b), p. 5. This same sentence appears in Pole (1930a), p. 4.
129. White (1981, 1982, 1983) reviews the historical connections between deposit insurance and bank chartering.
130. Sen. Glass, *Congressional Record* (1933), p. 3728.
131. See the interchange between Sen. Glass and Sen. Couzens (R-MI), *Congressional Record* (1933), p. 3727.
132. Section 17 of the Glass bill 'provides for the amount of capital of national banks depending upon the population of the places where they are to be located and also *prohibits the admission of a bank into the Federal Reserve System unless it possesses a paid-up unimpaired capital sufficient to entitle it to become a national bank*'. See Glass (1933b), p. 16, (emphasis added). The population schedule for minimum capital was: \$25 000 for areas under 3000 persons; \$50 000 for 3000 to 6000 persons; \$100 000 for 6000 to 50 000 persons; \$200 000 for areas over 50 000 persons; see Steagall (1933a), pp. 18–19.
133. Quoted by Anderson (1932b), p. 678.
134. The opinion was published as Wyatt (1933). The Attorney General had felt it was not possible, and had told Glass that; see Anderson (1932b), p. 678.
135. Joint resolution S. J. Res. 18 was introduced by Sen. Gore (D-OK), *Congressional Record* (1933), p. 249.
136. Andrew (1934b), p. 95.
137. See Burns (1974), pp. 11–12.
138. See Anderson (1933a), p. 17. They were joined by Sen. Vandenberg, whose temporary plan extended insurance to state non-member banks upon certification of soundness by the relevant state banking authority.
139. There was little fondness connecting the two Southern Democrats. Smith and Beasley (1939), pp. 346–7, relate that, in the heat of the banking debate and in response to a series of Long's *ad hominems*, Glass unleashed a string of invective that literally chased the Kingfish – his hands clamped over his ears – off the Senate floor. This version of events is apocryphal, however.
140. Sen. Vandenberg, referring to the temporary insurance amendment, *Congressional Record* (1933), p. 5256. See also Vandenberg (1933), p. 43.
141. Anderson (1933a), p. 63.
142. Rep. Luce reported that bank structure issues predominated in the conference committee reconciling the Glass and Steagall bills: 'There were but two points of serious controversy in the discussions of the conferees – those to which I have just referred, branch banking, the membership requirement together with other details of insurance of bank deposits', *Congressional Record* (1933), p. 5896. Much of the force of Glass's requirements for Fed membership was lost when deposit insurance was revamped by the Banking Act of 1935; see, for example, Woosley (1936), pp. 24–6. See Table 3.3,

'the four that passed'. The membership requirement was dropped entirely in 1939; see Golembe (1967), pp. 1098–1100.

Opinions varied on the significance of the consolidation of bank regulation implicit in the final act. *Bankers Magazine* editorialized that, 'while this development will bring the state banks under a considerable degree of Federal control, it will not – for a time at least – result in that unification of banking regarded by many as desirable. The state banks, by coming into the deposit-guaranty scheme have escaped with their lives'. 'State Banks Qualifying for Insurance of Deposits' (1933), p. 490. Anderson (1933c), p. 17, warned that, 'with all this variation, this glorification of the unit bank principle, however, comes the hard fact that these institutions, for the first time in their history, will be under one direct control whose authority is such as practically to set aside all the principle privileges for which state banks have fought so long'.

143. Amberg (1935), p. 49.
144. Kaufman, for example, claims that the opinions of Emerson (1934) – and, by association, those of the banking community as a whole – regarding flaws in the actuarial basis for the plan were unheeded at the time. In particular, Kaufman (1990) states, pp. 1–2: 'Some of the problems are new, however many have been around for many years and were even clearly foreseen at the time they were forming or, worse yet, even earlier, at the time their underlying causes were put in place in the form of legislation or regulation. This is the case with the extant structure of federal deposit insurance. Among those forecasting the problems that this innovation would come to cause was Guy Emerson, a long-time economist for the Bankers Trust Company (New York). His warnings are evident in his article "Guaranty of Deposits Under the Banking Act of 1933", published in the February 1934 *Quarterly Journal of Economics* and reprinted in this volume. Much of this book is necessitated because policy makers did not listen to Emerson and others more than half a century ago'.
145. Association of Reserve City Bankers (1933), p. 7. They were, however, at pains not to appear eager in their praise: '*What we are recommending, therefore, is co-operation in an emergency measure of the sort that has been deemed necessary in almost all branches of our economic life, but we are not, directly or indirectly, endorsing the principle of deposit guaranty*', *ibid.*, p. 7, (emphasis in the original). The permanent plan was never operational; it was in fact ultimately superseded by a modified form of the temporary plan.
146. The technical legal question of the *de jure* liability of the United States government for deposit insurance is surprisingly complex, and the answer is not entirely clear. As a practical matter, however, the question is neither complex nor unclear. See FDIC (1990), pp. 4438–9.

References

'A Good Start' (1933) *Business Week* (22 March) 32.

Amberg, Harold V. (1935) 'The Future of Deposit Insurance', *Association of Reserve City Bankers: Proceedings, Twenty-fourth Annual Convention*, 49–61.

American Bankers Association (ABA) (1933a) 'The Guaranty of Bank Deposits' (Economic Policy Commission: American Bankers Association, New York).

American Bankers Association (ABA) (1933b) 'Forum Discussion – Uniform Banking Law – Guarantee of Deposits', *Commercial and Financial Chronicle* (American Bankers Convention Supplement, 23 September) 58–9.

American Bankers Association (ABA) (1933c) 'Report of Resolutions Committee – Insurance of Deposits Declared Unsound', *Commercial and Financial Chronicle* (American Bankers Convention Supplement, 23 September) 59.

American Savings, Building and Loan Institute (1933) *Guarantee of Bank Deposits and Building and Loan* (American Savings, Building and Loan Institute, Chicago).

Anderson, George E. (1932a) 'The Glass Bill is a Medley', *American Bankers Association Journal* (February) 498, 532–5.

Anderson, George E. (1932b) 'Washington Looks at the State Banks', *American Bankers Association Journal* (May) 677–8, 718.

Anderson, George E. (1933a) 'Bank Law Making', *American Bankers Association Journal* (May) 17, 63.

Anderson, George E. (1933b) 'The Price of Deposit Insurance', *American Bankers Association Journal* (October) 17–9, 51.

Anderson, George E. (1933c) 'Washington Epic: II. Prospectus – National Financial Control', *American Bankers Association Journal* (November) 16–7, 48.

Anderson, George E. (1934a) 'Deposit Insurance, First Phase', *American Bankers Association Journal* (January) 20–1.

Anderson, George E. (1934b) 'Bank Owners', *Banking* (November) 11–2.

Andrew, L. A. (1934a) 'Reconstruction: Individual Initiative', *American Bankers Association Journal* (January) 15–16, 53, 69.

Andrew, L. A. (1934b) 'The Future of the Unit Bank', *Proceedings of the Forty-fourth Annual Convention of the Missouri Bankers Association*, 91–101.

'Are State Banks to be Suppressed?' (1929) *Bankers Magazine* (November) 663–4.

Association of Reserve City Bankers, Commission on Banking Law and Practice (1933) 'The Guaranty of Bank Deposits', Bulletin No. 3, (Chicago, November).

Awalt, F. G. (1933) *Annual Report of the Comptroller of the Currency, 1932* (Washington, DC: US Government Printing Office).

'Bank Bill' (1933) *Business Week* (10 June) 8.

'Bank Reform' (1933) *Business Week* (4 January) 3–4.

'Banking Issues in the Campaign' (1932) *American Bankers Association Journal* (August) 22, 65.

'Banking Reform' (1933) *Business Week* (8 March) 32.

'The Banks Reopen' (1933) *Business Week* (22 March) 3–4.

Beebe, M. Plin (1931) 'A National View of State Banks,' *American Bankers Association Journal* (October) 217–18, 287.

Bell, Elliott V. (1934) 'The Bankers Sign a Truce', *Current History* (December) 257–63.

Bell, Elliott V. (1935) 'Who Shall Rule the Money Market?', *Current History* (July) 353–9.

Bennett, Frank P., Jr. (1931) 'A Word to National Banks', *American Bankers Association Journal* (October) 232–3, 272.

Benson, Philip A. (1932) 'Government Guaranty of Bank Deposits', *American Bankers Association Journal* (December) 14–15, 69.

Benston, George J. (1990) *The Separation of Commercial and Investment Banking: The Glass–Steagall Act Revisited and Reconsidered* (New York: Oxford University Press).

Berle, A. A., Jr. (1934) 'Reconstruction: Central Control', *American Bankers Association Journal* (January) 13–14, 52, 68–9.

Blocker, John G. (1929) 'The Guaranty of State Bank Deposits', Bureau of Business Research of the University of Kansas, Kansas Studies in Business No. 11 (Lawrence: Department of Journalism Press).

Boeckel, Richard M. (1932) *The Guaranty of Bank Deposits* (Washington DC: Editorial Research Reports).

Bogen, Jules I., and Marcus Nadler (1933) *The Banking Crisis* (New York: Dodd, Mead and Company).

Bradford, Frederick A. (1933) 'Futility of Deposit Guaranty Laws', *Bankers Magazine* (June) 537–9.

Brandeis, Louis D. (1933) *Other People's Money and How the Bankers Use It* (Washington, DC: National Home Library Foundation).

Bremer, C. D. (1935) *American Bank Failures* (New York: Columbia University Press).

Burns, Helen M. (1974) *The American Banking Community and New Deal Banking Reforms 1933–1935* (Westport: Greenwood Press).

Calomiris, Charles W. (1989) 'Deposit insurance: Lessons from the record', Federal Reserve Bank of Chicago *Economic Perspectives* (May/June) 10–30.

Calomiris, Charles W. (1990) 'Is Deposit Insurance Necessary? A Historical Perspective', *Journal of Economic History* (June) 283–95.

Calverton, V. F. (1933) 'Is America Ripe for Fascism?', *Current History* (September) 701–4.

Carter, W. E. (1934) 'Annual Address of the President', *Proceedings of the Forty-fourth Annual Convention of the Missouri Bankers Association*, 21–7.

Chernow, Ron (1990) *The House of Morgan: An American Banking Dynasty and the Rise of Modern Finance* (New York: Atlantic Monthly Press).

Collins, Charles W. (1931) *Rural Banking Reform* (New York: MacMillan).

Colt, Charles C., and N. S. Keith (1933) *28 Days: A History of the Banking Crisis* (New York: Greenberg).

'Comptroller Pole's Views on Rural Unit Banking', *Bankers Magazine* (April) 463–9.

'Congress Passes and President Roosevelt Signs Glass–Steagall Bank Bill as Agreed on in Conference' (1933) *Commercial and Financial Chronicle* (17 June) 4192–3.

Congressional Record (1933) (daily edition), 73rd Congress, 1st Session.

Crowley, Leo T. (1934) 'The Benefits of Deposit Insurance', *Proceedings of the Forty-fourth Annual Convention of the Missouri Bankers Association*, 101–10.

Crowley, Leo T. (1935) 'The Necessity of Cooperation Between State Supervising Authorities and the F.D.I.C'. (with discussion), *Proceedings of the Thirty-fourth Annual Convention of the National Association of Supervisors of State Banks* (New Orleans: Brandao Printing) 65–8.

Cummings, Walter J. (1933) 'The Federal Deposit Insurance Corporation', *Bankers Magazine* (November) 577–8.

Daiger, J. M. (1933) 'Toward Safer and Stronger Banks', *Current History* (February) 558–64.

Danielian, N. R. (1933) 'The Stock Market and the Public', *Atlantic Monthly* (October) 496–508.

'Death of Francis H. Sisson, Vice-President Guaranty Trust Co. of New York and Former President American Bankers Association' (1933) *Commercial and Financial Chronicle* (23 September) 2195.

De Long, J. Bradford (1990) '"Liquidation" Cycles: Old-Fashioned Real Business Cycle Theory and the Great Depression', NBER Working Paper (October).

'Deposit Insurance' (1933a) *Business Week* (12 April) 3.

'Deposit Insurance' (1933b) *Business Week* (31 May) 20.

'Deposit Insurance Draws Near' (1933) *Review of Reviews and World's Work* (December) 50–1.

'Depositors Want Insurance' (1933) *Business Week* (7 June) 12.

Dyer, Gus W. (1933) 'Federal Control of Business', *Proceedings of the Forty-third Annual Convention of the Missouri Bankers Association*, 91–8.

Elliott, W. S. (1935) 'State Banks and the Future Thereof' (with discussion), *Proceedings of the Thirty-fourth Annual Convention of the National Association of Supervisors of State Banks* (New Orleans: Brandao Printing) 80–5.

Emerson, Guy (1934) 'Guaranty of Deposits Under the Banking Act of 1933', *Quarterly Journal of Economics* (February) 229–44.

'Extension of Branch Banking' (1929) *Bankers Magazine* (November) 661–3.

Federal Deposit Insurance Corporation (FDIC) (1951) 'History of Legislation for the Guaranty or Insurance of Bank Deposits', *Annual Report of the Federal Deposit Insurance Corporation, 1950* (Washington, DC: FDIC) 61–101.

Federal Deposit Insurance Corporation (FDIC) (1953) 'Insurance of Bank Obligations Prior to Federal Deposit Insurance', *Annual Report of the Federal Deposit Insurance Corporation, 1952* (Washington, DC: FDIC) 57–72.

Federal Deposit Insurance Corporation (FDIC) (1957) 'State Deposit Insurance Systems, 1908–1930', *Annual Report of the Federal Deposit Insurance Corporation, 1956* (Washington, DC: FDIC) 45–73.

Federal Deposit Insurance Corporation (FDIC) (1983) *Deposit Insurance in a Changing Environment* (Washington, DC: FDIC).

Federal Deposit Insurance Corporation (FDIC) (1984) *Federal Deposit Insurance Corporation: The First Fifty Years* (Washington, DC: FDIC).

Federal Deposit Insurance Corporation (FDIC) (1990)'Are Deposits in Financial Institutions Guaranteed Directly by the Federal Government or by the FDIC and its Resources', FDIC Advisory Opinion FDIC-90-6, in: *Federal Deposit Insurance Corporation: Law, Regulations and Related Acts*, Volume 1 (Prentice-Hall) 4438–9.

Federal Deposit Insurance Corporation (FDIC) (1992) 'Federal Deposit Insurance Corporation', *Federal Register* (21 May) 21617–33.

'Federal Guaranty of Bank Deposits' (1932) *Bankers Magazine* (April) 380–2.

Federal Reserve Board (1925a) 'Guaranty of Bank Deposits', *Federal Reserve Bulletin*, (September) 626–40.

Federal Reserve Board (1925b) 'State Laws Relating to Guaranty of Bank Deposits', *Federal Reserve Bulletin* (September) 641–68.

Federal Reserve Board (1932) 'Recent Amendments to the Federal Reserve Act (Glass–Steagall bill)', *Federal Reserve Bulletin* (March) 180–1.

Federal Reserve Board (1933a) 'Review of the Month', *Federal Reserve Bulletin*, (March) 113–33.
Federal Reserve Board (1933b) 'Banking Act of 1933', *Federal Reserve Bulletin* (June) 385–401.
Federal Reserve Board (1933c) 'Review of the Month', *Federal Reserve Bulletin* (July) 413–8.
Federal Reserve Board (1934a) *Twentieth Annual Report of the Federal Reserve Board, Covering Operations for the Year 1933* (Washington, DC: US Government Printing Office).
Federal Reserve Board (1934b) 'Act of June 16, 1934, Extending for 1 Year the Temporary Plan for Deposit Insurance, etc.', *Federal Reserve Bulletin* (July) 486–8.
Federal Reserve Board (1935) 'Banking Act of 1935', *Federal Reserve Bulletin* (September) 602–22.
Federal Reserve Board (1943) *Banking and Monetary Statistics, 1914–1941* (Washington, DC: US Government Printing Office).
'Final Chapter in the History of Bank Deposit Guaranty' (1930) *Bankers Magazine* (April) 472.
Fisher, Irving (1932) 'Statement of Prof. Irving Fisher, Professor of Economics, Yale University, New Haven, Conn.', in *To Provide a Guaranty Fund for Depositors in Banks*, US Congress, House of Representatives, Committee on Banking and Currency. Hearings, 72nd Congress, 1st Session (Washington, DC: US Government Printing Office) 143–54.
Flynn, John T. (1933) 'The Wall Street Water Pump', *Harper's Monthly Magazine* (September) 404–13.
Flynn, John T. (1934) 'Wanted: Real Banking Reform', *Current History* (January) 394–401.
'For Better Banks' (1933) *Business Week* (17 May) 5.
Ford, Henry (1933) 'Essentials of Sound Banking', *The Rotarian* (April) 6–9, 56–7.
Fox, Mortimer J. (1936) 'Deposit Insurance as an Influence for Stabilizing the Banking Structure', *Journal of the American Statistical Association* (March) 103–12.
Friedman, Milton, and Anna Jacobson Schwartz (1963) *A Monetary History of the United States 1867–1960* (Princeton: Princeton University Press).
Galbraith, John K. (1961) *The Great Crash, 1929* (Boston: Houghton Mifflin).
Gayer, A. D. (1935) 'The Banking Act of 1935', *Quarterly Journal of Economics* (November) 97–116.
Glass, Carter (1933a) 'Carter Glass Urges the Need of Banking Reform', *Review of Reviews and World's Work* (January) 20–2.
Glass, Carter (1933b) 'Operation of the National and Federal Reserve Banking Systems: Report to accompany S. 1631', 73rd Congress, 1st Session, Senate, Report No. 77 (15 May).
'The Glass and Steagall Bills' (1933) *American Bankers Association Journal* (June) 22–3.
'The Glass Bill' (1933) *Business Week* (24 May) 32.
Golembe, Carter (1960) 'The Deposit Insurance Legislation of 1933: An Examination of its Antecedents and its Purposes', *Political Science Quarterly* (June) 181–200.

Golembe, Carter (1967) 'Our Remarkable Banking System', *Virginia Law Review* (June 1967) 1091–1114.

Greer, Guy (1933a) 'Why Canadian Banks Don't Fail', *Harper's Monthly Magazine* (May) 722–34.

Greer, Guy (1933b) 'Wanted: Real Banking Reform', *Harper's Monthly Magazine* (October) 533–46.

Grodsky, Marcia (1990) 'Charles Ponzi', in Larry Schweikart (ed.), *Encyclopedia of American Business History and Biography, Banking and Finance, 1913–1989* (New York: Facts On File) 355–9.

'Guaranty of Deposits: How Can This Threat To Sound Banking Be Met?' (1933) *American Bankers Association Journal* (September) 96.

Hapgood, Norman (1933) 'Protect the Depositor', *The Nation* (15 March) 283.

Harris, S. E. (1932) 'Banking and Currency Legislation, 1932', *Quarterly Journal of Economics* (May) 546–57.

Hecht, Rudolf S. (1935) 'The Banking Outlook' (with discussion), *Proceedings of the Thirty-fourth Annual Convention of the National Association of Supervisors of State Banks* (New Orleans: Brandao Printing) 42–9.

'The Ideal Bank' (1933) *Business Week* (19 April) 16.

Ives, Mitchell (1931) 'How Banks Have Been Saved', *American Bankers Association Journal* (August) 71–4, 112–13.

Jamison, C. L. (1933) 'Bank Deposit Guaranties: The Insurance Aspects of the Problem', *Bankers Magazine* (May) 451–5.

Jones, Homer (1938) 'Insurance of Bank Deposits in the United States of America', *Economic Journal* (December).

Kane, Edward J. (1991) 'The S&L Insurance Mess', Center for the Study of American Business, Contemporary Issues Series, No. 41 (February).

Kaufman, George G. (1990) 'Purpose and Operation of the Shadow Financial Regulatory Committee', in George G. Kaufman (ed.), *Restructuring the American Financial System* (Boston: Kluwer Academic Publishers).

Kelly, Edward J., III (1985) 'Legislative History of the Glass–Steagall Act', in Ingo Walter (ed.), *Deregulating Wall Street* (New York: John Wiley) 41–65.

Kennedy, Susan Estabrook (1973) *The Banking Crisis of 1933* (Lexington: University Press of Kentucky).

Kent, Frank R. (1932) 'The Next President', *Scribner's Magazine* (November) 257–61.

Keynes, John M. (1973) in Donald Moggridge (ed.), *The General Theory and After: Part 1 Preparation* (London: Macmillan).

Kiplinger, Willard M. (1932) 'The Reconstruction Workshop', *American Bankers Association Journal* (April) 619, 634, 644.

Landon, Alf. M. (1933) 'The Necessity of a Strong State Banking System Without a Deposit Guaranty', *Commercial and Financial Chronicle* (American Bankers Convention Supplement, 23 September) 50–3.

Law, Francis M. (1934) 'Banking and the Country', *Proceedings of the Forty-fourth Annual Convention of the Missouri Bankers Association*, 37–44.

Lawrence, Joseph Stagg (1930) *Banking Concentration in the United States: A Critical Analysis* (New York: The Bankers Publishing Company).

Lawrence, Joseph Stagg (1931) 'Are Big Banks More Profitable?', *Bankers Magazine* (January) 9–13.

Lawrence, Joseph Stagg (1934) 'Burying the Banker', *Review of Reviews and World's Work* (June) 19–23.
Love, J. S. (1932) 'President's Address', *Proceedings of the Thirty-first Annual Convention of the National Association of Supervisors of State Banks* (New Orleans: Brandao Printing) 25–31.
Martin, Tiarr (1990) 'Louis Thomas McFadden', in Larry Schweikart (ed.), *Encyclopedia of American Business History and Biography, Banking and Finance, 1913–1989* (New York: Facts On File) 248–50.
McLaughlin, George V. (1933) 'The Need for Revision of the Glass–Steagall Act and a Sane Legislative Program for Banking', *Commercial and Financial Chronicle* (American Bankers Convention Supplement, 23 September) 16–19.
McWhirter, Felix M. (1932) 'The Unit Bank Accepts the Challenge', *American Bankers Association Journal* (July) 11–13, 61–2.
'Modern Paradoxes' (1933) *Bankers Magazine* (August) 119.
Nahm, Max B. (1934) 'Report of Resolutions Committee – Tributes in Memory of Francis H. Sisson, Peter W. Goebel and Melvin A. Traylor', *Commercial and Financial Chronicle* (American Bankers Convention Supplement, 17 November) 30.
National Industrial Conference Board (1932) *The Banking Situation in the United States* (New York: National Industrial Conference Board).
'The Need of a New Banking Policy' (1929) *Bankers Magazine* (November) 659–61.
'New Bank Bills' (1933) *Business Week* (24 May) 5–6.
'The New Banking Picture' (1933) *American Bankers Association Journal* (April) 11–13, 37.
'New Banks – Model T' (1933) *Business Week* (8 March) 5–6.
'The "New Deal" in Banking' (1933) *Business Week* (24 June) 22–3.
'New Deal, New Money, New Banks' (1933) *Business Week* (15 March) 3–4.
O'Connor, James F. T. (1933) 'Defense of Banking Act of 1933 – Deposit Insurance Provision', *Commercial and Financial Chronicle* (American Bankers Convention Supplement, 23 September) 23–7.
O'Connor, James F. T. (1934) 'Temporary Deposit Insurance', *American Bankers Association Journal* (January) 21.
O'Connor, James F. T. (1935) 'Address by J. F. O'Connor, Comptroller of the Currency' (with discussion), *Proceedings of the Thirty-fourth Annual Convention of the National Association of Supervisors of State Banks* (New Orleans: Brandao Printing) 95–105.
Ogg, Frederic A. (1932) 'Does America Need a Dictator?', *Current History* (September) 641–8.
'Opinions on the New Banking Act, Charted from West to East' (1933) *American Bankers Association Journal* (September) 22–3, 50, 52, 58.
'Other People's Money' (1933) *Business Week* (5 April) 9.
'Our Orgy of Speculation' (1929) *Bankers Magazine* (December) 907–8.
Paton, Thomas B. (1932) '16 Deposit Guaranty Bills in Congress', *American Bankers Association Journal* (April) 621, 652.
Pecora, Ferdinand (1939) *Wall Street Under Oath* (New York: Simon and Schuster).
'Permanent Bank Reform' (1933) *Business Week* (29 March) 3.

Phillips, Ronnie J. (1993) 'The "Chicago Plan" and New Deal Banking Reform', Jerome Levy Economics Institute Working Paper No. 76 (June) and chapter 5, this volume.

Platt, Edmund (1932) 'Branch Banking: A Reply', *American Bankers Association Journal* (August) 13–15, 62–5.

Pole, John W. (1929) 'Plight of National Banking System', *Bankers Magazine* (July) 23–6.

Pole, John W. (1930a) *Report of the Comptroller of the Currency, 1929* (Washington, DC: US Government Printing Office).

Pole, John W. (1930b) 'Statement of Hon. John W. Pole, Comptroller of the Currency', in *Branch, Chain, and Group Banking*, US Congress, House of Representatives, Committee on Banking and Currency, Hearings, 71st Congress, 2nd Session, Volume 1 (Washington, DC: US Government Printing Office) 3–419.

Pole, John W. (1931) *Report of the Comptroller of the Currency, 1930* (Washington, DC: US Government Printing Office).

Pole, John W. (1932a) *Report of the Comptroller of the Currency, 1931* (Washington, DC: US Government Printing Office).

Pole, John W. (1932b) 'Statement of Hon. John W. Pole, Comptroller of the Currency', in *To Provide a Guaranty Fund for Depositors in Banks*, US Congress, House of Representatives, Committee on Banking and Currency. Hearings, 72nd Congress, 1st Session (Washington, DC: US Government Printing Office) 6–56.

Preston, Howard H. (1933) 'The Banking Act of 1933', *American Economic Review* (December) 585–607.

Preston, Thomas R. (1932) 'As a Southern Banker Views the Situation', *American Bankers Association Journal* (August) 15.

'Protecting Bank Depositors' (1931) *Bankers Magazine* (April) 433–5.

Robb, Thomas B. (1921) *The Guaranty of Bank Deposits* (Boston: Houghton Mifflin).

Robinson, A. C. (1931) 'The Moral Values of Thrift', *American Bankers Association Journal* (October) 209–11, 285–6.

Roosevelt, Franklin D. (1938) *The Public Papers and Addresses of Franklin D. Roosevelt: Volume Two, The Year of Crisis, 1933* (New York: Random House).

Salter, Sir Arthur (1933) 'A New Economic Morality', *Harper's Monthly Magazine* (May) 641–9.

Schlesinger, Arthur M. (1960) *The Age of Roosevelt: The Politics of Upheaval* (Boston: Houghton Mifflin).

Sisson, Francis H. (1932) 'The Strength of Our Banking System', *Review of Reviews and World's Work* (December) 30–2, 71.

Sisson, Francis H. (1933a) 'How We May Have Safer Banks: The Solution Does Not Lie in the Government Guaranty of Deposits', *Bankers Magazine* (June) 563–5.

Sisson, Francis H. (1933b) 'Annual Address of the President', *Commercial and Financial Chronicle* (American Bankers Convention Supplement, 23 September) 30–3.

Smith, Rixey, and Norman Beasley (1939) *Carter Glass: A Biography* (New York: Longmans, Green and Co.).

'Start' (1934) *American Bankers Association Journal* (January) 80.

'State Banks Qualifying for Insurance of Deposits' (1933) *Bankers Magazine* (November) 489–90.
Steagall, Henry B. (1933a) 'Banking Act of 1933: Report to accompany H.R. 5661', 73rd Congress, 1st Session, House of Representatives, Report No. 150 (19 May).
Steagall, Henry B. (1933b) 'Banking Act of 1933: Conference Report to accompany H.R. 5661', 73rd Congress, 1st Session, House of Representatives, Report No. 251 (12 June).
Stephenson, Rome C. (1931) 'Providing Safety for Future Banking', *Bankers Magazine* (May) 591–4.
Stephenson, Rome C. (1934) 'Making Banks Safe', *The Rotarian* (September) 34–5, 46–8.
Taggart, J. H., and L. D. Jennings (1934) 'The Insurance of Bank Deposits', *Journal of Political Economy* (August) 508–16.
Taussig, F. W. (1932) 'Doctors, Economists, and the Depression', *Harper's Monthly Magazine* (August) 355–65.
Timmons, Bascom N. (1948) *Garner of Texas: A Personal History* (New York: Harper & Brothers).
'Unit Banking Not So Bad After All' (1930) *Bankers Magazine* (April) 470.
US Congress, House of Representatives, Committee on Banking and Currency (1930) *Branch, Chain, and Group Banking*, Hearings, 71st Congress, 2nd Session (Washington, DC: US Government Printing Office).
Upham, Cyril B., and Edwin Lamke (1934) *Closed and Distressed Banks: A Study in Public Administration* (Washington DC: The Brookings Institution).
Vandenberg, Arthur H. (1933) 'A Defense of the Bank Deposit Insurance Law and an Answer to the American Bankers Association' (with discussion), *Proceedings of the Thirty-second Annual Convention of the National Association of Supervisors of State Banks* (New Orleans: Brandao Printing) 38–67.
Warburg, Paul M. (1929) 'A Banking System Adrift at Sea', *Bankers Magazine* (March) 569–73.
Warburton, Clark (1959) *Deposit Insurance in Eight States During the Period 1908–1930*, unpublished manuscript (FDIC).
Warburton, Clark (1967) 'Origin, Development, and Problems of Deposit Insurance', *Lectures in Monetary Economics*, mimeo, University of California at Davis.
'Washington and the Banks' (1933) *Business Week* (8 March) 3–4.
'Washington Reads the Signs' (1933) *Business Week* (15 March) 4–5.
Watkins, Myron W. (1933) 'The Literature of the Crisis', *Quarterly Journal of Economics* (May) 504–32.
Westerfield, Ray B. (1931) 'Defects in American Banking', *Current History* (April) 17–23.
Westerfield, Ray B. (1933) 'The Banking Act of 1933', *Journal of Political Economy* (December) 721–49.
'What'll We Use For Money?' (1933) *Business Week* (11 January) 10–11.
Wheelock, David C. (1992a) 'Monetary Policy in the Great Depression: What the Fed Did, and Why', *Review*, Federal Reserve Bank of St Louis(March/April) 3–28.

Wheelock, David C. (1992b) 'Deposit Insurance and Bank Failures: New Evidence from the 1920s', *Economic Inquiry* (July) 530–43.

Wheelock, David C. (1992c) 'Regulation and Bank Failures: New Evidence from the Agricultural Collapse of the 1920s', *Journal of Economic History* (December) 52, 806–25.

Wheelock, David C., and Subal C. Kumbhaker (1991) 'Which Banks Choose Deposit Insurance? Evidence of Adverse Selection and Moral Hazard in a Voluntary Insurance System', Federal Reserve Bank of St Louis Working Paper 91–005A (September).

White, Eugene Nelson (1982) 'The Political Economy of Banking Regulation, 1864–1933', *Journal of Economic History* (March) 33–40.

White, Eugene Nelson (1983) *The Regulation and Reform of the American Banking System, 1900–1929* (Princeton: Princeton University Press).

White, Eugene Nelson (1984) 'A Reinterpretation of the Banking Crisis of 1930', *Journal of Economic History* (March) 119–38.

Willis, H. Parker (1932) 'What Shall We Do with Our Banks?', *The Nation* (13 April) 422–5.

Willis, H. Parker (1934) 'The Banking Act of 1933 – An Appraisal', *American Economic Association: Papers and Proceedings* (March) 101–10.

Willis, H. Parker, and John M. Chapman (1934) *The Banking Situation* (New York: Columbia University Press).

Woollen, Evans (1933) 'The Insurance of Bank Deposits', *Atlantic Monthly* (November) 609–11.

Woosley, John B. (1936) 'The Permanent Plan for the Insurance of Bank Deposits', *Southern Economic Journal* (April) 20–44.

Wyatt, Walter (1933) 'Constitutionality of Legislation Providing a Unified Commercial Banking System for the United States', *Federal Reserve Bulletin* (March) 166–86.

4 Supervision and the Great Deposit Insurance Debacle

Richard W. Nelson

The great deposit insurance debacle of the 1980s and 1990s has prompted a number of recent studies of the debate surrounding the creation of federal deposit insurance. (Barth, 1991; Barth and Bartholomew, 1992; and Flood, Chapter 3 of this volume). These studies show that the members of Congress who created the FDIC during the New Deal were well aware of the potential risks. Flood, for instance, concludes as follows:

> It is obvious from an examination of the record that the debate surrounding the adoption of federal deposit insurance was both wide-ranging and well-informed.

Though well-informed, Congress was not of one mind on the risks of deposit insurance. Many in Congress were openly skeptical that a new system would be able to avoid the risks which had caused many prior state-sponsored deposit insurance systems to fail. One interpretation of the recent debacle is that these skeptics were correct.

Flood's conclusions suggest an alternative interpretation. Flood points out that the creators of the federal deposit insurance system sought to limit its risks by withholding an explicit federal guarantee and by building checks into the system, including conservative coverage limits, high chartering standards, and wider supervisory authority. He further suggests that the recent deposit insurance debacle resulted from erosion of these checks. Flood cites the emergence of a *de facto* federal guarantee, expanded coverage, relaxed chartering, and relaxed supervision as examples of the weakening of the deposit insurance system. The result is to place the responsibility for the debacle of the 1980s not on flaws in the original system, but on flaws which developed over time, after its New Deal origins.

In what follows, we seek further insight into these alternative interpretations. First, we review deregulation and expanded insurance coverage as contributors to the great deposit insurance debacle of the 1980s. Second, we analyze the interrelations between supervision and deposit insurance and trace their interaction to colonial times.

4.1 DEREGULATION AND THE RECENT DEPOSIT INSURANCE DIFFICULTIES

Bank failures were very low from the mid-1930s through the 1970s, and then rose precipitously during the 1980s. Whether banks also became riskier over this period is a much more complex question (Nelson, 1988). However, there is significant evidence that this also was the cause.

For commercial banks, the greatest increase in risk resulted from a major shift in bank portfolios after 1950, from US government securities into loans. Government securities had constituted about one-half of bank assets at the end of World War II, reflecting the dominance of federal military spending in economic activity during the War period and the decision to finance this spending largely with debt. After the War, financing demands shifted back toward the private sector, and bank portfolios responded.

A second major factor in the increased post-war risk was the decline in capital ratios. Thus, the ratio of equity to risk-assets (excluding cash and government securities) declined significantly during the 1950s and 1960s, at the same time as risk assets were increasing rapidly.

Increased risk in bank portfolios and decreased capital both increased the riskiness of banks. Economic and financial instability also increased. The rate of increase in prices rose sharply from relatively low levels of the 1950s and early 1960s, hitting double-digit levels in the inflationary 1970s. Inflation then diminished equally sharply in the 1980s. Interest rates followed a similar roller-coaster. The interest rate on three-month US Treasury bills rose from the one to three per cent range in the 1950s and early 1960s to over 15 per cent in 1981, before returning to 3 per cent in 1992. Finally, the severity of economic recessions increased significantly, first in 1973–5 and culminating in the severe recession of 1979–82.

Deregulation had very little to do with the increased risks in banking between 1950 and 1980. In the S&L (Savings and Loan) industry, most of the deregulation occurred in 1980 and 1982, after sharply rising interest rates had already rendered, practically, the entire industry market-value insolvent. (Barth *et al.*, 1985, provide early estimates of the size of the S&L problem.) These problems had nothing to do with deregulation, but rather resulted from an extreme mismatch between the durations of assets and liabilities (Nelson, 1993). In turn, the mismatch arose from S&Ls portfolios of single-family mortgage loans, which they had been making since 1831. The mismatch would have caused as severe a problem in the 1950s as it did in 1979–80 had interest rates risen as sharply at that time. Deregulation was not responsible for the S&L crisis.

Whereas deregulation did not cause the maturity mismatch which set off the S&L debacle, regulation did play a significant contributing role. The maturity mismatch at S&Ls developed after the 1930s as the result of government encouragement and regulation. Prior to the New Deal, the standard mortgage instrument had been relatively short-duration, balloon-payment loans. Because of the liquidity problems associated with these mortgages during the Great Depression, New Deal reformers encouraged the long-term, fixed-rate, self-amortizing loan, which subsequently became the standard. It was this regulation-encouraged mortgage instrument which created the maturity mismatch.[1] Subsequently, S&Ls failed to alter their maturity structures to match the new, longer-duration loans, or to develop adjustable rate mortgages. However, again regulation contributed to the problem by prohibiting adjustable rate loans at Federal associations.

After 1981, unsupervised expansion into deregulated activities did contribute to the ultimate losses in the S&L industry and to the deposit insurance debacle. However, the problem had as much to do with lax supervision as with deregulation and, in any case, came after the deposit insurance system had already failed. We shall return to the supervisory elements in the following section.

What about commercial banks? There was very little deregulation during the 1950s and 1960s, when banks began increasing their asset risk and reducing their capital ratios. Banks have long had the power to make risky loans, and capital levels were in the domain of supervision, not regulation. Deregulation gained momentum in the late 1970s, but initially focused on the elimination of interest-rate ceilings on deposits, not expanded powers.

Falling agricultural, energy, commodity and real-estate prices had a lot to do with bank losses in the 1980s. So did the higher proportion of loans in their portfolios and reduced capital ratios. In contrast, deregulation had little impact.

An increasingly competitive banking environment probably did contribute to increased risk. Here, however, there are clear gains to be measured from increased competition, and it is possible that any increased risk that occurred was optimal.

4.2 EXPANDED DEPOSIT INSURANCE COVERAGE LIMITS

At its inception, the FDIC insured deposits only to a limit of $2500. Coverage limits of deposit insurance were expanded sharply in subsequent years, to the present limit of $100 000. However, the greatest increase came in 1980, when coverage was increased from $40 000 to $100 000, without debate, through a parliamentary maneuver.

Again, the S&L problem emerged prior to the major increase in insurance coverage. The increase in coverage may have reflected ill-conceived hopes of dealing with the crisis, or manipulation by bankrupt S&Ls, but it certainly did not cause the crisis. The maturity mismatch, which underlays the S&L crisis, developed when insurance coverage limits were still low, and there is no reason to believe that S&Ls would have reduced their interest rate risk or increased their capital had deposit insurance coverage remained low.

During the 1980s, the higher deposit insurance limits, coupled with advances in telecommunications and computer technology, facilitated a rapid growth of brokered and telemarketed deposit markets. These markets were used widely, sometimes with supervisory approval, to keep failed S&Ls going when there were insufficient funds to close them. They also were used to finance risky investments and yield curve plays that ultimately increased the size of the debacle. However, modern computer technology probably would have permitted much of the growth to occur even with lower deposit insurance limits.

Similarly, increases in commercial bank asset risk and declines in their capital ratios began when insurance coverage was still relatively low. It is, consequently, difficult to relate the banking crisis to this development.

4.3 SUPERVISION AND DEPOSIT INSURANCE IN HISTORICAL CONTEXT

By banking supervision, we mean oversight of the safety and soundness of banks and other depository institutions. Banks also are subject to other varieties of regulation and oversight, including oversight of mergers and acquisitions to promote competition, oversight of lending and deposit-taking practices to ensure meaningful disclosure or to limit discrimination or unethical practices, and regulation and oversight of activities to separate banking and commerce and limit geographical expansion. These areas are beyond the scope of this chapter.

Supervision and deposit insurance may be viewed as alternatives from the perspective of protecting depositors against possible loss in banking failures. Supervision reduces the likely loss to depositors by reducing banking risk and, thus, the likelihood and possible magnitude of losses that banks may incur. In the absence of deposit insurance, any such losses in excess of the bank's capital would be passed on to depositors. Supervision also produces information that can be used to close depository institutions, again reducing the magnitude of losses at failure.

While deposit insurance obviates the need for supervision to protect depositors, it reintroduces supervision in another role. Both theory and historical experience suggest strongly that supervision is necessary to make deposit insurance workable or to limit its cost. First, insurers, generally, must evaluate the insurability of risks and sort them into actuarial categories. This requires pre-insurance supervision. Second, the actions of bank management affect the level of risks after insurance is granted. This creates a moral hazard in transferring risk from the depositor to the insurer which must be removed to make insurance workable. Continuing supervision of banks operations under an insurance regime is one approach to controlling the moral hazard in deposit insurance.

In historical context, supervision developed before deposit insurance. Government supervision of banking in the United States has historically been closely associated with the chartering of banks. The Continental Congress granted the first US bank charter to the Bank of North America in 1781. The directors of this bank reported on the operations of the bank each day to the Superintendent of Finance. This rudimentary form of oversight marks the beginning of banking supervision in the United States, even prior to the Constitution.

It is notable that bank supervision began with the chartering of banks rather than the first appearances of banking activity. Functional banking actually began earlier, but was performed privately and as an adjunct to other business activities, without government charters. For instance, merchants with idle balances or currency reserves were known to lend to merchants who needed funds. These forms of banking were extremely rudimentary, however, and early governments wanted to encourage the development of a more specialized banking system.

Government's principal instrument of encouraging banking was the corporate charter. Charters granted a number of privileges to their recipients, including limited liability. Early bank charters also granted the right to issue bank notes which circulated as money. This was regarded as a government function.

In the eighteenth and early nineteenth centuries, corporate charters were all granted by special acts of government and were highly specialized. In addition to a few banking corporations, US corporations were chartered to build roads and canals and to construct toll bridges. Not many corporate charters were granted, and these charters were not broad licenses to do business. Rather, they restricted the business of the corporation to specific activities deemed worthy of the privilege of a charter. Oversight was regarded as necessary to enforce charter restrictions and as a useful way of ensuring that the desired services were provided. Thus, supervision of banks was not unique, but fell within the broader pattern of oversight of corporate activity prevalent at the time.[2]

Oversight of early corporate activity, including banking, was a rather simple affair. The small number of corporations with limited powers, presented no need for specialized government officials or agencies to provide supervision. Charters were typically granted for a limited period of time, and the necessity of renewal of the charters constituted the most basic form of oversight. Oversight through charter renewal was performed by the legislature, itself. The presumption was that the corporation would have shown itself worthy of the continued grant of government privileges through continued public service.

The number of chartered banks grew rapidly in the early nineteenth century. Many of the bank charters that were granted contained restrictions on the issuance of notes. The First Bank of the United States, chartered by the US Congress to operate between 1791 and 1811, was limited to issuing total debt not more than the capital and moneys deposited for safekeeping. The states, which chartered most early banks, also imposed restrictions on note issuance and capital levels, and sometimes required the redemption of notes on demand.

The earliest focus of bank supervision, thus, centered on establishing a specialized banking system, ensuring a sound currency, and protecting bank creditors in general. Supervision of banks was common, although not universal, and restrictions were often not strictly enforced. Oversight varied a great deal in its intensity.

The growth of banks in the early 1800s brought increasing bank failures and triggered a cycle of escalating supervision that has continued through the present. The cycle developed as follows. Banking failures were perceived as a significant problem. A number of states, led by New York in 1825, responded by creating note or deposit insurance to provide the protection that supervision had failed to provide. However, recognizing the interdependence of insurance and supervision, they also further increased bank supervision. Thus, with its insurance system, New York State established specialized government officials to supervise the banks. These officials introduced bank examination as a way of gathering information on the soundness of banks, going beyond the reporting and *ad hoc* oversight that had characterized the previous period.

The establishment of free banking ratified the rapid expansion of banks in the early 1800s and encouraged even more rapid expansion, thereafter.

Again, New York State led the way with its Free Banking Act of 1838. Free banking provided standard bank charters widely available to financially responsible parties. Because banking charters were the principle vehicle used to restrict banking activities, the free banking laws established a general framework for bank supervision. The New York Act, for instance, required banks to hold collateral in mortgages or state notes against the banks' own notes and, again, regulated bank capital. The rapid growth of banks under free banking also heightened the need for specialized supervisory agencies.

The experience of note insurance systems during the period prior to 1860 is instructive. Most of these systems eventually were closed. But, it is not correct to say that they all failed. A number of these systems flourished, and were closed when the National Bank Act of 1863 created a national currency guaranteed by the Federal government and taxed state bank notes. These systems were driven out of business by federal note insurance, which represented a competing technology. Studies of this period have suggested that many of these systems should be regarded as financial successes, not failures. They further suggest that the distinguishing feature of the successful note insurance systems was adequate supervision.

The preceding analysis leads to three conclusions:

(1) Historically, supervision preceded deposit insurance.
(2) Historically, deposit insurance developed because supervision failed to protect depositors and note holders.
(3) Historically, deposit insurance systems failed when not associated with adequate supervision.

4.4 SUPERVISION DURING THE EARLY HISTORY OF THE FDIC

The early actions of the FDIC suggest that it recognized the limited government backing of its operations. In its 1938 *Annual Report*, the FDIC devoted an entire section to the 'Objectives of Supervision of Insured Banks'. Here, it stated:

> Commercial banks have operated under the supervision of State or Federal agencies for more than a century. Supervision was established primarily to protect creditors of banks. The Federal Deposit Insurance Corporation was created in 1933 for the same purpose following the most severe crisis in banking affairs that had occurred during that

century. It was established to provide safety which had not been provided through previously existing supervisory and rediscount systems. In creating the Corporation, provision was made: (1) to distribute losses resulting from bank failures over the entire banking system instead of allowing them to concentrate upon certain individuals, groups, or communities; and (2) *to improve bank supervision with a view to preventing, insofar as possible, an accumulation of weak or hazardous banking situations* (emphasis added).[3]

The FDIC's discussion in its 1938 Annual Report also clearly recognized the key role of supervision in supporting deposit insurance:

> The Federal Deposit Insurance Corporation has a more direct interest in the prevention of bank failures than any other bank supervisory authority for the reason that the Corporation must bear the financial burden resulting from such failures... For this reason, it is essential that the Corporation have ample powers to determine the financial condition of, and the character of banking practices being pursued by, any insured bank, and to take steps to secure correction of unsound situations.[4]

Continuing, the FDIC identified a number of steps to do so, including maintaining bank capital, requiring banks to carry assets at their 'reasonable worth', and keeping self-dealing at a minimum. It also recognized the importance of prompt closure:

> Banks which are in hazardous condition or show undesirable tendencies should be closely watched, and if improvement is not forthcoming during periods of favorable business and financial conditions they should be reorganized, merged, or liquidated before losses to creditors accumulate.[5]

The FDIC was given the power to withdraw insurance from depository institutions which did not meet its standards. Withdrawal of insurance from national banks, which were required to join the FDIC system, required that the Comptroller of the Currency liquidate the bank. Withdrawal of insurance from a state-chartered bank that was a member of the Federal Reserve System required that the Federal Reserve act to terminate membership. In its early years, the FDIC did utilize its supervisory powers to terminate deposit insurance of operating banks as well as to force the liquidation of those banks by the chartering authorities.

4.5 SUMMARY AND CONCLUSIONS

The framers of the FDIC knew the risks of deposit insurance and took measures to provide effective supervision. Yet, the supervision did not succeed in preventing the deposit insurance crisis that developed 50 years later, partly because of supervisors' failure to appraise risk accurately, partly because of political interference, and partly because of unanticipated economic and financial instability.

What is at issue, thus, is not deregulation or increased deposit insurance coverage, but rather the ability of supervisors to control banking risk. Historical context shows that the current supervisory failure is not unique. Indeed, the early origins of deposit insurance are tied to the prior failure of supervision to provide the desired amount of protection.

If the New Deal deposit insurance system failed to solve the problem of effective bank supervision, it may be that its only innovation was getting the taxpayers involved. The Federal government is the only entity with sufficient resources to back an unequivocal guarantee when supervision proves inadequate. Private insurance companies fail when they make mistakes or get a bad draw from the economic card deck. That is what has given the deposit insurance system the success that it has had in protecting depositors. And that success can be argued to have had great benefits to our economy.

Benefits notwithstanding to the contrary, unless we find new ways to deal with the fundamental defects of deposit insurance, it is likely to continue to be a costly system. As for the future, developing better analytical methods for appraising risk and reducing political interference with supervision remains an important element of the research agenda. Other important issues include whether more of the costs of deposit insurance should be shared by depositors and borrowers than by taxpayers. These issues, of course, are not new, but continue to pose serious problems for deposit insurance.

Notes

1. In sharp contrast, Canada did not encourage the fixed-rate self-amortizing loan, and it did not develop to the extent that it did in the US. As a result, the Canadian financial system was spared a debacle comparable to our S&L crisis.
2. What is interesting, here, is that oversight of general business corporations diminished over time, in opposition to the trend of expanding supervision over banking corporations.

3. FDIC (1939), pp. 22–3.
4. *Ibid*, p. 23.
5. *Ibid*, p. 25.

References

Barth, James R., R. Dan Brumbaugh, Daniel Sauerhalf, and George H. K. Wang (1985) 'Insolvency and Risk Taking in the Thrift Industry: Implications For the Future', *Contemporary Policy Issues* (Fall), 1–32.

Barth, James R. (1991) *The Great Savings and Loan Debacle* (Washington, DC: American Enterprise Institute).

Barth, James R. and Philip Bartholomew (1992) 'The Thrift Industry Crisis: Revealed Weaknesses in the Federal Deposit Insurance System', in James R. Barth and R. Dan Brumbaugh, Jr. (eds), *The Reform of Federal Deposit Insurance* (New York: Harper Business).

Benston, George J., Robert A. Eisenbeis, Paul M. Horvitz, Edward J. Kane, and George G. Kaufman (1986) *Perspectives on Safe and Sound Banking: Past, Present, and Future* (Cambridge, MA: The MIT Press).

Board of Governors of the Federal Reserve System (1941) *Banking Studies* (Washington, DC).

Federal Deposit Insurance Corporation (1939) 'Objectives of Supervision of Insured Banks', *Annual Report, 1938*, 22–8.

Federal Deposit Insurance Corporation (1951) 'History of Legislation for the Guaranty of Insurance of Bank Deposits', *Annual Report, 1950*, 63–101.

Federal Deposit Insurance Corporation (1953) 'Insurance of Bank Obligations Prior to Federal Deposit Insurance', *Annual Report, 1952*, 59–72.

Federal Deposit Insurance Corporation. (1954) 'Bank-Obligation Insurance Systems, 1829 to 1866,' *Annual Report, 1953*, 45–67.

Federal Deposit Insurance Corporation (1957) 'State Deposit Insurance Systems, 1908–1930', *Annual Report, 1956*, 49–73.

Gruchy, Allan G. (1937) *Supervision and Control of Virginia State Banks* (New York: D. Appleton-Century Company, Inc.).

Nelson, Richard W. (1989) 'Management Versus Economic Conditions as Contributors to the Recent Increase in Banking Failures', in Courtenay C. Stone (ed.), *Financial Risk: Theory, Evidence, and Implications* (Boston, MA: Kluwer Academic Publishers), 125–48.

Nelson, Richard W. (1993) 'Regulatory Structure, Regulatory Failure, and the S&L Debacle', *Contemporary Policy Issues* (January) 108–15.

5 The 'Chicago Plan' and New Deal Banking Reform

Ronnie J. Phillips

The history of the legislative changes in the financial system, which occurred during the 28 months from Franklin D. Roosevelt's inauguration, in March 1933, until the passage of the Banking Act of 1935 has been well documented (Burns, 1974; Kennedy, 1973). This period saw the enactment of the Emergency Banking Act, the Banking Acts of 1933 and 1935, as well as reforms of the stock market and agricultural credit. The existing histories have given us detailed examinations of the political maneuvering involved in the passage of the legislation, but they have neglected the role of the 'Chicago plan' – the 1933 proposal put forward, in a series of memoranda by economists at the University of Chicago, to abolish the fractional reserve system and impose 100 per cent reserves on demand deposits. The proposal was known to the Roosevelt administration prior to the passage of the Banking Act of 1933, and later led directly to legislation introduced by Senator Bronson Cutting of New Mexico, and other Progressives, as part of the debate over the Banking Act of 1935. The influence of the Chicago plan was felt even before Irving Fisher's more widely known, and largely unsuccessful, efforts to enlist Roosevelt's support for the 100 per cent reserve plan (Allen, 1977, 1991).

The Chicago plan was a proposal to radically change the structure of our financial system and, as such, its best chance of passage was in the period of the early New Deal. The objective of this chapter is to document the role of the Chicago plan in the debates over New Deal banking legislation, and provide an assessment of why the Chicago plan ultimately lost out to the alternative measures embodied in the Banking Act of 1935. The failure of the Chicago plan in the 1930s is also of interest in the contemporary debates over banking reform. The Chicago plan, by restricting bank assets, would not have saddled the taxpayers with an enormous liability from federal deposit insurance. Recently, proposals have been put forward for 'narrow' or 'core' banks, which restrict bank assets, and embody many of the components of the Chicago plan (Tobin, 1985, 1987; Bryan, 1988, 1991).

5.1 THE BANKING CRISIS AND THE MARCH MEMORANDUM

When Roosevelt came into office, he faced a myriad of problems related to the economy. Farmers, workers, bankers and politicians, were all demanding action. On the financial front, there were three critical issues which had to be dealt with: (1) the safety of the medium of exchange; (2) the financing of the capital development of the economy; and (3) the control of money and credit by the Federal Reserve. In response to the widespread bank holidays which had already been declared by many states, Franklin Roosevelt's first act as President was to declare a national bank holiday for the period 4–9 March 1933. In his inaugural address, Roosevelt, referring to the financial collapse, stated that 'The money changers have fled from their high seats in the temple of our civilization' (Schlesinger, 1957, p. 7; Tugwell, 1957, p. 289).

The Emergency Banking Act, which was passed in less than an hour, did not provide any permanent solutions to the problem, it only gave the Congress and the President a breathing spell in which to formulate a plan. During his first fireside chat, Roosevelt explained his reasons for closing the banks and announced their reopening. It is a tribute to Roosevelt's charisma that when the banks reopened on Monday, 13 March, the runs had virtually ended. Walter Lippmann remarked that 'In one week, the nation, which had lost confidence in everything and everybody, has regained confidence in the government and in itself' (Schlesinger, 1958, p. 13). Raymond Moley, one of the original Brain Trusters wrote: 'Capitalism was saved in eight days' (Moley, 1939, p. 155).

It is within this historical context that economists at the University of Chicago presented their proposal for reform of the banking system. The six page memorandum on banking reform was given limited and confidential distribution to about 40 individuals on 16 March 1933 (Knight, 1933). A copy of the memorandum was sent to Henry A. Wallace, then Secretary of Agriculture, with a cover letter signed by Frank Knight. The letter listed the following supporters of the plan: F. H. Knight, L. W. Mints, Henry Schultz, H. C. Simons, G. V. Cox, Aaron Director, Paul Douglas, and A. G. Hart. The authors anticipated skepticism about their plan as evidenced by a typed postscript which stated: 'We hope you are *one* of the forty odd who get this who will not think we are quite looney [sic], I think Viner really agrees but doesn't believe it is good politics'.

The proposal opens with the statement: 'It is evident that drastic measures must soon be taken with reference to banking, currency, and federal fiscal policy'. The general recommendations were: (a) federal guarantee of deposits; (b) the guarantee only be taken as part of a drastic program of banking reform which will certainly and permanently prevent any possible recurrence of the present banking crisis; and (c) the Administration announce and pursue a policy of bringing about, and maintaining, a moderate increase in the level of wholesale prices, not to exceed 15 per cent (Knight, 1933, p. 1).

The detailed suggestions advocated outright ownership of the Federal Reserve Banks; the guarantee of the deposits of member banks which were open for business 3 March 1933 but subject to full supervisory *control* over the management of these banks by the Fed. They advocated the issue of Federal Reserve Notes, which should be declared legal tender, in any amounts which may be necessary to meet demands for payment by depositors. Further, the Federal Reserve Banks should liquidate the assets of all member banks, pay off liabilities, and dissolve all existing banks; and new institutions should be created which accept only demand deposits subject to a 100 per cent reserve requirement in lawful money and/or deposits with the Reserve Banks. Saving deposits would be handled through the incorporation of investment trusts. Present banking institutions would continue deposit and lending functions under Federal Reserve supervision until the new institutions can be put into place. The government should then undertake to raise the price level by 15 per cent by fiscal and currency means, but further inflation (beyond 15 per cent) should be prevented. Finally, there should be suspension of free-coinage of gold, embargo upon gold import, prohibition of private export of gold, call in all gold coins in exchange for Federal Reserve notes, suspension of the gold-clause in all debt contracts, and substantial government sale and export of gold abroad (Knight, 1933).

Henry Wallace, then Secretary of Agriculture, gave the Chicago plan to Roosevelt less than a week after it was distributed. Wallace hoped FDR would give the plan serious consideration, though the plan was a radical break with the past. Wallace wrote to Roosevelt:

> The memorandum from the Chicago economists which I gave you at [the] Cabinet meeting Tuesday, is really awfully good and I hope that you or Secretary Woodin will have the time and energy to study it. Of course the plan outlined is quite a complete break with our present banking history. It would be an even more decisive break than the founding of the Federal Reserve System.
>
> (Wallace to Roosevelt, 23 March 1933, Roosevelt Library, POF #230)

During the first 100 days of the Roosevelt administration, numerous measures were passed to deal with the economic situation, especially the crisis of the banking system and agriculture. On 20 March, the Economy Act was passed; on 31 March, the Civilian Conservation Corp was created; and on 19 April, the US went off the gold standard. These measures were followed by the sweeping reforms of the Agricultural Adjustment Act (AAA), in May, which sought to raise agriculture prices through output restrictions. An amendment to the AAA gave the President the power to issue greenbacks and to monetize gold (Schlesinger, 1958, pp. 199–200). Congress also passed the Emergency Farm Mortgage Act in May which provided for the refinancing of farm mortgages. The month of June saw the passage of the Home Owners's Loan Act, providing for the refinancing of home mortgages, the National Industrial Recovery Act (which included a public works program), the Farm Credit Act, the joint resolution by Congress to suspend the gold standard and abrogate the gold clause and, perhaps most importantly, the Banking Act of 1933, which separated investment and commercial banking, established temporary federal deposit insurance, and made an official body the previously informal Federal Open Market Committee.

Thus by June, many of the proposals contained in the March memoranda had been enacted. Though there was a separation of commercial and investment banking, 100 per cent reserve deposit banks had not been created. Federal Reserve notes had not been declared legal tender, and, though liberalized, the Federal Reserve still did not have full use of its policy tools to affect monetary aggregates. The Fed had long had the discount rate, though it could vary regionally, and now as a result of the Thomas Amendment to the AAA, the suspension of the gold standard, and the Banking Act of 1933, it could issue Federal Reserve notes. However, the Fed was not yet totally free to set reserve requirements.

There was also widespread support for the separation of commercial and investment banking because it was believed that bankers had speculated with depositors funds in the stock market, and, when the stock market speculation spree ended, many banks became insolvent. The separation of investment and commercial banking was supported by prominent bankers such as Winthrop Aldrich (Leuchtenburg, 1963, p. 60).

The two proposals, for federal insurance and separation of commercial and investment banking, were linked in the Banking Act of 1933. The linking of these two reforms is vital in the understanding of the subsequent evolution of the debates and reforms. Though they became identified as administration measures, the crisis nature of 1933 and the support of a new administration merely facilitated their passage. Deposit insurance made banks 'safe' not by direct restrictions on their assets, but rather by the promise that the government would guarantee *all* banks, both good and bad. The separation of commercial and investment banking removed some abuses resulting from the use of depositors funds in stock market speculations, but it did not address directly the issue of financing for the capital development of the economy.

On passage of the Act, J. P. Morgan predicted that the separation would have dire effects on his firm's ability to supply capital 'for the development of the country' (Schlesinger, 1958, p. 443). William O. Douglas observed that the Act was a nineteenth-century piece of legislation which ignored the problem of capital structure and the need to manage investment (Schlesinger, 1958, p. 445). While it is true that the RFC had undertaken the role of providing capital funds for industry, the banking legislation attempted to restore credit availability by restoring confidence in the medium of exchange and, therefore, an increase in bank deposits. The Banking Act of 1933 attempted to kill two birds with one stone. Though it succeeded in stopping bank runs, the fractional reserve nature of the banking system, coupled with a lack of power on the part of the Federal Reserve Board, effectively undermined the ability of the financial system to supply adequate investment funds. In 1929, the ratio of loans to total assets for all commercial banks was 58 per cent. By 1934, that ratio had fallen to 38 per cent, as total bank assets began increasing after falling steadily from 1929 to 1933. This was also in spite of the fact that total bank failures went from 4000 in 1933 to 61 in 1934. Clearly, though bank numbers were increasing and total assets were increasing, bank loans remained at about the same level from 1933 to 1936. The economy was in a credit crunch.

Though much had been accomplished by November 1933, the central problem which remained was the Federal Reserve's ability to use all means available to it to affect monetary aggregates. In order to do this, changes would have to be made to the Federal Reserve Act which would restrict the power of individual Reserve Banks, especially New York, while strengthening the power of the Federal Reserve Board in Washington. This was the focus of the November Chicago memoranda, and it was to become the crucial issue in the Banking Act of 1935.

5.2 THE NOVEMBER 1933 MEMORANDA

During the period March to November, the Chicago economists received comments from a number of individuals on their proposal and, in November 1933, another memorandum was prepared. The memorandum was expanded to 13 pages, there was a supplementary memorandum on 'Long-time Objectives of Monetary Management' (seven pages) and an appendix titled 'Banking and Business Cycles' (six pages). Though signed by the same group of economists, this document was evidently written by Henry Simons. The proposal began by noting that government had failed in its primary function of controlling currency by allowing banks to usurp this power. Such 'free banking' in deposit creation 'gives us an unreliable and inhomogeneous medium; and it gives us a regulation or manipulation of currency which is totally perverse'. What was necessary was a 'complete reorientation of our thinking and a redefinition of the objectives of reform' (Simons, 1933, p. 1). The solution was the 'outright abolition of deposit banking on the fractional-reserve principle' (Simons, 1933, p. 2).

The proposal included many of the items in the March reform: (i) Federal ownership of the Federal Reserve Banks; (ii) exclusive Congressional powers to grant charters for deposit banking; (iii) suspension of all powers of existing corporations to engage in deposit banking within two years; (iv) creation of a new type of deposit bank with 100 per cent reserves in the form of notes and deposits at the Federal Reserve Banks; (v) abolition of reserve requirements for Federal Reserve Banks; (vi) replacement of private-bank credit with Federal Reserve bank credit over a two-year transition period; and restricting currency to only Federal Reserve notes. However, they went on to add: (vii) enacting a simple rule of monetary policy; and (viii) achievement of a price-level specified by Congress. There is no mention of federal deposit insurance which had already gone into effect in June.

As before, the plan would displace existing commercial banks by two types of institutions: deposit banks and investment trusts. If private companies failed to provide new deposits, then government, through the extension of a postal savings system, could offer such deposits (Simons, 1933, p. 6). Investment trust banks would acquire funds exclusively by sale of their own securities, thereby limiting their lending capacity to the funds so obtained. Investment trust banks would provide a service by bringing borrowers and lenders together, and could, therefore, charge for this service (Simons, 1933, p. 7). The memorandum also evaluated a return to the gold standard (which was rejected unless it was a 100 per cent gold standard) and various rules to guide monetary policy, including price-level stabilization (Simons, 1933, pp. 8–11). The proposal noted that a monetary rule which set money supply growth could be carried out by conversion of interest-bearing federal debt into non-interest bearing debt, open market operations by the Reserve banks, an increase in federal expenditures, or a reduction in federal taxes (Simons, 1933, p. 12).

In summary, the memoranda stated that the Federal Reserve Act had faulty objectives because commercial paper offered no real liquidity, and that the answer lay in the abolition of fractional reserve banking, so that a reconstituted Federal Reserve would have precise power over the money supply. However, monetary management was not to be discretionary, but subject to definite rules laid down by Congress.

This version of the proposal was given to Gardiner C. Means, who worked for Assistant Secretary of Agriculture, Rexford G. Tugwell. Means responded to the Chicago plan in a three-page, single-spaced memo (Means, 'Comment', c1933). Given the Administration's concern over the relationship between farmers and bankers, it is no surprise that the Agriculture Department would be interested in monetary reform. Means praised the Chicago memorandum's primary objective, of placing control of the monetary medium in the exclusive hands of government, and the method by which the transition would be effected (Means, 1933, p. 1). He thought the Chicago proposal provided a 'relatively simple and direct method of dealing with the deposits aspect of our banking system', though it would likely be opposed by bankers (Means, 1933, p. 2). Means' only disagreement with the plan was that he would allow the Federal Reserve banks to purchase high-grade commercial paper in order to establish 100 per cent reserves, and Means argued that monetary policy should be discretionary, and not subject to a rule (Means, 1933, p. 3). It is interesting that the Chicago proposal had found greatest favor with Rexford Tugwell (who advocated a similar scheme to expand the postal savings system) and Gardiner Means, both institutional economists and planners.

In January 1934, Roosevelt sent a message to Congress asking for legislation to organize a sound and adequate currency system. Roosevelt requested that Congress enact legislation to vest, in the United States Government, sole title to all American owned monetary gold and 'other monetary matters [which] would add to the convenience of handling current problems in this field'. FDR further indicated that the Secretary of the Treasury was prepared to submit information concerning changes to the appropriate committees of the Congress (Krooss, 1969, p. 2791). It was soon after FDR's address to Congress that there was direct involvement by the Chicago group in the drafting of legislation to enact the Chicago plan for banking reform.

5.3 LEGISLATING THE CHICAGO PLAN

Robert M. Hutchins, the President of the University of Chicago, mailed a copy of the November Chicago plan to Senator Bronson Cutting of New

Mexico in December 1933. Cutting was a progressive Republican in the mode of Robert La Follette, Sr. He was highly critical of the role of private bankers in the economy and an advocate of greater government involvement in banking and credit and national planning. As Schlesinger has noted, this emphasis on planning and the role of government was very much in line with New Dealers such as Tugwell, Means, Adolph Berle, and others (Schlesinger, 1960, pp. 389–91). Cutting was one of the radicals in the Senate, mostly old Progressives, which included: George Norris, Robert La Follette, and Gerald P. Nye, all Republicans, and Democrats Burton K. Wheeler of Montana, Edward P. Costigan of Colorado and Homer Bone of Washington, all of whom started as Progressive Republicans (Schlesinger, 1960, pp. 134–5).

Cutting was quite interested in the Chicago proposal and largely in agreement. He replied to Hutchins:

> I may say at once that I agree decidedly with most of the views expressed by the members of your faculty. I wonder if any of them has considered the idea of drafting a bill embodying their views? I suspect that Bob La Follette would be as much interested in this matter as I am and, if we could get a draft in tangible shape, it would at least give us something to shoot at.
>
> (Cutting to Hutchins, 15 December 1933, Cutting Papers)

Hutchins replied 'we'll set to work drafting a bill' (Hutchins to Cutting, 22 December 1933, Cutting Papers); however, in March 1934, Cutting wired Hutchins inquiring about the status of the proposed bill (Cutting to Hutchins, 7 March 1934, Cutting Papers). As a result, Henry Simons traveled to Washington and met with Cutting on 16 March to discuss the essential features of a bill (Simons to Cutting, 10 March 1934; Cutting to Simons, 14 March 1934, Cutting Papers). Simons did not feel that he was qualified to draft an entire bill, since he would not be familiar with many of its technical features. His outline for a bill was given to Cutting and Senator Robert La Follette, Jr. The actual bill was written by Robert H. Hemphill, a writer for the Hearst newspapers.

To kick off the campaign for his bill, Cutting published an article in the 31 March 1934 issue of *Liberty* magazine entitled 'Is Private Banking Doomed?' Cutting's answer, of course, was that it was doomed by the New Deal because government should control money and credit without the interference of private banks. Cutting remarked that unless the administration introduced such legislation to deprive private bankers of this power, that he would introduce such a measure (Cutting, 1934, p. 10).

Banks could remain, in Cutting's view, if they held 100 per cent reserves against deposits, but they would not be allowed to create credit. Cutting expected that a battle against the bankers would not be easy, and lamented FDR's failure to nationalize the banks in March 1933. He wrote: 'It was President Roosevelt's great mistake. Now the bankers will make a mighty struggle' (Cutting, 1934, p. 12).

On 19 May 1934, Senator Cutting gave a speech to the People's Lobby in which he announced his intention to introduce a bill to create a national bank which would have a monopoly of credit, and that private bankers should not make profits from credit.

Business Week, noting that radical ideas for banking reform were receiving wide support, wrote in reference to Cutting's remarks:

> The fact that the more radical opinions are so widespread as to be reflected in the House indicates that the banks have not resold themselves to the public ... But unless the banks convince the people the present system is best or unless business picks up markedly by the start of 1935, Congress may go beyond the small changes of the deposits insurance bill and alter the whole banking setup – despite the anguished wails of established banks.
>
> (*Business Week*, 2 June 1934, p. 27)

The bill, S. 3744, was introduced by Cutting and Congressman Wright Patman of Texas (H.R. 9855) on 6 June 1934, and had as its stated objective to 'provide an adequate and stable monetary system; to prevent bank failures; to prevent uncontrolled inflation; to prevent depressions; to provide a system to control the price of commodities and the purchasing power of money; to restore normal prosperity and assure its continuance' (US Congress 1934). To achieve these goals, the bill proposed to (1) segregate demand from savings deposits; (2) require the banks to keep 100 per cent reserves against their demand deposits; (3) require them to keep 5 per cent reserves against their savings deposits; (4) set up a Federal Monetary Authority with full control over the supply of currency, the buying and selling of government securities, the gold price of the dollar; (5) have the FMA take over enough of the bonds of the banks to provide 100 per cent reserves against their demand deposits; and (6) have the FMA raise the price level to its 1926 position and keep it there by buying and selling government bonds. As a consequence of this bill, the only money that would exist would be either currency issued by the Federal Monetary Authority, or in demand deposits backed 100 per cent by lawful money (gold) or government securities. The legislative bill would retain, squarely within the federal government, the power given to it in the Constitution to create money and maintain its value. This bill would also achieve the other long-run New Deal objectives of raising the price level and strengthening government influence on economic activity, in this case, through monetary policy.

Cutting, who shared Roosevelt's background as a graduate of Groton and Harvard, and should have been a natural political ally, had alienated Roosevelt over the issue of payment of the veterans' pensions. Cutting had worked hard against Roosevelt's attempt to reduce veterans' pensions (Schlesinger, 1960, p. 140). Whether warranted or not, Roosevelt personally disliked Cutting, who was the only Progressive that Roosevelt failed to endorse for re-election in 1934. There was little doubt that the animosity between Roosevelt and Cutting would mean little likelihood of administration support for Cutting's bill.

Cutting's bill served to put the Roosevelt administration on notice that there were those in Congress prepared to take drastic and extreme measures if the administration's reforms did not go far enough toward complete government control of money and credit. The goal of the bill was to correct the shortcomings of the Banking Act of 1933. The Act had not addressed the problem of the availability of credit, nor had it dealt with the issue of the Federal Reserve's control over the money supply. The Cutting bill sought to make both the money supply and credit availability subject to government control.

5.4 THE BANKING ACT OF 1935

The Administration strategy for the final phase of banking reform began with studies directed under Jacob Viner. William Woodin was Roosevelt's first Secretary of the Treasury, but when he resigned for health reasons in November 1933, Roosevelt nominated an old friend, Henry Morgenthau, to take his place. The appointment was confirmed in January 1934 and, soon afterward, Morgenthau suggested to Jacob Viner, who was a special assistant to the Secretary, that he assemble a group of the best minds he could find in monetary, banking and public finance, to see what they could come up with.

The group would include Viner, four senior staff, four junior research staff, and clerical and secretarial staff. On 27 June 1934, Secretary Morgenthau announced that the Treasury was undertaking a number of studies in preparation for next year's legislative program in the areas of currency and banking and taxation and revenue (Treasury Department

Press Release, 27 June 1934). Those temporarily employed by the Treasury to work on the Monetary and Banking Survey studies were: Lauchlin Currie, Harry D. White, Albert G. Hart, Benjamin Caplan, Virginius F. Coe, and Edward C. Simmons. It is important to note that two of this group, Currie and Hart, were already known advocates of the 100 per cent reserve plan, while Viner appears to have been at least strongly sympathetic.

In his book, *The Supply and Control of Money in the United States*, Currie presented a model of the money supply mechanism in which the major source of variation in the money supply was the level of excess reserves, while the Federal Reserve's primary means of control of the money supply was the level of required reserves (Steindl, 1992, pp. 452–3). At the time Currie wrote, the Federal Reserve did not have the power to change reserve requirements. The Federal Reserve actions were firmly grounded in the 'real bills doctrine'. The Fed was allowed to discount only real bills and, thus, its monetary policy was pro-cyclical. Currie saw this as a major limiting factor in effective monetary control. Currie then went on to discuss the 'ideal conditions' for monetary control, which he argued was a system with 100 per cent reserve requirements on demand deposits. In a footnote in his book, Currie stated that Albert Hart had brought the Chicago proposal to his attention after the book had gone to press (Currie, 1968, p. 156).

In September 1934, Lauchlin Currie submitted a comprehensive proposal for monetary reform to the Secretary of the Treasury, Henry Morgenthau. The fundamentally faulty structure of the monetary system was attributed by Currie to the unsatisfactory nature of the compromise between private creation of money with governmental control (Currie, 1968, p. 197).

Currie did not provide an elaborate theoretical rationale, as the Chicago economists had in their appendix on 'Banking and Business Cycles', but rather noted that the monetary system had been acting as a 'maladjustment-intensifying factor' due to the 'unsatisfactory nature of the compromise of private creation of money with government control' (Currie, 1968, p. 197).

Currie proposed that the reserve ratio for checkable deposits be 100 per cent, that for non-checkable deposits zero per cent, and an end to interbank deposits unless subject to 100 per cent reserves. During the transition to the new system, Currie sought to insure that banks would not see a loss of income with the increase in the reserve requirements. When the new policy was announced, banks would initially meet the 100 per cent requirement with a non-interest bearing note from the Reserve banks. This note might be left outstanding indefinitely, or only retired upon suspension or merging of the bank. Alternatively, the debt might be retired over a period of time from five to 20 years by the member banks turning over to the reserve banks Government bonds (Currie, 1968, pp. 200–1). Any excess reserves held at the time of the imposition of 100 per cent reserves could be loaned out, but there would be no multiplier effect because of the 100 per cent reserve requirement (Currie, 1968, p. 202).

If it was decided that banks must repay the Fed loans made at the time of the implementation of the 100 per cent reserve system, the interest earned on those bonds would be paid to the commercial banks. Again, there would be no impact on the current income/expense situation of the bank. However, once those initial loans were repaid, banks could no longer acquire earning assets by selling checkable deposits. As a final policy recommendation, Currie proposed that banks be allowed to make service charges for their checkable accounts to avoid incurring a loss (Currie, 1968, p. 204).

In the event that the implementation of the 100 per cent reserve plan created a shortage of loanable funds in a particular area, then the Reconstruction Finance Corporation (RFC) would be empowered to subscribe to the capital of local loaning agencies, to make secured loans, or to establish loaning agencies (Currie, 1968, p. 219).

Currie's views are important because he was soon to become intimately involved with drafting the administration version of the Banking Act of 1935. The key figure in the administration's strategy for banking reform in 1935 was Marriner Eccles, a banker who had impressed Tugwell and Henry Morgenthau, and who had been brought to Washington in early 1934 to work in the Treasury Department. It was Morgenthau who suggested to Roosevelt that Eccles would be the perfect choice as the head of a restructured Federal Reserve System.

Eccles agreed to take the job if certain changes were made to enhance the power of the Federal Reserve Board and, therefore, reduce the power of the regional banks. Roosevelt agreed, and Eccles, along with Lauchlin Currie, prepared a memorandum for Roosevelt with their desirable reforms in the Federal Reserve System (Eccles, 1951, p. 166). The central concern of the memorandum was the Federal Reserve's ability to set and control monetary aggregates, precisely the problems Currie had addressed in his book. Eccles shared the view that the real bills constraint on the Federal Reserve was absolutely the crucial constraint on any attempt to undertake an appropriate monetary policy. The memorandum was drafted by Currie and generally reflected his views on the problems of controlling the money supply. Sandilands notes that one point was added by Eccles that he considered important, but Currie was less interested in. Eccles thought that an extension of bank assets available for rediscount by the Fed was vital. This point boiled down to the substitution of 'sound assets' for the Federal Reserve Act's 'eligible paper'. The significance of this is that it would allow banks to continue making long-term loans, but at the same time provide some incentive to assure the quality of those loans, since such loans could potentially be available for rediscount in the event of a run on the bank (Eccles, 1951, p. 173; Sandilands, 1990, p. 63).

Though Eccles' appointment was announced in late 1934, he was not confirmed until April 1935. Roosevelt, in selecting Eccles, had not conferred with Carter Glass, Chairman of the Senate banking committee. Glass was a powerful senator and a Jacksonian Democrat who feared increased centralization of government. Glass held up the confirmation of Eccles and, in the end, was not present when the Committee voted to confirm him; and Glass was the lone dissenting vote when the matter was voted on by the entire Senate. The sometimes strained and confrontational relationship between Eccles and Glass undoubtedly had an impact on the ability of the administration to get its bill passed. Eccles himself recognized this in his memoirs (Eccles, 1951, pp. 177–81; Schlesinger, 1960, pp. 291–301).

The important amendments to the Federal Reserve Act which were contained in the so-called Eccles bill on banking reform were with regard to the makeup of the Federal Reserve Board (section 4), expansion of assets which could be discounted by the Fed (section 13), legal tender status for Federal Reserve notes (section 6), and power to change reserve requirements (section 19). In amending section 19 of the Federal Reserve Act with regard to reserve requirements, section 209 of Title II of the bill stated:

> Notwithstanding the other provisions of this section, the Federal Reserve Board, in order to prevent injurious credit expansion or contraction, may by regulation change the requirements as to reserves to be maintained against demand or time deposits or both by member banks in any or all Federal Reserve districts and/or any or all of the three classes of cities referred to above.

In line with his Treasury proposal for reform, according to Sandilands, Currie intended that the Board be given unlimited power to alter reserve requirements with the view of eventually raising them to 100 per cent (Sandilands, 1990, p. 66).

The Administration bill was introduced by Senator Duncan Fletcher in the Senate (S. 1715) and Congressman Steagall in the House (H.R. 5357) on 5 February 1935. Title I of the bill made Federal Deposit Insurance permanent, Title II contained amendments to the Federal Reserve Act, and Title III included technical amendments. The debate over the bill centered on Title II, which sought to give greater powers to a revised Federal Reserve Board whose members would be appointed by the President. Senator Carter Glass denounced Eccles' bill as the most dangerous and unwarranted measure of the entire New Deal (Sandilands, 1990, p. 64).

On 4 March 1935, Senator Cutting reintroduced his bill to create a Federal Monetary Authority and require 100 per cent reserve banking (S. 2204). Just a few days before, the *New York Herald Tribune* ran an article entitled: 'Many Withhold Opposition to Present Banking Bill Lest Legislators Put Forward Measure Requiring 100% Reserves for Demand Deposits' (*New York Herald Tribune* 25 February 1935, p. 41). The article stated that many on Wall Street, though opposed to Title II of the bill, were reluctant to voice their opposition. The fear was that a 'worse bill' would be put forward which 'might be a bill embodying the theories of that group advocating 100 per cent reserves for demand deposits'. The article went on to note that the plan had gained wide academic support. Though no one in the Administration had gone on record in support of the plan, the paper noted that 'should there be a resurgence of New Dealism the 100 per cent reserve scheme might possibly get some attention in the high quarters'. Though some might view the proposed bill as radical, according to the *Tribune* article, 'Compared with the 100 per cent reserve plan, it will be seen, the banking act of 1935 is weak tea' (*New York Herald Tribune*, 25 February 1935, p. 41).

A revised version of the Banking Act of 1935 was introduced on 19 April 1935 by Congressman Steagall (H.R. 7617). The version introduced by Steagall included section 209 unchanged from the earlier version. Fletcher, as Chairman of the Senate Banking Committee, was deluged with letters opposing Title II of the proposed Banking Act of 1935 (H. R. 5357 and S. 1715). In a statement read into the *Congressional Record*, Fletcher asserted that the changes in the Federal Reserve System embodied in Title II did not 'involve a radical change in the present powers and functions of the Federal Reserve Board and the Federal Reserve System as it is now constituted' (*Congressional Record*, 22 April 1935, p. 6103). He explicitly stated that this applied unequivocally to section 209 granting the Board the power to change reserve requirements. Fletcher was clearly concerned that the banking system remained subject to wild fluctuations as a result of bankers influence on the creation and destruction of credit. He stated:

> It is common knowledge, however, that there now lies within the hands of bankers the potential makings for one of the most stupendous inflations this or any other Nation has ever experienced. And experience teaches us that banker control of monetary policy will probably give us an equally devastating financial whirlwind when that bubble is pricked.
>
> (*Congressional Record*, 22 April 1935, p. 6104)

In May, Eccles testified that the most effective way to achieve the goals of centralization, without undue political influence or banker influence, would be to have outright ownership of the Federal Reserve banks (Schlesinger, 1960, p. 299). Though not advocated by Currie, it was part of the Chicago plan for banking reform.

A significant blow to the Chicago plan came in May, when Senator Bronson Cutting died in an airplane crash. Cutting's re-election in 1934 turned out to be a very dirty campaign, with those actively opposing him. After Cutting emerged as the apparent victor over Dennis Chavez by slightly over one thousand votes, the election results, with Roosevelt administration approval, were contested. It was during a trip back to New Mexico, to get affidavits in connection with the contested election, that Cutting's plane crashed in Missouri. Schlesinger reports that some of the Progressives blamed Roosevelt for Cutting's death (Schlesinger, 1960, pp. 140–1).

The bill passed easily in the House in early May, where Alan Goldsborough had assumed responsibility for Title II, and then went to the Senate where hearings were held (Burns, 1974, p. 169). In the House, the only significant amendments were Alan Goldsborough's proposals to create a Federal Monetary Authority, along the lines presented by Cutting, and to mandate an explicitly declared policy of the United States to restore the average purchasing power of the dollar to the level of the period 1921–9 (Leuchtenburg, 1963, p. 159; Burns, 1974, p. 130). After this restoration, the purchasing power of the dollar would be maintained substantially stable in relation to a suitable index of basic commodity prices (*Congressional Record*, 8 May 1935, p. 7163). The amendment was defeated by a vote of 128 to 122 (*Congressional Record*, 8 May 1935, p. 7185).

The last attempt to explicitly introduce 100 per cent reserves in the Senate, as part of the overhaul of the Federal Reserve System, came on

25 July when Senator Nye of North Dakota introduced a substitute for Title II of H.R. 7617 (the revised Banking Act of 1935). The amendment embodied most of the Cutting bill (S. 2204) introduced in March. In addition to the 100 per cent reserves and the creation of a central monetary authority, price stabilization was also included, as it had been in the original Cutting bill outlined by Simons. The amendment was defeated on a vote of 10 yes, 59 no, and 27 not voting (*Congressional Record*, 25–26 July 1935, pp. 11842–906).

Glass set out to rewrite H.R. 7617 to remove those elements which he thought increased, unduly, the government's role. As an example, the final version of the Banking Act of 1935 limited the Fed's ability to change reserve requirements by adding the following to section 209:

> but the amount of the reserves required to be maintained by any such member bank as a result of any such change shall not be less than the amount of the reserves required by law to be maintained by such bank on the bank of enactment of the Banking Act of 1935 nor more than twice such amount.
>
> (Section 207 of H.R. 7617)

This effectively prohibited any move to raise reserve requirements to 100 per cent. Glass also had removed a statement which mandated the government to 'promote conditions conducive to business stability' in so far as it was possible with the 'scope of monetary action and credit administration' (Egbert, 1967, p. 152).

Despite Glass's later boast that 'We did not leave enough of the Eccles bill with which to light a cigarette,' the bill provided for a significant shift toward centralization of monetary policy and, thus, achieved what Currie believed to be a necessary reform if monetary policy was to be effective (Leuchtenburg, 1963, p. 160). The administration had achieved its goal of enhancing the Federal Reserve's ability to manage the money supply and, therefore, hopefully, the economy (Schlesinger, 1960, p. 301).

5.5 CONCLUSION

The Chicago plan for radical banking was well known at the highest levels of government during the period 1933–5 and, though the plan called for radical changes, the early New Deal probably offered the best chance for radical reforms to be undertaken. The question is, thus, why did the Chicago plan lose out?

The answer, on one level, should be of no surprise: it lost as a matter of pure political expediency. It is important to note that it did not lose because the principles of the plan were rejected. In fact, the banking legislation passed during the period moved in part toward the Chicago plan reforms. Tugwell thought that radical reform seemed like such a remote possibility, that Roosevelt abandoned any such attempts and opted for 'simple restoration of a system people understood under conditions which would assure them of future safety' (Tugwell, 1957, p. 264).

The Banking Act of 1933 was successful in restoring confidence in the banking system. It did so by institutionalizing Federal Deposit Insurance and by the separation of commercial and investment banking. By 1935, few politicians opposed doing away with deposit insurance. The economy did not recover fully in 1934, and the administration was convinced that it was due to a lack of centralized control over monetary policy. Given the determined resistance of Carter Glass, the administration got as much as it could in the Banking Act of 1935 in the way of enhanced Federal Reserve Board control. The Chicago plan played a role here by being viewed as an extreme position and, therefore, bolstered the administration bill.

The key player for the administration appears to be Lauchlin Currie, who, though an advocate of 100 per cent reserves, sought to achieve measures that would be politically acceptable. In doing so, he compromised on the 100 per cent reserve goal and, in the end, his compromise prohibited any possibility that such reform could be achieved in the future.

There is evidence that Currie believed that Hemphill and Fisher were politically naive. In his unpublished memoirs, Currie, reflecting on the battle over the Banking Act of 1935, says: 'An adviser in Washington is of limited usefulness unless he acquires some sense of what is feasible and how projects and policies should be presented to have the best chance of being adopted' (Sandilands, 1990, p. 65). In a letter to Viner written in early 1935, Currie stated:

> You will be tickled by Hemphill's childlike naivete in suggesting that instead of his bill being introduced and then sent to the Board for comments it would save time if we drafted the bill together at the Board! I pointed out that such a procedure would make his bill in effect an administration measure, and he said very seriously he would not mind that!
>
> (Currie to Viner, 18 January 1935, Viner Papers)

The fact that the Chicago plan was supported by the early New Deal planners and then by the Progressives, though it may have helped the administration, at the same time, reduced the possibility that the legislation would have been passed. However, there were attempts, especially after Cutting's death, to create both a Federal Monetary Authority, reflation, and price-level stabilization. This indicates that support for the ideas embodied in the plan went beyond the radical and Progressive members of Congress.

Roosevelt came into office with the intent of restoring the safety of the banks and increasing government control over monetary policy. The legislation passed during the period 1933–5 gave Roosevelt most of what he wanted: safety of the payments system, separation of commercial and investment banking, and enhanced control over monetary policy by a reconstituted Federal Reserve. Safety of the bank deposits came at the price of a system of contingent liabilities with inherent problems, which all came to a head decades later. The separation of commercial and investment banking eliminated the problem of banks using depositors funds to speculate in the stock market, but it did not prevent banks from making risky loans.

Still, the legislation passed in the early New Deal must be viewed as a success as judged by the fact that little change was made in the system for nearly 50 years. Though passage of the Chicago plan might have advocated the large-scale bailouts of financial institutions we are seeing today, there is no guarantee that it would have been equally successful.

The Chicago plan, without an appropriate transition period, could have worsened the credit crunch. The crucial action would have been the supplanting of fractional reserve bank credit with the credit of new investment trusts and, if necessary, credit supplied by the RFC. One possible evolution could have been the complete socialization of investment as Bronson Cutting and others advocated.

Control of M-1 could have accelerated the expansion of money substitutes and deposit banking could have been reborn, perhaps in a relatively short period of time. However, one response to this is that technology seems to have driven the developments of near monies in recent years and it is unlikely that 100 per cent reserve banking could have affected the development of computers which, as we have seen in recent years, enable the creation of financial assets which would have been technologically impossible in the past.

The problems we face today are in large part a direct result of the programs that were implemented during the early New Deal. The first, and most obvious, is federal deposit insurance. The amount of money necessary to pay off all depositors is unknown. We have done nothing to fundamentally change the situation. Even modest reforms to limit the amount of federal deposit insurance have been difficult to implement.

The 100 per cent reserve idea did not disappear after the passage of the Banking Act of 1935, in fact, Irving Fisher spent the remainder of his life lobbying Congress and the public on the need for 100 per cent reserves (Allen, 1991). It is also not surprising that, in recent years, we have seen the emergence of 'narrow banking' or 'core banking' proposals which are in the tradition of the 100 per cent reserve plan. If we are ever again faced with economic, and particularly financial, problems on the level of the Great Depression, the clamor for the separation of the depository and lending functions of banks may reappear.

It is also clear that the Federal Reserve can do little to cajole banks into lending when they do not wish to do so. What we are seeing is banks buying more government debt, which is available today on a scale far beyond the 1930s. The Federal Reserve can effectively restrain activity during a boom, but during a business downturn can do little to stimulate the economy beyond cutting interest rates to historically low levels. This is precisely the situation we face today.

References

Allen, William R. (1991) 'Irving Fisher and the 100% Reserve Proposal', unpublished paper, UCLA.

Allen, William R. (1977) 'Irving Fisher, F.D.R., and the Great Depression', *History of Political Economy*, **9**, 560–87.

Bryan, Lowell L. (1988) *Breaking Up the Bank* (Homewood, IL: Business One Irwin).

Bryan, Lowell L. (1991) *Bankrupt: Restoring the Health and Profitability of Our Banking System* (New York: Harper Collins).

Burns, Helen (1974) *The American Banking Community and New Deal Banking Reforms: 1933–1935* (Westport, Connecticut: Greenwood Press).

Business week, 2 June 1934, 27.

Chicago. The University of Chicago Law Library. The Henry Simons Papers.

Currie, Lauchlin (1934) *A Proposed Revision of the Monetary System of the United States* (submitted to the Secretary of the Treasury, Henry Morgenthau, September. Reprinted in Currie, 1968).

Currie, Lauchlin (1968) *The Supply and Control of Money in the United States* (New York: Russell and Russell, originally published by Harvard University Press, 1934).

Cutting, Bronson (1934) 'Is Private Banking Doomed?', *Liberty* (May).

Egbert, Arch O. (1967) 'Marriner S. Eccles and the Banking Act of 1935', Ph.D. Dissertation, Brigham Young University.

Eccles, Marriner (1951) *Beckoning Frontiers* (New York: Knopf).

Hyde Park. The Franklin D. Roosevelt Library. President's Official Files (Box 230).

Hyde Park. The Franklin D. Roosevelt Library. The Papers of Gardiner C. Means. Jacob Viner to Henry Morgenthau, Interdepartmental Communication, Department of the Treasury, 10 May 1934. FDR Library. Morgenthau Papers, Box 301, File Jacob Viner 1933–34.

Kennedy, Susan (1973) *The Banking Crisis of 1933* (Louisville: University of Kentucky Press).

Knight, Frank (1933) 'Memorandum on Banking Reform' (March).

Krooss, Herman E. (1969) *Documentary History of Banking and Currency in the United States* (New York: McGraw-Hill).

Leuchtenburg, William E. (1963) *Franklin D. Roosevelt and the New Deal* (New York: Harper and Row).

Means, Gardiner C. 'Comment on the Chicago Plan for Banking and Currency Reform', n.d., Box 1 The Papers of Gardiner C. Means, Franklin Roosevelt Library, Hyde Park.

Moley, Raymond C. (1939) *After Seven Years* (New York: Harper and Brothers).

New York Herald Tribune, 25 February 1935, 41.

New York Times, 20 May 1934, **32**(1).

Princeton, N. J. Mudd Library, Princeton University. The Jacob Viner Papers.

Sandilands, Roger J. (1990) *The Life and Political Economy of Lauchlin Currie* (Durham: Duke University Press).

Schlesinger, Arthur M. (1957) *The Crisis of the Old Order* (New York: Houghton Mifflin).

Schlesinger, Arthur M. (1958) *The Coming of the New Deal* (New York: Houghton Mifflin).

Schlesinger, Arthur M. (1960) *The Politics of Upheaval* (New York: Houghton Mifflin).

Simons, Henry (1933) 'Banking and Currency Reform'. Manuscript, reprinted in Warren Samuels (ed.) (1990), *Research in the History of Economic Thought and Methodology* (Greenwich, CT: JAI Press).

Steindl, Frank G. (1991) 'The Monetary Economics of Lauchlin Currie', *Journal of Monetary Economics*, **27**, 445–61.

Tobin, James (1985) 'Financial Innovation and Deregulation in Perspective', *Bank of Japan Monetary and Economic Studies*, **3**(2), 19–29.

Tobin, James (1987) 'The Case for Preserving Regulatory Distinctions', in *Restructuring the Financial System*, Federal Reserve Bank of Kansas City, 167–83.

Tugwell, Rexford G. (1957) *The Democratic Roosevelt* (New York: Doubleday and Son).

US Congress, Senate, *A Bill to Regulate the Value of Money*, S.3744, 73rd Congress, 2nd session, 6 June 1934.

US Congress, House, *A Bill to Provide for the Sound, Effective, and Uninterrupted Operation of the Banking System*, H.R. 5357, 74th Congress, 1st session, 5 February 1935.

US Congress, Senate, *A Bill to Provide for the Sound, Effective, and Uninterrupted Operation of the Banking System*, S. 1715, 74th Congress, 1st session, 5 February 1935.

US Congress, House, *A Bill to Provide for the Sound, Effective, and Uninterrupted Operation of the Banking System* (Banking Act of 1935) H.R. 7617, 74th Congress, 1st session, 5 February 1935.

US Congress, Senate, *A Bill to Regulate the Value of Money*, S. 2204, 74th Congress, 1st session, 4 March 1935.

US Congress, Senate, statement by F. A. Vanderlip on S. 1715, 74th Congress, 1st session, 4 March 1935, *Congressional Record*.

US Congress, House, radio address by Congressman Steagall regarding H.R. 5357, 74th Congress, 1st session, 24 January 1935, *Congressional Record*.

US Congress, Senate, text of Senate bill 1715, 74th Congress, 1st session, 6 February 1935, *Congressional Record*.

US Congress, Senate, text of article by Senator Cutting, 'Is Private Banking Doomed?', 73rd Congress, 1st session, 4 May 1935, *Congressional Record*.

US Congress, Senate, statement by Senator Fletcher on S. 1715, 74th Congress, 1st session, 22 April 1935, *Congressional Record*.

US Congress, Senate text of article,'Fletcher Attacks Bankers', *New York Times*, 21 April 1935. 74th Congress, 1st session, 22 April 1935, *Congressional Record*.

US Congress, House, Amendment by Senator Goldsborough to H.R. 7617 (Banking Act of 1935), 74th Congress, 1st session, 8 May 1935, *Congressional Record*.

US Congress, Senate, statement by Senator Glass on H.R. 7617 (Banking Act of 1935), 74th Congress, 1st session, 25 July 1935, *Congressional Record*.

US Congress, Senate, Amendment by Senator Nye to H.R. 7617 (Banking Act of 1935), 74th Congress, 1st session, 25 July 1935, *Congressional Record*.

Washington, DC, National Archives, US Treasury, press release, 27 June 1934.

Washington, DC, Library of Congress Manuscript Collection, Bronson Cutting Papers.

Part II

Issues of Financial Reform

6 The Political Economy of Financial Reform in the US and the UK[1]

Gillian Garcia

Analysts and participants remark on the seeming inability of the political system in the US to enact legislation to modernize the financial system. The conventional wisdom is that there must be a crisis in the US to act as a catalyst for action. Only in a crisis can a consensus be reached: and consensus is a *sine qua non* for US legislative action. Laws enacted during a crisis run the risk of being reactionary and not designed to anticipate the economy's future financial needs.

As this chapter will show, it is much easier to pass legislation in the UK. Parliament in Britain has enacted a substantial reconfiguration of the financial system during the past decade. (Britain is also a member of the European Community, whose Parliament has also enacted sweeping financial modernization. Nevertheless, this chapter does not examine the political process in the EC.)

Ease in passing legislation does not, of course, guarantee better legislation or a superior financial system. Evaluation of relative merits and demerits of legislation enacted in recent years in the two countries and Europe must remain a subject for future investigation.

6.1 THE MEANING OF FINANCIAL REFORM

For the Concise Oxford Dictionary, 'to reform' is to 'make (person, institution, procedure, conduct, oneself) ... become, better by removal or abandonment of imperfections, faults, or errors'.

Financial reform, in this sense, can happen in many ways; by changes made by firms in the industry (in managerial practices, types of products offered, or operating procedures); by the agencies that supervise them (via new capital standards and other regulations); by legislation; or the courts' interpretations of the laws. My current experience puts me in a better position to discuss reform by legislation than by other routes and legislation as seen from a Senate perspective.

So, the agenda for this chapter is to: (a) describe, very briefly in section 6.2, the political system in Great Britain for comparative purposes; (b) enumerate and give brief examples of the different routes to financial reform in the US in section 6.3; (c) speculate in section 6.4 about the effects of different party configurations in the US on financial reform through legislation; (d) examine, in section 6.5, the numerous stages that legislation follows in the US, with particular reference to the Financial Institutions Reform, Recovery and Enforcement Act (FIRREA) of 1989, and the FDIC Improvement Act (FDICIA) of 1991; and (e) conclude with some remaining questions in section 6.6.

6.2 THE PARLIAMENTARY SYSTEM IN GREAT BRITAIN

In Britain, the party that controls Parliament (that is, controls the House of Commons) forms the Administration. There is no split between the legislative and executive branches. It is easier, therefore, to enact legislation in Great Britain. That is not an accident; the US deliberately built in checks and balances into its constitution to avoid ill-considered legislation. It may or may not be harder to implement the legislation that is passed in Britain than in the US.

6.2.1 The Loyal Opposition

New laws can be passed quickly in Britain. The opposition party operates a shadow government, with shadow cabinet ministers and policies 'ready to go' as soon as it is returned to power. So, there is none of the delay between Administrations that is so evident in the US system, at the time when this paper was written. An election in the UK lasts for only three weeks and ends with polling on a Thursday. The vote is counted; if the opposing party wins a clear simple majority in the House of Commons, the Queen summons the leader of the opposition to form a government. The prime minister that loses moves out (of 10 Downing Street) that Saturday. The new government is up and running on Monday.[2]

6.2.2 Party Whips

The party in power is able to get its agenda passed because of the system of Whips. Whips are party officials, but the term is also applied to the written instructions that the officials send to party members informing them how they are expected to vote in an imminent division.[3] Instructionwhips are underlined (to a maximum of three times) depending on the urgency of compliance. Members can vote according to their conscience on unlined or one-lined whips, but to vote against a three-line whip endangers continued membership in the party.

There are no primaries in Britain. The party chooses who will run under its banner in each election and who belongs to the party in the interim. Without endorsement by a party, the candidate has only the funds s/he can raise to spend in a campaign and no party resources to rely on while in Parliament. (The misadventures of a new woman Labour MP in the Public Broadcasting System's (PBS's) television program 'No Job For A Lady', illustrate this problem.)

What any candidate can spend in an election today is heavily circumscribed at no more than (roughly) $10 000 per election.[4] A member disowned by his party has to run as an independent, unless he is welcomed into the opposing party (typically, an unlikely event) and is able to run under its banner.

6.2.3 British Courts

The courts prove no obstacle to legislation in Britain. The House of Lords is the highest court in the land. There is no written constitution and no concept of an 'unconstitutional' law. Rather, the doctrine of 'the supremacy of Parliament' means that what Parliament passes (and the Queen signs) is law, period.[5] So, the courts do not challenge legislation.[6] In the PBS's television program, 'Rumpole of the Bailey', Rumpole and his barrister partners never draw swords against the legislature.

6.2.4 The House of Lords

Other potential obstacles to the majority party's getting its way with regard to legislation have been whittled down over the centuries. The membership of the House of Lords has been diluted by the appointment of 'life peers'. Its authority has been reduced in successive onslaughts over the centuries. Now, at best, it can delay legislation for one year.[7]

6.2.5 The Crown

Similarly, the powers of the sovereign have been diminished over the centuries. The monarch has the right to be informed and to ask questions. The extent of the crown's influence when the government has to make policy choices depends on the holder as an individual. The Queen has earned her right to be heard as a result of 40 years of daily discipline of reading 'dispatches' (that is, memos in American) and always being informed. It is now ironic that her lifetime of hard work is being dissipated by the misdeeds of the younger generation.

So, there are considerably fewer obstacles to passing legislation in Britain as compared to the US under divided government. There are also fewer impediments than in the US under unified, supposedly gridlock-free, government. Consequently, there has been more legislation in the past 15 years to structurally reform the British financial system than the American.

There have been at least six pieces of major financial legislation in Britain since 1979: the Banking Acts of 1979 and 1987, the Building Societies Act of 1986, the Financial Services Act of 1986 ('Big Bang'), the Insurance Industry Act of 1986, and the Friendly Societies Act of 1990. These laws have changed the regulatory system, granted additional powers, and broken down some of the industry-protective oligopolistic walls that surrounded different segments of the financial system in Britain. Fundamental financial reform is also taking place as a result of legislation in the European Parliament to open national borders to competition from financial firms from other EC countries.

6.2.6 Implementing Legislation

The civil service in London is staffed entirely by career employees. This stoutly defended tradition arose from public outcry over the abuses of the patronage system before the Reform Act of 1832. With a change in administration, only the minister-in-charge of an agency is replaced. Moreover, the Governor of the Bank of England, which is the bank regulatory agency, stays in place when governments change. Everyone, except ministers, keep their jobs, and so are ready to implement the laws passed by the new administration immediately.

In Britain, however, the entrenched civil service can be an impediment to successful legislation. Consciously, or not, it may obstruct implementation. The significance and full irony of the PBS program 'Yes, Prime Minister', is lost on American viewers. If a US cabinet servant played just one such game with the President, he would soon be dismissed.

6.3 DIFFERENT ROUTES TO FINANCIAL REFORM IN THE US

The financial services industry, the regulatory agencies and the federal government have each had an important impact on the process of financial reform in the US. Each will be examined in this paper. State governments and the courts have also been influential. The States of California and Texas, for example, allowed thrifts that they had chartered to use a more extensive set of powers than were permitted to federal thrifts. Glendale Federal Savings Bank is successfully suing the government for compensation following the limitations placed on the use of goodwill on thrift balance sheets in FIRREA. Nevertheless, I will not analyze developments in the states and the courts further in this essay.

6.3.1 Reform by Legislation

Since 1968, there have been eight pieces of US legislation affecting banks and thrifts that were enacted and have had far-reaching consequences: (1) the 1970 Amendments to the Bank Holding Company Act of 1956; (2) the 1978 Act allowing the General Accounting Office (GAO) to oversee the financial regulatory agencies; (3) the Foreign Banking Act of 1978, which established the criterion of 'national treatment'; (4) the Community Reinvestment Act (CRA) also of 1978; (5) the Depository Institutions Deregulation and Monetary Control Act (DIDMCA) of 1980; (6) the Garn–St Germain Act of 1982; (5) the Competitive Equality Banking Act (CEBA) of 1987; (7) the Financial Institutions Reform, Recovery, and Enforcement Act (FIRREA) of 1989; and (8) the FDIC Improvement Act (FDICIA) of 1991. Many of these laws extended regulation and supervision over banks and thrifts, but the 1980 and 1982 Acts granted some additional powers.

Numerous other attempts at financial reform have failed during this period. For example, Senate, but not the House, voted to repeal the Glass–Steagall Act in 1988. In addition, there have been numerous commissions on, and proposals for, legislative reform that have not reached fruition (Cargill and Garcia, 1982 and 1985). I will examine the legislative route to reform in detail in section 6.5 below.

6.3.2 Reform by Regulatory Change

Individual regulatory agencies have, from time to time, acted unilaterally when adopting a regulatory change. Since 1988, for example, the Federal Reserve has approved the applications of some large bank holding companies to exercise 'section 20' powers to engage to a limited extent in previously banned securities activities.[8]

6.3.2.1 *Joint Action*

More often, the regulators band together when they want to effect an important change. The Inter-Agency Coordinating Committee (ICC) that ran until 1980 and its successor, the Depository Institutions Deregulation Committee (DIDC), consisting of representatives from the Federal Reserve, the Office of the Comptroller of the Currency (OCC), the FDIC, and the Federal Home Loan Bank Board, for example, tried to alleviate the disintermediation resulting from caps on the interest rates that banks and thrifts could pay on their deposits. The two Committees allowed some limited exceptions to Regulation Q, before they were able to persuade the Carter and Reagan Administrations and Congress to phase it out (except on business demand deposits).

6.3.2.2 *International Cooperation*

Another example of reform-via-regulation is the Basle capital standards. The financial regulators of the Group of Seven Countries were concerned in the mid-1980s that bank capital ratios were too low, took no account of off-balance sheet activities or different risk-exposures among classes of assets, and were difficult for any country to raise unilaterally because to do so would prejudice the international competitiveness of its banks. So, they made an international agreement to accomplish what they could not do unilaterally.

These capital standards, introduced since 1990, are now at risk, however. They are being criticized for causing or exacerbating the credit crunch. Congress could override them in legislation if enough Congressmen and Senators decided to do so. That event would be the more likely if the Clinton Administration were to support the override. A major concern to Committee staff, currently, when this chapter was written, was whether forbearance would return in the name of regional economic recovery.

6.3.2.3 *Political Issues*

Two political questions arise, whether: (1) is it easier for the regulators to initiate reform-via-regulation in some countries' political systems than in others and (2) is it easier to make regulatory changes in the US under some party configurations than others. I would expect regulatory changes to be easier to make in Parliamentary systems than in the US and, within the US, under same-across-the-board configurations than others.

I would, for example, expect that the regulators in the US can make changes independently of legislation only when the Administration approves them and Congress does not strongly oppose them. Regulation Q removal and the Basle capital standards illustrate the process of change and the constraints operating on reform by regulation.

6.3.2.4 Political Appointees in the US

The fact that the Administration nominates and the Senate confirms the top political appointees both enables and restrains the Administration's ability to implement its policies. In general, political appointees will do the Administration's bidding, even when they are appointed to 'independent agencies'. But appointees' ability to carry out the Administration's agenda is limited. For example, the Senate Banking Committee refused to approve the nomination of Robert Clarke for a second term as Comptroller of the Currency. The Committee held Clarke partly responsible for the large number of national banks, particularly national banks in Texas, that failed in the mid and late-1980s. The Comptroller was, however, implementing the Administration's policies of deregulation and economized supervision.

The system of political appointments appears to be something of an anomaly in the US, particularly as political appointees sometimes 'burrow' into the career civil service when their leader loses the presidency.

In addition, even when senior agency positions are not schedule C appointments, office-holders sometimes act as though they were. For example, experience has shown that a request to either of two particular congressional liaisons at the 'independent' regulatory agencies resulted in a fruitless run-around, while requests to others produced prompt results. This, I believe, is not a question of the competence of the office-holder, but rather his and her political allegiance. The question arises whether there be greater cooperation from all congressional liaisons with requests from Democrats now that the Administration is Democratic.

6.3.2.5 Mistaken Regulatory Changes

In the early 1980s, as the condition of the thrift industry deteriorated, the Bank Board reduced the ratio of required capital to assets from 5 per cent to 3 per cent and then emasculated the 3 per cent by allowing accounting gimmicks (goodwill, deferred losses and income capital certificates) to count as capital. The Administration applauded these fig leaves and so did Congress. Members of Congress justified this forbearance by comparing insolvent thrifts to wounded animals deserving time to recover.

The Bank Board, I believe, also sanctioned fast growth as a remedy for insolvency, although I have not found a citation to this effect in the speeches of Chairmen Pratt and Gray. The Banking Committee called former Bank Board Chairmen, Richard Pratt, Ed Gray, and Jay Janis, to account for the condition of the thrift industry in hearings in the summer of 1988.

Fast growth was supposed to produce high profits from new assets in large enough quantities to arithmetically bury losses on old fixed-rate mortgages. The dangers of this practice were not initially self-evident to the regulators or to Congress. In the summer of 1988, I wrote a memo for Senator Proxmire, then Chairman of the Senate Banking Committee, on the dangers of 'Fast Growth at Insolvent Institutions'. Convinced, the Senator made a statement on the floor of the Senate (Proxmire, 1988) in the summer of 1988 that began a new 'received doctrine' in Congress on the dangers of forbearance.

6.3.2.6 Bucking the Administration

Another way to examine political control over the heads of supposedly independent agencies is to ask when such political appointees have 'bucked' the Administration's policies. Ed Gray claimed in his 1988 testimony before the Senate Banking Committee that he tried to do so with regard to the number of thrift examiners in the mid 1980s. (OMB reduced them.) But Gray was forced out of office, he says, because he deviated, or wanted to deviate, from the Administration's policies of deregulation and reduced federal supervision, which largely reflected industry wishes.

There may be examples, where the career staff of a regulatory agency have strongly opposed a change proposed by the Administration. But, I am personally aware of only one instance. A career employee at the Bank Board complained to the Committee through me and one other congressional staffer about agency practices. He was fired soon afterwards. Neither the Administration nor the dissenters find it in their interests to air their disputes publicly. Maybe some complain to the press just before or after they move to jobs in the private sector. Dissent has, no doubt, occurred but is likely to have been kept confidential.

6.3.3 Industry-Induced Changes

The credit card, automatic teller machine (ATM), the wire transfer system for large payments (especially the Clearinghouse Interbank Payments System, or 'CHIPS'), options and derivative products markets, are but some examples of sweeping industry-induced advances that spring to mind. The press and the public are aware of most of these changes and their consequences as they happen. But that is not true of all changes. In general, Congress does not intervene in these developments unless it perceives dangers to the safety and soundness of the financial system or the abuse of market power.

The industry is more likely to be able to carry out changes it desires and offer the new products it wants when the Administration approves them. Even so, in general, banks still cannot underwrite securities even though the Reagan and Bush Administrations and the Senate would have permitted them, because the House balked. In the past, to my perception, Republicans have been more sympathetic to industry proposals than the Democrats, many of whom harbor populist suspicions of the banking industry's intentions. Populist prejudice does not extend to thrifts or credit unions, however. The Clinton Administration's predispositions are still unknown.

6.3.3.1 Industry Consolidation

One industry-generated change that is going on behind the scenes is consolidation. Consolidation occurred much earlier in Great Britain than in the United States, where it is an ongoing process. I suspect that Britain acquired its cartelized banking and building society industries without ever making a conscious decision to do so (Garcia, 1980).[9] It happened years ago when stronger institutions took over weak and failing ones with government blessing. With no system of insurance for depositors until 1979, the government was only too eager to avoid the scandal of consumers and small businesses losing some of their funds if their bank failed. The government was willing to accept the resulting enhanced market power of the acquirer as an easy price to pay for the 'cost-less' resolution of a failed bank.

The public did not complain and neither did their Members of Parliament. MPs are not delegates from their constituency in the British system; rather, their job is always to consider the good of the country as a whole and not just their district.

The US system is very different, so I hope that there will be an out-in-the-open discussion of the benefits of consolidation and the costs of market power.[10] But this is not now happening. To date, the banks appear to have won a public relations campaign that there are too many banks in the US and that the number must be reduced. Politicians are acquiescing. Few, in and out of Congress, appear to know where we now stand in the consolidation process. The Federal Reserve's analysis of competition focuses on local markets, so the introduction of an out-of-state bank into a state, such as Nevada, appears to be a benefit. Yet, last September, three major out-of-state bank holding companies already owned 84 per cent of bank assets in that State. They have market power!

Will US citizens wake up one morning and realize that a few large, initially regionally dominant, bank holding companies own the vast majority of the nation's banking assets? This can happen, whether or not interstate branching is allowed. In a sense, the debate over branching is distracting attention away from the regional consolidation via holding companies that is already far advanced.[11]

6.4 LEGISLATION AND PARTY CONFIGURATIONS IN THE US

I hypothesize that legislation is easier to pass when one party controls both the Administration and Congress, but this has happened for only four of the past 24 years. I speculate that the ease of enactment during years of divided government depends on the particular configurations of the two parties in the Administration, House and Senate.

With two parties to arrange in three locations (the House, the Senate and the Administration), there are eight possible configurations. Not all of them have been operative in the past century. (Tables 6.1 and 6.2 show the party configurations since 1867, when the current two-party system became established.) For the 100 years following the Civil War, one party often controlled both Houses and the Administration. That situation has been rare in the recent quarter-century, however. My thesis is that it is easier to pass legislation under one-party configurations than others. That is taken for granted in popular analysis, so I will attempt to go further and say what is different in some of these cases.

During the past 25 years that I have been in the US, there have been mostly Republican Administrations (1969–77 and 1981–93). The Democrats held the White House from 1977 to 1981 and now do so again. During the period since 1968, the House has been consistently Democratic. The Democrats have also controlled the Senate, except for the period 1981–87.

6.4.1 Legislative Reforms

Some financial legislation was passed under the Democratic Administration, some under the Reagan Administration with a Republican

Table 6.1 Political configurations 1867–1993

Administration	*Senate*	*House*	*Recent Years*
R	R	R	1867–73 1881–83 1889–91 1921–33 1953–55
R	R	D	1875–79 1891–93 1911–13 1981–87
R	D	R	
R	D	D	1879–81 1883–85 1955–61 1969–77 1987–93
D	R	R	1895–97 1919–21 1947–49
D	R	D	1885–89
D	D	R	
D	D	D	1893–95 1913–19 1933–47 1949–53 1961–69 1977–81 1993–94

R – Republican ; D – Democrat
Sources: Clerk of the House of Representatives and Secretary of the Senate, US Department of Commerce, *Historical Statistics*, (1971, Y204–210), and US Department of Commerce *Statistical Abstract*, (1987, 247)

Senate and the remainder under a Republican Administration and Democratic Congress. In all situations, but, particularly under divided government, two factors are required for passage: (1) an agreement that a serious problem exists and must be dealt with immediately by legislation, and (2) a consensus on what needs to be done about the core problem. With this framework in place, members of Congress will try to attach

Table 6.2 Political configurations 40th Congress–103rd Congress

Congress	*Years*	*Administration* *R–Republican D–Democrat*	*Senate*	*House*
40*	1867–9	R	R	R
41*	1869–71	R	R	R
42*	1871–3	R	R	R
43*	1873–5	R	R	R
44	1875–7	R	R	D
45	1877–9	R	R	D
46	1879–81	R	D	D
47*	1881–3	R	R	R
48	1883–5	R	R	D
49	1885–7	D	R	D
50	1887–9	D	R	D
51*	1889–91	R	R	R
52	1891–3	R	R	D
53*	1893–5	D	D	D
54	1895–7	D	R	R
55*	1897–9	R	R	R
56*	1899–901	R	R	R
57*	1901–3	R	R	R
58*	1903–5	R	R	R
59*	1905–7	R	R	R
60*	1907–9	R	R	R
61*	1909–11	R	R	R
62	1911–3	R	R	D
63*	1913–5	D	D	D
64*	1915–7	D	D	D
65*	1917–9	D	D	D
66	1919–21	D	R	R
67*	1921–3	R	R	R
68*	1923–5	R	R	R
69*	1925–7	R	R	R
70*	1927–9	R	R	R
71*	1929–31	R	R	R
72*	1931–3	R	R	R
73*	1933–5	D	D	D
74*	1935–7	D	D	D
75*	1937–9	D	D	D
76*	1939–41	D	D	D
77*	1941–3	D	D	D
78*	1943–5	D	D	D
79*	1945–7	D	D	D
80	1947–9	D	R	R
81*	1949–51	D	D	D
82*	1951–3	D	D	D

Table 6.2 Continued

Congress	*Years*	*Administration R–Republican D–Democrat*	*Senate*	*House*
83*	1953–5	R	R	R
84	1955–7	R	D	D
85	1957–9	R	D	D
86	1959–61	R	D	D
87*	1961–3	D	D	D
88*	1963–5	D	D	D
89*	1965–7	D	D	D
90*	1967–9	D	D	D
91	1969–71	R	D	D
92	1971–3	R	D	D
93	1973–5	R	D	D
94	1975–7	R	D	D
95*	1977–9	D	D	D
96*	1979–81	D	D	D
97	1981–3	R	R	D
98	1983–5	R	R	D
99	1985–7	R	R	D
100	1987–9	R	D	D
101	1989–91	R	D	D
102	1991–3	R	D	D
103*	1993–5	D	D	D

Note: * Represents a Congress where one party controlled the House, Senate and Administration.
Sources: Clerk of the House of Representatives, Secretary of the Senate, US Department of Commerce, *Historical Statistics* (1971, Y204–210), and US Department of Commerce *Statistical Abstract*, (1987, 247).

other pieces of less urgent, not-agreed, and possibly extraneous, legislation to the structure, like ornaments on a Christmas tree.[12]

6.4.1.1 Democratic Legislation

During the late 1970s, the House, Senate and Administration were all Democratic. Three pieces of industry-restrictive legislation were passed – the Foreign Bank Act, the Community Reinvestment Act (CRA), and the GAO oversight legislation, all in 1978. The laws, respectively, extended regulation to foreign banks, began federal action against discriminatory lending practices by banks and thrifts, and gave GAO an oversight role over the federal financial regulators. Although I was not in Washington to observe it, the last two passed surely over industry opposition. The GAO legislation, no doubt, encountered regulatory and industry opposition. I observed the lingering industry resentment toward GAO when I worked at the agency between 1984 and 1988. Moreover, responses to GAO oversight from the regulatory agencies varied between angry obstruction and polite obfuscation.[13]

The most important piece of legislation passed by the Democrats was DIDMCA. It came about as a result of the regulators' assessments that changes needed to be made and made urgently. The problem requiring urgent attention was the set of ceilings on the interest rates that banks and thrifts could pay to their depositors. As market interest rates rose with inflation, the fixed ceilings lead to disintermediation, which curtailed lending by banks and thrifts and, on occasions, plunged the economy into recession.

Industry interests were divided on the subject of what should be done to end their problem with disintermediation. Both banks and thrifts hoped that their competitors' activities would be circumscribed so that they could continue to obtain deposits at bargain rates. But, the 'Grey Panthers' demanded market rates for their retirement savings. The industry obtained a delay – a phased-in removal over six years. Thrifts also hoped that they would retain 'the thrift differential' – a cap that was 25 basis points higher than the banks'. They retained that for a period, too.

In other respects, the legislation was responsive both to regulatory concerns and industry wishes. For example, the extension of reserve requirements to nonmember banks and thrifts came because the Federal Reserve claimed that it would help to meet its money growth targets more closely. The Act's requirement that Federal Reserve banks charge market rates for the services previously provided free to member banks, came in response to pressure from banks offering such correspondent services to nonmember banks in competition with the Fed.

The source of the extension of the insurance coverage of deposits from \$40 000 to \$100 000 is currently a source of finger-pointing at the Congressional Commission that is studying the origins of the S&L crisis.

In many respects, I find the DIDMCA surprisingly pro-industry given that it was passed by an all Democratic government. On further reflection, I believe the populist strand of the Democratic party was/is anti-bank, but pro-thrift. DIDMCA was mainly pro-thrift.

DIDMCA did meet two criteria for the passage of major legislation – urgency and consensus with respect to the core problem of disintermediation. There was also concern over the health of the thrift industry but this was not regarded as a crisis in early 1980.[14] Many other of the provisions, including raising the deposit insurance limit to $100 000, were 'Christmas tree' ornaments.

6.4.1.2 *Republican Administration and Senate*

The Garn–St Germain Act (GSGA) was passed in Fall 1982 under a Republican Administration, a Republican Senate and a Democratic House. I believe it to be the most industry-sympathetic of the legislation passed in the past 15 years. This raises the question of why the House permitted such a bill to pass. But, like DIDMCA, the GSGA was more pro-thrift than pro-bank. Press analysis of the current S&L Commission hearings attributes the legislation to pro-thrift industry bias on the part of House Banking Committee Chairman, Fernand St Germain.

6.4.1.3 *Republican Administration, Democratic Congress*

Despite gridlock elsewhere, the Bush Administration passed two major pieces of banking legislation – FIRREA and FDICIA. In FIRREA, the two central factors were in place – an agreement that something must be done urgently about the S&L debacle and a consensus that the FSLIC's guarantee to depositors should be made good. But everyone agreed that 'never again' should such a problem be allowed to occur.

Unfortunately, however, that pledge was not kept: the Bank Insurance Fund (BIF) became insolvent in 1991 and needed legislation to permit it to extend its authority to borrow from the Treasury. The industry is to repay any borrowings within 15 years.[15] The need to refinance BIF was the driving force for FDICIA. There was a consensus that prompt corrective action provided a basis for reforming the system of deposit insurance. It appeared, for example, in the Administration's, the House's and the Senate's initial bills.

6.5 THE LEGISLATIVE PROCESS IN THE US

For someone brought up in the British political system, democracy, as practiced in the US, is a constant source of wonder. Absolutely everyone in the US who is interested can get involved in the legislative process, if s/he takes the trouble. Sometimes foreigners' interests are also considered. In Britain, the majority party can and does, from time to time, ride roughshod over opposition.[16] An Administration in the US, on the other hand, runs a risk when it tries to act unilaterally. A filibuster in April 1993, for example, prevented the Clinton Administration from unilaterally pushing its $16 billion economic stimulus package through the Senate.

There has been, perhaps, only one exception to universal inclusion in financial legislation in the US over the past decade. That omission was unintentional. The taxpayer was excluded from much of the early financial legislation, because he did not realize he was involved. Now, the National Taxpayers' Union speaks for him or, most recently he speaks for himself by picking up the telephone and calling a talk show, his Congressman and Senator.

6.5.1 Legislative Stages

Legislation in the US goes through a large number of stages and can fail at any step. In fact, the pitfalls are so great that it is surprising that legislation gets enacted. The energy expended in the process of building consensus and overcoming the checks and balances is remarkable.

6.5.1.1 The Sources of Legislative Proposals

The sources of proposed legislation are numerous. Initial drafts may be written by staff, the regulators, lobbyists on behalf of a client, GAO, or Legislative Counsel (each House has its own).[17] Legislation is introduced by a member into one or other of the Houses. Often legislation is introduced simultaneously by cooperating Senators and Congressmen as two separate bills into both Houses. Each House then refers its bill to its relevant committee or committees.

6.5.1.2 Precursors to Action

Sometimes attention is drawn to a problem needing redress by complaints from constituents and in the press. The Senate Banking Committee's annual oversight hearings have recently focused on some problems in banks' real estate lending that need to be resolved by legislation.[18] A '60 Minutes' program on abusive use of second mortgages by out-of-state banking organizations in Georgia started the Senate Banking Committee's investigation into 'reverse redlining'.

Frequently, the regulators complain that they need more authority to do their jobs properly. The monetary provisions of DIDMCA and the Foreign Bank Supervision title of FDICIA (written by Fed lawyers in response to its perceived failure to contain the BCCI scandal) are prime examples. The staff director's job description almost requires him to ask the regulators what they want to achieve in any financial legislation and how they plan to obtain it.

The regulators do not always get what they want, however. In many ways, FDICIA curtails the regulators' prized discretion. In the past, the regulators' stance had been, 'leave the problem to us, we will take care of it'. But that Congressional trust in the regulatory agencies dissipated in the 1980s, when regulators appeared to have used their authority for other than the public good and taxpayer protection.[19]

6.5.1.3 Staff Investigative Work

Behind the scenes, the Committee Chairman has his staff investigate whether a problem is real or not.[20] Staff phone the industry experts, industry analysts and academics; and ask the Congressional Research Service (CRS) to search the literature, supply briefing materials, and/or investigate some legal issues. They call in the regulators' staff for a 'briefing' on their research, conclusions, opinions and recommendations. They contact the personal staff of Senators on the Committee to exchange views.

During the summer and fall of 1988, there was a frustrating period after the extent of the S&L problem had been revealed in the Senate's hearings in June and July, but while action awaited the results of the election and the installation of the new Administration. Senator Riegle, anticipating that he would become Chairman of the Senate Banking Committee in the 101st Congress after Senator Proxmire retired, asked Senator Proxmire to request his on-staff expert on domestic financial legislation and a GAO-staff-expert to quietly study the S&L crisis in depth, list options for resolving the problem, and make recommendations. In this way, Senator Riegle was able to introduce legislation into the Senate very quickly in 1989 and get it passed promptly.

While the staff are doing the ground work, Senators talk to their confidants and discuss issues with like-minded colleagues.

6.5.1.4 Beginning to Go Public

More visibly, a Chairman will ask the General Accounting Office, sometimes the Congressional Budget Office (CBO), and the regulators to study the issue. (As a case in point, in 1992 Chairman Riegle asked GAO and the banking and thrift regulators to study the use and possible abuse of derivative products in the banking and thrift industries. The Agriculture Committee has asked the CFTC, the SEC, and the Federal Reserve to do a separate study.)

6.5.1.5 *Investigative Hearings*

Hearings are held to notify all concerned that the Committee perceives a problem and plans to do something about it. Good examples are the Senate Banking Committee's hearings on the S&L crisis in June and July 1988, its oversight hearings on the condition of the banking industry in Fall 1989, when Comptroller General, Charles Bowsher, and CBO Director, Robert Reischauer testified on successive days about BIF's approaching insolvency in 1990 and the reverse redlining hearing in February 1993.

The first hearing established that the S&L problem was much bigger than had previously been perceived or admitted and that the band-aids applied in the Competitive Equality Banking Act (CEBA) of 1987 were entirely inadequate. The second examined three problems confronting the banking industry, overinvestment in real estate, junk-bond financing, and remaining problems with LDC lending. The third successfully disputed Administration complacency on the condition of the banking industry and its insurance fund.[21] At the reverse redlining hearing, Senator D'Amato, the ranking minority member, announced his intention to introduce legislation to stop the abusive practice.

6.5.1.6 *Choosing the Best Solution*

The criteria for choosing the best solutions are typically not laid out. When conducting analysis, a staffer starts by stating his/her objectives. In general, however, I believe that I observe a shift of emphasis in the late 1980s away from endorsing the industry wish-list toward protecting the taxpayer.

For example, in the summer and fall months of the pre-election hiatus in 1988, Senator Proxmire made floor statements, introduced 'Sense of the Congress' motions that reiterated the full faith and credit of the US behind the insolvent FSLIC's failed thrift resolutions, legitimized FSLIC notes and placed a limit on their use. He also decried the 1988 deals and searched for other constructive actions in face of a general conclusion that nothing definitive would be done until after the 1988 Presidential election.

After reading the Committee staff's Fall 1988 analysis in late 1988, Senator Riegle discussed the study with staff, and then sought the advice of friends and advisors that he trusted. When he had decided on the correct course of action, he gave instructions to the Committee's lawyers to draft legislation.

Staff, particularly the lawyers, write the legislation. Non-lawyers on the Committee staff certainly, and lawyers possibly, will call on the services of the Senate's Legislative Counsel, a stable of in-House expert lawyers.

Senate Banking Committee staff sent their first draft of the FDICIA legislation out to academics and other experts for review, comment, and suggested amendments in the Fall of 1990. As a result of the critiques received, Senator Riegle introduced a revised bill, early in 1991. The Administration and the House bills were introduced afterwards.

6.5.1.7 *Introducing the Legislation into the Senate*

Any Senator can introduce a bill into the Senate. It is then referred to the committee or committees that have jurisdiction over it.

In principle, any MP in Britain can introduce a bill into the House of Commons. But, in practice, the opportunity to do so is severely limited. There is a lottery to establish priority for a private member's right to introduce bills. Only a handful will get the opportunity.[22] Bills can also originate in the House of Lords. The bill may be referred to a committee, specially constituted for this purpose, between its second and third readings.

In the US, the House and Senate typically each produce their own bills, as they did in FIRREA and FDICIA. The Administration also had its own, third bill in each case. In Britain there is only one bill, usually introduced by the majority into the House of Commons.

In 1989 and 1991, the Senate Banking Committee wanted to introduce its bill first and it succeeded. It introduced its versions of FIRREA in January 1989 and of FDICIA in September 1990, before both the Administration and the House. Going first, however, was later revealed to be less of an advantage than the Senate Committee first thought. The House, for example, went last on both bills. It waited for public scrutiny of the bills in play in order to avoid some of the pitfalls that close public examination revealed. Consequently, the House won the competition for good press. In each case, the Administration's bill fell by the wayside and the final product ended as a compromise between the House and Senate bills with more weight going to the House's version, particularly in FIRREA.

6.5.1.8 *Airing the Bill: Legislative Hearings*

Committees with jurisdiction call formal hearings to consider the bill. Each House holds legislative hearings on its bill, where witnesses are asked to express their support for, and explain any concerns regarding, the legislation. Virtually anyone who wishes to testify at such hearings is allowed to testify, subject to some limitations. The Chairman of the party in control of each House sets the hearing agenda and chooses the witnesses. The Committee's ranking Republican and other members from either side sometimes request that a person they recommend be included on a panel. (The Republicans, for example, requested that Bert Ely be included on the second panel at the Senate's 'December Surprise' (non-legislative) hearing just before the 1992 election.)

The majority has a substantial advantage in choosing topics, dates and witnesses for hearings. It also has an advantage with respect to legislation. Any Senator, but only a Senator, can introduce a bill into the Senate. The Administration can usually persuade one or more members to introduce its bill into each chamber. Nevertheless, a Republican Administration usually asks the chairman and ranking member of a Democratic chamber to jointly introduce the legislation on its behalf.[23] The need for bipartisan support gives the Senate and the House leadership and the members that control the relevant Committees an opportunity to be heard by the Administration, to opine what can and cannot be passed, and thus to influence the content. This process has also been evident during the confirmation hearings for the Clinton Administration's Attorney General.

In the US, those who can convince the Chairman that they have a viewpoint worth hearing, will, in my observation, be given a chance to testify. Tables 6.3 and 6.4 lay out the names of the witnesses that testified at the FIRREA and FDICIA legislative hearings, respectively. Included in this set of likely witnesses are:

- All trade associations involved. In the banking and thrift legislation that included the American Bankers Association (ABA), the Independent Bankers Association of America (IBAA), the Conference of State Bank Supervisors (CSBS), the US League of Savings Institutions, the National Council of Savings Institutions, and others.
- Consumer groups, such as the Association of Community Organizations for Reform Now (ACORN), the Consumers Union, Public Citizen, the Center for Community Change, and the American Association of Retired Persons.
- Regulators from each agency directly involved. It is interesting to me that the Federal Reserve stayed out of deliberations on the S&L mess, even though its staff were highly informed.[24]
- GAO is almost always asked to give its analysis and recommendations, first privately in briefings and then in testimony. Sometimes, and increasingly, CBO is asked to testify. CRS has not testified on financial issues, to my knowledge.
- Role-model industry participants. At the 1989 thrift hearings, World Savings' Chairman, Herb Sandler, poured water from one bucket to another to demonstrate the industry's and FSLIC's solvency con-

Table 6.3 101st Congress – Senate banking committee hearings on savings and loans problems and related issues

1989		
1.	31 Jan	Lowell Bryan, McKinsey & Co. Andrew Carron, First Boston Corp. Paul Horvitz, University of Houston *Topic*: Problems of the Savings and Loan industry, the deposit insurance fund, and related matters
2.	2 Feb	Charles Bowsher, GAO *Topic*: Problems of the Savings and Loan industry, the deposit insurance fund, and related matters
3.	7 Feb	Paul Volcker, Princeton University *Topic*: Problems of the Savings and Loan industry, the deposit insurance fund, and related matters
4.	9 Feb	Richard Thornburgh, Attorney General Joe Selby, former Chief Regulator, Federal Home Loan Bank of Dallas David Gleeson, Lincoln Asset Management Co. *Topic*: Fraud in the savings and loan industry
5.	22 Feb	Nicholas Brady, Treasury Secretary *Topic*: The President's proposed savings and loan legislation
6.	23 Feb	Alan Greenspan, Fed Chairman *Topic*: Problems of the savings and loan industry, the FSLIC, and the President's proposed savings and loan legislation
7.	28 Feb	William Seidman, FDIC Chairman Robert Clarke, Comptroller of the Currency *Topic*: Problems of the savings and loan industry, the FSLIC, and the President's proposed savings and loan legislation
8.	1 March	Danny Wall, Federal Home Loan Bank Board Chairman *Topic*: Problems of the savings and loan industry, the FSLIC, and the President's proposed savings and loan legislation
9.	2 March	Richard Darman, OMB Director *Topic*: Problems of the savings and loan industry, the FSLIC, and the President's proposed savings and loan legislation
10.	3 March	James Blum, Congressional Budget Office William Ferguson, Ferguson & Co. Peter Treadway, Smith Barney *Topic*: Problems of the savings and loan the FSLIC, and the President's proposed industry, savings and loan legislation

Table 6.3 Continued

11.	7 March	Charles Koch, National Council of Savings Institutions Barney Beeksma, U.S. League of Savings Institutions *Topic*: Problems of the savings and loan industry, the FSLIC, and the President's proposed savings and loan legislation
12.	8 March	William Haraf, Financial Services Council Thomas Rideout, American Bankers Assn. Jay Tomson, Independent Bankers Assn. *Topic*: Problems of the savings and loan industry, the FSLIC, and the President's proposed savings and loan legislation
13.	9 March	Frank McKinney, Assn. of Bank Holding Companies H.M. Osteen, Jr., Assn. of Thrift Holding Companies Charles Zwick, Reserve City Bankers *Topic*: Problems of the savings and loan industry, the FSLIC, and the President's proposed savings and loan legislation
14.	10 March	Jerome Blank, National Assn. of Realtors Kent Colton, National Assn. of Home Builders Willard Gourley, Jr., Mortgage Bankers Assn. *Topic*: Problems of the savings and loan industry, the FSLIC, and the President's proposed savings and loan legislation
15.	14 March	Charles Bowsher, GAO *Topic*: FSLIC's 1988 deals
16.	15 March	Robert Gnaizda, Public Advocates, Inc. Michelle Meier, Consumers Union Peggy Miller, Consumer Federation of America Al Williams, Credit Union National Assn. Kenneth Robinson, National Assn. of Federal Credit Unions *Topic*: Consumer impacts of the President's proposed savings and loan legislation

Table 6.3 Continued

17.	16 March	Eugene Kuthy, Conference of State Bank Supervisors John Seymour, American Council of State Savings Supervisors *Topic*: State regulatory perspectives on the President's proposed savings and loan legislation	19.	4 Oct	RTC Oversight Board Brady, Greenspan, Kemp, Seidman *Topic*: Establishment and implementation of the RTC provisions of FIRREA
18.	17 March	Herb Sandler, World Savings and Loan Assn. Ernest Fleischer, Franklin Savings Assn. Lewis Ranieri, Ranieri Wilson *Topic*: Thrift industry perspectives on the President's proposed savings and loan legislation			

Table 6.3 Continued

1990			
1. 31 Jan	Robson (for Brady), Greenspan, Kemp, Seidman *Topic*: Semi-annual report of the RTC; implementation of the RTC strategic plan	5. 6 April	GAO's Final Audit of FSLIC Charles A. Bowsher, GAO *Topic*: Cost of the S&L problem
2. 23 Feb	John J. Adair *Topic*: Confirmation hearing: nomination of witness to be Inspector General of the RTC	6. 23 May	Brady, Greenspan, Kemp, Seidman, Larson and Jackson *Topic*: RTC Oversight -- semi-annual report of the RTC; oversight of RTC resolution and asset disposition efforts
3. 28 March	T. Timothy Ryan *Topic*: Confirmation hearing: nomination of witness to be Director of the Office of Thrift Supervision	7. 29 June	Andrew C. Hove
4. 3 April	Robert C. Larson and Philip C. Jackson, Jr. *Topic*: Confirmation hearing: nominations of witnesses to be members of the Oversight Board of the RTC		

Table 6.4 Senate banking committee hearings on bank reform, 1991

Date	*Topic*	*Witness*
1. 26 Feb	Administration's Reform Proposal	Nicholas Brady, Treasury
2. 5 March	CBO's Analysis of Treasury Proposal	Robert Reischauer, CBO
3. 7 March	GAO's Analysis of Treasury Proposal	Charles Bowsher, GAO
4. 12 March	Deposit Insurance Reform and Prompt Corrective Action	• James Barth, Auburn Univ. • Robert Eisenbeis, University of North Carolina, Chapel Hill • Robert Litan, Brookings Institute
5. 20 March	Interstate Banking	• Robert Carswell, Sherman & Sterling. Deputy Treasury Secretary, 1977–81 • Ken Littlefield, Texas Banking Comissioner, representing Conference of State Bank Supervisors • Hugh McColl, Jr., NCNB • Edwin Gordon Hebb, Jr., Hebb & Gitlin and Chairman, Connecticut Commission on Inter-State Banking 1979–83.
6. 21 March 10.00 a.m	BIF Recapitalization	William Seidman, FDIC
7. 21 March 2:00 p.m.	BIF Recapitalization	Robert Glauber, Treasury

Table 6.4 Continued

Date	*Topic*	*Witness*	*Date*	*Topic*	*Witness*
8. 9 April	RTC Reform Proposals	• Anthony Frank, Postmaster General • Martin Mayer, Author, *The Greatest Ever Bank Robbery* • Marshall Breger, Chairman, the Administrative Conference of the United States • David Braun, Director, The Nature Conservancy • Jim Davidson, Chairman, National Taxpayers Union • Chris Lewis, Co-Chair, Financial Democracy Campaign	10. 19 April	Risk-Based Premiums	• Roger Watson, FDIC • Roberto Mendoza, Morgan Guaranty Trust • Robert Clements, Marsh and McLennan, Inc. • John Caouette, Capital Markets Assurance Corporation
			11. 23 April	Deposit Insurance Reform and Regulation	• Alan Greenspan, Fed • William Seidman, FDIC • Robert Clarke, OCC
9. 11 April	Regulatory Restructuring	• Sen. William Proxmire, Former Chairman, Senate Banking Committee • Steve Roberts, KPMG Peat Marwick • Bernard Shull, Hunter College • David Holland, Boston Federal Savings Bank • Wolfgang Reinicke, Brookings *Also attending:* • Hon. John Chafec, R.I. • Hon. Claiborne Pell, R.I. • Hon. Bruce Sundlun, Gov of RI • Hon. Bob Kerrey, Nebraska • Hon. Bruce Vento, Minnesota	12. 25 April 10:00 a.m.	Public Interest Group's Perspectives	• Michele Meier, Consumers Union • Sherry Ettleson, Public Citizen • Allen Fishbein, Center for Community Change • Ed Mierzwinski, US PIRG
			13. 25 April 2:00 p.m.	Public Interest Group's Perspectives	• Michael Aronstein, National Taxpayer's Union • Joan King, AARP • Sharon Bush, ACORN

Table 6.4 Continued

Date	Topic	Witness	Date	Topic	Witness
14. 26 April	BIF Recapitalization	• Charles Bowsher, GAO • Felix Rohatyn, Lazard Freres and Company • Lloyd Cutler, Wilmer, Cutler and Pickering • Christopher James, University of Florida • Roger Kormendi, University of Michigan	16. 8 May	Financial Modernization	Paul Volcker, James D. Wolfensohn, Inc. and former Federal Reserve Chairman
15. 7 May	Pending Legislation for Deposit Insurance Reform	• Richard Breeden, SEC • Timothy Ryan, OTS • Roger Jepsen, NCUA	17. 9 May 10:00 a.m.	Industry Perspectives	• Richard Kirk, United Bank of Denver, representing the American Bankers Association • David Ballweg, Community States Bank, representing the Independent Bankers Association of America • Eugene Miller, Coamerica, representing and Association of Holding Companies • James Daniel, The Friendly Bank, representing the Community Bankers Association

straints to the astonished amusement of all who saw it (including C-SPAN viewers).

- Competitors that are acknowledged to have legitimate concerns. Industry associations such as National Association of Securities Dealers, the National Futures Association and the Securities Industry Association and their regulators testified in the legislative hearings on Glass–Steagall repeal in 1987 and 1988.
- Industry analysts have made valuable contributions to cleaning up the country's financial messes. For example, Bill Ferguson's testified on bank and thrift problems; Alex Sheshunoff foretold banks' real estate woes at the 1989 Senate oversight hearings; Standard and Poor's convincingly estimating the value of the implicit federal subsidies to Government Sponsored Enterprises at the GSE hearings; Bert Ely has testified on numerous occasions on bank, thrift, and their insurers' problems; and Martin Weiss drew attention to problems in the insurance industry in 1991.
- Academics have also contributed to the legislative deliberations on Glass–Steagall repeal in the 1987 and 1988 Senate hearings. But, without doubt, their greatest coup has been to convince the Senate, the Administration, and the House that the deposit insurance system could best be reformed in 1991 through prompt corrective action to resolve bank and thrift problems.
- Other private, expert panels are heard from time to time. For example, the Financial Accounting Standards Board (FASB) has been consulted over market value accounting on numerous occasions and selected think tanks have sent witnesses.
- Since the S&L scandal, the Senate Committee has been careful to consult the National Taxpayers' Union and obtain its testimony, for example, when preparing for FDICIA.
- Individuals with either a grievance or useful recommendation can help to resolve a problem. The Senate Banking Committee's (non-legislative) hearings on 'reverse redlining' in February 1992 are a good example of such testimony.

6.5.1.9 Others Involved in Consensus-Building

Not everyone testifies, but others can attend the hearings or watch them on C-SPAN. Many attend; in the audience an observer can pick out:

- The press, assisted by the Committee's press secretary. Except for the press secretary, staff interact with the press on an irregular basis. A staffer is called when he has inside information on something of interest, particularly if it is something obscure and complex, like derivative products.

- Domestic and foreign interests and their lobbyists. Staff will engage in, usually, cautious and circumspect discussions of the issues with them, but almost always only 'on background'.
- The interested public. Letters and calls from constituents and others are becoming increasingly vociferous. Calls and correspondence on the subjects of gays in the military and nominations to Attorney General, provide good examples.
- Newspaper articles and TV shows have made valuable assessments of what has gone wrong on financial issues; for example, the '60 Minutes' antecedent to the reverse redlining hearing.

6.5.1.10 Working Toward Consensus

In fact, both the FIRREA and FDICIA legislation had a large common core of legislation in the House, Senate, and Administration bills. It is these consensus items that are most likely to pass.

Staff check support among members of the Committee. Members and senior staff work out compromises and 'do deals'.

6.5.1.11 Mark-Up

If support is adequate on both sides of the aisle, the Chairman schedules a mark-up. In the US, unlike GB, there are usually enough maverick Democrats to require some Republican support for passage.[25] For example, Senator Cranston voted with the Republicans and against the Democrats on several important issues in the mark-up and conference on FIRREA.[26]

The Senate Banking Committee's rules of procedure say that amendments to the bill are due at the Committee's office at least two business days before the mark-up. For recent financial mark-ups in the Senate, amendments have numbered in the hundreds, due partly to the 'Christmas tree' phenomenon.

Members and staff, on separate tracks, negotiate with Democrats and Republicans to obtain support for the vote. The managers of the bill make a managers' amendment (which may include agreements and compromises that are necessary to obtain enough votes for passage) on the day of the Committee's vote. (The Chairman and Ranking Minority Member were the managers in FIRREA and FDICIA.)

At the mark-up, the press sit at side tables and are attended by the press secretary. The regulators have reserved seats. Everyone else has to queue for seats. Lines typically form outside before the Senate opens to visitors. Line-sitters earn over $10 an hour to wait in line for lobbyists.

The Chairman calls the Committee to order and the members make opening statements. The list of amendments are offered in order, discussed and voted on. Some amendments have disappeared into the managers' amendment and others are withdrawn. Compromises are made; sometimes a recess is called to allow negotiations to take place. Lobbyists do their best to influence the result.[27] Staff sit at the witness table to explain the legislation when asked and answer questions. Finally, the bill is voted on, as amended by the Committee.

6.5.1.12 Clean-Up

If the bill passes, the staff execute the changes in the legislation that were agreed to in the mark-up. Much of the legislative language is written obscurely in the form – amend section x of statute y to say z. Consequently, staff also write a 'section-by-section' analysis that actually says what the legislation does. A subsequent broader analysis provides the 'legislative history' that explains why the legislation was passed and what it seeks to accomplish.

The legislation, the amendments adopted in Committee, and accompanying report should be available in printed form at least a day before the bill is scheduled to reach the Senate floor. But that is not always possible; then, the responsibility falls on staff to make sure their member knows what is included in the legislation.

6.5.1.13 On the Senate Floor

In the case of the FIRREA and FDICIA legislation, the Committee Chairman and Ranking Minority member jointly managed the bill on the Senate floor. The majority leader controls the Senate's agenda. Under a unanimous consent agreement, he stipulates, for example, how much time will be allocated for debate and when the bill will be taken up. The bill's managers allocate the time allotted among Senators who have indicated that they wish to speak in the debate.

The amendments adopted in the mark-up are called first, debated and put to a vote. Additional amendments are introduced and debated. Deals are made, and the final vote is put. Senate rules do not limit debate nor do they exclude non-germane amendments. Such restrictions are usually imposed by unanimous consent, however. Without that agreement, a filibuster can occur.

Providing taxpayer funds to repay depositors at failed S&Ls is an unpopular vote. Senators and Representatives fear criticism and losing votes as a result of supporting RTC funding. For example, freshman Senator Carol Moseley Braun called supporting the funding bill 'a vote from hell' during debate on the Senate Banking Committee's mark-up of RTC funding on 25 March 1993.

Senate and House leadership have had to be creative, therefore, in order to secure passage of some of the RTC funding bills. There are four options regarding the form the vote can take: (1) unanimous consent; (2) a voice vote; (3) a division;[28] and (4) a roll-call vote. All but the roll-call allow an member to remain anonymous when voting for funding. Voting by consent, voice or division makes it harder for the press and constituents to identify a member's position and criticize him for authorizing or appropriating taxpayer funds for S&Ls.

Strong and visible pressure from the President to support a particular measure can provide a justification for a member's support of otherwise unpopular legislation. The Democratic leadership in the House, for example, says that the House did not pass the RTC refinancing bill in 1992, because President Bush did not personally call on Republicans, individually and collectively, to vote for the bill. Absent this justification, many Republicans opposed the bill and Democrats did too, because they feared that they would be punished by the electorate if Democrats were the only members to vote for the bill. The bill failed as a result.

All four voting options have been used in the 13 votes on RTC funding that have taken place in the House or Senate chambers during the past five years. Table 6.5 shows that, in the Senate there were five roll-call votes, one unanimous consent, and one division. The House has had four recorded votes, one division, and one voice vote.

6.5.1.14 The Exchange of Bills

When it has passed its bill first, the Senate usually sends its bill to the House for consideration. Typically, an equivalent-in-many-respects process has been underway in the House. The House can accept a Senate bill or amend it. The House can also wait until its own bill has passed, strike out the contents of the Senate's bill and substitute the material in its own bill and send the package back to the Senate.[29]

Sometimes, as in the case of FIRREA and FDICIA, these inter-House maneuvers end in stalemate, and a Conference between the House and Senate is called to resolve differences between the two bills.

Table 6.5 RTC funding

Bill title	*Bill number*	*Date of action*	*Vote*	*Public law number*
		Senate votes		
Thrift Depositor Protection Act of 1993	S. 714	13 May 1993	61 yeas to 35 nays	
1992 RTC Funding	S. 2482	26 March 1992	52 yeas to nay	
November 1991 RTC Restructuring and Funding	H.R. 3435	11 November 1991	44 yeas to 33 nays	P.L. 102–233
March 1991 RTC Funding	S. 419 S. 419	7 March 1991 20 March 1991	69 yeas to 30 nays Unanimous Consent	P.L. 102–18
FIRREA	S. 774 H.R. 1278 (Conference Report)	19 March 1989 4 August 1989	91 yeas to 8 nays Division Vote	P.L. 101–73
		House votes		
RTC Completion Act of 1993	H.R. 1340	Pending		
1992 RTC Funding	H.R. 4704	1 April 1992	125 yeas to 298 nays	
November 1991 RTC Restructuring and Funding	H.R. 3435	26 November 1991	Division Vote	P.L. 102–233
March 1991 Funding	H.Res. 112 S. 419 (Conference Report)	13 March 1991 21 March 1991	Voice Vote March 21, 1991	P.L. 102–18
FIRREA	H.R. 1278 H.R. 1278 (Conference Report)	15 June 1989 4 August 1989	320 yeas to 97 nays 201 yeas to 175 nays	P.L. 101–73

Source: Timothy Mitchell's records for the Senate Banking Committee.

6.5.1.15 Conference

The Conference typically first meets some days after it is called. In the meantime, staff write a 'side-by-side' analysis which, in tabular format analyses every provision of the legislation, section by section. It shows where provisions are identical, where and what are any differences, and where one bill contains issues that the other does not.

Conferees on a bill that has been amended by the other House are supposed to negotiate a resolution of differences within the bounds of the House and Senate bills (Bach 1991). If they move outside these bounds they become subject to a point of order when the bill returns to the two Houses. The boundaries do not apply so sharply, where one House has substituted its own bill into the shell of the other, however. Conferees then can have more latitude. In FIRREA, the Senate struck out the House material and substituted its own bill. In FDICIA, the reverse occurred. Thus, the two conferences received the broader mandate for negotiation.

Banking bills' conferences usually convene in the Rayburn Building, because the House Banking Committee room is bigger than the Senate's. The party leadership in each House, after receiving the recommendations of the Committee's Chairman, appoints the conferees. In FIRREA, this produced highly disparate numbers of members. The House had almost 100 conferees including all 51 from the House Banking Committee and almost as many from the several other Committees of the House that had jurisdiction over the bill. The Senate Banking Committee, with almost (but not quite) sole jurisdiction[30] over the bill in the Senate had just five conferees (three Democrats and two Republicans). The number of conferees does not directly affect the outcome, however, because each House's conferees vote as a unit (Hilldenbrand and Dove, 1982).

Members of a Banking Committee Conference sit round a special conference table set up in the well of room 2129 in the Rayburn Building. The press sit in the members' tiered seats, and staff sit (if they are senior enough) round the edges of the members' table and the public squeeze in where they can. Most observers end up in an overflow room that broadcasts the sounds of the Conference. Typically, they have no video, because C-SPAN does not usually broadcast mark-ups or conferences, which may appear too technical and dry to attract interest.

The Conference appoints a chairman. In fact, the House and Senate Banking Committee Chairmen take turns at chairing their Conferences. The Conference Chairman then directs staff to settle what issues it can (the most technical and least contentious ones) and report back at a certain day and time.

The majority and minority staff directors for each Committee in each House delegate to their staff the responsibilities for doing the ground work. Staff rise up from both Houses like ants and swarm over the hill. (Usually House and Senate staff work independently and have little opportunity to mingle.) Legislative counsel are busy monitoring the staff negotiations and keeping track of proposed changes in the wording of the legislation.

In due course, committee staff report back to the staff director and the Chairman, personal staff to their Senator. The principals meet, often in their 'hideaways' in the Capitol.

The Conference reconvenes. Staff report progress and describe the compromises that they recommend as the outcomes of their efforts to compare notes across Houses. Members debate the recommendations, offer other solutions, and vote to approve or reject them. Conferees discuss items where staff have been unable to reach agreement. (The most contentious item in FIRREA was whether RTC funding should be accounted for on or off budget. That issue was debated long and hard.) Staff may be directed to work again on the outstanding issues and report back again at the next scheduled meeting of the principals. The process may be repeated. Typically, a conference leader from one House or the other offers a compromise package that proposes solutions to the items that the staff have not been able to resolve. There will probably be a counter offer and a counter-counter offer. In FIRREA, negotiations were hard and protracted; but agreement was reached more readily in FDICIA.

Ultimately, if the bill is to pass, agreement is reached and the resulting bill is then reported back and voted on in each House.[31]

6.5.1.16 Passage

The bill has to be passed by both Houses in the same form. Then staff and 'legal counsel' produce the final form of the legislation; staff write the section-by-section analysis and the legislative intent and history.

6.5.1.17 Signing the Bill

In the case of the FIRREA and FDICIA legislation, the bills were passed in forms acceptable to the President, so there was little concern that he would veto either bill.

In the case of important legislation, the President signs the bill in a private ceremony in the White House Rose Garden. He invites members and staff who have worked on the legislation to the ceremony.

6.5.1.18 Technical Amendments

The bill is now law. It is recess and members and staff take a vacation to rebuild their energy. As the federal regulatory agencies work to implement the law, they may find some errors and inconsistencies that will be removed a few months later in 'technical amendments' to the law.

The bill's lawyers are reluctant to admit that technical amendments are needed; they serve as a criticism to their drafting ability. The bill's managers are also reluctant to reopen the legislation, because it gives opponents another change to effect additional changes.[32]

6.6 CONCLUDING QUESTIONS

The description above of legislative processes raises several questions. First, is my inference correct that financial reform is easier to implement (as well as to pass) in Britain than in the US? If so, does the same thing hold in other Parliamentary systems, such as Canada's? Does the system of political appointments in US government service help or hinder implementation as compared to the independent Civil Service in Britain. Second, is it indeed easier to pass pro-banking industry legislation in the US under Republican configurations than Democratic ones? Is thrift legislation also easier to pass under Republican authority than Democratic? To what extent do the personalities of Committee Chairmen influence legislation? Is my suggestion that all interests can be heard in the US system accurate? If so, what is it that determines whose interests will carry the day in the legislation?[33] Are the factors that determine who wins, changing? If they are changing, in what ways and why?

Clearly, this chapter raises more questions about the political economy of financial reform than it answers. But I hope that these questions will be considered worthy of further study.

Notes

1. The author thanks Richard Carnell, former Senior Counsel to the Senate Banking Committee, and now Assistant Secretary for Financial Institutions, Department of the Treasury for help in understanding US legislative procedures, Richard Saunders of the British Embassy in Washington for information on recent financial legislation in Britain, Amy Kostanecki for assistance in tracking US political configurations, and Professor Thomas

Mayer of the University of California at Davis for his comments on an earlier draft.

2. 'The principle of unbroken continuity of Parliament is, for all practical purposes, secured by the fact that the same proclamation which dissolves a Parliament provides for the election and meeting of a new Parliament' (May, p. 259).
3. Votes are called 'divisions,' in the House of Commons, because MPs (seated by party and facing each other on opposite sides of the House) vote by exiting the floor of the House through either the government or opposition lobby. This arrangement is also the origin of the term 'crossing over', that is, crossing over the floor of the chamber.
4. A typical candidate in an urban constituency can spend £4144 plus 3.5 pence per elector. A typical constituency has 70 000 voters, which entitles the candidate to spend up to £6600 (or $10 000 at an exchange rate of $1.52 per pound) per election. 'Candidates' election expenses are strictly regulated, breaches of the law are punishable by severe penalties. If the winning candidate is involved, a fresh election may be called' (HMSO, 1991, p. 32).
5. There is a convention, however, that Parliament will not pass retrospective legislation, something that seems to happen all the time in the US.
6. The courts' challenges to Parliament have occurred mostly where a member has abused his 'Parliamentary privilege'.
7. The Parliament Acts of 1911 and 1949 determined that the House of Lords cannot amend or defeat a 'money bill'. It can amend other bills sent to it by the Commons. A bill amended by the Lords then returns to the Commons, which can accept or reject the amendment. The process can be repeated, but only once.
8. When his attempt to repeal the Glass–Steagall Act failed in the last hours of the 100th Congress, Senator Proxmire wrote to the Federal Reserve to encourage it to relax the restrictions on banks' securities activities by regulation.
9. The Building Societies' cartel weakened when the commercial banks began to offer residential mortgages in the early 1980s and was formally abolished in the 1986 Act.
10. A question on undue market power for banks, prepared for the Banking Committee's nomination hearing of Frank Newman as Under Secretary of the Treasury for Domestic Finance, will provide an opportunity to raise this issue.
11. The popular Ferguson data base for banks lulls the user into complacency. A state may register, say, 400 individual, apparently independent, banks. It is possible to find how many belong to any particular holding company only after considerable extra effort.
12. In the House of Representatives, only 'germane' amendments are in order. That restriction does not hold in the Senate except for the Budget Act or under 'unanimous consent' agreements.
13. Two of my most extraordinary experiences with agency responses to GAO involved meeting with senior Treasury staff on GAO's lender-of-last-resort work in 1985, and with Gerald Corrigan (then President of the Federal Reserve Bank of New York) on GAO's study of the 1987 stockmarket crash in late 1987.

14. The OCC was already questioning the viability of the thrift industry in 1979.
15. The BIF has borrowed $12 billion from the Federal Financing Bank (and repaid $2 billion). It has not used its line of credit to the Treasury.
16. Ignoring opposition is punishable, however. Margaret Thatcher's poll-tax in the UK was forced through Parliament over great opposition. It was, perhaps, the most important single factor that led to her ouster.
17. Until recently, the Senate Banking Committee's fax machine was next to its xerox. Sometimes, while waiting for copies, one observed legislative language spewing from the fax. It is not so surprising, therefore, that sometimes draft legislation was intercepted before it reached its intended destination. An aide from the Housing Subcommittee, for example, working closely with Fannie Mae, was believed to have diverted draft legislation to require a study of risk-taking by Government Sponsored Enterprises during FIRREA.
18. The easing on restrictions on real-estate lending by commercial banks is an example.
19. Professor Edward Kane has been influential in questioning the regulators' motives.
20. Both Chairmen of both the House and Senate Banking Committees are male, and that is true of the subcommittees too. The Senate Committee now has three women members – Barbara Boxer, Carol Moseley Braun, and Patty Murray.
21. Some republican Senators ignored the warnings witnesses gave of the severity of the banking industry's problems at the Senate Banking Committee's oversight hearings in October 1989. They debated whether they should conclude, 'Don't worry. Be happy' (Senate Banking Committee, 1989, p. 381–5).
22. PBS's freshman lady MP won a high place in the lottery and then set out hurriedly to find a bill worthy of that priority.
23. It is too early to observe whether the Clinton Administration will rely solely on Democrats to introduce its legislation. Its misadventure with the $16 billion stimulus package that fell to a filibuster in the Senate suggests that the Administration will need to court bipartisan support.
24. Earlier, the Fed had taken the lead in research on thrift issues in the interagency ICC and DIDC deliberations in 1979 and 1980.
25. It is risky for an MP in the majority party to vote against a three-lined whip in Britain. If he does, and his party loses the vote, the government may be forced to resign.
26. The situation was so pronounced that his principal aide had her photograph taken with the Republican staff at the signing ceremony in the Rose Garden at the White House.
27. During a recess in the mark-up of the Senate's Glass–Steagall Repeal bill in 1988, staff had to be locked into a room when they were drafting an agreed compromise amendment in order to keep the lobbyists out.
28. When the presiding officer is unable to judge the relative strengths of the yeas and nays in a voice vote, members may be asked to stand, divided into two groups, and be counted.
29. In the 98th Congress, 63 per cent of the 623 bills passed 'when one chamber adopted without amendment the version sent to it by the other' (Nickels, p. 21). A chamber amended a version sent by the other in 25 per cent of the

bills in the 98th Congress. The remaining 12 per cent were reconciled in conference.

30. The Senate Judiciary Committee was also involved in FIRREA.
31. Late in the night, after the final version of the FIRREA legislation had passed the Senate, Senate staff returned to the Dirksen Building to a party in the office of the minority staff director while they watched the final debate and vote in the House of Representatives on C-SPAN.
32. Counsel likes to boast that no technical amendments were needed to FIRREA. The few that were necessary for FDICIA were included in Title XVI-A of the Housing and Community Development Act of 1992.
33. *False Profits*, by Peter Truell and Larry Gurwin, the story of BCCI, illustrates the power that securing political influence across the globe can have.

References

Bach, Stanley (1980) 'The Amending Process in the Senate' (Congressional Research Service).

Bach, Stanley (1986) 'An Introduction to the Legislative Process on the Senate Floor' (CRS).

Bach, Stanley (1991) 'Resolving Legislative Differences in Congress: Conference Committees and Amendments Between the Houses' (CRS).

Cargill, Thomas F. and Gillian Garcia (1982) *Financial Deregulation and Monetary Control* (Stanford, CA: Hoover Institution Press).

Cargill, Thomas F. and Gillian Garcia (1985) *Financial Reform in the 1980s* (Stanford, CA: Hoover Institution Press).

Committee on Banking, Housing, and Urban Affairs (1991) *Rules of Procedure and Jurisdiction* (June).

Committee on Banking, (1989) *Oversight Hearings on the Condition of the Banking System*, 101–512.

Garcia, Gillian (1980) 'The British Way with Thrifts', Federal Home Loan Bank Working Paper.

Her Majesty's Stationary Office (HMSO) (1991) *Parliamentary Elections*.

Hilldenbrand, William F. and Robert B. Dove (1982) *Enactment of a Law: Procedural Steps in the Legislative Process*, US Senate, 97th Congress, 2nd Session, Document No. 97–20.

Kane, Edward J. (1989) *The S&L Insurance Mess* (Washington, DC: The Urban Institute Press).

May, Thomas Erskine (1976) *Parliamentary Practice: The Law, Privileges, Proceedings, and Usage of Parliament*, 19th edition, ed. Sir David Lidderdale (London: Butterworth).

Nickels, Ilona B. (1986) 'Guiding a Bill Through the Legislative Process: Considerations for Legislative Staff' (CRS).

Proxmire, Senator William (1988) Statement on Senate Resolution 452, 'To Stop the Growth of Insolvent Thrift Institutions', *Congressional Record*, S 9712–14.

Truell, Peter and Larry Gurwin (1992) *False Profits* (Boston, MA: Houghton-Mifflin).

7 The Limits of Prudential Supervision: Economic Problems, Institutional Failure and Competence[1]

Bernard Shull

7.1 INTRODUCTION

Bank supervision typically receives little, if any, attention when banks are operating without difficulty. But when banks fail in large numbers, or large banks fail, and the system itself is threatened, supervision becomes a focal point for criticism and reform (Conference Report, 1989, Title I, IX; Pecchioli, 1987, pp. 11 ff.; and Comptroller General of the US, 1977).[2] On such occasions, institutional changes may take equal billing with the 'improvement' of supervision. But as often as not, the only thing Congress can agree on is that supervision needs to be better. This usually translates into more supervisors operating with more authority.

The repeated augmentation of bank supervision may give the impression that it is a solution rather that a symptom of recurring banking problems; and it is in the interest of supervisors to suggest that this is the case. Repeated disappointments about past performance never seem to undermine the promise that more and better supervisors, with more authority, will make things better in the future.

The historical record suggests that this is not true. There are, however, independent reasons for questioning whether, in and of itself, more supervisors with more restrictive authority will help very much. It is argued below that the promise of supervisory enhancement is an illusion traceable to the belief that recurring banking problems are caused by bad bankers, and that ignores the limitations of supervision in dealing with the problems that actually exist. These limitations include: (1) the existence of an intractable economic problem confronting depository institutions; (2) at least two distinct institutional failures, a fragmented regulatory system composed of multiple agencies and the growth of opportunism among banking organizations, that make it difficult to formulate and implement appropriate policies; and, finally, (3) the inability of the existing supervisory establishment to deal with these economic and structural issues.

The nature of supervision is discussed in the next section. The limitations are reviewed in section 7.3, and the inadequacy of the current supervisory establishment to deal with the problems it must deal with to be successful is considered in section 7.4. Some proposals to remedy the existing difficulties are presented in section 7.5. These include the consolidation of the 'stand-alone' supervisory agencies with the monetary authority.

7.2 SUPERVISION AND BANKING PROBLEMS

Bank supervision in a rudimentary form accompanied the inception of chartered banking in the United States (Hammond, 1957, p. 187). The early bank charters granted banks exclusive privileges, particularly the right to issue notes payable on demand that would circulate as currency. Banks were also understood to be 'private establishments employed as public agents' (Dunbar, 1904, p. 91). Among other things, they were employed to provide credit to the government. A symbiotic bank–government relationship implied government support of one kind or another (Shull, 1983). Government supervision was a logical outcome.

The substance of the bank–government relationship has changed over the past two hundred years, but special charters, effectively defining and limiting banks activities, still exist; and other firms are restricted in providing depository services. Banks are still perceived as serving public functions, such as participation in the payments mechanism, and are supported by what, in recent years, has been referred to as a 'safety net' that includes deposit insurance and the Federal Reserve's discount mechanism.

7.2.1 Supervisory Objectives and Operations

The objectives of supervision are sometimes specified in terms of protecting depositors, and/or protecting the insurance funds, and/or protecting the payments mechanism, and/or protecting the money supply and/or assuring that banks abide by laws that constrain the private use of their resources; for example, the Community Reinvestment Act. In general, each of these objectives may be viewed as involving a public function which banks perform.

While it is often said that it is not the purpose of supervision to keep banks from failing, these functions cannot be served by failing or failed banks, particularly if problems are system-wide. It is understandable, then, that supervisors are not simply concerned with closing insolvent banks, but also aim at sustaining banks as viable institutions. This objective is reflected in activities that range from advice given to bankers on how to solve problems, to financial aid provided by the supervisory agencies (particularly the FDIC and the Federal Reserve), to advocacy by supervisory agencies for legal changes that are seen as supporting bank earnings; for example, providing banks with the authority to underwrite securities and sell various types of insurance. Bank capital, as noted, is viewed as a protection against failure; and earnings are the basis for increased capital. The twin obligations of supporting banks and restraining them, the ultimate restraint being closure, implies a potential conflict of objectives that at best can confuse supervisors in responding to changing bank and market conditions.

The functioning of supervision has also changed over the past two hundred years, from the collection of sporadic reports to sophisticated techniques for monitoring, evaluation and enforcement. By the middle of the twentieth century, supervision had developed into an examination of the condition of banks on a given date, their policy procedures and management competence, as well as a determination of compliance with applicable statutes and regulation. (Crosse, 1962, p. 109). At the Federal Reserve Bank of New York, for example, the principal concerns were that banks would have sufficient liquidity to meet their contractual obligations to provide funds, that they would have sufficient capital to prevent the threat of insolvency in the face of potential losses, and sufficient earnings to absorb losses and raise new capital when needed (Crosse, 1962, p. 158).

Currently, the principal work of the supervisory agencies includes the establishment of regulations in accordance with law, and the evaluation of 'safety and soundness' of the institutions supervised. When a bank's condition is deemed 'weak' or 'troubled', that is, approaching insolvency, they attempt to bring about improvements; if unsuccessful, they are expected to close the bank promptly. The principal tool of the supervisory agencies is bank examinations.

In recent years, with the collapse of the S&L industry, the high rate of commercial bank failure, and the depletion of the FDIC's deposit insurance funds, there have been some notable changes in supervisory technique. There has been movement toward measuring the net worth of banks on a market, rather than a book, basis, toward adjusting capital requirements to risk, and incorporating interest-rate risk measures and interest-rate change scenarios into supervisory calculations (Houpt and Embersit, 1991). But a principal legislative remedy, as has typically been the case, has been more supervision and tougher constraints, including earlier intervention and closure of weak banks. This approach derives from the venerable idea that bank management is almost invariably responsible for bank failure.

7.2.2 Bank Management, Supervision and Bank Failure

Mismanagement as a cause of bank failure was a recurrent theme in the nineteenth and early twentieth centuries (*Legislative History*, 1855, pp. 58 ff.; House Committee on Banking and Currency, 1913, pp. 11, 31). (For an early example of the incipient 'supervisory attitude', see Hammond, 1957, p. 201.) It has emerged repeatedly in studies by supervisory agencies in a succession of banking problems and crises over the last 70 years. In 1926, Federal Reserve officials identified bad management as a principle cause of the high rate of bank failure (Friedman and Schwartz, 1963, pp. 269–70). In 1930, the Comptroller of the Currency reported roughly half the failures of national banks then in receivership could be attributed to incompetent management and dishonesty, while the other half could be attributed to local financial depression (Comptroller of the Currency, 1930, pp. 307–21). The economist Walter Spahr epitomized the 'supervisory attitude' when he wrote that 'it is probably not possible to separate [the]...failures due to incompetent management from those due to local business depressions since it is the purpose and test of good bank management to avoid the effects of local financial depressions' (Spahr, 1932, p. 220). This appears to have been the view of the Federal Reserve which, in the early years of the Great Depression, again found bad management to be principally at fault for bank failures (Friedman and Schwartz, 1963, pp. 358–59).

In the mid-1970s, the reemergence of large bank failures evoked the traditional supervisory response. The federal banking agencies again pointed to inept management and/or fraudulent practices as the principal cause (*First Meeting on the Condition of the Banking System*, 1977, pp. 1022–5, 1077–81, 1154–67). In the early 1980s, the FDIC discounted the significance of regional economic problems and found mismanagement to be the most important cause of bank failures (FDIC, 1984, p. 13). In the late 1980s, the Comptroller indicated a 'long held belief' that bank management and boards of directors bear ultimate responsibility for bank problems and that management-driven weakness were the underlying cause of most of the bank failures studied (Comptroller of the Currency, 1988, p. 1).

It is a small step from identifying management deficiencies as a principal cause of bank failure to finding that supervision needs to be improved.

The currently active Federal agencies provide a living historical record of the continuing efforts to provide such improvement. The perceived deficiencies of state bank supervision was an important element in passage of the National Banking Act in 1863 and the establishment of the Office of the Comptroller of the Currency (OCC) (Robertson, 1968, pp. 42–52). Reviewing a succession of banking crises in the latter half of the nineteenth century under the National Banking Act, the National Monetary Commission complained in 1912 that '[w]e have no power to enforce the adoption of uniform standards with regard to capital, reserves, examinations and the character and publicity of reports of all banks in different sections of the country' (National Monetary Commission, 1912, p. 9). An explicit purpose of the Federal Reserve Act of 1913 was 'to establish more effective supervision of banking in the United States'. It extended Federal supervision to state (member) banks.

The massive bank failures of the early 1930s were attributed by many both to inadequate bankers and inadequate supervision. W. F. Gephart, of the First National Bank of St Louis, reflected a common sentiment when he wrote in the *American Economic Review* in 1935:

> For many decades, the states and even the federal government have permitted banks to be organized with small capital...and by individuals with no banking or business experience to qualify them to conduct a banking business... Chief reliance has...been placed on bank examinations... In many cases, these examiners were less qualified for their jobs than the bankers were for theirs.
>
> (Gephart, 1935, p. 84)

The measures required to remedy the 'constitutional weaknesses' of the system, as seen by the Senate Banking Committee in reporting the Glass Bill to the full Senate in May 1933 have a familiar ring:

> (a) Strengthen the capital of banks; (b) Provision for closer and stronger supervision; (c) More careful restriction of investments; (d) Requirements for the truthful valuation of assets; (e) Protection of depositors and limitation of their losses through a bank deposit insurance corporation'.
>
> (Senate Banking Report, 1933, p. 11)

The FDIC was established in the early 1930s not simply to provide deposit insurance, but to further extend an upgraded federal supervision to state (insured) banks; and the Federal Home Loan Bank System (FHLBS) was established to provide Federal supervision for the reorganized savings and loan industry.

In more recent years, the National Credit Union Administration (NCUA) was established in 1970 to provide Federal supervision for credit unions. And the Federal Financial Institution Examination Council (FFIEC) was organized in 1977 as a coordinating agency to improve the 'improved' supervision provided by the other Federal agencies.

Comprehensive banking reform, typically including improved supervision, has typically evoked a transcendent and, in retrospect, unwarranted optimism. For example, the Comptroller of the Currency announced in 1914 that, with the new Federal Reserve Act, 'financial and commercial crises, or "panics"...with their attendant misfortunes and prostrations, seem to be mathematically impossible' (Comptroller of the Currency, 1914, p. 10). Seventy-five years later, confronting the S&L disaster with yet another comprehensive reform, the Financial Institutions Reform, Recovery and Enforcement Act (FIRREA), Nicholas Brady , the Secretary of the Treasury, proclaimed '[t]wo watch words guided us as we undertook to solve this problem – "Never Again"' (Brady, 1989, p. 1).

7.2.3 Recent Banking Reform

Notwithstanding its general emphasis on liquidating insolvent S&Ls and regulatory reorganization, a stated purpose of FIRREA was '[t]o promote... a safe and stable system of affordable housing', that is, to sustain the public functioning of savings associations. It increased the required proportion of assets to be held by S&Ls in loans and securities related to residential housing (qualified thrift lender test; Title III, Sec. 301); and it established two new subsidized housing programs (Title VIIA, Sec. 721).

FIRREA provided for the liquidation of failed savings institutions through the Resolution Trust Corporation (RTC). It abolished the Federal Home Loan Bank Board and the Federal Savings and Loan Insurance Corporation (FSLIC), transferred supervisory authority over savings associations to a newly established Office of Thrift Supervision (OTS) in the Treasury and established a new Savings Association Insurance Fund (SAIF) to be administered by the FDIC. Despite its emphasis on 'picking up the pieces' and reorganization of the S&L regulatory structure, FIRREA did not neglect the public functions of S&Ls. FIRREA also included major changes in supervision that affected not only savings associations, but other depository institutions and bank holding companies. In general, it tightened constraints on federal savings associations, extended federal constraints to state-chartered associations, and imposed other restrictions applicable to national and member banks.

Specifically, among other things, it prohibited savings associations from the acquisition and retention of junk bonds, and limited their equity investments (Title II, Sec. 222). It raised their capital requirements to levels no less stringent than those applicable to national banks (Title III, Sec. 301) and imposed National Bank and Federal Reserve Act limits on lending to one borrower, lending to insiders and on inter-affiliate transactions (Title III, Sec. 301). It prohibited certain activities to institutions not meeting capital requirements ('troubled institutions'); these prohibitions included accepting brokered deposits, offering above-market interest rates on deposits, lending to business development corporations, increasing assets, and, for state associations, exercising 'expanded powers' permitted under state law. The FDIC was given 'backup enforcement authority' over all savings associations, permitting it to intervene in situations representing a risk to the insurance funds.

In addition, FIRREA augmented the authority of all the federal agencies to ferret out potential problems, impose timely restrictions and discipline recalcitrant bank officials (Title IX). For example, it expanded agency authority to appoint a conservator on the determination that a bank is unsafe or unsound, or that it has 'willfully' violated an order issued against it. It expanded agency authority to remove bank officials, and to order restitution for violations of law or regulation. The agencies were given veto power over new directors and senior executive officers of relatively new banks, banks experiencing recent change in control and those not meeting capital requirements. It provided for substantial civil money penalties, up to $1 million per day, for violating written agreements or orders, or for filing false or misleading reports. It also beefed up criminal penalties and appropriated additional funds to the Department of Justice to undertake civil and criminal prosecutions (Seidman, 1990).

The new powers to discipline and penalize banks did not prevent high levels of commercial bank failure in 1990 and 1991, or the emerging insolvency of the Bank Insurance Fund (BIF). Comprehensive reform was again proposed by the Treasury in 1991 (*Treasury Report*), and an 'Administration bill', based on the *Report*, was introduced in Congress. The bill provided for the recapitalization of the Bank Insurance Fund (BIF); it included measures to relax restrictions on interstate branching, lift restrictions on securities and insurance activities, and permit ownership of bank holding companies by commercial firms. Finally, it contained measures to further modify supervision.

The Act that was passed, the Federal Deposit Insurance Corporation Improvement Act of 1991 (FDICIA), did not adopt the Administration's proposals on branching, new activities or holding company ownership, measures expanding bank powers, aimed at increasing bank market value and, in general, extending deregulation. It did, however, reaffirm the public interest in banks by recapitalizing the insurance funds and, among other 'public function' measures, providing depository institutions with an incentive to offer 'lifeline banking accounts' and to make loans in 'distressed communities' (Title II, Secs. 231–34). It augmented supervision in a number of ways: by requiring federal supervisors to perform additional on-site bank examinations, and through annual independent audits for larger institutions (Title I, Secs.111–12); by giving supervisors authority to prescribe and enforce detailed managerial and operational standards for purposes of 'safety and soundness' that seem to run the gamut from loan documentation to compensation for tellers; and by further extending Federal authority to state banks by imposing the limits on insurance underwriting and equity investments applicable to national banks (Title III, Sec. 303).

FDICIA coupled the reaffirmation of public interest in banks and the augmentation of supervision with the requirement that rules be substituted for discretion in evaluating bank condition and dealing with weak institutions. Past agency practice had supported large banks deemed 'too big to fail'. FDICIA restricted such policies by prohibiting the FDIC from extending insurance coverage to uninsured creditors after 1994 unless the President, the Secretary of the Treasury and the FDIC jointly determine that doing so involves a 'least cost' resolution or that there is a systemic risk. In the latter case, the Congressional banking committees must be notified (Title I, Sec. 141). FDICIA further restricted the Federal Reserve from lending to 'undercapitalized' institutions unless the institution were certified 'viable' by its federal bank supervisory agency. If a 'certified' institution to whom the Federal Reserve makes loans were subsequently to fail, with losses to the insurance fund, the Federal Reserve Board could incur a liability to the FDIC (Title I, Sec. 142).

FDICIA further limits supervisory discretion on a case-by-case basis through what has been termed 'prompt corrective action', involving the imposition of escalating constraints on undercapitalized banks (Title I, Section 131). In an elaboration of the 'troubled institution' category of FIRREA, five capitalization categories are established: 'well-capitalized', 'adequately capitalized', 'undercapitalized', 'significantly undercapitizlized', and 'critically-undercapitalized'. A determination by the relevant federal supervisory agency that a bank is in one of the lower three categories automatically triggers the requirement that it submit an acceptable capital restoration plan. 'Undercapitalized' banks failing to submit and implement an acceptable plan are subject to constraints on asset growth, non-traditional activities, transactions with affiliates, and deposit rates of interest, among others. Those 'critically undercapitalized' are subject to additional constraints and, under the law, must be closed promptly.

Despite the establishment of 'prompt corrective action', discretionary authority remains for the agencies in key areas. In defining the five categories, FDICIA specifies the use of both a leverage and a risk-based capital requirement.[3] It also specifies a minimum requirement for 'critically undercapitalized' institutions; the agencies must impose a leverage requirement of tangible equity-to-total assets of not less than 2 per cent, and not more than 65 per cent of the minimum leverage requirement established (by the agencies) for 'adequately capitalized' banks. But within these legislated limits, the federal supervisors have been given authority to develop the capital adequacy thresholds that activate supervisory constraints.[4] Even the required closing of a 'critically undercapitalized' bank, is subject to agency-determined exceptions; it need not be closed if the bank's federal supervisor and the FDIC jointly determine that it has an acceptable capital restoration plan and is viable.

It was recently noted that '...the regulators have opted for a narrow definition of "undercapitalized" that sticks less than 5% of the industry with the unwanted label'. Andrew Hove, Chairman of the FDIC, was reported to have acknowledged that 'We could have set the capital levels a lot higher' (Rehm, *American Banker*, 2 December 1992).

The establishment of rules for dealing with weak banks can be seen as an effort to encourage higher levels of capital and provide a basis for further deregulation. Risk-adjusted deposit insurance premiums and risk-adjusted capital requirements (both required by FDICIA) are aimed at reducing incentives for excessive risk-taking emanating from government support through deposit insurance, forbearance, and 'too-big-to-fail' policies. Closure rules run parallel by precluding, for the most part, bank operations with little or no capital (at least on a book basis). If risk-adjustment and closure rules can effectively neutralize undesirable incentives and, thereby, limit FDIC and taxpayer exposure, regulatory restrictions on bank activities should not be needed to curb excessive risk-taking. With Federal support for large banking organizations curtailed by restrictions on 'too-big-to-fail,' the growth of large organizations through interstate branching and merger should not derive from unfair advantages in capital markets or further expose the insurance funds.

Whether the specific rules established by FDICIA (or any set of rules) can be effective in protecting the insurance funds and taxpayers, without jeopardizing other public policy objectives, are questions that have yet to be fully examined. Any system of rules raises the specter of a *deus ex machina* that unthinkingly closes (or keeps open) large numbers of banks on the basis of arbitrary calculations that can have little relationship to bank condition.

On close examination, however, FDICIA establishes 'rules' over 'authorities' in a illusory way. In fact, the legislation provides the authorities – that is, the federal supervisory agencies – with enormous discretion. They have been authorized to establish standards for bank management that extend into areas that had long been considered management prerogatives. They have been directed to visit and examine banks more often, and to implement legislative provisions requiring considerably more rule-making and regulation-writing. In the case of weak banks, they have been given the power to establish, for the most part, the 'rules' for activity-restrictions and closure which, presumably, may be changed if, in their discretion, it seems reasonable to do so. Even in restricting 'too-big-to-fail' policies, Congress left the door open for discretion. (The supervisors may, nevertheless, find it advantageous in dealing with bank officials to emphasize that they now have less flexibility to go easy on undercapitalized banks.)

In the venerable 'rules v. authority' debate on the conduct of monetary policy, the establishment of a 'rule' for money growth was to be through legislation that would tie the hands of the central bank, eliminate 'fine-tuning', and even permit its reorganization as a small agency, largely composed of technicians. FDICIA, on the other hand, calls for more, not less agency activity and 'fine-tuning'. Larger, not smaller, agencies, are a result. In mid-1992, the Comptroller announced that to meet the more frequent bank examination requirements of the Act, he would soon hire 300 additional bank examiners, and another 300 in 1993 (Comptroller of the Currency, 27 May 1992). In fact, all the federal agencies have substantially expanded their staffs over the past year and project further substantial increases in 1993 (Rehm, *American Banker*, 2 December 1992).

FIRREA and FDICIA reflect well-established trends and tendencies in banking legislation, including the expansion of supervisory authority to meet bank failure problems and the extension of federal supervision to state banks. 'Prompt corrective action' is also consistent with the historic tendency to expand supervision. The operational questions raised concern the capacity of supervisors to 'co-manage' as opposed to monitor and 'nurse' sick banks; and the capacity of a more constrained bank management to raise capital and sustain traditional lending functions. The strategic questions concern a seeming failure to recognize the inherent limitations of supervision.[5]

7.3 LIMITATIONS

The reform of supervision in recent legislation reflects the failures of supervision over the last decade. It continues to focus on misguided, inept and dishonest bank management as the principal cause of bank failure. It does not address the inherent deficiencies in the supervisory process that have contributed to the historical record of repeated failure.

7.3.1 Monetary Policy and Exogenous Shock[6]

It has long been understood that banks are vulnerable to macro-economic disruption. It is somewhat less widely recognized that banks may also be vulnerable to monetary policy designed to ameliorate disruptions. The Federal Reserve appears to have been cognizant of the latter from the early 1920s when it began to use open market operations as a tool of policy.

7.3.1.1 Federal Reserve Policy

When the Federal Reserve was established, the discount window was much more actively used than it is currently. Discounts and advances as a proportion of Federal Reserve credit reached a peak of 82 per cent in 1921; in 1929 they were still over 60 per cent. During the 1920s, the proportion of member banks borrowing from the Reserve Banks was consistently around 60 per cent (Shull, 1971, pp. 36–8).

The Federal Reserve's view of supervision reflected its position as a creditor, and also its understanding that the credit it extended was intended, by Congress, to serve the 'needs of trade'; that is, to provide commercial banks with funds that would be extended to business in the form of short-term credit for current operations. The Reserve Banks, therefore, needed to '...be acquainted with the loan policies and credit extensions of their member banks...' (Federal Reserve Board, 1923, p. 35).

In the early 1920s, monetary policy was transformed from the provision of credit at the discount window, on the demand of banks having short-term commercial paper eligible for discount, to recurrent pressure on bank reserves implemented through open-market operations. This transformation required new constraints on borrowing at the discount window. A set of non-price rationing rules, limiting use of the discount window to short-term borrowing for unanticipated outflows of funds, were developed; banks were encouraged to be 'reluctant to borrow', that is, the Federal Reserve 'turned to "gadgets" and conventions...without any overt alteration of the law' (Keynes, 1930, pp. 239–40).[7]

The reformulation of monetary policy, of necessity involved a reevaluation of supervision. Like other bank supervisors, the Federal Reserve might focus on the integrity and competence of bank management, the adequacy of bank capital in light of past experience, and the bank's current condition. But it would also have to consider whether banks had the capacity to meet predictable needs for funds without reliance on the window, and other unexpected needs for funds with only short-term reliance on the window. If not, do they have sufficient capital to absorb the losses they might incur as the result of monetary restraint.

The compelling need to supervise with these questions in mind could be traced to recognition of a potential bind in exerting monetary restraint. If many banks or important banks did not have the capacity to tolerate the pressure imposed, the Federal Reserve would have the choice of maintaining restraint and permitting banks to fail, or easing restraint and abandoning the objectives of the policy it had adopted, for example, price stability.

The problem was addressed through a supervisory policy that served as a companion to its new discount policy. The lessened availability of discount credit to meet reserve drains, some at least imposed by monetary restraint, implied that banks would have to maintain higher levels of liquidity and/or capital to meet the new needs. The new supervisory policy was, in part, implemented through discount window surveillance where, with about 60 per cent of member banks typically indebted, discount officials could influence bank behavior.[8]

Elements of the Federal Reserve's distinctive supervisory policy over the past 40 years can be seen in its approach to capital adequacy. An 'adjusted risk asset' approach was originally adopted by the Federal Reserve Bank of New York in 1952. In 1956 a liquidity test was added that required more capital from banks which were less liquid (Crosse, 1962, pp. 173 ff.). The Federal Reserve Board amended its capital adequacy approach in 1972 to consider the experience of banks in the 1969–70 period of disintermediation (Vojta, 1973, p. 11; see Appendix 2 for the revised ABC form developed by the Federal Reserve Board). The Federal Reserve Board's approach has sometimes been contrasted with that of the Comptroller of the Currency who de-emphasized 'ratio analysis' in favor of general guidelines '...appropriate for banks operating in normal conditions' (Vojta, 1973, p. 11).

In general terms, the policy problem confronting the Federal Reserve, and distinguishing its supervisory efforts from that of other supervisory agencies, can be briefly described as follows: (1) the condition of banks will be affected by unexpectedly intense monetary restraint and/or other exogenous shocks; (2) the degree of restraint that can be imposed by monetary policy *may* be affected by worsened conditions of banks developing out of the surprise or shocks; and (3) if policy is eased because the condition of banks worsens, the inflation rate will rise; but if pressure is sustained, the bank failure rate will rise.

7.3.1.2 Surprise and Shock

It seems likely that bank managements are now well aware of the problems created by alterations in Federal Reserve policy, and have adjusted their operations accordingly, at least within the limits of their experience. Nevertheless, unanticipated changes, whether emanating from sudden and drastic shifts in monetary policy (monetary surprise) or from exogenous shocks to bank-sensitive sectors and markets, may still produce an escalation of pressure to which banks are unable to adjust quickly.

The onset of a shock may be due to the inability of one or more large banks to replace volatile liabilities (for example, Continental Illinois, 1984; Bank of New England, 1990), with many other banks excessively exposed. A similar shock may be generated by severe monetary restraint to control inflation that abruptly elevates market rates of interest and pushes banks into insolvency as in 1979–82. The imposition of severe monetary restraint in the early 1980s, and the rise in bank failure rates during the last decade has indicated just how vulnerable banks can be.

'Shocks', such as defaults by major classes of borrowers, become increasingly likely during long periods of prosperity without crises (Minsky, 1957, pp. 181–7; Minsky, 1971, pp. 114–7; Guttentag and Herring, 1986, pp. 1–5; 1988, p. 607). During such periods, which may appear to be characterized by successful monetary policy, the banking system is likely to become increasingly 'fragile', with institutions 'excessively exposed' to insolvency (Minsky, 1971; Guttentag and Herring, 1986).[9] And ultimately, monetary policy will be constrained by the fragility of the system.

Shocks have been defined as low probability hazards carrying high potential costs (Guttentag and Herring, 1986, pp. 2, 32–3). It has been observed that 'the continuing potential for credit crunches has usually been underestimated...' And at the same time, it is not possible to know before the event when or how hard it is going to hit (Kaufman, 1991).

Bank management, then, will have no basis on which to calculate probabilities; the events, in Davidson's terms, do not emerge from an ergotic process (Davidson, 1988, pp. 332–3; Davidson, 1991). Even in the case where management took an 'outside observer's' view and attached a 'prudent' probability to such possibilities, competition could drive the institution from the market. In these circumstances, rational expectation and efficient market axioms do not apply.[10]

The development of bank vulnerability has also been viewed as a 'perceptual problem'. There is evidence in the psychological literature to suggest that when a probability reaches some critically low level, it is treated as if it were zero (Guttentag and Herring, 1986, pp. 3–4).

During a long period of expansion, then, managements' assessments of the probability of 'shocks' tends to be biased downward. As a result, bankers will take greater risks than an objective assessment, if such were possible, would warrant. In the late 1960s, Minsky referred to this phenomena as 'the economics of euphoria', and, more recently, Guttentag and Herring have labeled it 'disaster myopia' (Minsky, 1971, pp. 100–3; Guttentag and Herring, 1986, pp. 3–4). When vision is cleared by events, many banks are likely to be threatened with insolvency. There is evidence that with less capital, excessive risk-taking will be further encouraged and that the rate of insolvency is likely to rise (Barth, Bartholomew and Labich, 1990; Golbe and Shull, 1990).

7.3.1.3 Policy Implications

The problem outlined above implies that bank supervisors need to be aware of developing fragility; and, in particular, to the growing vulnerability of banks to both monetary surprise and other shocks during periods of expansion. It is necessary that they separate themselves from what may seem the 'reasonable' risk evaluations of bank management in developing supervisory policy. The monetary authority needs a capacity to establish minimum standards for bank condition, through supervision, in accordance with the effects of likely, and sometimes abrupt, changes in monetary policy. It also needs a continuous stream of current information on the condition of banks in order to ascertain the likely effects of its policies.

In contrast, traditional supervision has not focused on identifying vulnerable or fragile banks and leaning against their fragility (Minsky, 1975; Guttentag and Herring, 1988, p. 602). There are reasons why bank supervisors might have difficulty doing so. First, they too may believe it rational to ignore potential hazards of low probability. Supervisors and bankers live in the same emotional climate. Second, supervisory efforts to strengthen weak banks and sustain healthy ones focus on earnings from which most new bank capital has come. Restraining weak, much less seemingly healthy, banks in a vigorously growing economy, and in the face of unrestrained competitors, conflicts with traditional supervisory aims to support bank earnings and not to interfere with successful bank management. There is some evidence that supervisory myopia has been a problem (Guttentag and Herring, 1986, p. 33; Petersen, 1977, pp. 27–8).

Political difficulties are also created for a supervisory agency that is sensitive to growing system fragility during long periods of prosperity. An agency that 'leans against' the developing institutional, operational and perceptual changes that impair the system and, in particular, what it views as myopic risk-taking, places itself in the way of banks and others, that literally do not see the reasons for supervisory foot-dragging. The Federal Reserve has found itself in this position from time to time and has been subjected to severe criticism. It has been accused, for example, of deferring desirable 'innovative' regulatory action to avoid controversy that could generate political opposition to its 'independence' (C. Golembe as quoted in Horvitz, 1983, p. 259); and of using its regulatory authority in a way that 'offends one's sense of fair play and equal regulatory treatment under the law' (Petersen, 1977, p. 36). Bank associations have sought to eliminate the Federal Reserve entirely from a supervisory role (*Federal Reserve Bulletin*, 1984, p. 551).[11]

In fact, in a boom characterized by 'euphoria' and 'disaster myopia', the strength of the criticism may be a measure of a supervisory agency's value as a supervisor. Despite strong opposition by banking associations and others, recent government studies, with the *Treasury Report* being the latest, have reserved a supervisory role for the Federal Reserve. In 1984, the Task Group headed by then Vice President Bush concluded '...that the FRB should maintain...supervisory and regulatory authority to back up its responsibilities as the central bank' (*Blueprint for Reform*, p. 48). The conclusion is not unreasonable; but, as discussed below, it is inadequate.

Recent legislation and supervisory reform has, as noted, taken some steps toward dealing with bank vulnerability, as opposed simply to existing weakness. Risk-adjusted capital standards, as they have developed, are, however, seriously deficient. They apply relatively arbitrary weights to individual assets independently of their contribution to risk in each bank's portfolios. They apply to book capital which may differ significantly from capital based on market values, and they do not confront the problem of myopia in any systematic way. Risk-adjusted deposit insurance premiums and interest-rate risk evaluations are at a very early stage and have yet to be tested.

While it is not possible to anticipate a particular surprise or shock, more can be done in preparation. It is possible to create accounting systems that reveal bank exposure to non-specific events of varying impact that would also inform supervisors and give them some leverage in confronting bank managements (Minsky, 1971, pp. 124–9; Minsky, 1975; Guttentag and Herring, 1988). It should also be possible to develop more complex models, with regional as well as national banking sectors, and to simulate economic and financial shocks.

The risk evaluation approaches currently underway in the supervisory agencies are limited by the absence of an explicit model of the relationship between the banking firm, financial markets, real markets and monetary policy. It is noteworthy that even the Federal Reserve's elaborate MPS model does not include an explicit banking sector. In the formal analysis and forecasting framework of the Board of Governors, the interactions between monetary policy and bank condition are ignored.

7.3.2 The Fragmented Regulatory System

The continued existence of multiple regulatory agencies has precluded uniformity, made planning nearly impossible and diminished accountability. The system has repeatedly been perceived as deficient. Unification of federal bank supervision was proposed in Congress as early as 1919, again in the 1930s, and on numerous occasions subsequently (Robertson, 1966, p. 686).[12] Among other things, the system involves overlap and duplication that is excessively costly and imposes differential costs on competing depository institutions (*Blueprint for Reform*, 1984, p. 29, note 16; Huston, 1985; Hackley, 1969). By the end of the 1970s there was both anecdotal and empirical support for many of its shortcomings (Shull 1992; Hackley, 1969; Robertson, 1966). Case studies have indicated conflicts among different regulators with overlapping authority (Shull, 1980; Huston, 1985).[13]

In the late 1970s, the Federal Financial Institution Examination Council (FFIEC), composed of the heads of the five principal federal banking agencies and a small staff, was commissioned to institute uniform standards and to coordinate the work of the five federal agencies. There has yet to be a full evaluation of the FFIEC.[14] But without authority to impose negotiated recommendations, this organization cannot be viewed as a reasonable substitute for consolidation.

Events of the last decade have further exacerbated the problems. Differentially permissive federal and state regulation of S&Ls provides a morbid illustration of destructive regulatory competition and differential cost problems. With excessively lax S&L regulation in the early 1980s some commercial banks opted to become S&Ls (Isaac, 1984, pp. 1667–8). Forbearance for insolvent thrifts, in one form or another, and the relatively high rates they were willing to pay for deposits, injured not only solvent thrifts but also commercial banks (Brumbaugh, 1988, pp. 70 ff.).

With an intensification of competition, differential regulatory costs, of necessity, assume an increasing importance. A higher probability of bank failure makes confusion generated by overlaps less acceptable. Timely supervisory policies to assist bank adaptation to rapidly changing financial markets, unburdened by agency conflicts, becomes increasingly important and difficult to achieve. Global banking and international regulatory agency deliberations, for example, to establish uniform capital standards, place new demands on agency coordination.

The principal arguments in favor of a continuation of the fragmented system has been that it promotes regulatory innovation, in particular, deregulation, and that it affords a check against excessive concentration of regulatory power (Scott, 1977). Events have made these arguments less important in recent years. The value of agency competition was higher when there were more anticompetitive regulations to erode. With interest-rate restrictions on deposits eliminated, and branch banking and activity restrictions in process of elimination, the benefits of further erosion are, for the time being at least, dubious. Moreover, it is now clear that the check afforded by multiple agencies are just one of several types, including litigation and Congressional oversight, that constrain each regulatory agency. For example, the transfer of authority from the Federal Home Loan Bank Board, an independent agency with exclusive jurisdiction over S&Ls, to the OTS in the Treasury Department was justified on the basis of evidence that the Board had been excessively 'checked' by industry and Congressional pressure, and needed to be 'insulated' (Greenspan, 1989, p. 6).

The system that now exists tends, itself, to undermine the efficacy of supervision. First, it has induced competing institutions to seek out the most attractive regulatory regime, permitted escape from supervisory restraints imposed on individual institutions and, thereby, eroded constraints in general (Burns, 1974; Shull, 1980). In addition, it has made it difficult, if not impossible, to achieve certain policy objectives that require cooperation. As noted by Vice President Bush's 1984 Task Group, the banking agencies have difficulties in 'shared responsibilities' and '...problems of interagency coordination may...(undermine) confidence in the financial system' (*Blueprint for Reform*, 1984, p. 31).

Examples of one agency's policy being frustrated by other agencies are readily available. In the 1960s, the Comptroller of the Currency adopted a distinctive chartering, acquisition and new powers policy; it was frustrated, in part, by agency conflict. In the 1970s, the Federal Reserve Board adopted a policy aimed at restoring competition in local market areas by restricting market-extension acquisitions; it was frustrated, in part, by other agencies also having merger and acquisition authority, but with different views on competition (Shull, 1975, p. 110). Beginning in 1980, nonbanking firms found it possible to establish 'nonbank banks' by exploiting a 'loophole' in the Bank Holding Company Act that the Comptroller, but not the Federal Reserve, was willing to accommodate. It required roughly seven years of Congressional deliberations before further nonbank bank acquisitions were prohibited by the Competitive Equality Banking Act of 1987. Thus, major changes in banking structure have also resulted from divided authority and agency conflict.

The fragmented system may, moreover, result in some important issues not being addressed at all. The deficiencies of the 'too-big-to-fail' policies of the Federal Reserve and FDIC are now reasonably clear. But because of divided merger and acquisition authority, no one agency has been in a position to prevent new banks from becoming 'too-big-to-fail'. In fact, no agency has ever proposed to incorporate this consideration into its merger and acquisition standards. As noted, a proper focus on the macro problems confronting banks suggests the need to develop analyses that increases supervisory awareness of institutional vulnerabilities. Of the agencies, only the Federal Reserve appears to be clearly aware of the problem (*Federal Reserve Bulletin*, 1984). But none have dealt with it effectively.

As a practical matter, we should expect the agencies to focus on what can be accomplished and generally disregard what is beyond their capacity. In the absence of unification, capacity is limited and important issues fall through the cracks.

At the practical level, the effects of agency differences can spill over from one group of banks to another. A recent staff report of the House Banking Committee contended that national banks had imposed a disproportionate drain on the federal deposit insurance fund because of supervisory deficiencies of the Comptroller of the Currency (Staff Report, 1991).[15] Other banks would be affected even if their condition and their supervisors were superior.

Under the dual banking system, banks have been able to choose the most attractive (least costly) supervisory domain. Even if there were no overlaps, with each supervisory agency confined to a separate depository institutions, a competition among supervisors to attract banks would exist.

Arthur Burns believed that such competition promoted laxity, that is, a relaxation of supervisory restrictions to attract 'constituents' (Burns, 1975).

The fragmented system, moreover, attacks its own effectiveness and legitimacy. Agency competition, if not agency differences alone, imply that supervision is arbitrary; and supervisors can, therefore, be viewed as capricious in insisting on any particular set of rules. Evading supervision and regulation takes on the character of an activity for which the social consequences are trivial.

Some of the problems of the fragmented system may be attenuated by the growing uniformity of Federal regulation, limitation on supervisory discretion, and the extension of the new rules to state banks. But to the extent this development is effective, it leaves the existing agencies as artifacts. And it does not integrate supervision and monetary policy.

7.3.3 Insider Abuse and Criminal Misconduct: Opportunism

In recent years, there has been a substantial increase in insider abuse and criminal misconduct in banking.[16] The growth is evidenced in Congressional reports, written orders by regulatory authorities, criminal referrals, civil suits, and the expansion of bank examination staffs and costs (*Fraud in America's Insured Depository Institutions*, 1991; Seidman, 1990; *Federal Response to Criminal Misconduct*, 1984). Over the last decade, the number of criminal referrals to the Justice Department by the supervisory agencies have risen dramatically. In 1986, the Justice Department notified all US attorneys that fraud in the banking industry was a national priority. The number of failed financial institutions with ongoing FBI investigations have increased each year since 1986 (*Effectiveness of Law Enforcement Against Financial Crime*, 1990, pp. 397–8, 444). The legislative response has been to establish more extensive supervision and harsher penalties.

Widespread insider abuse and criminal misconduct constitutes a substantial burden on supervision. Like any form of appraisal, supervision is simpler when those being appraised recognize the legitimacy of the evaluation, believe it is of benefit to them, view themselves as participants with common interests, and generally govern their institutions with an attitude of 'stewardship'.[17] It is more difficult when those being appraised are intent on distortion and obfuscation. There has, from time to time, been a sense of stewardship among bankers that has been encouraged by supervisors.[18] The upsurge in misconduct can be viewed as an institutional failure.

There has been no definitive study of the causes for an increase in misconduct in banking. But some plausible ones may be suggested within a 'contractual' framework.

Bank regulation may be viewed as a 'contract.' The government-bank relationship is permeated by mutuality. Depository institutions receive the 'privilege' of offering liabilities payable on demand that serve as 'money' and also government support of various types. The government obtains a stable supply of banking services for itself and for other politically influential groups. The underlying basis for the exchange has historically involved both a shift in risk from banks to the government (taxpayers), and government efforts to control its exposure.

This continuing exchange suggests the existence of a contract that can be characterized as: (1) long-term, (2) incomplete, and (3) with important implicit elements (Goldberg, 1976, pp. 427–9; Williamson 1985, Ch. 2). The long-term nature of the banking contract is reflected in charters of indefinite duration; it is incomplete in the sense that neither law nor regulation can spell out precisely how banks and regulators will behave in all possible circumstances. The implicit elements include informal 'understandings' about behavior, and particularly, but not exclusively, in the face of unspecified contingencies (such as exogenous shock) that affect the net benefits of both parties. The relationship that supports such cooperation can be traced to the first chartered banks in the US that were organized on the Bank of England model in the seventeenth century. As noted above, they were considered 'private establishments employed as public agents'.

Long-term contracts with implicit elements invariably create concerns among parties about each other's good faith performance. In banking, the complexity of the transactions and the potential for false reporting creates a particular problem. Hiding information, distorting and lying, to say nothing of stealing, cheating and embezzling, needs to be controlled by a proper structuring of incentives and/or in other ways. This type of behavior has been referred to as 'profit seeking with guile', and termed 'opportunism'. It has been contrasted with simple profit maximization, within the established rules, and with stewardship (Williamson, 1985, pp. 47–9; and 1975, p. 26).[19]

Concerns about deceit and guile are reflected in vague bank regulatory requirements such as 'meeting fiduciary duties' and 'protecting safety and soundness'. Such terms are not subject, *ex ante*, to precise definition; and even *ex post* are frequently difficult to evaluate. They support, however, a necessary understanding that bankers will curb opportunistic behavior; and they do give regulatory agencies a legal basis for proceeding against banks that are perceived in violation. Experience suggests that the government and supervisory agencies are also expected to act in good faith in adjusting laws and regulations to changing circumstances that create unexpected difficulties for banks, and to honor its informal pledges of *ad hoc* support.

The increase in misconduct that has developed has paralleled the deterioration of the old regulatory arrangement that had been established in the 1930s. The changes over the period of 'deregulation' placed enormous pressures on banks, as reflected in the S&L debacle, the high rate of commercial bank failure and the low levels of profits in recent years.

The good faith of the government may be questioned, as it was in the early 1980s when the Federal Reserve's anti-inflation policy produced interest rate levels and volatility that, for S&Ls, created a 'financial holocaust' (Gray, 1984, p. 1598).[20] Risk-taking incentives emanating from Federal deposit insurance and other elements of the safety net have existed since their inception. But with a reduction in charter values resulting from an intensification of competition, a counterweight appears to have been removed (Keeley, 1990). In these circumstances, stewardship may simply be untenable.

The transition to opportunism can be viewed as including increased incentives and lowered costs. In the market environment that existed in the 1980s, the potential gains from misreporting, distortion, violating restrictions, and so forth, appear to have been enormous compared to the potential gains from abiding by the rules. Opportunistic activities, of course, involve risks, and are sometimes equated to risk-taking within the 'rules'. But the identification is not complete, either conceptually or with regard to the effect on the institutions involved.[21] Conventional risk-taking is associated with higher expected profits for the institution and might or might not be associated with an increased probability of insolvency. Misconduct would always be associated with lower expected (true) profits for the institution and an increased probability of insolvency. For example, 'lending' excessive amounts to associates on the basis of inflated collateral values would have the effect of producing bad loans, likely to be hidden on financial statements, and, thereby reduce expected profits and capital. The institution's risk may also be increased indirectly by reducing asset diversification, without any increased profit expectation.

A principal difference between risk-taking within and outside the rules, then, relates to the expected future of the institution. The conventional risk-taker knows that there is a chance that the institution will fail; but also that there is a chance it will succeed and prosper. The abusive risk-taker knows that, in the long-run, the institution has no chance at all.[22]

While restraints on opportunistic behavior may have weakened with the disorganization of the old regulatory arrangements, other factors appear simultaneously to have made opportunism 'safer', that is, the expected cost of discovery lower. First, the demand on supervisory resources has been increasing as the result of increased numbers of problem banks, bank failures, and mergers (Comptroller General of the US, 1984, p. 74). In addition, much of the deregulation that has occurred in recent years has been conditional. From a supervisory point of view 'just say no' is less demanding than 'yes on condition'. The latter requires far more careful monitoring. Despite growth in resources, supervision may, at any point in time, be insufficient. Finally, while the capacity for misreporting and distortion has always been great in banking, growth in the complexity of markets, instruments and banking institutions has probably make it easier to escape detection.

Opportunism among bankers tends to compromise supervision. Supervisors become torn between their obligations to support bank profitability and to prevent dubious practices which, *ex ante*, are not obviously abusive, and which seem to contribute to profitability. In periods of prosperity, they may be reluctant to substitute their judgement for that of bank management, and reluctant to restrict the banks they supervise when their competitors, supervised by others, are not restricted. In times of bank distress, difficulties arise for the same underlying reason. Moreover, when supervisors are confronted with banks at or near insolvency, they become understandably anxious to find buyers who will inject new capital. The S&L experience of the 1980's suggests that standards for evaluating the character of new owners can suffer in the anxiety to find investors.

Recent legislation, like FIRREA and FDICIA, have attempted to make the expected cost of discovery much greater. They may also be steps in the process of establishing a new regulatory contract. But the process is not yet complete. It remains to be seen just what effect more supervision and harsher penalties have in and of themselves.

7.4 COMPETENCE

Given the problems of supervision and its track record, it is reasonable to ask whether supervisors are sufficiently competent. This question needs to be considered on two levels. First, are supervisors competent to do what they have traditionally been assigned to do; that is, to appraise the condition of banks at a point in time, identify weak institutions and institute corrections as needed. Second, even if they are, can they prevent system-wide periodic deterioration in safety and soundness of the banks they supervise.

There is evidence to suggest that supervisors have been reasonably successful in identifying weak institutions, but less successful in correcting their problems (Comptroller General of the US, 1977, Ch. 4). Oversight by Congressional banking committees has resulted in severe criticism from time to time, for example, in the cases of the Continental Bank insolvency, failure of the United American Bank (and other banks controlled by Jake Butcher), and more recently in the case of the Bank of New England. However, criticism has typically been directed toward sluggishness in supervisory reaction after weaknesses have been uncovered.

There is reason to believe that, as a general matter, supervisors, with some notable exceptions, would be competent to detect trouble as it develops. Those that head the principal agencies are well educated in business and, some, in law. They have had successful careers as bankers, in bank examinations or the legal departments of the regulatory agencies. Their staffs have similar backgrounds, for the most part with less experience. Training at the regulatory agencies appears to have become reasonably sophisticated in the areas of financial markets and financial analysis.

Failure to effectively implement remedies is evidenced by a long list of floundering institutions that have ultimately failed. Over the past decade, troubled banks have imposed enormous costs on the insurance funds. Supervision has been condemned for yielding to political and industry pressure. Supervisors have been modeled as subordinating the public interest to their own career interests. It has been Congressional distrust of supervision, based on recent experience, that has resulted in constraints on supervisory discretion and the establishment of tripwires requiring intervention.

Whether or not the curtailment of supervisory discretion and the substitution of rules will improve supervisory performance remains to be seen. If the only aim of supervision was protection of the insurance funds, the new rules, or some variant, might serve well. But traditional supervision is also designed to conserve banks as going concerns and it is not clear that the current approach will facilitate this aim.

Supervisory competence can be questioned at another level. Even if supervisors are competent in identifying weak institutions, and the new rules for intervention are successful in protecting the deposit insurance funds, problems will remain. Supervisors are not competent, at present, to resist the pressures toward increasing fragility during periods of expansion. The institutional failures of the current system would strain the most competent agency in developing and implementing appropriate policies. The new rules could, moreover, impose draconian measures in a financial crisis.

Supervisors have not dealt effectively with these problems in the past, and there is nothing in the recent legislation that suggests they will come to grips with them in the future. It is reasonable to infer that they cannot.

7.5 POLICY

The problems faced by supervision are interrelated and reinforcing. These include an economic problem involving monetary surprises and exogenous shocks. The fragmentation of regulatory system makes the development and implementation of reasonable polices almost impossible. An increase in opportunistic behavior has made effective supervision considerably more difficult. The supervisory establishment does not appear capable of dealing with the economic and institutional problems that tend to undermine its best efforts.

Given the proper circumstances, it might be possible to deal with the economic problem. But it is far more difficult to do so when authority is divided and opportunism drains substantial resources. Any solution to the difficulties has to begin with unification of the regulatory structure. It is not possible to develop and implement appropriate policies with numerous quasi-independent supervisory agencies for competitive depository institutions. It is certainly more difficult to 'lean against fragility' when other supervisory agencies are not. This implies that there is a need to work toward coordination and unification of policies. It is necessary, moreover, to integrate supervision more fully with monetary policy. As discussed, the impact of monetary policy on the condition of banks is such that it makes no sense to view supervision and central banking as separate functions. Monetary policy as it has been conducted and is likely to be implemented in the future, requires the authority to evaluate and influence the condition of commercial banks. Consolidation within the Federal Reserve, or within a new agency that incorporates the monetary authority, is needed.

A second step is a fuller integration of supervision with economic analysis that goes beyond early warning to potential vulnerabilities. Efforts toward this end seem to be underway. Integration would facilitate these efforts and produce the kinds of information that arm supervisors to 'lean against fragility'.

A third step is to raise the level of qualification and expectation for the top supervisory officials. With expanded goals, supervision should command leadership of the first rank, no less qualified in economic and financial market analysis than Federal Reserve Board chairmen.

Notwithstanding the qualities that some high-level supervisors bring to the job, they have been insufficient to deal with the problems supervision must deal with if it is to be successful. The integration of central banking and supervision would help produce this result.

To the extent possible, it is necessary to reestablish a reasonable regulatory contract. It would be of considerable help if stewardship behavior could be promoted. What can be done, however, in a relatively deregulated, competitive and rapidly changing banking system is unclear.

7.6 CONCLUSIONS

Supervision has repeatedly failed in preventing recurrent episodes of systemic deterioration in bank safety and soundness. The solution, repeatedly endorsed by Congress, with the support of supervisors, has been to augment supervision and improve the quality of bank management. Because periods of systemic fragility typically occur after long intervals of seeming successful bank operations, each episode appears to occur independently of the ones that preceded it.

We are now in a period of supervisory augmentation that is focusing on what happened during the last decade. This focus is, at best, distorted because it does not consider why 'improved supervision' has repeatedly failed.

As in most cases of repeated failure, there exist systemic problems that produce inherent limitations. For supervision, the problems include monetary surprises and exogenous shocks, the effects of which seems only dimly appreciated. The fragmentation of regulatory system undermines the development of reasonable polices. And, in recent years, an upsurge in opportunistic behavior has confused supervisory efforts and drained resources. Supervisors appear competent to uncover weak banks, but not to deal with their inherent limitations.

To correct the difficulties, it would first be necessary to unify the regulatory agencies and integrate them with monetary policy, either in the Federal Reserve or in a new institution that included monetary policy authority. Such a consolidation would almost invariably produce a research initiative to develop a better understanding of the interrelationship between macro-economic policy, economic and financial markets and the condition of banks. This elevation of supervision, as a component, of banking policy, implies an upgrading of top officials whose background and experience should be, at a minimum, on par with what is currently expected of Federal Reserve Board chairmen. And this implies a better chance of dealing successfully with the enormous difficulties that supervision confronts.

Notes

1. The author wishes to acknowledge the helpful comments of Hyman Minsky of the Jerome Levy Economic Institute of Bard College, Joe Cleaver of the Federal Financial Institution Examination Council, and Gerald Hanweck of George Mason University.
2. Unless otherwise specified, commercial banks, savings associations, including S&Ls and savings banks, credit unions, all providing transactions deposits and subject to more or less similar regulation and supervision, are referred to as 'banks' throughout this paper. Holding companies that control these institutions, and are similarly regulated and supervised, are, in general, not distinguished.
3. The 'leverage' requirement refers to the ratio of tangible equity capital-to-total assets. Tangible capital excludes intangibles, principally 'goodwill'; equity capital is the principal component of what has been termed 'Tier 1' (or 'core') capital and distinguished from 'supplementary capital', including subordinated debt, loan loss allowances and preferred stock ('Tier 2'). The risk-based capital requirement currently derives from a weighing of the credit risk in specific types of assets on bank balance sheets and in off-balance sheet items, such as standby letters of credit. FDICIA, however, requires the Federal supervisory agencies to augment their risk-based capital computations by developing interest rate risk, 'concentration' risk and 'non-traditional activity' risk components (Title III, Sec. 305). Advanced notice of changes, subject to comment, was issued in July, 1992 (Federal Reserve Board, 'Press Release', 30 July 1992). Final regulations are to go into effect in mid-1993.
4. The final rules, including the definitions developed by the federal supervisory agencies, were issued in September 1992 and went into effect on 19 December 1992.
5. While not discussed here, it is worth noting that limitations of the supervisory process would also support proposals to confine the Federal 'safety net' to 'minimal banks', in which safety is assured by asset restrictions (Litan, 1987, Ch. 5 and Pierce, 1991, Ch. 5).
6. This section is adapted from Hanweck and Shull, 1992 which provides a review of the literature and empirical tests of hypotheses that monetary surprise and exogenous shock substantially affect the condition of banks.
7. There is an irony in the Federal Reserve's encouraging banks to be reluctant to borrow that corroborates Keynes' perception of what the Federal Reserve was doing. An important aim of the Federal Reserve Act of 1913 had been to promote the secondary market for commercial paper and *to overcome* the reluctance of banks to borrow. In establishing the discount window, few restrictions, other than those required to define 'commercial paper', were initially imposed by the Act and by the Federal Reserve (Hackley, 1973, Chs. 2, 3).

8. In the aftermath of the great depression, the discount window became far less important to banks as a source of reserves than in the 1920s. In the 1950s, the development of alternative sources of short-term funds, first through the federal funds market, and associated with the decline in bank holdings of government debt, made supervision through the window less effective. These developments did not, however, change the need for a supervisory policy coordinated with monetary management.
9. Hyman Minsky recognized such institutional changes early. 'If during a long prosperity, monetary policy is used to restrain inflation, a number of...velocity-increasing and liquidity-decreasing money-market innovations will take place...these compounded changes will result in an inherently unstable money market so that a slight reversal of prosperity can trigger a financial crisis' (Minsky, 1957, p. 184). Examples of excessive exposure from the 1960s to the 1980s are readily available (Minsky, 1986, pp. 51 ff; Guttentag and Herring, 1986, pp. 16 ff.).
10. This is not to suggest that policy will have no effect if changes are anticipated. There is evidence that the Federal Reserve's relief of seasonal pressure on banks in the 1920s, by definition an anticipated pressure, had a significant effect in reducing the frequency and severity of the banking crises that had plagued the economy in the late nineteenth and early twentieth centuries (Miron, 1986).
11. Such efforts have been supported by some who suggest that monetary policy can be executed without financial regulation. But such analyses view the Federal Reserve's supervisory needs as emerging from an unnecessary role as a creditor at the discount window (Goodfriend and King, 1988), or from informational requirements that can be satisfied by other agencies (Benston, 1983). In fact, as discussed above, the Federal Reserve's distinctive supervisory role emerged from its use of open-market operations and countercyclical policy, not from discount window lending. Further, the information obtained in the course of supervision is needed not only to inform monetary policy, but also as the basis for regulatory revision.
12. For reviews of past proposals see US Treasury Department, 1991, pp. IX-6 to IX-8 (*Treasury Report*); *Blueprint for Reform: Report of the Task Group on Regulation of Financial Services*, 1984, pp. 32–3 (*Bush Report*); and Horvitz, 1982, pp. 44–5.
13. A recent review of the arguments on both sides of the issue is provided in Shull, 1992.
14. A GAO study in 1984 was critical of its performance (Comptroller General of the US, 1984). For a history of the FFIEC from an insider's point of view, see Lawrence, 1992.
15. The House Banking Committee's Staff Report is highly critical of OCC supervision. The Comptroller of the Currency disputed the findings of the Staff Report, but simultaneously announced the expected hiring of 300 new examiners over the next two years (Clarke, 1991).
16. The term 'insider abuse' refers to a wide range of 'misconduct' by officers, directors and other insiders of depository institutions for purposes of personal enrichment, without regard to the safety and soundness of the institution, and in violation of civil banking laws or regulations and/or criminal banking laws. Criminal misconduct ('fraud') refers to criminal acts

committed by 'insiders' for the same purpose (*Federal Response to Criminal Misconduct*, 1984, p. 2).

17. Stewardship has been defined as a involving a trust relationship in which the word of a party can be taken as its bond (Williamson, 1975, p. 26); it suggests some degree of self-denial, at least in the short-run, and obedience to rules.
18. An explicit example of an older supervisory attitude urging bankers to abide by the rules and to exercise self-restraint can be found in a 19th Century circular letter sent by Comptroller Hugh McCulloch to each national bank. 'Every banker ... (should) feel that the reputation of the system ... depends on the manner in which his particular institution is conducted ... Never be tempted by the prospect of large returns to do anything but what be properly done... "Splendid financiering" is not legitimate banking, and "splendid financiers" in banking are generally humbugs or rascals' (as quoted in Kane, 1922, pp. 29–30).
19. For any one individual, these types of behavior need not be taken as mutually exclusive over time; nor need one, the other or some blend be uniform across an entire industry.
20. Brumbaugh states: 'In October 1979, the Federal Reserve made a decision with ruinous results for the thrift industry. The Federal Reserve changed from a policy of stabilizing interest rates to ... slowing money growth rates to combat inflation. This led to ... an unprecedented increase in thrifts' costs ... with almost no corresponding increase in revenues ...' (Brumbaugh, 1988, p.15).
21. For a discussion of the conceptual differences, see Williamson, 1985, pp. 64–7.
22. Regulatory forbearance encourages conventional risk-taking by permitting bank managers to operate with little or no capital. But this does not directly encourage opportunistic risk-taking; penalties for misconduct do not increase as capital is reduced. If forbearance encourages misconduct, it does so by keeping open institutions run by opportunistic managers. Opportunism may also extend to political activity that delays closure of insolvent institutions and would, therefore, tend to promote risk-taking of both types.

References

Barth, James, Philip Bartholomew and Carol Labich (1990) 'Moral Hazard and the Thrift Crisis: An Empirical Analysis', *Consumer Finance Law, Quarterly Report* (Winter) 22–34.

Benston, George (1983) 'Federal Regulation of Banking: Analysis and Policy Recommendations', *Journal of Bank Research* (Winter).

Berle, A. A. and G. C. Means (1940) *The Modern Corporation and Private Property* (New York: Macmillan).

Brady, Nicholas (1984) *Blueprint for Reform: Report of the Task Group on Regulation of Financial Services* (July) (Washington, DC: US Government Printing Office).

Brady, Nicholas (1989) 'Statement', *Treasury News*, 6 February 1988 in Brumbaugh, R. Dan, *Thrifts Under Siege* (Cambridge, MA: Ballinger).
Bryant, Ralph C. (1984) *Eurocurrency Banking: Alarmist Concerns and Genuine Issues* (The Brookings Institution).
Brumbaugh, R. Dan (1988) *Thrifts Under Siege* (Cambridge, MA: Ballinger).
Burns, Arthur (1975) 'Maintaining the Soundness of Our Banking System', Address to the Convention of the American Bankers Association, Honolulu, Hawaii (21 October).
Clarke, Robert L., Comptroller of the Currency (1991) 'Letter' to Henry B. Gonzalez, Chairman, Committee on Banking, 'Finance and Urban Affairs, US House of Representatives (22 September).
Comptroller General of the United States (1977) 'Federal Supervision of State and National Banks' (January).
Comptroller General of the United States (1984) 'Federal Financial Institutions Examination Council Has Made Limited Progress Toward Accomplishing Its Mission', GAO (3 February).
Comptroller of the Currency (1914) *Annual Report.*
Comptroller of the Currency (1930) *Annual Report.*
Comptroller of the Currency (1988) 'Bank Failure: An Evaluation of the Factors Contributing to the Failure of National Banks' (June).
Comptroller of the Currency (1992) 'News Release', No. 92–42 (27 May).
Conference Report to Accompany *Financial Institutions Reform, Recovery and Enforcement Act of 1989*, Report 101–209, U.S. House of Representatives, 101st Congress, 1st Session, August 1989
Crosse, Howard D. (1962) *Management Policies for Commercial Banks* (Englewood Cliffs, NJ: Prentice Hall).
Davidson, Paul (1988) 'A Technical Definition of Uncertainty and the Long-run Non-neutrality of Money', *Cambridge Journal of Economics*, **12**, 329–37.
Davidson, Paul (1991) 'Is Probability theory Relevant for Uncertainty? A Post-Keynesian Perspective', *The Journal of Economic Perspectives* (Winter) 129–43.
Dunbar, Charles Francis (1904) 'Some Precedents Followed by Alexander Hamilton', *Economic Essays* (New York: Macmillan).
Federal Deposit Insurance Corporation (1983) *Deposit Insurance in a Changing Environment* (15 April) (FDIC, Washington, DC).
Federal Deposit Insurance Corporation (1984) *Annual Report.* (FDIC, Washington, DC)
Federal Reserve Board (1923) *Annual Report* (U.S. Government Printing Office, Washington, DC).
Federal Reserve Board (1992) 'Press Release' (Risk-Based Capital Standards) (30 July) (Board of Governors of the Federal Reserve System, Washington, DC).
Federal Reserve Board (1984) 'The Federal Reserve Position on Restructuring of Financial Responsibilities', *Federal Reserve Bulletin* (July) 547–57 (Board of Governors of the Federal Reserve System, Washington, DC).
Friedman, Milton and Anna J. Schwartz (1963) *A Monetary History of the United States* (Princeton, NJ: Princeton University Press).
Gephart, W. F. (1935) 'Our Commercial Banking System', *American Economic Review: Supplement* (March).

Golbe, Devra and Bernard Shull (1991) 'Risk Taking by Thrift Institutions', *Contemporary Policy Issues* (July) 105–15.

Goldberg, Victor, P. (1976) 'Regulation and Administered Contracts', *The Bell Journal of Economics* (Autumn) 426–48.

Goodfriend, M. and R. G. King (1988) *Economic Review*, Federal Reserve Bank of Richmond (May/June) 3–32.

Gray, Edwin J. (1984) 'Testimony', before the Committee on Banking, Finance and Urban Affairs, US House of Representatives (11 April).

Greenspan, Alan (1989) 'Testimony', before the Committee on Banking, Housing and Urban Affairs, US Senate (23 February).

Guttentag, Jack (1975) 'Reflections on Bank Regulatory Structure and Large Bank Failures', *Proceedings of a Conference on Bank Structure and Competition*, Federal Reserve Bank of Chicago, 136–49.

Guttentag, Jack and Richard Herring (1986) *Disaster Myopia in International Banking*, Essays in International Finance, No. 164, International Finance Section (Princeton University) (September).

Guttentag, Jack and Richard Herring (1987) 'Prudential Supervision to Manage Systemic Vulnerability', *Proceedings of a Conference on Bank Structure and Competition*, Federal Reserve Bank of Chicago, 602–33.

Guttentag, Jack and Richard Herring (1988) 'Prudential Supervision to Manage Systemic Vulnerability', *Proceedings of a Conference on Bank Structure and Competition*, Federal Reserve Bank of Chicago (May) 602–33.

Hackley, Howard (1969) 'Our Discriminating Banking System', *Virginia Law Review*, **55**, 1421.

Hackley, Howard (1973) *Lending Functions of the Federal Reserve Banks: A History*, Board of Governors of the Federal Reserve System (May).

Hammond, Bray (1957) *Banks and Politics in America* (Princeton, NJ: Princeton University Press).

Hanweck, Gerald and Bernard Shull (1991) 'Monetary Policy and the Condition of Banks', unpublished paper.

Harvard Law Review (1920) (March) 718–21.

Horvitz, Paul M. (1983) 'Reorganization of the Financial Regulatory Agencies', *Journal of Bank Research* (Winter).

Horvitz, Paul M. (1982) 'Consolidation of the Regulatory Agency Structure: Has the Time for It Come', *Economic Review*, Federal Reserve Bank of Atlanta (December).

Houpt, James V. and James A. Embersit (1991) 'A Method for Evaluating Interest Rate Risk in U.S. Commercial Banks', *Federal Reserve Bulletin* (August) 625–37.

Hurst, J. Willard (1973) *A Legal History of Money, 1774–1970* (Lincoln: University of Nebraska Press).

Huston, Thomas H. (1985) 'Dual Standards in Soundness and Safety Regulation', *Proceedings of a Conference on Bank Structure and Competition*, Federal Reserve Bank of Chicago, 542–51.

Isaac, William, Chairman, Federal Deposit Insurance Corporation, *How the Financial System Can Best Be Shaped to Meet the Needs of the American People*, Hearings before the Committee on Banking, Finance and Urban Affairs, 98th Congress, 2nd Session (April/May/June).

Kane, Thomas P. (1932) *The Romance and Tragedy of Banking* (New York: The Bankers Publishing Co).

Keeley, Michael C. (1990) 'Deposit Insurance, Risk and Market Power in Banking', *American Economic Review* (December) 1183–200.

Kaufman, Henry (1991) 'Credit Crunches: The Deregulators Were Wrong', *Wall Street Journal* (9 October).

Keynes, J. M. (1960) *A Treatise on Money, Vol. II* (London: Macmillan)

Lawrence, Robert (1992) *Origin and Development of the Examination Council*, Federal Financial Institutions Examination Council (February).

Legislative History of Banking in the State of New York (1855) (New York: Wm. C. Bryant & Co).

Litan, Robert E. (1987) *What Should Banks Do?* (Washington, DC: The Brookings Institution).

Mauskopf, Eileen (1987) 'Structure and Uses of the MPS Quarterly Econometric Model of the US', *Federal Reserve Bulletin* (February) 93–109.

Mauskopf, Eileen (1990) 'The Transmission Channels of Monetary Policy: How Have They Changed', *Federal Reserve Bulletin* (December) 985–1008.

Minsky, Hyman P. (1957) 'Central Banking and Money Market Changes', *Quarterly Journal of Economics*, LXXI(2) (May).

Minsky, Hyman P. (1971) 'Financial Instability Revisited', *Reappraisal of the Federal Reserve Discount Mechanism*, **3** (Federal Reserve Board) 95–136.

Minsky, Hyman P. (1975) 'Suggestions for a Cash-Flow Oriented Bank Examination', *Proceedings of a Conference on Bank Structure and Competition* (Federal Reserve Bank of Chicago) 150–84.

Minsky, Hyman P. (1986) *Stabilizing an Unstable Economy* (New Haven: Yale University Press).

Pecchioli, R. M. (1987) *Prudential Supervision in Banking*, OECD (Paris).

Peterson, Manfred O. (1977) 'Conflicts between Monetary Policy and Bank Supervision', *Issues in Bank Regulation* (Autumn).

Pierce, James L. (1991) *The Future of Banking* (New Haven: Yale University Press).

Posner, R.A. (1974) 'Theories of Economic Regulation', *The Bell Journal of Economics and Management Science*, **5**(2) (Autumn) 335–58.

Rehm, Barbara A. (1992) 'Regulators Loosen FDICIA's Handcuffs', *American Banker* (2 December).

Robertson, J. L. (1966) 'Federal Regulation of Banking: A Plea for Unification', *Law and Contemporary Problems*, **31**(4) (Autumn) 673–95.

Robertson, Ross M. (1968) *The Comptroller and Bank Supervision*, Office of the Comptroller of the Currency (Washington DC).

Scott, Kenneth E. (1977) 'The Dual Banking System: A Model of Competition in Regulation', *Stanford Law Review*, **30**(1) (November) 1–49.

Scott, Kenneth E. (1979) 'The Dual Banking System: A Model of Competition in Regulation', *Issues in Financial Regulation*, F. R. Edwards (ed.) (New York: McGraw Hill).

Shull, Bernard (1971) 'Report on Research Undertaken in Connection with a System Study', *Reappraisal of the Federal Reserve Discount Mechanism I*, Board of Governors of the Federal Reserve System (August) 27–75.

Shull, Bernard (1975) 'Statement', *Federal Bank Commission Act*, Hearings before the Committee on Banking, Housing and Urban Affairs, US Senate, 94th Congress, 1st Session (31 October).

Shull, Bernard (1983) 'The Separation of Banking and Commerce: Origin, Development and Implications for Antitrust', *The Antitrust Bulletin*, **28**(1) (Spring) 255–79.

Shull, Bernard (1993) 'How Should Bank Regulatory Agencies Be Organized,' *Contemporary Policy Studies*, (January) 99–107

Seidman, L. William (1990) 'Testimony on the Prosecution of Financial Crimes', Subcommittee on Criminal Justice, Committee on the Judiciary, US House of Representatives (11 July).

Spahr, Walter E. (1932) 'Bank Failures in the United States', *American Economic Review: Supplement* (March).

US Department of the Treasury (1991) *Modernizing the Financial System* (February) (cited as *Treasury Report*, 1991).

US. House of Representatives (1913) *House Banking Report, Changes in the Banking & Currency System of the United States*, Committee on Banking and Currency, 9 September of 1913.

US House of Representatives (1984) Federal Response to Criminal Misconduct and Insider Abuse in the Nation's Financial Institutions, Committee on Government Operations, 4 October 1984 (Cited as *Federal Response to Criminal Misconduct Report*, 1984).

US House of Representatives (1989) Conference Report to Accompany *Financial Institutions Reform, Recovery and Enforcement Act of 1989*, Report 101–209, 1 August 1989.

US House of Representatives (1990) *Effectiveness of Law Enforcement Against Financial Crime*, Field Hearing before the Committee on Banking, Finance and Urban Affairs, 12 April 1990.

US House of Representatives (1991) Staff Report, *Analysis of Bank Deposit Insurance Fund Losses*, Committee on Banking, Finance and Urban Affairs, 9 September 1991.

US Senate (1912) *Report of the National Monetary Commission*, 9 January 1912.

US Senate (1933) Senate Banking Report, *Operation of the National and Federal Reserve Banking Systems*, 15 May 1933.

US Senate (1977) *First Meeting on the Condition of the Banking System*, Hearings before the Committee on Banking, Housing and Urban Affairs, 10–11 March 1977.

Vojta, George (1973) *Bank Capital Adequacy*, First National City Bank (New York, NY).

Williamson, Oliver E. (1975) *Markets and Hierarchies: Analysis and Antitrust Implications* (New York: The Free Press).

Williamson, Oliver E. (1985) *The Economic Institutions of Capitalism* (New York: The Free Press).

8 The Current State of Banking Reform[1]

George G. Kaufman

Banking reform, or changes in banking regulations because of dissatisfaction with existing regulations, has been on the political agenda since the earliest days of the United States. This reflects a number of factors, including:

- Banking is an old industry that has existed throughout US history;
- Banking has always been under some government regulation and control;
- Banks provide a large part of the country's money supply, changes in which affect economic welfare importantly and are viewed as a government responsibility;
- Banks have periodically performed poorly causing large losses to depositors, disruptions to borrowers, and societal damage;
- Banks are the single largest supplier of total credit to the economy and also the largest supplier of credit to a number of important individual sectors and perceived to have the power to 'make or break' households and business firms in need of credit; and
- Widespread fear of excessive economic power by banks.

Indeed, in some early years of US history, banking was an important and emotional political issue; for example, the chartering and subsequent termination of the First and Second Banks of the United States. The large number of bank and thrift institution failures in recent years, with large losses to some large depositors, solvent institutions and, in the case of the thrift institutions, the taxpayers, has brought banking reform to the front burners of the political agenda in the late 1980s and early 1990s. Because banking deals largely with intangibles and is highly technical, it is not well-understood by the general public. Except in periods of crisis, the public is generally willing to delegate the formulation of public policy towards banking to experts. As a result, banking reform frequently becomes the province of bankers themselves and their government regulators.

Public policy towards banking, like public policy towards any other sector or issue, reflects the primary public concerns at the time. As the public's concerns change, so does public policy. Thus, in the early days of the US, public concern about banking focused on the fear of excessive economic power. This resulted in restrictions on the products and services banks may offer and, in many states, on their ability to branch. What easier way to restrict bank size than to restrict the number of offices and product line. In 1933, public concern focused on the large number of bank failures with losses to a large number of depositors and serious disruptions to loan customers. In response, the federal government imposed additional restrictions on bank activities perceived to be risky and introduced government insurance (guaranty) on some deposits.

In the early 1980s, the combination of high and volatile interest rates and advances in computer and telecommunications technology provided both the reason and the means for bypassing price restrictions on bank deposits and permitted non banks to offer traditionally exclusive banking services. The sharp increase in interest rates also drove almost the entire S&L industry, which had financed its long-term loans primarily with short-term deposits, into economic insolvency. As a result, public concern focused on the inefficiency and the threat to the viability of the banking system from excessive regulation, which was interfering with market forces. Government responded by reducing restrictive regulations, particularly on thrift institutions. In the later 1980s, the large losses associated with the large number of bank and thrift failures, a major part of which was borne by the taxpayers, shifted public concern to reducing the future cost of failure to the taxpayer. This implied deposit insurance reform.

This chapter reviews bank reform in the 60 years since the Banking (Glass–Steagall) Act of 1933, and speculates on the likelihood and direction of further reform in the near future.

8.1 BACKGROUND

With rare exception, the Banking Act of 1933 significantly increased restrictions on bank activities in an attempt to increase bank safety and soundness. Among other things, the Act:

- Prohibited interest payments on demand deposits;
- Limited interest payments on time deposits;
- Restricted bank underwriting of and trading in private and some municipal securities;

- Introduced margin requirements on bank financed security purchases;
- Restricted entry by new banks;
- Introduced federal deposit insurance; and
- Liberalized national bank branching restrictions within state boundaries.

Following its enactment, the rate of bank failures dropped to nearly zero and the banking and thrift industries recovered, first, slowly through the 1930s and, then, more rapidly in the post-World War II period. But the thrust of public policy, particularly at the federal level, continued to be restrictive. The Bank Holding Company Act of 1956 both increased the separation of banking and commerce by expanding it to holding companies that owned two or more banks and restricted bank holding companies from circumventing the prohibition on interstate branching by expanding across state lines through establishing full-service bank subsidiaries. The Bank Merger Act of 1960 reinforced the anti-competitiveness criteria for bank mergers. Amendments to the Bank Holding Company Act in 1970 further expanded the separation of banking and commerce to holding companies that owned only one bank.

At the same time, however, a successive series of major government and private commissions – for example, the Commission on Money and Credit, 1961; the Advisory Committee on Banking to the Comptroller of the Currency (Saxon Committee), 1962; the President's Committee on Financial Institutions (Heller Committee), 1963; the President's Commission on Financial Structure and Regulation (Hunt Commission), 1971; the Federal Institutions and the Nation's Economy (FINE) Study, 1975; and the Vice President's Task Group on Regulation of Financial Services Commission (Bush Commission), 1984 – that analyzed the performance, structure and regulation of banking and depository institutions all concluded that banks were overregulated and recommended liberalization of the restrictions on product and geographic powers, particularly for thrift institutions, and the elimination of restrictions or interest payments on, at least, time deposits. These studies laid the groundwork for the deregulation of the early 1980s.[2] But enacting reform of regulations generally requires more dramatic causes than recommendations of a commission alone, no matter how prestigious the commission. The remainder of this chapter reviews the changes in bank and, to a lesser extent, thrift regulation since 1980 in three areas:

- Deposit insurance;
- Powers – product, geographic and price; and
- Regulatory agency structure.

8.2 DEPOSIT INSURANCE REFORM

Since 1933, government deposit insurance was the last banking reform to be recommended, but the first to be seriously overhauled by federal legislation. For many years, the introduction of federal deposit insurance was viewed as one of the major banking reforms in history. For example, in their seminal, *A Monetary History of the United States: 1867–1960*, Friedman and Schwartz, not known as great lovers of government intervention, highlight the contribution of the FDIC in achieving what had been a major objective of banking reform for at least a century, namely, the prevention of bank panics, and in reducing bank failures and depositor losses.[3] But the large losses to the insurance funds, associated with the bank and thrift failures in the 1980s, produced an abrupt change in opinion. By the late 1980s, the extant structure of deposit insurance was viewed as a major culprit of the debacle. The bad side of deposit insurance had surfaced.

This should not have been a surprise. Reviews of the debate surrounding the enactment of federal deposit insurance in 1932 and 1933 clearly show that most participants, including many of the legislative sponsors, bankers and the Roosevelt Administration, were keenly aware of the perverse incentive and moral hazard problems associated with misstructured deposit insurance.[4] The evidence both from the numerous state deposit insurance plans throughout US history and from private life, casualty, and property insurance companies clearly demonstrated the importance of these potential dangers. Most supporters viewed deposit insurance as the right political solution in 1933, but not necessarily the right economic solution.

8.2.1 History of Federal Deposit Insurance

In the Great Depression, the US was traumatized by the bank failure crisis and demanded quick action by the new Roosevelt Administration and the Congress. Politically, this was not a time for emphasizing the longer-term drawbacks of proposed policies nor for calls for further study. The public only rewarded action. Numerous Congressmen had pet reform proposals that they had been unable to enact in previous sessions. These included many of the components of the Banking Act of 1933. Indeed, some 150 proposals for federal deposit insurance or guaranty had been introduced in Congress between 1886 and 1933.[5] Spurred by the public's demand for action, supporters of many of these projects were able to horsetrade sufficient votes to ensure passage of the omnibus Banking Act in the first 100 days of the new Congress.[6]

The deposit insurance program enacted for commercial banks reflected the designers' familiarity with the potential pitfalls of such plans. Two insurance plans were included in the Banking Act; a temporary plan through 1 July 1933 and a permanent plan, thereafter. The temporary plan called for full insurance coverage up to $2500 per account, which included 97 per cent of all accounts and 24 per cent of all deposits, and flat premiums of 0.5 per cent of insured deposits, with a provision for an extra assessment if necessary. The permanent plan called for graduated account coverage – 100 per cent up to $10 000, 75 per cent for the next $40 000, and 50 per cent for amounts in excess of $50 000. The permanent premium structure was a flat 0.5 per cent of total deposits, which shifted much of the cost to larger banks, again with a provision for extra assessments if necessary. Proposals for 100 per cent account coverage were defeated. However, the permanent plan was never put in operation. The temporary plan was extended in 1934 through mid-1935, with an increase in account coverage to $5000 and then enacted permanently in the Banking Act of 1935. The premiums were reduced to $\frac{1}{12}$ of 1 per cent, with a provision for rebating surpluses.

From the late 1930s through the early 1950s, the FDIC resolved almost all insolvencies through purchase and assumptions in which an acquiring bank purchased the good assets of a failed bank, assumed all of its deposits, and received cash from the FDIC for any difference. Uninsured as well as insured depositors were fully protected. In 1957, as it would again 30 years later, Congress questioned this procedure and the FDIC agreed to choose between assumption and payoff resolutions, including not protecting uninsured depositors, on the basis of lower cost.[7] Because of the widespread satisfaction with insurance in nearly eliminating bank runs and failures as well as most depositor losses, account coverage was increased to $10 000 in 1950, $15 000 in 1966, $20 000 in 1969, $40 000 in 1974, and finally $100 000 in the Depository Institutions Deregulation and Monetary Control Act (DIDMCA) of 1980.

With the resolution of the Continental Illinois National Bank in 1984, the seventh largest bank in the country at the time, the FDIC reverted to its old policy of protecting all depositors. But the rationale was changed to protecting against systemic or spillover risk from the failure of a large money center bank, particularly if it was also an important correspondent bank or a bank considered 'too big to fail'. This rationale was quickly expanded to banks considered 'too important to fail' and even to 'too political to fail', in the protection of all depositors at the National Bank of Washington, the 250th largest bank in the country.[8] The losses to the FDIC from these policies were enlarged further by a policy of forbearance in which economically insolvent banks were not resolved for many months after they first were identified as seriously troubled institutions by examiners.[9] The FDIC did this both in the hopes that the banks would recover and because it did not have sufficient cash to pay off the depositors or an acquiring bank. Forbearance was particularly costly for the FSLIC and, ultimately, the taxpayers in the S&L debacle.[10]

8.2.2 History of Deposit Insurance Reform

Deposit insurance reform proposals effectively began with the publication in 1965 of an argument for risk-based insurance premiums over flat per cent of deposit premiums by Thomas Mayer.[11] In the 1980s, this proposal was joined, first, by proposals to reduce insurance coverage sharply, to replace government insurance with private insurance or a system of bank cross-guarantees, and to restrict insured deposits to 'narrow banks' that would invest only in safe assets. In the late 1980s, a plan was developed that would make deposit insurance effectively redundant by requiring earlier and progressively harsher and more mandatory structured intervention by regulators in the affairs of troubled institutions as their performance declines and resolving the institutions before their capital is fully depleted. The plan would maintain the extant *de jure* structure of federal deposit insurance, but impose a system of regulatory intervention that would mimic and reinforce existing creditor discipline on troubled institutions. Thus, at least in theory, there would be fewer bank failures and small, if any, losses to uninsured depositors or the FDIC when banks did fail.

This plan, entitled Structured Early Intervention and Resolution (SEIR) was first developed by George Benston and George Kaufman for the American Enterprise Institute in 1988 and refined by both the Shadow Financial Regulatory Committee and a Brookings Institution Task Force on Financial Institutions Restructuring in 1989.[12] Although a radical departure from other deposit insurance reform proposals, this plan did not require major changes in either deposit insurance coverage or bank operations. Deposit insurance would, effectively, become redundant. Moreover, because FDIC losses would be minimal, deposit insurance premiums would be low.

The large losses associated with the S&L failure in the 1980s suddenly elevated consideration of deposit insurance reform ahead of other, longer-discussed banking reforms. Coming on the heels of widespread public outrage over the S&L debacle and the insolvency of FSLIC, the large number of commercial bank failures and troubled banks in the early 1990s, which threatened to also bankrupt the FDIC and involve another taxpayer contribution, finally spurred Congress to undertake fundamental deposit insurance reform. The idea of possibly eliminating all losses from failures appealed greatly to it and won acceptance over the alternative proposals. In 1990, the Senate Banking Committee, chaired by Senator Donald Riegle, introduced an omnibus banking reform bill that included broader product and geographic powers, as well as deposit insurance reform in the form of SEIR. The bill did not make it through the Senate and was introduced again in the next session. Also in the 1991 session, Chairman Henry Gonzalez of the House Banking Committee introduced an approximately similar bill and the Treasury Department released a study required by the Financial Institutions Reform Recovery and Enforcement Act (FIRREA) of 1989 that made similar recommendations.

The expanded product and geographic powers permitted by these bills drew the greatest attention and attracted the heaviest lobbying. As will be discussed later in this chapter, neither expanded product nor geographic powers were enacted. The final bill, the Federal Deposit Insurance Corporation Improvement Act (FDICIA) of 1991, included a modified and weakened version of SEIR and risk-based insurance premiums as deposit insurance reform as well as a large number of other wide-ranging provisions. SEIR is incorporated in the prompt correct action (PCA) and least cost resolution (LCR) provisions of the Act.

FDICIA is the most important banking legislation since the Banking Act of 1933. The SEIR provisions fundamentally change the incentive structure under deposit insurance for bankers to take excessive risk and for regulators to forbear taking corrective actions on troubled and even insolvent institutions. But for reasons discussed below, the Act is unlikely to either reduce the number of failures or reduce losses to the FDIC as much as possible. As a result, further deposit insurance reform is required both to correct the weaknesses in the present legislation and to provide intensified oversight of the regulatory agencies in implementing and enforcing the intent of the Act.[13]

8.2.3 Reform Incomplete

FDICIA provides incomplete deposit insurance reform because, among other things, it mismeasures the economic capital position of banks, particularly of troubled banks; permits overly long delays in resolving insolvent or near-insolvent banks; provides exceptions to least cost resolution for banks still considered 'too big to fail'; and, perhaps most importantly, delegates to the regulatory agencies both the interpretation of many of the provisions and the drafting and implementation of the accompanying regulations.

8.2.4 Mismeasures Capital Position

To be most effective in implementing PCA and LCR, the capital position of banks should be measured in market or current value terms. Substantial evidence suggests that banks, particularly those in financial distress, tend to delay reserving for loan losses and to underreserve when they do.[14] In addition, book measures do not adjust for changes in values from changes in interest rates. A recent study of large banks that failed between 1986 and 1990, by the Office of Management and Budget, showed that while their capital was, on average, positive until they were closed on a book-value basis, it was already negative on a market-value basis 3 $\frac{1}{2}$ years before closure, and substantially negative at closure (Figure 8.1).[15] SEIR could work with book values, but the trigger levels for prompt corrective action and resolution would need to be increased sufficiently to compensate for the overstating of net worth. The Act also requires that the:

> accounting principles applicable to reports or statements required to be filed with Federal banking agencies ... should ... result in financial statements ... that accurately reflect ... capital ..., facilitate effective supervision ... and facilitate prompt corrective action to resolve institutions at the least cost to the insurance funds.

The agencies are to review their accounting principles and modify them if they do not comply with the above objectives. In addition, the agencies should develop methods for insured banks to provide supplementary market-value reports 'to the extent feasible and practicable'. The agencies were given until one year after enactment (19 December 1992) to review their procedures for conformity with these objectives and to make appropriate changes. To date, the agencies have not released any reports that they have done so. Nor have any research studies been published. Indeed, for years, the agencies have been dragging their feet with respect to introducing market-value accounting or reporting and do not appear ready to make meaningful changes in their position.[16]

The reluctance of the agencies to move towards quicker market-value reporting is particularly disturbing in light of their ongoing attacks on the

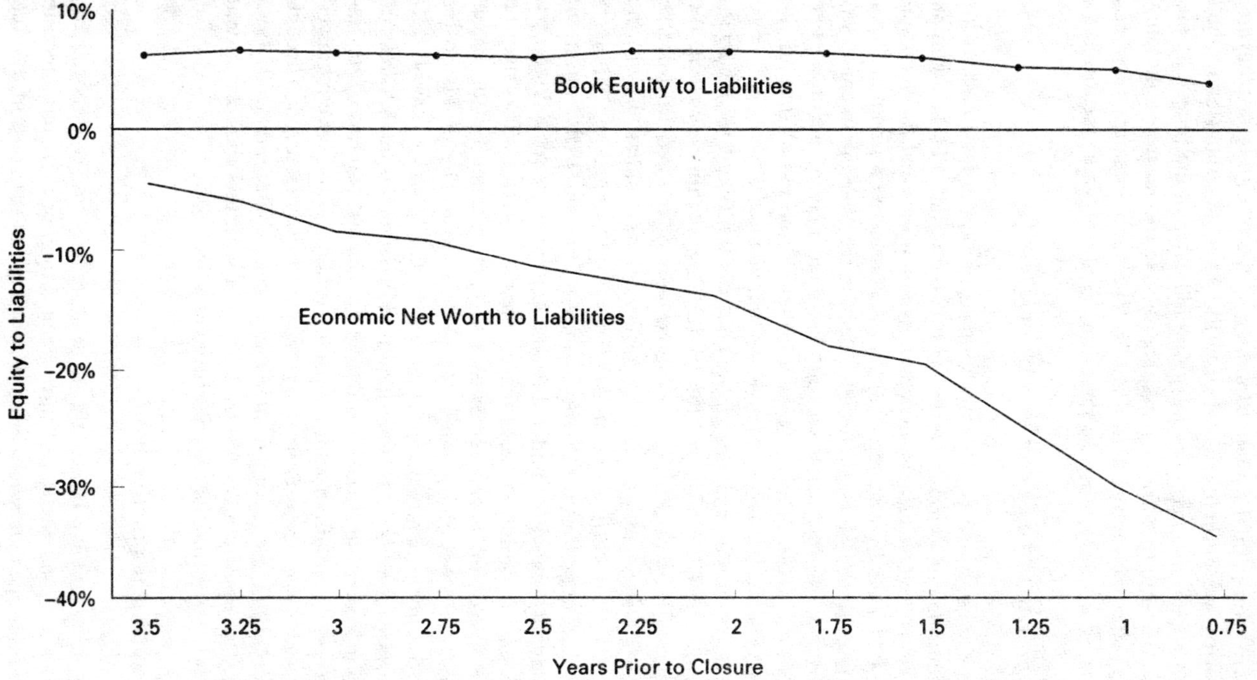

Source: Justine Farr Rodriguez, Richard L. Cooperstein and F. Stevens Redburn, 'Assessing the Cost of Government Guarantees', *Credit Markets in Transition*, Chicago: Federal Reserve Bank of Chicago, May 1992, p. 32.

Figure 8.1 Book equity vs economic net worth averages for large failed banks: 1986–1990

supplementary non-capital tripwires included in the Act. In large measure, these tripwires were included because the agencies themselves had testified that book-value capital is a lagging indicator of the financial condition of a bank and, therefore, is an inappropriate trigger to use in delineating the prompt corrective action zones. The supplementary tripwires were an attempt to compensate for the failings of book-value measures.

8.2.5 Exceptions to Least-cost Resolution

The Act permits two exceptions to prompt resolution at least cost to the insurance fund: (1) institutions viewed as 'too big to fail' (TBTF) without causing 'serious adverse effects on economic conditions and financial stability'; and (2) critically undercapitalized institutions with less than 2 per cent tangible equity capital need not be placed in receivership to conservatorship for 90 days after being classified so, and may be accorded two additional 90-day extensions or even an indefinite period of time, if the agency views the institutions as recovering and viable.

The first exception does appear to make it more difficult for the agencies to invoke TBTF. To do so, the FDIC must obtain in writing the consent of a majority of the Board of Governors of the Federal Reserve System and of the Secretary of the Treasury after consultation with the President. All must certify that making uninsured depositors whole is necessary to avoid serious economic harm. Any loss the FDIC suffers in making all depositors whole under the exception must be recaptured by a special assessment on all banks based on their total assets. This may be expected to evoke increased opposition to such rescues by the larger banks, who would pay the greater share of the cost. The provision for delays in resolving critically undercapitalized banks, however, has no self-limiting or restraining aspects other than that the agencies have to restrict the institution's activities, file periodic reports or certifications of its viability, and need to explain in writing, disclose publicly, and have reviewed by the General Accounting Office any material losses incurred. Through mid-February 1993, two months after the so-called 'December 19, 1992 surprise', only one of the 25-odd banks caught with less than 2 per cent equity capital at that time had been resolved by the FDIC.

8.2.6 Foot-dragging by Regulators

During the legislative process, the regulators vigorously opposed the enactment of a strong SEIR and have been dragging their feet since in adopting regulations that would effectively carry out the spirit of the Act.

They fear that the reductions in their discretionary powers and flexibility in disciplining troubled banks and resolving insolvent banks might, among other things, reduce their visibility and importance. This may adversely impact both their current career advancement and their post-career opportunities. The revolving door between bank regulators and the industry revolves at least as fast as does the better-publicized door in the Defense Department. In advancing their personal careers, bank crises may be said to be to regulators what wars are to generals. They put them in the spotlight.

Thus, as has already been noted, regulators have moved slowly in introducing market-value accounting. They have also adopted numerical definitions of adequate-capitalization for prompt corrective action on a book-value basis that are both far too low for ensuring safety, particularly in relation to either the riskier portfolios banks have selected in recent years or the more volatile regional economic shocks, and considerably lower than at the banks' uninsured 'unregulated' competitors.[17] The agencies' definition encompasses 98 per cent of all banks, holding 97 per cent of all bank assets as of mid-1992. At the same time, however, some 8 per cent of all banks with 14 per cent of all banking assets were on the FDIC's problem bank list; nearly 25 per cent of the so-called adequately-capitalized banks had received CAMEL ratings of 3 or less on their examinations; and some 5 per cent had ratings of 4 or 5. Since then, the substantial improvement in bank earnings has depleted the lower capitalization categories even further. In light of the low values for capital ratios that were established by the agencies as qualifying a bank as well-capitalized, it is apparent that the regulators' definitions may be generating a false sense of security if macroeconomic shocks have not diminished greatly. Indeed, it appears that the market place is a stricter capital regulator than are the regulators.

The adequately-capitalized category in mid-1992 also encompassed all 46 banks with assets in excess of $10 billion. This is particularly important because it is the largest banks that provide most of the correspondent bank services to smaller banks and thereby are the counterparty to the interbank exposure of smaller banks. The critical role of interbank exposure in transmitting bank shocks was repeatedly cited as particularly worrisome in the Congressional testimony of the regulators. In response, the Act requires the agencies to draft regulations to reduce the probability of systemic risk occurring through interbank exposure. It is, thus, ironic that after Congress accepted their argument, the regulators failed to take the opportunity to follow through and limit the exposure of smaller banks to large correspondent banks by requiring the large banks, who wish to maintain the correspondent business, to be more than adequately-capitalized. This would have provided a strong incentive for large banks that were not better than adequately-capitalized, that is, well-capitalized, to become so. It would also have been consistent with the carrot–stick approach of the Act, which provides greater freedoms and less supervision to better-capitalized banks.

It is even more ironic that the regulators had proposed this in their draft regulation, but then modified it in their final regulation to permit unlimited exposure by smaller banks to only adequately-capitalized larger banks. This represents another major weakening of the Act. The final irony is that if the regulators had not been so attached to systemic risk and had not successfully argued for a TBTF exception, the interbank exposure section of the Act may not have been included, and an interbank exposure regulation would not have been necessary. Banks would have monitored each other automatically. And who is better qualified to monitor banks than other banks?

The Act also requires the regulators to expand the risk-based capital standards to incorporate interest rate and asset concentration risks. This had been a glaring failure in the existing capital requirements. Particularly in 1992, when the yield curve was exceptionally steeply upward-sloping, banks increased their relative holdings of longer-term securities sharply. This has greatly increased their exposure to interest-rate risk. Yet, the regulators' draft interest-rate risk regulation is badly deficient in four areas. First, the measurement of exposure is inadequate. Because the regulators wanted to impose a minimum reporting burden on the banks, the exposure computation requires minimum information in. As a result, it also generates nearly useless information out. Indeed, most fair-sized banks already collected more information in measuring their exposure internally.

Second, additional capital is to be required only of the outlying 20 per cent of the banks with the greatest interest-rate risk exposures. In the example presented in the draft proposal, this would include only banks whose capital has a duration of more than 12 years. At this exposure, a 200 basis-point adverse change in interest rates would reduce the bank's capital by 25 per cent. Third, the additional capital required is greatly insufficient for the risk assumed.

Fourth, and lastly, the requirement is static. There is no provision for the replenishment of capital if interest rates change adversely to reduce the market value of the bank's capital, although not its book value. Unlike losses from credit defaults, losses from adverse interest-rate changes are not recognized.

The regulators are also weakening FDICIA by specifying risk-based insurance premiums required by the Act that, on the one hand, have too narrow a spread between healthy and sick banks in comparison to the differences in deposit rates imposed by the market and, on the other hand, are too high on healthy banks in relationship to the current value they receive from the insurance coverage. As a result, sick banks are not sufficiently discouraged from taking excessive risk at the expense of healthy banks, and healthy banks and their customers are encouraged to search for less costly alternatives.

In sum, enacted in response to the high cost to the taxpayer of regulatory failure stemming from the extant structure of government deposit insurance, FDICIA represents the first major step forward in reforming federal deposit insurance since its inception in 1933. Nevertheless, the reforms are only potentially effective for, among other reasons, those discussed above. To make the Act more effective and prevent back-sliding requires strong and ongoing Congressional and public oversight to see that the regulators are not sabotaging the Act, and some strengthening of the Act itself.

8.3 POWERS REFORM

Although, because of the rush of events, deposit insurance reform was the most urgently required reform in recent years, powers reform has been discussed for much longer and had received the majority of attention in most of the earlier commissions, committees and studies on financial reform.[18] But the costs of regulatory failure in this area were much smaller and less directly visible. Thus, reform was not perceived as urgent. If deposit insurance reform is perceived to be effective, attention is likely to refocus on powers reform.

8.3.1 Product and Service Powers

Little, if any, reform has occurred to date in expanding the product and service lines for commercial banks. The Depository Institutions and Monetary Control Act of 1980 and the Garn–St Germain Act of 1982 greatly broadened the product powers of S&Ls to more closely resemble those permitted banks. Once deposit insurance is reformed to discourage banks from shifting excessive risk on to the FDIC, many reformers would permit banks to offer a nearly unlimited range of financial services, generally within the bank, and also some nonfinancial services but, generally, outside the bank itself through holding company affiliates. FDICIA makes permitting additional powers more rational both by potentially repairing deposit insurance and by permitting regulators to award new powers only to better-capitalized institutions. Arguments for permitting commercial banks a broad range of financial powers, that is, universal banking, include greater efficiencies of scale and scope, reduced risk through diversification, and more intensive competition with the benefits passed through to consumers in the form of lower prices and higher quality. Arguments against focus on small, if any, economies, the potential for increased risk through permitting new riskier powers, unfair competition from access to underpriced federal deposit insurance, and excessive economic concentration.[19]

The new financial powers most often discussed are insurance and securities. Most studies suggest that insurance brokerage is relatively riskless, amenable to meaningful scope economies, and quite inefficient in its present form of delivery. Insurance underwriting involves greater risks, smaller synergies, and probably small returns. In most states, insurance was separated from commercial banking relatively early in banking. This separation was reinforced by the Board of Governors in its determination of permissible bank holding company powers and periodically broadened by federal legislation. The insurance agency lobby is one of the more powerful lobbies in the country. It has lost few battles to keep banks out of insurance brokerage. Indeed, the latest in a series of challenges to general insurance offerings by banks is a challenge to the legal ability of national banks to offer such services in cities under 5000 in population. This authority appeared to be on the books almost since the National Banking Act in 1863, but may have been inadvertently erased by Congress in amendments to the Act in the early 1900s.

8.3.2 Securities Activities

Banks have always been involved in some aspect of securities activities – as investors, underwriters and/or dealers. Until the enactment of the Glass–Steagall Act in 1933, most states permitted their banks to engage in all three activities for a wide range of securities, including both debt and equity. National bank regulations were vaguer, until the enactment of the McFadden Act in 1927. Many national banks engaged in all three activities in their bond departments. At the time, equity issues were relatively minor to debt issues and most banks could not hold equities in their portfolios. Other national banks conducted these activities in holding company affiliates or separate entities under common ownership. The McFadden Act codified these activities to explicitly give national banks the same in-bank powers as state banks, subject to approval by the Comptroller of the

Currency. The latter denied national banks the power to underwrite or trade equities.

The Glass–Steagall Act prohibited institutions that accepted deposits (commercial banks) and belonged to the Federal Reserve System from underwriting and trading all private securities and municipal revenue bonds, and vice versa for investment banks. But banks could continue to invest, underwrite, and trade federal and general obligation municipal securities. Congress liberalized the Glass–Steagall restrictions only once, in 1968, when some municipal revenue bonds were added to the list of bank-eligible securities.

Nevertheless, through reinterpretation of the Act by the courts and the regulatory agencies one activity at a time, banks have slowly been permitted to engage, effectively, in underwriting and trading through holding company affiliates all securities, including equities, and mutual funds that they also manage.[20] Indeed, a major regional bank in Michigan recently purchased a full-service investment bank. But the restrictions imposed by the agencies on how some of these activities can be conducted, both increase the cost of the activities and limit them primarily to large banks. For example, underwriting and dealing in newly-permitted so-called 'ineligible' securities must be conducted in a separately capitalized holding company affiliate and is restricted to a maximum percentage of the affiliate's activity in 'eligible' securities. Because smaller banks underwrite and trade only small amounts of eligible securities, most would be permitted to deal in ineligible securities in amounts too small to be economic. Ironically, it could be that few large banks will be able to compete successfully with large investment banks, while some smaller regional banks, which generally have been slower at entering into securities activities other than brokerage, may be more successful in competing with large investment banks headquartered elsewhere in underwriting securities of local private and government entities.

Opposition to expanded bank securities powers from the securities industry association has weakened considerably in recent years. Indeed, the major opposition appears to come from smaller banks, which are more afraid of Citicorp and BankAmerica than of Merrill Lynch and Salomon. Repeal of Glass–Steagall has passed the Senate twice, but has been stalled in the House.

8.3.3 Banking and Commerce

Combining full-service banking with commerce (nonfinancial products), which was effectively stopped by the Bank Holding Company Acts of

1956 and 1970, is even more controversial. Some opponents fear excessive bank concentration, a fear that was basic throughout much of US history until recently. Moreover, studies show few scope economies in such combinations, although risk reduction may be possible through diversification. Studies of combinations of banking and commerce in other countries report little evidence of adverse impact. On the other hand, the benefits include not only intensified competition for many services, but improved corporate governance, longer investment time horizons, and lower failure rates for affiliated nonbank firms. Permitting the combination of banking and commerce through holding company affiliation was recommended in the 1991 Treasury study and included in the 1991 Bush Administration's draft bank reform bill, but did not make it through Congress.

Although most studies conclude the new product powers would permit banks to reduce their risk exposure through diversification, recent evidence from the S&L industry also suggests some institutions may misuse the new powers to increase their risk. As a result, some oppose granting banks additional powers, at least, until they are financially stronger and the public cost of potential misuse is smaller.

The chances appear poor for little immediate legislative relief for new financial or nonfinancial powers, but good for greater use of securities activities through the door opened by the courts and the regulators. Because the fastest growing assets in the financial sector are those generally owned by individuals and managed by institutions, for example, pension and mutual funds, rather than those owned by institutions, it is unlikely that even if banks receive new product powers that they would be able to reverse greatly the reported secular decline in their market share of all financial assets since the end of World War II. The assets of mutual funds managed by banks, for example, are classified as mutual funds not as banks in the flow of funds data. Moreover, except for insurance brokerage, it is also unlikely that any new financial services by themselves would add greatly to the industry's aggregate profitability, although it might boost that of a number of individual banks. Indeed, competitive forces may insure that much, if not all, of any potential gains in profitability would be passed through to consumers in the form of lower prices.

8.3.4 Geographic Powers

The drive to expand geographic powers through branching and holding company acquisitions began, in earnest, in the early 1900s with the development of the automobile and suburbia. A number of states liberalized their branching laws but, by the late 1920s, branching opponents succeeded in stalling further liberalization. In 1930, branching was still permitted in only 19 of the 48 states. National banks, which, effectively, were not permitted to branch, were first given city-wide branching authority, in states permitting branching, by the McFadden Act of 1927, and then full equity with state banks by the Banking Act of 1933. No state permitted branching across state lines, and the McFadden Act specifically prohibited it for national banks.

That is where matters stood until the 1950s, when the drive to expand geographically was renewed. Some bank holding companies began aggressively to expand across state lines into states that did not prohibit such acquisitions. But Congress viewed this as a circumvention of the prohibition against full-service interstate branching and effectively prohibited further such expansion in the Douglas Amendment to the Bank Holding Company Act of 1956. The Amendment permitted interstate holding company expansion only if the host state specifically permitted it. At the time, no state did. However, holding companies continued to expand rapidly across state lines on a limited service basis, such as loan production and consumer credit offices. At the same time, states began to liberalize their intrastate branching laws. By the mid-1960s, about two-thirds of the states permitted some form of branching, about one-half statewide (primarily on the West Coast) and the other half more limited (primarily on the East Coast). The Midwest remained, predominantly, unit banking. By 1992, all states permitted some branch banking, and only a handful permitted less than statewide branching.

8.3.5 Interstate Holding Company Expansion

In the early 1980s, in response to the large number of interstate limited-service offices, advances in telecommunications and computer technology (some as simple as the 800 telephone number) that permit quick and low-cost interstate transfers of funds, and the need to attract buyers for troubled institutions, states began to enact legislation specifically permitting acquisition of full-service domestic banks by out-of-state holding companies, generally on a reciprocal and, at first, regional basis. By 1992, all states but one (Montana) permitted some form of full-service interstate holding company banking, most on a national basis. It appears likely that full nationwide interstate holding company banking will be a reality in the next few years.

It is of interest to note that, despite the national ramifications of this change, interstate holding company banking has occurred without any changes in federal legislation. Indeed, the states were forced to enact enabling legislation to remove restrictions imposed by federal legislation. More recently, a small number of relatively small states and New York have enacted some form of interstate branching, generally on a reciprocal basis. This does not affect national banks. Little such branching has, however, occurred to date. In 1991, the Treasury Banking Study recommended and the Bush Administration introduced legislation phasing in interstate branching for national banks. The proposal was opposed primarily by smaller banks, who feared intensified competition. The opponents carried that day. But it appears likely that they will not carry all future days and that interstate branching is not far away.

Does it matter whether interstate banking is provided through branching or holding companies? Efficiency arguments suggest that organizations be permitted to choose the form they consider optimum for them. In states where both forms of geographic expansion are permitted, banks have generally preferred the branching route. Some analysts also argue that, as a result of the more intense competition, improved management and economies of scale, interstate banking would generate annual savings as large as $15 billion. Although these claims appear high, savings from an expanded reduction in the number of independent small banks should occur.[21] Perhaps more importantly, interstate branching will permit even greater geographic and product diversification than interstate holding company banking and improve bank safety. It appears reasonable that if interstate banking had been permissible a number of years earlier, the number of bank and thrift failures in the 1980s would have been considerably smaller and possibly less costly.

8.3.6 Prices

As noted earlier, the Banking Act of 1933 restricted interest rates banks could pay on time deposits (Regulation Q) and prohibited interest payments on demand deposits, primarily, to reduce interbank competition and, thus, enhance bank safety and soundness. But, in time, markets developed to permit depositors to circumvent these ceilings when binding. In the early 1960s, banks innovated large negotiated certificates of deposits (CDs) to permit them to compete for funds on the national money market. CDs were first subject to higher Q ceilings than consumer deposits and then exempted from ceilings altogether in the early 1970s. As market interest rates increased sharply in the late 1970s, many depositors disintermediated out of banks, and particularly thrifts, into short-term Treasury securities and newly-developed money-market funds. To permit the depository institutions to compete, the ceilings were progressively removed from consumer deposits. The process was accelerated first by DIDMCA of 1980, which called for a six-year orderly phaseout of all ceilings, and then by the Garn–St Germain Act of 1982, which permitted banks to offer money-market deposit accounts (MMDAs) without any ceilings. Moreover, starting in the mid-1970s, checks were permitted to be written on some interest-bearing consumer deposits (NOW accounts), so that consumers could effectively avoid the restrictions of interest payments on demand deposits.

But the prohibition on interest payments on non-consumer demand deposits remained in effect. However, technology has often permitted it to be effectively avoided through such means as sweep accounts, which automatically invest a large depositor's excess day-end balances overnight every night. As a result, there appears to be little, if any, groundswell for an early renewal of the prohibition on interest payments on demand deposits.

In the past, state usury laws have also restricted rates charged on some types of loans made by depository institutions, particularly on residential mortgage and consumer loans. These laws significantly curbed the flows of such credit when market rates of interest increased sharply in the late 1970s. In response, most states relaxed their usury ceilings on all but small, high-risk consumer loans and in 1980, DIDMCA, effectively, overrode some state usury laws. Few states have reimposed meaningful usury ceilings since.[22]

8.4 REGULATORY AGENCIES

Probably no banking area has received as much attention with respect to reform through the years than has restructuring the bank regulatory agencies; and no area has seen as little change. In part, according to Kenneth Scott, this may reflect the failure to have a:

> comprehensive and powerful theory of the political process and regulation. A large body of rather elegant theory and accumulated date can be brought to bear on the functioning of economic markets, but not on the working of political markets.[23]

Is one regulatory agency per industry better than a number of competing agencies? History also is of little guide. Industries regulated by a single agency – for example, ground transportation by the Interstate Commerce

Commission, air transportation by the Civil Aeronautics Board, and S&Ls by the Federal Home Loan Bank Board – have not had a better performance rating than multi-agency regulated commercial banks, particularly in introducing innovations. If competition is good for private firms, is it less good for government entities?

Every banking commission since World War II has recommended consolidation in their reorganization plan. None have recommended maintaining the status quo. Yet, until 1989, no reorganization has occurred. And when the Federal Home Loan Bank Board was eliminated in 1989 by FIRREA, and its powers divided among the newly created Office of Thrift Supervision (OTS) within the Treasury Department (supervisory authority), the newly created Savings Association Insurance Fund (SAIF) within the FDIC (insurance protection), and the Federal Home Loan Banks under the newly created Federal Housing Finance Board (thrift liquidity), it was basically done to punish the Board for permitting the S&L debacle to grow to the extent that it severely embarrassed Congress. The winning agencies were those that were less tainted at the time and had lobbied the hardest for the additional powers. A number of commissions recommended consolidating the deposit insurance and regulatory functions in a single agency so that the insurer could better protect the insurance fund. That structure existed in the S&L industry. The FSLIC was a division of the Federal Home Loan Bank Board. But the Board not only failed to protect the fund, but acted to endanger it. As a result, this experience led to recommendations that the two functions are better served separately. Likewise, most regulators prefer 'independent' banking agencies. Yet, the supervisory powers of the old independent Board were shifted to the OTS in the 'political' Treasury Department.

Most commissions also recommended diminishing the role of the Federal Reserve System in bank supervision and regulation. That would permit it to concentrate its full attention to monetary policy, over which it has sole responsibility. Separation would also remove any potential conflicts between its monetary policy and regulatory responsibilities. But to date, the Fed has fought this reduction in authority long, hard and successfully. When a late draft of the Bush Commission Report in 1984 recommended transferring much of the Fed regulatory power to the FDIC and the Comptroller of the Currency, the Chairman of the Federal Reserve, Paul Volcker, personally went before the Commission to lobby against this change. He successfully argued that, without the ability to directly monitor large banks, the Fed could not be held responsible for any monetary or financial crisis that might ensue. No commission can be expected to be willing to shoulder the burden of such a possibility and be charged as acting irresponsibly. Indeed, from a relatively minor bank regulatory agency in the early 1950s, with primary responsibility for a relatively small number of state chartered member banks, the Federal Reserve has grown rapidly until FDICIA into the premier bank regulatory agency. Its regulatory responsibilities were enhanced greatly by being delegated primary responsibility over all bank holding companies by the Bank Holding Company Acts of 1956 and 1970 and by subjecting all depository institutions to Federal Reserve requirements by DIDMCA in 1980, all of which the Fed lobbied for vigorously. By granting it broad powers to resolve undercapitalized banks, FDICIA, however, is likely to elevate the FDIC to equal regulatory, although not overall, importance.

In part, because there appears to be no widely agreed upon underlying logical rhyme or reason for a particular bank regulatory structure, the arguments come down to which agencies are sufficiently strong and sufficiently acute at lobbying to absorb the powers of the weaker and less efficient lobbiers; for example, the FDIC and Treasury Department over the FHLBB in 1989. Moreover, because banking is generally viewed as technical and beyond the ability and interest of much of the public, even the most educated members, the public makes little attempt to understand the issues. Other than at major financial crises, there is thus little, if any, public sentiment or emotion for change. Outside the industry and its regulators, basically no one cares about regulatory agency restructuring. It is primarily an inside the beltway issue. Thus, the outlook for restructuring the regulatory agencies for good or for bad is not bright. Nevertheless, both the Senate and House Banking Committees have announced that they will take another try at it this session. Most likely, as they are now both housed in the Treasury Department, there may be an attempt to consolidate the OCC and the OTS. If the Clinton Administration wishes to do so, it would be easiest to leave the open OTS Director position vacant. Once it is filled, the new incumbent and the S&L industry are likely to join forces to maintain the status quo.

8.5 SUMMARY

What is the current state of banking reform? As with most important reforms in any area, it takes a perceived crisis to occur. Otherwise, the status quo philosophy of 'if it ain't broke but only inefficient, don't fix it' wins hands down. Thus, even though many of the potential causes of financial crises had been identified in earlier studies and reforms proposed, banking reform made slow progress until the crisis actually occurred. This is clearly evident for the recent S&L and commercial banking debacles. Because deposit insurance was identified as the major culprit of the debacle, the highest priority was, rightly so, given to deposit insurance reform. The lesser culprits of bank powers and regulatory agency structure, which had been recommended for reform for considerably longer periods of time, were accorded lower and less urgent priority. In practice, regulatory changes generally follow, rather than precede, market changes. Because major financial crises occur only periodically, major financial reform occurs only periodically. Lesser regulatory reforms follow lesser regulatory failures.

FDICIA represents potentially effective reform of the previous perverse incentive structure for bankers to take excessive risk under deposit insurance and for regulators to forbear taking appropriate corrective actions. As was discussed, whether FDICIA lives up to its potential depends largely on the willingness of the regulators to implement its provisions and of Congress and the Administration to hold their feet to the fire if they do not do so.

Significant legislative action to expand product and geographic powers in the near-term is unlikely, at least until the banking industry is healthier and less likely to require taxpayer support. If FDICIA is successful in reducing or eliminating altogether the perceived threat to taxpayers of losses from bank failures, expanded powers are a distinct possibility. But broadened product powers would add only marginally to aggregate bank market share and profitability and does not have the unanimous approval of the banking industry itself. It is caught between the opposition of many smaller banks and the support of fewer but more influential larger banks. Expanded geographic power in the form of interstate branching is more likely, although it also is caught in the middle of the two warring bank factions. But, because nationwide bank holding company banking is now almost a reality and is eroding local banking monopolies and because it not only does not appear to increase risk but should actually promote safety through improved diversification, nationwide branching is probably more inevitable than are greatly expanded product powers. Because it permits regulators to limit expanded powers only to better capitalized banks, thereby providing an incentive for banks to improve their capital ratios, FDICIA is a good vehicle for introducing additional powers. Regulatory agency reform is probably least needed, least likely to reach agreement on, furthest away for major changes, and least likely to resemble 'reform' if and when it does occur.

Notes

1. An earlier draft was presented at a conference on *Financial Prosperity in the 21st Century*, Jerome Levy Economics Institute of Bard College, Annandale-on-Hudson, New York, 4–6 March 1993.
2. For a review of the contribution of these studies to financial reform see Sidney L. Jones, *The Development of Economic Policy: Financial Institution Reform*, Ann Arbor, MI: University of Michigan, 1979 and Thomas R. Saving *et al.*, 'Toward a More Competitive Financial Sector' and following articles, *Journal of Money, Credit and Banking*, November 1972, pp. 897–1009.
3. Milton Friedman and Anna J. Schwartz, *A Monetary History of the United States, 1867–1960*, Princeton, NJ: Princeton University Press, 1963, pp. 11, 437, 440.
4. Mark D. Flood, 'The Great Deposit Insurance Debate', *Review* (Federal Reserve Bank of St Louis), July/August 1992, pp. 51–77; James R. Barth, John J. Feid, Gabriel Riedal, and H. Hampton Tunis, 'Alternative Federal Deposit Insurance Regimes' in US Senate Committee on Banking, Housing and Urban Affairs, *Problems of the Federal Savings and Loan Insurance Corporation: Hearings*, Washington, DC: 101st Congress, 1st Session, Part IV, 1989; and Charles W. Calomiris, 'Getting the Incentives Right in the Current Deposit-Insurance System: Successes From the Pre-FDIC Era' in James R. Barth and R. Dan Brumbaugh, Jr. (eds), *The Reform of Federal Deposit Insurance*, HarperBusiness, 1992, pp. 13–35.
5. Federal Deposit Insurance Corporation, *The First Fifty Years*, Washington, DC, 1984, p. 29.
6. A similar deposit insurance plan for savings and loan associations under FSLIC was enacted in 1934, both to maintain equality between banks and S&Ls and to protect the flow of funds into home buying.
7. FDIC, pp. 86–7.
8. George G. Kaufman, 'Lender of Last Resort, Too Large To Fail, and Deposit Insurance Reform' in James R. Barth and R. Dan Brumbaugh, Jr. (eds), *The Reform of Federal Deposit Insurance*, HarperBusiness, 1992, pp. 256–7.
9. James R. Barth, R. Dan Brumbaugh, Jr., and Robert Litan, *The Future of American Banking*, Armonk, NY: M. E. Sharpe, 1992, pp. 110–3.
10. James R. Barth and Philip F. Bartholomew, 'The Thrift Industry Crisis: Revealed Weaknesses in the Federal Deposit Insurance System', in James R. Barth and R. Dan Brumbaugh Jr. (eds), *The Reform of Deposit Insurance*, HarperBusiness, 1992, pp. 36–116 and Edward J. Kane, *The S&L Insurance Mess*, Washington, DC: Urban Institute Press, 1989.
11. Thomas Mayer, 'A Graduated Deposit Insurance Plan', *Review of Economics and Statistics*, February 1965, pp. 114–6. See also Thomas Mayer and Kenneth Scott, 'Risk and Regulation in Banking', *Stanford Law Review*, May 1971, pp. 857–902.
12. For a history of the SEIR proposal, see George J. Benston and George G. Kaufman, 'The Intellectual History of the Federal Deposit Insurance Corporation Improvement Act' Working Paper, Loyola University of Chicago, January 1993. A briefer version appears in *Assessing Bank Reform:*

FDICIA One Year Later, Washington, DC: Brookings Institution (forthcoming).

13. George J. Benston and George G. Kaufman, 'Improving the FDIC Improvement Act: What Was Done and What Still Needs to be Done to Fix the Deposit Insurance Problem', Working Paper, Loyola University of Chicago, January 1993.
14. US General Accounting Office, *Bank Failures: Independent Audits Needed to Strengthen Internal Control and Bank Management*, Washington, DC, 31 May 1989, and US General Accounting Office, *Failed Banks: Accounting and Auditing Reforms Urgently Needed*, Washington, DC, 22 April 1991; and US General Accounting Office, *Depository Institutions: Flexible Accounting Rules Lead to Inflated Financial Reports*, Washington, DC, 1 June 1992.
15. Justine Farr Rodriguez, Richard L. Cooperstein, and F. Steven Redburn, 'Assessing the Cost of Government Guarantees', *Credit Markets in Transition*, Chicago: Federal Reserve Bank of Chicago, May 1992, pp. 14–32.
16. The General Accounting Office has recently concluded that:

> Because neither FASB nor the regulators appear willing to address the serious deficiencies in existing accounting standards for non-performing loans, we have suggested that the Congress consider legislating regulatory accounting principles for non-performing loans and financial reporting to the regulators... If the regulators do not adequately address our recommendations to correct the serious weaknesses, the Congress may wish to enact legislation to mandate such improvements.
>
> (General Accounting Office, *Bank Insurance Fund*, Washington, DC, December 1992, pp. 37–8)

The agencies are currently working on revising and clarifying standards for loan loss allowances.

17. George G. Kaufman, 'Capital in Banking: Past, Present and Future', *Journal of Financial Services Research*, April 1992, pp. 385–402.
18. For a discussion of the state of bank powers reform in the early 1980s see George G. Kaufman, Larry R. Mote, and Harvey Rosenblum, 'Consequences of Deregulation for Commercial Banking Reform', *Journal of Finance*, July 1984, pp. 789–803. See also Franklin R. Edwards, 'The Future Financial Structure: Fears and Policies', in William S. Haraf and Rose Marie Kushmeider (eds), *Restructuring Banking and Financial Services in America*, Washington, DC: American Enterprise Institute, 1988, pp. 113–55; and Anthony Saunders, 'Bank Holding Companies: Structure, Performance and Reform', in William S. Haraf and Rose Marie Kushmeider (eds), *Restructuring Banking and Financial Services in America*, Washington, DC: American Enterprise Institute, 1988, pp. 156–202.
19. A thorough review of all issues related to universal banking appears in Thomas A. Pugel, Anthony Saunders, and Ingo Walter, *Universal Banking in the United States*, New York: Oxford University Press, forthcoming.
20. Thomas G. Fischer, William H. Gram, George G. Kaufman, and Larry R. Mote, 'The Securities Activities of Commercial Banks: A Legal and Economic Analysis', *Tennessee Law Review*, Spring 1984, pp. 467–578;

George G. Kaufman, 'Securities Activities of Commercial Banks: Recent Changes in the Economic and Legal Environments', *Journal of Financial Services Research*, January 1988, pp. 183–99; and George G. Kaufman and Larry R. Mote, 'Glass–Steagall: Repeal by Regulatory and Judicial Reinterpretation', *Banking Law Journal*, September–October 1990, pp. 388–421.

21. Robert E. Litan, 'Interstate Banking and Product-Line Freedom: Would Broader Powers Have Helped the Banks', *Yale Journal of Regulation*, Summer 1992, pp. 521–42.
22. Donna C. Vandenbrink, 'Usury Ceilings and DIDMCA', *Economic Perspectives*, Federal Reserve Bank of Chicago, September/October 1985, pp. 25–30.
23. Kenneth E. Scott, 'The Patchwork Quilt: State and Federal Roles in Bank Regulation', *Stanford Law Review*, April 1980, p. 742. Good reviews of the arguments for and against restructuring appear in Bernard Shull, 'How Should Bank Regulatory Agencies Be Organized', *Contemporary Policy Issues*, January 1993, pp. 99–107; George J. Benston, Robert A. Eisenbeis, Paul M. Horvitz, Edward J. Kane, and George G. Kaufman, 'Perspectives on Safe and Sound Banking', Cambridge, MA.: MIT Press, 1986, Chapter II, 'Centralization or Decentralization of Regulation, Supervision and Examination', and US Treasury Department, *Modernizing the Financial System*, Washington, DC, February 1991, Chapter 19, 'Reform of the Regulatory Structure'.

References

Barth, James R. and Philip F. Bartholomew (1992) 'The Thrift Industry Crisis: Revealed Weaknesses in the Federal Deposit Insurance System', James R. Barth and R. Dan Brumbaugh Jr. (eds), *The Reform of Deposit Insurance* (New York: HarperBusiness) 36–116.

Barth, James R. and R. Dan Brumbaugh, Jr. (eds) (1992) *The Reform of Deposit Insurance* (New York: HarperBusiness).

Barth, James R., R. Dan Brumbaugh, Jr. and Robert Litan (1992) *The Future of American Banking* (Armonk, NY: M.E. Sharpe).

Barth, James R., John F. Field, Gabriel Riedal and H. Hampton Tunis (1989) 'Alternative Federal Deposit Insurance Regimes', US Senate Committee on Banking, Housing and Urban Affairs, *Problems of the Federal Savings and Loan Insurance Corporation: Hearings* (Washington, DC: 101st Congress, 1st Session, Part II, 22, 23, 28 February and 1, 2 March) 300–36.

Benston, George J., Robert A. Eisenbeis, Paul M. Horvitz, Edward J. Kane and George G. Kaufman (1986) *Perspectives on Safe and Sound Banking* (Cambridge, MA: MIT Press) Chapter II.

Benston, George J. and George G. Kaufman (1993) 'The Intellectual History of the Federal Deposit Insurance Corporation Improvement Act', Working Paper (Loyola University, January).

Benston, George J. and George G. Kaufman (1993) 'Improving the FDIC Improvement Act: What Was Done and What Still Needs to be Done to Fix the

Deposit Insurance Problem,' Working Paper (Loyola University of Chicago, January).

Calomiris, Charles W. (1992) 'Getting the Incentives Right in the Current Deposit-Insurance System: Successes From the Pre-FDIC Era', in James R. Barth and R. Dan Brumbaugh, Jr. (eds), *The Reform of Federal Deposit Insurance* (New York: HarperBusiness) 13–35.

Edwards, Franklin R. (1988) 'The Future Financial Structure: Fears and Policies', in William S. Haraf and Rose Marie Kushmeider (eds), *Restructuring Banking and Financial Services in America* (Washington, DC: American Enterprise Institute) 156–202.

Federal Deposit Insurance Corporation (1984) *The First Fifty Years* (Washington, DC).

Fisher, Thomas G., William H. Gram, George G. Kaufman and Larry R. Mote (1984) 'The Securities Activities of Commercial Banks: A Legal and Economic Analysis', *Tennessee Law Review* (Spring) 467–578.

Flood, Mark D. (1992) 'The Great Deposit Insurance Debate', *Review* (Federal Reserve Bank of St Louis, July/August) 51–77.

Friedman, Milton and Anna J. Schwartz (1963) *A Monetary History of the United States, 1987–1960* (Princeton, NJ: Princeton University Press).

Jones, Sidney L. (1979) *The Development of Economic Policy: Financial Institution Reform* (Ann Arbor, MI: University of Michigan).

Kane, Edward J. (1989) *The S&L Insurance Mess* (Washington, DC: Urban Institute Press).

Kaufman, George G. (1988) 'Securities Activities of Commercial Banks: Recent Changes in the Economic and Legal Environments', *Journal of Financial Services Research* (January) 183–99.

Kaufman, George G. (1992) 'Lender of Last Resort, Too Large to Fail, and Deposit Insurance Reform', in James R. Barth and R. Dan Brumbaugh, Jr. (eds), *The Reform of Federal Deposit Insurance* (New York: HarperBusiness) 246–58.

Kaufman, George G. (1992) 'Capital in Banking: Past, Present and Future', *Journal of Financial Services Research* (April) 385–402.

Kaufman, George G. (1993) 'The Intellectual History of the Federal Deposit Insurance Corporation Improvement Act', in *Assessing Bank Reform: FDICIA One Year Later* (Washington, DC: Brookings Institution).

Kaufman, George G. and Larry R. Mote (1990) 'Glass–Steagall: Repeal by Regulatory and Judicial Reinterpretation', *Banking Law Journal* (September–October) 388–421.

Kaufman, George G., Larry R. Mote and Harvey Rosenblum (1984) 'Consequences of Deregulation for Commercial Banking Reform', *Journal of Finance* (July) 789–803.

Litan, Robert E. (1992) 'Interstate Banking and Product-Line Freedom: Would Broader Powers have Helped the Banks', *Yale Journal of Regulation* (Summer) 521–42.

Mayer, Thomas (1965) 'A Graduated Deposit Insurance Plan', *Review of Economics and Statistics* (February) 114–6.

Pugel, Thomas A., Anthony Saunders and Ingo Walter (1994) *Universal Banking in the United States* (New York: Oxford University Press).

Rodriguez, Justine Farr, Richard L. Cooperstein and F. Steven Redburn (1992) 'Assessing the Cost of Government Guarantees', *Credit Markets in Transition* (Chicago, May) 14–32.

Saunders, Anthony (1988) 'Bank Holding Companies: Structure, Performance and Reform', in William S. Haraf and Rose Marie Kushmeider (eds), *Restructuring Banking and Financial Services in America* (Washington, DC: American Enterprise Institute) 156–202.

Saving, Thomas R. (1972) *et al*, 'Toward a More Competitive Financial Sector' and following articles, *Journal of Money, Credit and Banking* (November) 897–1009.

Scott, Kenneth E. (1980) 'The Patchwork Quilt: State and Federal Roles in Bank Regulation', *Stanford Law Review* (April) 687–742.

Shull, Bernard (1993) 'How Should Bank Regulatory Agencies Be Organized', *Contemporary Policy Issues* (January) 99–107.

United States General Accounting Office (1989) *Bank Failures: Independent Audits Needed to Strengthen Internal Control and Bank Management* (Washington, DC, 31 May).

United States General Accounting Office (1991) *Failed Banks: Accounting and Auditing Reforms Urgently Needed* (Washington, DC, 22 April).

United States General Accounting Office (1992) *Depository Institutions: Flexible Accounting Rules Lead to Inflated Financial Reports* (Washington, DC, 1 June).

United States General Accounting Office (1992) *Bank Insurance Fund* (Washington, DC, December).

9 A Comparison of Proposals to Restructure the US Financial System[1]

R. Alton Gilbert

Since the 1930s, commercial banks in the United States have been permitted to offer only a limited range of financial services. At the same time, firms engaged in non-financial activities, as well as some in financial industries, have not been permitted to own banks. Such restrictions were intended to limit the risk of bank failure, to avoid conflicts of interest and to prevent undue concentration of financial power.[2]

There have been many proposals in recent years to permit banking organizations to offer wider ranges of services. One major reason for permitting the common ownership of banks and firms in other industries is based on concern about the role of banks in financial intermediation in the future. Some bank customers have found cheaper sources of credit and other financial services outside the banking industry. Consequently, some analysts say, restrictions must be relaxed if banks are to survive.[3]

In 1991, the Bush Administration introduced legislation that would have permitted banking organizations to offer a wide range of financial services. Congress rejected that part of the proposed legislation. Instead, Congress enacted the Federal Deposit Insurance Corporation Improvement Act of 1991, which focuses on changes in supervision to limit the risk assumed by banks in their existing activities. Thus, arguments to broaden the range of services offered by banking firms remain as relevant as they were in the mid-1980s, when many of the proposals for restructuring the financial system were drafted. The purpose of this chapter is to describe several major proposals for changing banking restrictions and to examine the concepts that underlie these proposals.

9.1 CURRENT RESTRICTIONS ON BANKING ACTIVITY

At present, the activities of federally insured commercial banks are limited essentially to accepting deposits, holding relatively low-risk securities and making loans. Banking organizations may acquire firms engaged in financial activities through bank holding companies (BHCs) – corporations that own one or more banks. In the Bank Holding Company Act (BHCA), Congress authorized the Federal Reserve Board to determine what activities are permissible for BHCs; these activities, according to the act, should be 'so closely related to banking as to be a proper incident thereto'. Banks generally can engage in most activities that BHCs are allowed to pursue.[4] A major distinction between banks and the nonbank subsidiaries of BHCs involves opportunities for geographic expansion. The nonbank subsidiaries of BHCs may have offices throughout the nation, whereas nationwide branch banking is not permitted.

BHCs are subject to the supervision of the Federal Reserve, which periodically inspects them to determine whether they are operating in a sound manner and in compliance with regulations. Important regulations of BHCs include capital requirements set by the Federal Reserve and restrictions on transactions between banks and their affiliates designed to limit the risk assumed by banks. On several occasions, the Federal Reserve Board has ruled that BHCs could not undertake certain activities because they were not closely related to banking, might result in conflicts of interest or might have subjected the BHCs to greater risk.[5]

9.2 PROPOSALS FOR RESTRUCTURING THE US BANKING SYSTEM

This section describes seven proposals for restructuring the US banking system. Although others could be included, particularly those dealing with the entry of banks into specific industries, the following proposals encompass the range of options considered in the policy debates since the mid-1980s.

The key features of these seven proposals are summarized in Table 9.1. Each proposal would permit banking organizations to engage in a broader range of activities than currently allowed. Essentially, the proposals allow nonbanking services to be offered through corporate entities (affiliates or subsidiaries) distinct from the banks themselves.

There are two primary differences among the proposals. First, they differ on whether to permit nonfinancial firms to acquire banks or BHCs. These differences reflect conflicting views on the policies necessary to avoid conflicts of interest, decreased or unfair competition among firms offering financial services and undue concentration of economic resources. These issues have been discussed extensively elsewhere and, thus, they are not analyzed in this chapter.[6]

Table 9.1 Proposals to restructure the financial system

Features	*Association of bank holding companies (LaWare (1987))*	*Association of reserve city bankers (1987)*	*Robert Heller (1987)*	*Federal deposit insurance corporation (1987)*	*Gerald Corrigan (1987)*	*Robert Litan (1987)*
Corporate structure required of firms that own banks	FSHCs would own BHCs and holding companies that own firms engaged in financial activities in addition to banking	FSHCs would directly own banks and firms in other industries	BHCs could acquire banks and firms engaged in financial activities. Non-financial firms could acquire BHCs	Firm in any industry could buy banks, and banks could engage in non-banking activities through their own subsidiaries	Firms that engage in financial activities exclusively could purchase banks	Firms engaged in any activities could buy banks, subject to restrictions on the assets held by those banks
Ownership of banks by nonfinancial firms permitted	No	Yes	Yes	Yes	No	Yes
Restrictions on transactions between banks and their affiliates	Keep current restrictions	Eliminate section 23B of the Federal Reserve Act	Keep current restrictions	Impose uniform restrictions on dividends and lending limits of bank. Make these restrictions and those in sections 23A and 23B of the Federal Reserve Act apply to transactions between banks and their subsidiaries.	Keep current restrictions	Prohibit banks owned by nonbanking organizations from lending to affiliates

Table 9.1 Continued

Features	*Association of bank holding companies (LaWare (1987))*	*Association of reserve city bankers (1987)*	*Robert Heller (1987)*	*Federal deposit insurance corporation (1987)*	*Gerald Corrigan (1987)*	*Robert Litan (1987)*
Supervisory authority of regulatory agencies	Supervision of banks and BHCs unchanged. No one agency supervises FSHCs, which may own BHCs and holding companies that own firms in financial industries other than banking. Subsidiaries of FSHCs in nonbanking industries subject to supervision by their regulatory authorities	Same as for the Association of Bank Holding Companies	No comment on supervisory powers of the Federal Reserve over BHCs. Nonbank subsidiaries of BHCs subject to supervision by their own government authorities	Firms that buy banks not subject to supervision by bank supervisors. Banks required to report all transactions with affiliates or subsidiaries to bank supervisors, which could audit the terms of the transactions	Firms that own banks subject to supervision by the federal bank supervisors, including exercise of powers to limit risks (such as capital requirements) and aggregate concentration in the financial system	Nonbank firms that own banks not subject to bank supervisors except to verify that those banks held only the designated safe assets
Obligation to support bank subsidiaries	None	None	BHCs must absorb losses of bank subsidiaries. Non-banking firms must absorb lossess of of their BHCs	None	No formal obligation, but general commitment to be a source of strength for bank subsidiaries	None
Restrictions on assets of banks	Current restrictions	Current restrictions	Current restrictions	Current restrictions	Current restrictions	Bank subsidiaries of non-banking firms may hold only designated low-risk, liquid assets

Second, the proposals differ on the policies necessary to limit the risk assumed by banks. Note that the proposals have some common features designed to limit banking risk. Each proposal in Table 9.1 requires banking organizations to offer nonbanking services through subsidiaries or affiliates; moreover, each includes restrictions on banks lending to their nonbank subsidiaries or affiliates. These proposals rely in part on the legal concept of 'corporate separateness', under which the creditors of a corporation have no legal claim on the assets of a stockholder, even if that stockholder is another corporation. Thus, creditors of the nonbanking units of a firm that also owns banks would have no claim on its banks' assets.[7]

Several proposals include special features to limit the risk of bank failure that might result from affiliation of banks and nonbanking firms. The Heller proposal (Heller, 1987) requires BHCs to absorb all losses incurred by their bank subsidiaries; nonfinancial firms that acquire BHCs would absorb all losses incurred by their BHCs. The FDIC proposal (Federal Deposit Insurance Corporation, 1987) requires bank supervisors to audit transactions between banks and their nonbank affiliates or subsidiaries to determine whether they are detrimental to the banks. The Corrigan proposal (Corrigan, 1987) relies on direct supervision of the firms that buy banks to limit the risk they assume. Finally, the Litan proposal (Litan, 1987) requires banks purchased by nonbanking firms to hold only low-risk liquid assets.[8]

9.3 A FRAMEWORK FOR ANALYZING THE RISK OF BANK FAILURE

The proposals for changing bank regulations are concerned with their likely effect on bank failures. This section illustrates how the probability of bank failure is affected when banks and nonbanking firms combine.

9.3.1 Key Factors Affecting the Profits and Risks of Combining Banks and Nonbanking Firms[9]

If a bank offers nonbanking services, the effect on both the expected rate of return and the variability of returns to the bank's shareholders, as well as the risk of failure for the bank, depend on five factors. Suppose a bank merges with a nonbanking firm. *One* important factor is the average level of expected profits or rate of return for the nonbanking service. A *second* factor is the 'risk' associated with the prospective nonbanking service; risk is often measured by the standard deviation of the profits or rates of return.

A *third* factor is the correlation between the profit rates of the bank and nonbanking firm. A *fourth* factor is the size of the bank relative to the nonbanking firm. The third and fourth factors are important because the bank may actually reduce its risk by acquiring a nonbanking firm that has a higher coefficient of variation of profits than the bank. This possibility will be demonstrated later.

The *fifth* factor that must be considered is the 'synergies' (increase in profits) involved in combining banking and nonbanking services in the same organization. Offering banking and nonbanking services through the same firm may reduce the cost of providing the services and may attract customers who value the wider array of services offered by the combined bank–nonbank firm. These synergies could produce profit rates that exceed the sum of the profit rates of banks and firms in the nonbanking industry operating as separate corporations.

9.3.2 Some Empirical Estimates of Rates of Return and Risk

A number of studies have investigated the profit rates and risk in banking and selected nonbank activities.[10] One finding, demonstrated in Table 9.2, is that both the average profit rate and its standard deviation are lower in banking than in several industries that banks would be permitted to enter under the recent proposals.[11] Indeed, the standard deviation of return on equity, one measure of risk, is lowest in Table 9.2 for the banking industry. Another key finding of these studies is that the profit rates of banks are not positively correlated with the profits of firms in many industries that they would be permitted to enter. Thus, banks could diversify their risk by entering many nonbanking industries, even if the profits of firms in those industries are more variable than those of banks.

Table 9.3 illustrates the potential reduction in variability of bank profits possible through mergers with firms that offer other financial services. The table illustrates this with the coefficient of variation, a measure of relative risk that is calculated by dividing the standard deviation of the profit rates by the mean. The results demonstrate, using a hypothetical situation involving the relative size of banking and nonbanking components of the firm, that the combined firm can have the same or even lower risk than the bank itself, even though risk is higher in the nonbanking industries.

Boyd, Graham and Hewitt (1993) simulate mergers of banking firms with firms in other financial industries, using accounting and stock market data. Simulated mergers with life and property/casualty insurance companies reduce the risk of bankruptcy, but mergers with securities and real-estate firms increase the risk of bankruptcy of banking firms.

Table 9.2 Means and standard deviations of profit rates for firms in financial service industries, 1975–84

Industry	*Average after-tax return on equity (ROE)*	*Standard deviation of ROE*
Commercial banks	12.3%	1.3%
Thrift institutions	3.4	10.7
Securities brokers	13.0	4.0
Securities underwriters	16.4	5.7
Large investment banks only	21.5	7.7
Life insurance underwriters	13.7	2.3
Property–casualty insurance underwriters	11.9	6.4
Insurance brokers and agents	12.2	4.1
All manufacturing	13.1	2.0

Source: Litan (1987), p. 64.

Table 9.3 Variability of profits of hypothetical firms formed through the merger of banks and firms in various financial industries, 1962–82

Item	*Coefficient of variation*
Banks alone	0.22
Banks plus savings and loan associations	0.18
Banks plus personal credit agencies	0.24
Banks plus business credit agencies	0.22
Banks plus securities and commodities brokers	0.22
Banks plus life insurance	0.15
Banks plus mutual insurers	0.29
Banks plus insurance agents	0.15
Banks plus real estate operators and lessors	0.20
Banks plus subdividers and developers	0.20

Note: A time series of the profits of each hypothetical firm is formed by assuming that 75 per cent of the assets of the hypothetical firm are devoted to banking and 25 per cent are devoted to the nonbanking activity. The coefficient of variation is derived for the constructed time series.
Source: Litan (1987), p. 88.

Because banks have not yet entered the various nonbanking industries, there is little evidence on the magnitude of the synergies involved in combining banks with other firms.[12] There is evidence, however, of synergies for banks and selected financial activities. For example, before the separation of commercial banking and investment banking in the 1930s, securities affiliates of commercial banks held a large share of the investment banking business.[13] In nations where commercial banking organizations may offer investment banking services, commercial banking organizations have large shares of the investment banking business.[14]

9.3.3 An Illustration

The effects of permitting banking organizations to offer nonbanking services on the risk and returns in banking are analyzed using two probability

Table 9.4 Probability distributions of the profits of a bank and a nonbanking firm prior to merger or affiliation

		Bank	
Outcome	*Probability*	*Profits*	*Return to shareholders*
A	0.01	–$110	–$100
B	0.98	10	10
C	0.01	130	130
		Nonbanking firm	
Outcome	*Probability*	*Profits*	*Return to shareholders*
A	0.05	–$115	–$100
B	0.90	15	15
C	0.05	145	145

	Bank	*Nonbanking firm*
Expected return to shareholders as a percentage of capital	10.1%	15.75%
Coefficient of variation of returns to shareholders	1.6117	2.4637
Expected loss to the FDIC	$0.10	

distributions of profits, one for a hypothetical bank and another for a nonbanking firm. These probability distributions, presented in Table 9.4, are designed to reflect the results of studies of risk and returns in banking and various nonbanking industries summarized above. Profit distributions are combined in Table 9.5 under various assumptions that reflect the proposals for restructuring the financial system described in Table 9.1. Table 9.6 shows the returns to shareholders and the expected loss to the FDIC for the four cases analyzed in Table 9.5.

The illustration is designed to be simple. Differences among the four cases might change under assumptions that would make the analysis more complex. For instance, the management of the firm that buys the bank and the nonbanking firm is assumed to make no changes that affect the capital ratios or the probability distributions of profits. Analysis of the cases under alternative assumptions is beyond the scope of this chapter.

The bank begins the current year with book value of equity equal to \$100. The market value of the bank is assumed to equal its book value prior to financial restructuring, which permits the affiliation of the bank with the nonbanking firm. As presented in Table 9.4, the (discrete) probability distribution of the bank's profits in the current year has three possible outcomes: a 1 per cent chance of a loss of \$110, which would cause the bank to fail, a 98 per cent chance of a profit of \$10 (a 10 per cent return on equity) and a 1 per cent chance of a profit of \$130.[15]

Table 9.4 also presents the probability distribution of profits of a nonbanking firm that begins the year with book value capital of \$100. The market value of the nonbanking firm is also assumed initially to equal \$100. The nonbanking firm is riskier than the bank: the coefficient of variation of its profits is higher than that of the bank. This specification was chosen to reflect the greater variability of profits shown in Table 9.2 in some of the industries that banking institutions wish to enter.

The effects of combining the bank and the nonbanking firm in the same corporation are examined using three indicators: the expected return to shareholders as a per cent of capital, the coefficient of variation of returns to shareholders of the consolidated firm, and the expected loss to the FDIC from the bank's failure. These measures are calculated in Table 9.4 for both the bank and the nonbanking firm as separate organizations to provide benchmarks for comparison. The distribution of returns to shareholders differs from the distribution of profits because losses to shareholders are limited to the amount of their initial investment in the firm. Thus, losses to shareholders are limited to \$100 for the bank and \$100 for the nonbanking firm. The expected loss to the FDIC is calculated as follows. The bank fails in only one of the three possible outcomes: a loss of \$110,

Table 9.5 Distributions of returns to shareholders for various combinations of a bank and a nonbanking firm

Outcome	*Outcomes form underlying profit distributions (bank, nonbanking firm)*	*Probability (bank × nonbanking firm)*	(1) *Merger* *Return to shareholders*	(1) *Merger* *Loss to FDIC*	(2) *Affiliation, corporate separateness* *Return to shareholders*	(2) *Affiliation, corporate separateness* *Loss to FDIC*
1	A,A	0.01 × 0.05 = 0.0005	–\$100 –\$100 = –\$200	\$25	–\$100 – \$100 = –\$200	\$10
2	A,B	0.01 × 0.90 = 0.009	–110 + 15 = –95		–100 + 15 = –85	10
3	A,C	0.01 × 0.05 = 0.0005	–110 + 145 = 35		–100 + 145 = 45	10
4	B,A	0.98 × 0.05 = 0.049	10 – 115 = –105		10 – 100 = –90	
5	B,B	0.98 × 0.90 = 0.882	10 + 15 = 25		10 + 15 = 25	
6	B,C	0.98 × 0.05 = 0.049	10 + 145 = 155		10 + 145 = 155	
7	C,A	0.01 × 0.05 = 0.0005	130 115 = 15		130 – 100 = 30	
8	C,B	0.01 × 0.90 = 0.009	130 + 15 = 145		130 + 15 = 145	
9	C,C	0.01 × 0.05 = 0.0005	130 + 145 = 275		130 + 145 = 275	

Table 9.5 Continued

Outcome	(3) *Affiliation, Heller proposal* — *Return to shareholders*	*Loss to FDIC*	(4) *Affiliation, corporate separateness; bank lends $10 at a zero interest rate to its nonbank affiliate* — *Return to shareholders*	*Loss to FDIC*
1	–$100 – $100 = –$200	$10	–$100 – $100 = –$200	$20.50
2	–110 + 15 = –95		–100 + (15 + 1.053) = –83.947	10.50
3	–110 + 145 = 35		–100 + (145 + 1.053) = 46.053	10.50
4	10 – 100 = – 90		(10 – 0.50) – 10) – 100 = –100.500	
5	10 + 15 = 25		(10 – 0.50) + (15 + 1.053) = 25.553	
6	10 + 145 = 155		(10 – 0.50) + (145 + 1.053) = 155.553	
7	130 – 100 = 30		(130 – 0.50 – 10) – 100 = 19.500	
8	130 + 15 = 145		(130 – 0.50) + (15 + 1.053) = 145.553	
9	130 + 145 = 275		(130 – 0.50) + (145 + 1.053) = 275.553	

Table 9.6 Returns to shareholders and losses to the FDIC under various combinations of a bank and a nonbanking firm

Case number	*Means of combining the firms*	*Expected return to shareholders as a percentage of capital*	*Coefficient of variation of returns to shareholders*	*Expected loss to the FDIC*
1	Merger	12.51%	1.7754	$0.0125
2	Affiliation, corporate separateness	12.93	1.6278	0.1000
3	Affiliation, Heller proposal	12.88	1.6434	0.0050
4	Affiliation, corporate separateness; bank lends $10 at zero interest rate to nonbank affiliate	12.93	1.6860	0.1100

with a chance of 1 per cent. The loss to the FDIC in that outcome would be $10, since the initial capital of the bank is $100. Thus, the expected loss to the FDIC is $10 (loss to FDIC) × 0.01 (probability) = $0.10.

In deriving the distribution of returns to shareholders in Table 9.5, one must specify their investment, which determines their maximum loss and the denominator used in calculating their expected rate of return. The shareholders' initial investment is measured as the book value of the combined firms. The use of book value, net of any accounting goodwill resulting from the acquisition of the bank and the nonbanking firm, provides a basis for specifying bankruptcy. Book value also provides a common denominator for comparisons of expected rates of return in the various cases. The market value of the firm that buys the bank and the nonbanking firm will exceed their combined book value. If this were not the case, the combination of these firms in the same corporation would not benefit the shareholders.

The profits of the bank and the nonbanking firm are assumed to be statistically independent and, thus, uncorrelated. This assumption simplifies the analysis; it is also consistent with some of the evidence cited previously for several industries that banks could enter. For each outcome for the profits of the bank, there are three possible outcomes for the profits of the nonbanking firm. If combined into one firm, there would be nine possible outcomes for the returns to shareholders of the consolidated firm, as Table 9.5 illustrates.

Tables 9.5 and 9.6 ignore the existence of synergies from combining a bank with a nonbanking firm; they assume that there is no increase in the joint profits resulting from lower costs or a wider array of services to offer customers. As previously mentioned, it is difficult to determine the magnitude of such synergies, given that such combinations have been unlawful for many years. Such synergies, of course, must exist to make such combinations attractive to shareholders; investors can easily obtain the benefits of diversification by owning shares of firms with uncorrelated profits. In this chapter, however, assumptions about the size of the synergies are unnecessary; the relevant comparisons are made between the various cases. An increase in the levels of profits for each outcome would not alter the differences among the four cases examined in Tables 9.5 and 9.6, unless the synergies eliminate bankruptcy in all outcomes.

9.3.4 Merger of the Bank and the Nonbanking Firm: The Simplest Case

Each proposal described in Table 9.1 calls for the new activities of banking organizations to be conducted through corporate entities that are separate from banks. This feature of the proposals reflects the view that the chances of bank failure and the potential loss to the FDIC would be higher if the organizations that own banks offered nonbanking services through their bank subsidiaries, rather than through subsidiaries that are separate from the banks.

This view is not valid under all circumstances, as case 1 in Tables 9.5 and 9.6 illustrate. In this case, the bank begins offering nonbanking services by merging with the nonbanking firm that has the profit distribution presented in Table 9.4. The capital of the bank after the merger is $200. Given the underlying profit distributions in Table 9.4, there is only one outcome in which the bank fails: in outcome # 1, the returns from the banking and nonbanking activities yield the largest possible losses. In that outcome, the shareholders lose their total investment. The bank remains in operation in all of the other outcomes. In outcomes # 2 and # 3, in which the losses from banking operations are large enough to make the bank fail if operating as a separate corporation, the profits from the nonbanking operations and the increased capital of the bank resulting from the merger keep the bank from failing.

The expected loss to the FDIC in case 1 depends on what happens to the liabilities of the nonbanking firm after the merger. Suppose the nonbanking segment of the merged firm continues to borrow from the same sources it used before the merger. If the claims of these lenders are subordinated to the claims of depositors, the merger might reduce the expected loss to the FDIC, perhaps to zero.

In this illustration, however, the merged organization converts all of its liabilities to federally insured deposits. If the bank involved in the merger goes bankrupt, the FDIC absorbs losses above the capital of $200. In outcome # 1, because the bank's maximum loss after its merger with the nonbanking firm is $225, the loss to the FDIC is $25. Although the maximum loss to the FDIC is larger after the merger, the expected loss ($25 × 0.0005) is actually smaller after the merger (compare Tables 9.4 and 9.6).

The effects that a merger have on the possibility of bank failure and the expected loss to the FDIC depend on the size of the nonbanking firm relative to the bank. To illustrate, suppose the bank merges with a nonbanking firm whose distribution of profits is 10 times as large for each outcome as that presented in Table 9.4 and whose capital is $1000. In this case, which is not shown in the table, the expected loss to the FDIC would be $2.04, much larger than the expected loss shown in Table 9.6. Thus, in considering a restructuring of the financial system, the size of the bank relative to the nonbanking firm is an important determinant of the expected loss to the FDIC.

9.3.5 Affiliation of a Bank with a Nonbanking Firm

If banks combine with nonbanking firms, one way to limit the FDIC's expected loss is to require that banks remain separate corporations within their parent organizations and limit FDIC insurance only to the deposit liabilities of the banks. Within such structures, the principle of corporate separateness would prevent the nonbanking firm's creditors from claiming the assets of the bank.

The risk and return characteristics of a holding company that buys the bank and the nonbanking firm are presented in case 2. Under this case, labelled 'affiliation, corporate separateness', losses to shareholders of the holding company resulting from losses by the nonbank subsidiary are limited to the capital of the nonbank subsidiary. The bank does not rescue the nonbank subsidiary by absorbing the additional losses. In turn, if the bank has losses that exceed its capital, the nonbank subsidiary does not rescue the bank by absorbing the additional losses. There is assumed to be no lending among units of the holding company. The holding company lends to neither the bank nor the nonbank subsidiary, and the bank lends nothing to the nonbank affiliate. The nonbank affiliate borrows, instead, from nonaffiliated lenders; the liabilities of the bank are covered by FDIC insurance.

The expected return to the shareholders is higher and the variability of returns is lower in case 2 than under a similar combination of firms arranged through a merger. Thus, the shareholders benefit more from a combination of the bank and the nonbanking firm as affiliates of a holding company than through the merger of these firms.

The benefit to the shareholders, however, comes partly at the expense of the FDIC. The FDIC's expected loss is the same in case 2 as in the benchmark case in Table 9.4 but higher than under the merger. Under affiliation and corporate separateness, the outcomes in which the FDIC is exposed to losses are determined by the probability distribution of the bank's profits. Under the merger illustrated in case 1, in contrast, losses in outcomes # 2 and # 3 that would make the bank fail are absorbed by the profits of the nonbank segment of the merged firm and the capital contributed by the nonbanking unit. Under affiliation and corporate separateness, however, the expected loss to the FDIC does not depend on the size of the bank relative to its nonbank affiliate.

9.4 IMPLICATIONS FOR THE PROPOSALS

9.4.1 Merger or Affiliation

The cases in Tables 9.5 and 9.6 indicate that, under some conditions, the risk of FDIC loss would be lower if a bank engages in a nonbanking activity directly, rather than through affiliation with a nonbanking firm. In considering proposals for financial restructuring, therefore, it is unnecessary to prohibit the direct offering of nonbanking services through banks under all circumstances.

9.4.2 The Financial Services Holding Company (FSHC) Proposal

The proposals by the Association of Bank Holding Companies (LaWare, 1987) and the Association of Reserve City Bankers (1987) would permit FSHCs to acquire banks as subsidiaries under the condition of affiliation and corporate separateness. The bank could not use its assets to rescue a failing nonbank affiliate, and the FSHC would not be required to rescue a failing bank.

A comparison of case 2 in Table 9.6 with Table 9.4 shows how the formation of FSHCs can affect risk in banking. Affiliation of a bank with a nonbanking firm reduces the probability that the bank will fail only if affiliation yields synergies that raise the profits of the bank for each possible outcome. Thus, affiliations between banks and nonbanking firms that facilitate diversification of risk for shareholders of banking firms reduce the probability of bank failure and the expected loss to the FDIC *only* if there are synergies from combining banking and nonbanking firms in the same organization.

9.4.3 The Heller 'Double Umbrella' Proposal

The distribution of returns to shareholders under the Heller (1987) proposal is presented under case 3 in Table 9.5. The implications of this proposal can be illustrated by comparing the distribution of returns to shareholders under various outcomes in cases 2 and 3. Under the Heller proposal, the losses of the bank and nonbank subsidiary in outcome # 1 absorb all of the capital of the holding company. The FDIC has a loss of $10 in that outcome, the amount by which the loss of the bank exceeds its capital. In outcome # 2, the bank has a loss that exceeds its capital, but the holding company is required to cover that loss, drawing on its profit of $15 from the nonbanking subsidiary and its capital. The holding company also covers the large loss of the bank in outcome # 3. In outcomes # 4 and # 7, in contrast, the holding company does not absorb all of the losses of the nonbanking subsidiary. Instead, the nonbanking subsidiary goes bankrupt. The holding company writes off its investment of $100, and nonaffiliated lenders absorb the additional loss of $15 in each of these outcomes.

The minimum level of synergies necessary to make combinations of banks and nonbanking firms attractive to investors is higher under the Heller proposal than under the FSHC proposal. The diversification of risk illustrated in case 2 could be achieved through a mutual fund that buys shares in firms in banking and nonbanking industries. Any synergies would make the shareholders' expected rate of return higher with the bank and nonbanking firm combined in the firm under affiliation and corporate separateness than through a mutual fund. To make combinations of banks and nonbanking firms under the Heller proposal attractive to shareholders, synergies would have to exceed a level necessary to compensate the holding company for the expected cost of bailing out the failing bank subsidiary.

The synergies necessary to make the affiliation of banks with nonbanking firms profitable under the Heller proposal would be different for each potential combination of firms. For case 3, the synergies would have to raise the returns to shareholders by $0.095 to make them equal to the expected returns to shareholders in case 2, and even more to compensate shareholders for the higher variability of returns in case 3.[16]

9.4.4 The Corrigan Proposal

Corrigan (1987) assumes that the methods of insulating banks built into the proposals of FSHCs will be ineffective. This view is based on evidence that BHCs are integrated organizations that have used all of their resources, including those of their bank subsidiaries, to support any nonbank subsidiary in danger of failing. Corrigan also expresses concern that, in approving the acquisition of banks by nonbanking firms, the federal supervisory authorities will extend the federal safety net to the parent organizations themselves.

9.4.4.1 The Effects of Loans to Nonbank Affiliates on Stockholder Wealth

The Corrigan proposal reflects these views on the relationship between banks and their parent organizations. Case 4 in Tables 9.5 and 9.6 examines whether such concerns reflect rational, profit-maximizing behavior. The Corrigan proposal assumes that firms are willing to risk the assets of their bank subsidiaries to aid their nonbank subsidiaries. One way for a holding company to do this is to allow the bank to lend directly to the nonbank subsidiary. To illustrate this, the bank in case 4 lends $10 to the nonbank affiliate at a zero interest rate, thus subsidizing the nonbank subsidiary at the expense of the bank.

Several assumptions have been made to derive the probability distribution of returns for shareholders of the holding company. First, the bank loan is assumed to be subordinated to other debt of the nonbank affiliate. If the nonbank affiliate goes bankrupt, therefore, the bank absorbs the first $10 of losses to creditors. Second, the interest rate on riskless assets is assumed to be 5 per cent. The distribution of profits for the bank is derived by subtracting $0.50 from the profits for each possible outcome presented in Table 9.4; this reduction reflects the opportunity cost of foregoing an alternative investment of $10 at the riskless rate.

The nonbank subsidiary saves $1.053 in interest expense on the $10 it borrows from the bank; this is the amount that a risk-neutral lender charges to compensate for the risk-free rate of 5 per cent and the 5 per cent chance of losing the $10 principal and foregoing the interest income if the nonbanking firm goes bankrupt.[17]

The effects of this loan on the distribution of shareholders' returns are illustrated in Table 9.5 under case 4. In outcomes # 1, # 4 and # 7, the bankruptcy of the nonbanking firm imposes an additional loss of $10 on the bank. In outcome # 1, in which the bank has its largest losses, the

FDIC absorbs a loss of $20.50 ($10 loss from the underlying distribution in Table 5, $0.50 loss of interest income on the loan to the nonbank affiliate and $10 loss on the loan to the nonbank affiliate).

The cost saving by the nonbank affiliate due to the zero interest loan from the bank raises the returns to shareholders by $1.053 in all outcomes except those in which the nonbank affiliate goes bankrupt. The return to shareholders is $0.01 higher in case 4 than in case 2; this difference is not large enough, however, to raise the expected rate of return in Table 9.6 by 1 basis point. The important difference between the distributions of returns in case 4 and case 2 is that the coefficient of variation of the returns is higher in case 4. Thus, it is not in the shareholders' interest to have their bank lend to its nonbank subsidiary, even at a subsidized rate. Such loans make their returns more variable.

Typically, bank supervisors would make such a loan even less attractive to the shareholders. Because the loan to the nonbank affiliate raises the expected loss to the FDIC, bank supervisors would require the bank to maintain a higher capital ratio. Though the bank could raise its capital ratio by reducing its total assets while keeping its capital unchanged, the asset reduction would reduce the level of profits for each possible outcome the bank faces.

This analysis is consistent with evidence that few banks make loans to their nonbank affiliates up to the limits allowed by regulation. Rose and Talley (1983) examine transactions among affiliates of 224 of the 229 BHCs that filed reports with the Federal Reserve from the fourth quarter of 1975 through the fourth quarter of 1980. In 1980, 27 per cent of the BHCs had no transactions among affiliates. Among the 16 BHCs in which the bank subsidiaries made larger loans to the nonbank affiliates than the nonbank affiliates made to the banks, loans to the nonbank affiliates in 1980 were only 1.3 per cent of the capital of the bank subsidiaries.

9.4.4.2 Banking Risk under Assumptions Other Than Profit Maximization

The distribution of returns in cases 2 and 4 reflect the assumption that, if the bank does not lend to the nonbank affiliate, the affiliate's bankruptcy does not affect the bank's profits. In a few cases, however, the bankruptcy of a nonbank subsidiary of a holding company has induced depositors to withdraw their deposits from the bank subsidiary.[18] The management of a holding company, therefore, might justify loans from a bank subsidiary to a nonbank affiliate as a way to prevent the nonbank subsidiary from going bankrupt and thus make depositors less concerned about the safety of their deposits. In this case, the costs of bailing out the nonbanking subsidiary might be less than the cost of adverse reaction by depositors.

There have been several cases in which the management of a BHC used the resources of a bank subsidiary to aid a nonbank affiliate in distress. In the mid-1970s, for example, the holding company that owned the Hamilton National Bank of Chattanooga, Tennessee, arranged for the bank to buy low-quality mortgages from a mortgage banking affiliate. The mortgage purchase was an important factor that led to the failure of the bank.[19] In October 1987, to cite another case, the Continental Illinois National Bank made a loan that exceeded its limits for loans to one customer to a subsidiary that deals in options. The subsidiary suffered a large loss after the sharp fall in stock prices that month.

The rationalization behind bank loans to bail out the nonbank affiliate overlooks an alternative that might be more favorable to the shareholders of the holding company: let the nonbank subsidiary go bankrupt and sell the bank to another party. Losses to the holding company would be limited to its investment in the nonbank subsidiary, with nonaffiliated lenders forced to absorb any additional losses. If potential bidders are concerned that the bank made loans to the failing nonbank affiliate or in some way assumed responsibility for the debts of that affiliate, the FDIC could facilitate the sale by offering to reimburse the winning bidder for any losses resulting from the failure of the nonbank affiliate.

Management of the holding company may prefer to have the bank absorb the losses necessary to bail out the failing nonbank affiliate, rather than sell the bank, which will result in the loss of their jobs. It may be in management's interest to arrange for the bank to lend to the nonbank subsidiary and pray that some favorable outcome helps the holding company remain solvent. The possibility of such action is why government supervisors must remain aware of any financial problems in firms that own banks and must subject the bank subsidiaries of those firms to particularly close supervision.

The analysis in Tables 9.5 and 9.6 of a bank lending to its nonbank affiliate is based on the assumption that the loan is used for legitimate business purposes. Loans from a bank to a nonbank affiliate, of course, could be made for fraudulent purposes. Suppose a bank is permitted to make a loan of any amount to an affiliate. One method of stealing from a bank would be to buy the bank through a holding company, arrange for a loan that exceeded the investment of the holding company in the bank and disappear with the proceeds of the loan.

The potential for fraud indicates that it may be prudent to prohibit loans to affiliates that exceed the capital of a bank. This prohibition would not prevent all forms of fraud in banking, but its violation would indicate to the bank supervisors when a bank is vulnerable to this type of fraud. It is also prudent to screen the background of those who buy banks through holding companies, as the federal bank regulatory agencies do when individuals buy banks.

The FDIC (1987) proposal calls for greater authority to audit the terms of any loans banks make to affiliates or subsidiaries. This proposal does not indicate what bank examiners would look for in such audits. Audits to detect fraud would be appropriate.

9.4.5 The Safe Bank Proposal

The so-called safe bank proposal (Litan, 1987) is intended to reduce the expected level and standard deviation of profit rates of banks subject to the 'safe bank' asset restrictions. As the appendix indicates, for each $100 of assets shifted from business loans to Treasury bills, the revenue of the safe bank would decline by $1.26. The asset limitations for safe banks may be so restrictive that they would prevent many affiliations of banks with nonbanking firms that would promote diversification or benefit society through synergies.

One way to evaluate the safe banking proposal is to compare the size of the synergies necessary to make bank acquisitions profitable for nonbanking firms to the synergies necessary under alternative proposals. Suppose the bank had loans of $600.[20] If the bank becomes a safe bank by reinvesting the $600 in Treasury bills, its revenue falls by $7.56. It must, however, continue to pay competitive interest rates on deposits after becoming a subsidiary to avoid a decline in its deposits. Thus, synergies from the operation of the bank as a subsidiary must be worth at least $7.56 to the holding company. This amount can be compared to the synergies necessary to make the acquisition of a bank subsidiary profitable under the Heller proposal, which is $0.095 for the case examined above.

This large difference reflects the fact that the safe bank proposal imposes a significant opportunity cost on a nonbanking firm that buys a bank under each possible outcome. The Heller proposal, on the other hand, imposes a loss on the nonbanking firm under an unlikely outcome – the failure of the bank subsidiary. These comparisons suggest that fewer combinations of banking and nonbanking firms that would promote diversification of risk and, possibly, more efficient use of resources would be viable under the safe bank proposal than under the Heller proposal.

9.5 CONCLUSIONS

This chapter illustrates the potential for risk diversification through the common ownership of a hypothetical bank and nonbanking firm. The illustration has several implications for proposals for restructuring the financial system. Banks are not necessarily made safer by requiring that all nonbanking activities be conducted through separate subsidiaries. On the contrary, banks may be less vulnerable to failure if some nonbanking activities are offered through the banks directly. Moreover, the expected loss of federal deposit insurance funds may be lower even if the nonbanking activities are financed through insured deposits.

The major proposals for restructuring the financial system would permit firms in various industries to buy banks and operate them as separate subsidiaries. Some of the proposals build in safeguards to prevent nonbanking firms from using the resources of their bank subsidiaries in ways that would increase both the chance for bank failure and the expected loss of the federal deposit insurance funds. These restrictions are based on the presumption that, without such safeguards, nonbanking firms would use the resources of their bank subsidiaries to benefit their nonbank subsidiaries.

The analysis in this chapter indicates that the shareholders of a holding company generally do not benefit by having their bank subsidiary lend at a subsidized interest rate to the nonbank subsidiary. In fact, shareholders are made worse off by such transactions because the holding company profits become more variable. Transactions that benefit nonbank subsidiaries at the expense of bank subsidiaries do not increase the shareholders' wealth. The greatest danger in banks lending to affiliates involves management of holding companies attempting to save their jobs by bailing out nonbank subsidiaries and fraudulent schemes to steal from banks through loans to affiliates.

Two of the proposals place special constraints on the nonbanking firms that buy banks to limit the risks of bank failure. One proposal requires that the holding companies absorb all losses incurred by banks, up to the holding company's total capital. The other proposal requires the bank subsidiaries of nonbanking firms to hold only low-risk liquid assets. Both proposals raise the level of synergies necessary to make the acquisition of banks by nonbanking firms profitable. Of these proposals, the safe banking proposal is the more restrictive. Some consolidations of banking and nonbanking firms that would yield social benefits in the form of higher profits and reduced variation in stockholder returns would not be attractive to shareholders under the safe banking proposal but would be attractive under other proposals.

Appendix

The Opportunity Cost of Holding Safe Assets

The safe bank proposal (Litan, 1987) would put the bank subsidiaries of nonbanking firms at a disadvantage in competing for deposits by restricting the return on their investments. This disadvantage could be offset slightly by waiving deposit insurance premiums for the subsidiaries of nonbanking firms. Under the requirements for holding only safe assets, the subsidiaries of nonbanking firms would not expose the federal deposit insurance funds to potential losses; therefore, an argument could be made for exempting 'safe' banks from deposit insurance premiums.

The opportunity cost of investing in Treasury securities instead of loans is estimated using data from the functional cost analysis program of the Federal Reserve. A change in the composition of a bank's assets affects its interest revenue and expenses. The functional cost data includes information on interest income and expenses allocated to various categories of loans, as well as expenses involved in purchasing and holding securities. Table 9.A1 indicates that the gross yields on loans almost always exceed those on three-month Treasury bills. Net yields on loans, which reflect expenses and losses, are lower than the net yields on Treasury bills in some years for mortgage and installment loans.

Table 9.A2 isolates the comparisons between net yields on Treasury bills and those on three categories of loans. Net yields on mortgages and installment loans tend to fall below the net yields on Treasury bills in periods of sharp increases in interest rates. The most stable spread is that between the net yield on commercial and other loans and the net yield on Treasury securities. On average, banks lose $1.26 in net income before income taxes per dollar transferred from commercial loans to Treasury bills.

Notes

1. An earlier version of this chapter appeared in Gilbert (1988). The views expressed in this Chapter are those of the author and do not necessarily reflect those of the Federal Reserve System or the Federal Reserve Bank of St Louis.
2. These restrictions have not been applied to the ownership of banks by individuals. Individuals who own bank stock may own and operate firms in any other industry. Under the Change in Bank Control Act of 1978, individuals and groups of individuals acting in concert must apply to the appropriate federal supervisory agency for permission to acquire the stock of a bank over certain percentages of ownership (Spong, 1985, pp. 94–5). The bank

Table 9.A1 Gross and net yields on bank assets

		Treasury bills		*Real estate mortgages*		*Installment loans*		*Commercial and other loans*	
Year	*Number of banks*	*Gross*	*Net*	*Gross*	*Net*	*Gross*	*Net*	*Gross*	*Net*
1972	86	4.07%	3.92%	7.58%	6.82%	10.19%	6.54%	6.71%	5.35%
1973	96	7.04	6.88	8.11	7.35	10.29	6.65	8.44	7.21
1974	99	7.89	7.72	8.57	7.77	10.77	6.90	10.53	9.09
1975	98	5.84	5.67	8.17	7.36	11.01	6.81	8.88	7.17
1976	109	4.99	4.83	8.39	7.46	11.11	6.91	8.22	6.39
1977	102	5.27	5.11	8.84	7.89	11.05	7.31	8.21	6.46
1978	85	7.22	7.08	8.88	7.93	11.43	8.02	9.67	8.16
1979	80	10.04	9.86	9.32	8.39	12.00	8.57	12.23	10.68
1980	59	11.51	11.28	10.01	9.29	12.90	9.18	14.31	12.62
1981	63	14.03	13.81	10.80	9.88	14.90	10.94	16.85	14.86
1982	76	10.69	10.54	10.84	9.95	15.87	11.96	14.96	12.36
1983	90	8.63	8.47	11.02	9.95	14.98	11.07	11.93	9.26
1984	82	9.58	9.43	11.41	10.31	14.39	11.10	12.82	10.34
1985	81	7.48	7.31	11.60	10.33	13.41	10.16	11.30	8.91
1986	75	5.98	5.75	10.21	8.50	12.50	9.11	10.21	7.73

Note: Data on the gross and net yields for the three categories of loans are derived from the functional cost accounting data. These data are for the banks with total assets greater than $200 million. The second column indicates the number of banks in that size category that reported data for the investment function each year. The choice of this largest size category in the functional cost accounting reports is based on the assumption that the safe banks owned by relatively large nonbanking firms would tend to have assets above this dollar level. Net yields on loans reflect adjustments of the gross yields for expenses in making and servicing loans and loss rates on the various types of loans. The gross yields on Treasury bills are the annual averages of yields on three-month Treasury bills, new issues. Net yields on Treasury bills are the gross yields minus the costs of buying and holding investments per dollar of investments in the functional cost accounting data. Under the safe bank proposal, safe banks could hold longer-term Treasury securities, but the longer-term securities have greater potential for capital gains and losses. This exercise uses the yields on short-term Treasury securities and ignores capital gains and losses.

supervisory agencies may deny permission to purchase bank stock under the following conditions:

(1) The purchase would create a monopoly in any part of the banking industry;

Table 9.A2 Sacrifice of income before income taxes per $100 of loans shifted to treasury bills

	Loan Categories		
Year	*Real estate mortgages*	*Installment loans*	*Commercial and other loans*
1972	$2.90	$2.62	$1.43
1973	0.47	–0.23	0.33
1974	0.05	–0.82	1.37
1975	1.69	1.14	1.50
1976	2.63	2.08	1.56
1977	2.78	2.20	1.35
1978	0.85	0.94	1.08
1979	–1.47	–1.29	0.82
1980	–1.99	–2.10	1.34
1981	–3.93	–2.87	1.05
1982	–0.59	1.42	1.82
1983	1.48	2.60	0.79
1984	0.88	1.67	0.91
1985	3.02	2.85	1.60
1986	2.75	3.36	1.98
Mean	.768	.905	1.262

(2) The financial condition of the acquiring party could adversely affect the bank; or
(3) The competence, experience or integrity of the proposed ownership would not be in the interest of the bank's depositors.

3. Corrigan (1987), Federal Deposit Insurance Corporation (1987), Huertas (1986, 1987) and Department of the Treasury (1991).
4. Spong (1985), pp. 95–8. The major exception to this involves the nonbank banks. The BHCA, which gave the Federal Reserve jurisdiction over the acquisitions of banks by corporations, defined a bank as one that accepts demand deposits and makes commercial loans. Acquisitions of institutions that did not accept demand deposits or make commercial loans were not subject to the jurisdiction of the Federal Reserve in its capacity as regulator of BHCs. These limited-service banks are commonly called nonbank banks. The Competitive Equality Banking Act of 1987 (CEBA) closes that loophole in the law. It places restrictions on the growth and activities of nonbank banks acquired on or before 5 March 1987, and requires firms that acquired nonbank banks after that date to sell them or restrict their activities to those permissible for BHCs. The following restrictions apply to nonbank banks acquired on or before 5 March 1987:

(1) They may not engage in new activities;

(2) They may not market the goods or services of affiliates or have their banking services marketed through nonbank affiliates, except through those marketing arrangements in effect before 5 March 1987; and
(3) Beginning in August 1988, their assets may not rise by more than 7 per cent in any 12-month period.

CEBA also imposes restrictions on the daylight overdrafts of nonbank banks.

5. Volcker (1986), pp. 436–8. The following are some of the activities not permissible for BHCs and the dates of denials for those activities by the Federal Reserve Board: underwriting general life insurance (1971); real estate brokerage (1972); land investment and development (1972); operating a savings and loan association (1974); operating a travel agency (1976); and acting as a specialist in foreign exchange options on a security exchange (1986).
6. Rose (1985).
7. Black, Miller and Posner (1978).
8. Similar proposals have been made by Kareken (1986), Gilbert (1987), Tobin (1987) and Forrestal (1987). Tobin proposes limiting the assets of all banks to short-term, low-risk assets.
9. The factors that determine the expected value and variance of profits of a firm that buys a bank and a nonbanking firm can be expressed in the following equations:

$$E(B + N) = E(B) + E(N),$$
$$V(B + N) = V(B) + V(N) + 2Cov(B,N),$$

where E refers to expected value, V to variance, B to the profits of the bank, N to the profits of the nonbanking firms and Cov to the covariance of the profits of the bank and the nonbanking firm. Holding constant the covariance of the two profit streams, a higher variance in the profits of the nonbanking firm means a higher variance in the profits of the combined firms. The variance of the combined profit streams depends on the covariance of the two profit streams. Finally, as the size of the nonbanking firm rises relative to the size of the bank, the variance of the combined profit streams converges to the variance of the profits of the nonbanking firm.

An analysis of the proposals to restructure the financial system involves an analysis of the mean and variance of the returns to shareholders of a firm that buys a bank and a nonbanking firm and operates them under the conditions of the various proposals. One approach to this analysis might involve expressing the mean and variance of the profits of the firm that buys the bank and the nonbanking firm in terms of the mean and variance of the profits of the bank and the nonbanking firm separately, as indicated in the equations above. The problem with this approach is that the distribution of returns to shareholders is not the same as the distribution of profits. In some outcomes, losses exceed the investment of the shareholders; losses to shareholders, however, are no larger than their investment in the firm. The distinction between the distribution of profits and the distribution of returns to shareholders is especially important for this study, since the various proposals involve different rules for truncating the losses to shareholders. Analysis of the mean and variance of returns to shareholders must be based on specific distributions of the profits of the bank and the nonbanking firm, as presented in the text, not on the expected value and variance of the profits.

10. Eisenbeis and Wall (1984) survey these studies. For a summary of more recent studies, see Boyd, Graham and Hewitt (1993).
11. Some studies measure returns to shareholders using data on stock prices and dividends. These studies report similar patterns: mean rates of return and variability of returns to shareholders are higher in several of the industries that banking organizations would be permitted to enter than in the commercial banking industry (Boyd and Graham, 1988; Boyd, Graham and Hewitt, 1993; Eisemann, 1976; and Macey, Marr and Young, 1987).
12. Several studies estimate the effects of the combination of services offered by banks on their costs (Gilligan, Smirlock and Marshall, 1984; Benston, *et al.*, 1983; and Clark, 1988). The results of these studies are not relevant in estimating the effects of nonbanking services on the costs of banks, since the data are for banks subject to current limitations on the services they may offer.
13. White (1986).
14. Daskin and Marquardt (1983).
15. The large profit of the bank associated with the small probability might reflect the recovery on loans previously charged off as losses or a large favorable change in market interest rates on portfolios of assets and liabilities that do not have matched duration.
16. Returns to the firm in column 3 are lower than returns in column 2 by $10 in outcome # 2, with probability of 0.009, and lower by $10 in outcome # 3, with probability of 0.0005. Multiplying $10 by each of the probabilities and summing yields $0.095.
17. The interest rate that the nonbank affiliate would pay to borrow from a nonaffiliated lender is determined by calculating the rate that would make the expected return on such a loan equal to the risk-free interest rate. Let *rl* be the interest rate on the loan and *rs* the risk-free rate. In lending $10 to the nonbank affiliate, there is a 95 per cent chance of collecting the principal plus interest at the rate *rl* and a 5 per cent chance of losing the principal and collecting no interest. The expected returns on the alternative investments are calculated as follows:

$$rl \times \$10 \times 0.95 - \$10 \times 0.05 = rs \times \$10.$$

If *rs* is 5 per cent,

$$rl = [0.05 + 0.05] \div 0.95 = 0.1053.$$

18. Cornyn, *et al.* (1986).
19. *Ibid.*, p. 186.
20. Suppose the bank has a capital-to-asset ratio of 10 per cent. For all federally insured commercial banks, the average ratio of loans to assets is about 60 per cent. Thus, $600 is a reasonable level for loans of the hypothetical bank with capital of $100 and a 10 per cent capital ratio.

References

Association of Reserve City Bankers (1987) *Association of Reserve City Bankers Emerging Issues Committee Proposal for a Financial Services Holding Company* (March 19).

Benston, George J. (1983) 'Economics of Scale and Scope in Banking', *Proceedings of a Conference on Bank Structure and Competition* (Federal Reserve Bank of Chicago, 2–4 May) pp. 432–55.

Black, Fischer, Merton H. Miller and Richard A. Posner (1978) 'An Approach to the Regulation of Bank Holding Companies', *Journal of Business* (July) pp. 379–412.

Boyd, John H. and Stanley L. Graham (1988) 'The Profitability and Risk Effects of Allowing Bank Holding Companies to Merge With Other Financial Firms: A Simulation Study', *Quarterly Review* (Federal Reserve Bank of Minneapolis, Spring) pp. 3–20.

Boyd, John H., Stanley L. Graham and R. Shawn Hewitt (1993) 'Bank Holding Company Mergers with Nonbank Financial Firms: Effects on the Risk of Failure', *Journal of Banking and Finance* (February) pp. 43–63.

Clark, J.A. (1988) 'Economies of Scale and Scope at Depository Financial Institutions: A Review of the Literature', *Economic Review* (Federal Reserve Bank of Kansas City, September/October) pp. 16–33.

Cornyn, Anthony (1986) 'An Analysis of the Concept of Corporate Separateness in BHC Regulation from an Economic Perspective', *Proceedings of a Conference on Bank Structure and Competition* (Federal Reserve Bank of Chicago, 14–16 May) pp. 174–212.

Corrigan, E. Gerald (1987) *Financial Market Structure: A Longer View* (Federal Reserve Bank of New York, January).

Daskin, Alan J. and Jeffrey C. Marquardt (1983) 'The Separation of Banking from Commerce and the Securities Business in the United Kingdom, West Germany and Japan', *Issues in Bank Regulation* (Summer) pp. 16–24.

Department of the Treasury (1991) *Modernizing the Financial System* (February).

Eisemann, Peter C. (1976) 'Diversification and the Congeneric Bank Holding Company', *Journal of Bank Research* (Spring) pp. 68–77.

Eisenbeis, Robert A. and Larry D. Wall (1984) 'Bank Holding Company Nonbanking Activities and Risk', *Proceedings of a Conference on Bank Market Structure and Competition* (Federal Reserve Bank of Chicago, 23–25 April) pp. 340–57.

Federal Deposit Insurance Corporation (1987) *Mandate for Change: Restructuring the Banking Industry* (October).

Forrestal, Robert P. (1987) 'Regulations Must Evolve Along with Financial Services Industry', Address to the Economics Club of Connecticut, 4 December, reprinted in *American Banker* (23 December 1987) pp. 4–7.

Gilbert, R. Alton (1987) 'Banks Owned by Nonbanks: What is the Problem and What can be Done about It?', *Business and Society* (Roosevelt University, Spring) pp. 9–17.

Gilbert, R. Alton (1988) 'A Comparison of Proposals to Restructure the US Financial System', *Review* (Federal Reserve Bank of St Louis, July/August) pp. 58–75.

Gilligan, Thomas, Michael Smirlock and William Marshall (1984) 'Scale and Scope Economies in the Multi-Product Banking Firm', *Journal of Monetary Economics* (May) pp. 393–405.

Heller, H. Robert (1987) 'The Shape of Banking in the 1990s', Address before the Forecasters Club of New York (26 June).

Huertas, Thomas F. (1986) 'The Protection of Deposits from Risks Assumed by Non-bank Affiliates', *Structure and Regulation of Financial Firms and Holding Companies* (Part 3), Hearings before a Subcommittee of the Committee on Government Operations, House of Representatives, 99th Congress, 2nd Session (17–18 December) pp. 325–60.

Huertas, Thomas F. (1987) 'Redesigning Regulation: The Future of Finance in the United States', *Issues in Bank Regulation* (Fall) pp. 7–13.

Kareken, John H. (1986) 'Federal Bank Regulatory Policy: A Description and Some Observations', *Journal of Business* (January) pp. 3–48.

LaWare, John P. (1987) 'FSHCA – The Flexible Alternative for Financial Restructuring', *Issues in Bank Regulation* (Fall) pp. 25–7.

Litan, Robert E. (1987) *What Should Banks Do?* (The Brookings Institution).

Macey, Jonathan R., W. Wayne Marr and S. David Young (1987) 'The Glass–Steagall Act and the Riskiness of Financial Intermediaries', mimeo (Tulane University, November).

Rose, John T. (1985) 'Government Restrictions on Bank Activities: Rationale for Regulation and Possibilities for Deregulation', *Issues in Bank Regulation* (Autumn) pp. 25–33.

Rose, John T. and Samuel H. Talley (1983) 'Financial Transactions Within Bank Holding Companies', Staff Studies 123 (Board of Governors of the Federal Reserve System, May).

Spong, Kenneth (1985) *Banking Regulation: Its Purposes, Implementation, and Effects* (Federal Reserve Bank of Kansas City).

Tobin, James (1987) 'A Case for Preserving Regulatory Distinctions', *Challenge* (November/December) pp. 10–17.

Volcker, Paul A. (1986) Appendices to the Statement by Paul A. Volcker, Chairman, Board of Governors of the Federal Reserve System, *Structure and Regulation of Financial Firms and Holding Companies (Part 1)*, Hearings before a Subcommittee of the Committee on Government Operations, House of Representatives, 99th Congress, 2nd Session. (22 April, 11 June, and 23 July) pp. 391–510.

White, Eugene Nelson (1986) 'Before the Glass–Steagall Act: An Analysis of the Investment Banking Activities of National Banks', *Explorations in Economic History* (January) pp. 33–55.

Part III
Policy Options

10 Designing a Regulatory Structure for the Next Sixty Years

Catherine England

The financial markets have changed dramatically in the past 20 years. That change was most apparent in the number of failures among depository institutions. From 1943 through 1981, only 193 federally-insured commercial banks failed, and in only five of those years did failures number in the double digits.[1] By contrast, 1433 banks failed between 1982 and 1992.[2] This dramatic increase in bank failures was generally overlooked, however, because of the much more serious problems in the savings and loan industry.

By 1980, the liabilities of the savings and loan industry exceeded its aggregate assets by more than $100 billion. Despite some spotty and short-lived recoveries, the financial health of significant numbers of S&Ls deteriorated throughout the 1980s, eventually bankrupting the Federal Savings and Loan Insurance Corporation. The 1989 Financial Institutions Reform, Recovery and Enforcement Act formally committed taxpayers to covering the bulk of the clean-up costs. Although the full costs of the S&L fiasco are still unknown, estimates are that taxpayers will contribute some $200 billion before interest payments to reimburse insured S&L depositors. When interest payments are included, it is expected that taxpayers will be asked to ante up $500 billion. Nor did the bad news end in 1989. Two years later, Congress was required to commit taxpayers' funds to the Bank Insurance Fund.[3]

Policymakers and members of the general public were stunned by the events of the 1980s. How could a system that appeared stable for so long suddenly be on the verge of collapse? Newspaper articles, scholarly papers, and politicians' speeches all attempted to identify the lessons of the savings and loan debacle in an effort to determine whether a similar collapse of the banking industry could be avoided. Among the most important questions raised by events of the 1980s is whether a basic regulatory restructuring is needed. Or are the problems of banks and savings and loans simply evidence of market failure and deregulation gone awry?

Among policymakers there is little consensus about the answers to these questions. Academic observers come closer to agreeing on the causes of the depository institutions' difficulties, but when it comes to solutions there is less harmony. My task is to outline the dimensions of alternative reform proposals, but I do not believe we can begin to identify the regulatory design needed to assure financial prosperity in the 21st century without first reexamining the regulatory design established in the 1933–5 period.

The bank regulatory structure we have today was largely established during the Depression, and the system worked reasonably well for more than 40 years. It is a mistake, however, to assume that the sources of the 1980s problems are to be found only in the 1980s. Many of the problems banks and S&Ls face have much deeper roots. It is, therefore, important that we understand what went wrong if we are to establish a successful regulatory structure for the next century.

10.1 THE 1933–5 PACKAGE

The biggest banking problem facing Congress and the newly elected president in 1933 was massive failures. Indeed, bank stability had been a problem throughout the 1920s, and conditions worsened significantly after 1929. From 1921 through 1929, bank failures averaged 634.5 per year.[4] From 1930 through 1933, failures averaged 2274 per year, with 4000 bank suspensions occurring in 1933 alone. Losses to depositors remained surprisingly low, however. Throughout the 1920s, losses to depositors as a percentage of deposits in all commercial banks remained well below one per cent. It was not until 1930 that depositors' losses rose as high as one-half of one per cent, and in 1933, losses were still only 2.15 per cent of deposits in all commercial banks.[5]

Although depositor losses overall were less of a problem than we might assume given 4000 bank failures, there were reasons for concern. First, averages mask the fact that some individual depositors did lose substantial sums in bank failures. In addition, illiquidity was often a serious problem. Even when depositors ultimately recovered most of their funds, they sometimes had to wait for months while their banks' assets were liquidated. The lack of funds in the interim was a source of hardship for many households and businesses. In fact, Selgin (1988) suggests that many of the bank runs occurring in the 1930s resulted less from a loss of confidence in specific banks than from fears that one's state government was about to declare a bank holiday, creating general illiquidity problems.

Meanwhile, of course, the country was suffering from falling output and growing unemployment. At the depths of the Depression, GNP would fall by one-third, the price level would decline by some 30 per cent, and unemployment would top 25 per cent. A paralyzed banking system was clearly in no position to help reignite the general economy.

10.1.1 A Solution

By the time President Franklin Roosevelt took office in March 1933, it was apparent that something had to be done, but there was substantial disagreement about the preferred course. Despite the worldwide nature of the Depression, other countries were not suffering the same problems with their banking systems as the United States.[6] Branching restrictions clearly made it more difficult for US banks to survive the downturn, and President Roosevelt's new comptroller of the currency initially advocated a move to interstate branching as a solution to the nation's banking problems.[7] Other observers argued for a system of 100 per cent reserves.[8]

In the end, Congress and the Roosevelt administration took a different course. To shore up confidence immediately, Congress significantly expanded the government-sponsored safety net. Federal deposit guarantees were introduced through the creation of the Federal Deposit Insurance Corporation.[9] In introducing federal deposit insurance, however, the policymakers of the 1930s were clearly aware of what we now call 'moral hazard'.[10] Opponents of federal guarantees, including most of the major banking organizations of the day, repeatedly argued that federal deposit insurance would reduce the discipline faced by bank managers and lead to serious future problems. For example, Malburn (1934, p. 170) stated that:

> [Federal deposit guarantees] will doubtless, as charged by its opponents, encourage unsound banking. The reckless banker will offer greater inducements to the public than the conservative banker, and as the public will realize that it is equally well protected in either institution, it will be attracted by the more liberal promises of the less sound bank. This will draw business away from the sound banks and will increase the payments that the fund will be called on to make to reimburse depositors in failed banks. Careful, frequent, and intelligent examinations and a vigilant and strict supervision of insured banks will keep down losses. But whether they can be maintained in this character and whether they can hold losses down to a point that makes the continuance of the guaranty possible can be told only by putting the plan in actual operation.

Framers of the 1933 Banking Act attempted to address the moral hazard problem through several specific provisions. Coverage was limited to $2500, initially, although it was extended, in 1934, to $5000 per account. Even at $5000 per account, only 44.8 per cent of total deposits were insured during the 1930s.[11] In addition, 'chartering standards for national banks were raised, and supervisory authority was broadly increased' (Flood 1992, p. 73). Thus, the Banking Acts of 1933 and 1935 'succeeded in simultaneously protecting the small depositor and leaving the banker answerable to both supervisors and large depositors for the quality of his management' (Flood 1992, p. 73).

Whether or not it was intentional, the authors of the 1933 Banking Act also added another layer of protection against moral hazard. As banks and other businesses failed around them, many policymakers of the day concluded that 'excessive competition' was to blame for the all-too-apparent weaknesses. Much of the legislation adopted during the early 1930s contained measures designed to limit competition between market participants, thus assuring higher profits for surviving firms. Banking and finance were no exception. As noted, charters were made harder to come by. Geographic restrictions were also reaffirmed,[12] and, of course, the 1933 Banking Act forced the separation of commercial and investment banking.[13] The thrust of legislation during the 1930s was to leave every surviving financial institution in a clearly defined market in the products and services it offered and the place it operated. Finally, price controls were introduced through limits on the interest rates banks could offer for deposits.[14] This entire regulatory structure was designed to protect the profits of individual depository institutions and, thus, reduce the number of failures.[15]

White (1992, p. 106) sums up the 1930s efforts as follows: First, the Federal Reserve's role as lender of last resort was strengthened. Second, federal deposit insurance was introduced for both banks and savings and loan associations. Third, federal and state restrictions on entry were reinforced, thus limiting competition from newcomers. Fourth, new limits on banking activities were introduced at both the federal and state levels. These restrictions were later extended to bank holding companies through the 1956 and 1970 Bank Holding Company Acts. Finally, more systematic supervision of banks was introduced at both the federal and state levels.

In short, policymakers during the 1930s provided an expanded, but still limited, safety net that included market discipline from larger depositors. In addition, by creating a system of 'controlled' competition, the regulatory structure protected the profits of depository owners. With occasional adjustments, this package was reasonably successful for 40 years – at least if we measure success in terms of the numbers of bank failures. Regulators seemed able to respond to and control occasional problems, and bankers took a, generally, conservative approach in their lending and investment decisions. As time passed, however, the efficacy of this regulatory package was gradually undermined. As we debate the best course for future bank regulation, it is important that we understand why the structure established in the 1930s ultimately failed.

10.2 UNRAVELING THE 1930s PACKAGE

Federal deposit insurance was clearly viewed as the centerpiece of the 1930s banking legislation. Flood (1992, p. 62) reports that, 'Supporters (of federal deposit guarantees) argued that deposits *per se* required protection, to stabilize the medium of exchange and promote a renewed expansion of bank credit'. At the same time, however, policymakers understood the implications of deposit guarantees on the long-term risk characteristics of the banking and thrift industries,[16] and they took steps to limit the resulting moral hazard.

10.2.1 Reducing Depositor Discipline

The limited nature of the initial deposit insurance contract created a 'copayment' for individuals or businesses with more than $5000 in their bank accounts. Insured deposits continued to account for less than half of total bank deposits until 1950 when federal deposit insurance was increased to $10 000 per account. Uninsured deposits still represented more than 30 per cent of total bank deposits until 1980, when federal deposit guarantees were expanded to $100 000 per account.[17]

After 1980, increasing financial sophistication coupled with advances in telecommunications technology enabled depositors to expand their protection, even as official limits remained at $100 000 per account. Coverage expanded from 71.6 per cent of total deposits in 1980 to more than 75 per cent by 1987.[18] Even more important, however, was the fact that after 1984 the FDIC chose to close banks in ways that protected over 99 per cent of deposits in failed institutions.[19] As both explicit and implicit insurance expanded, copayments as a part of the deposit insurance contract became increasingly less important and depositor discipline was eroded.

10.2.2 Undermining Owner Discipline

In the deposit insurance context, equity capital can be thought of as a deductible attached to the guarantee contract. More equity implies a higher deductible, and thus more costs visited directly on the owners of a troubled depository. One lesson made apparent by the savings and loan debacle is that equity matters. Owners' willingness to take on risk clearly increases as their equity stake in the firm is reduced.

In the mid-1930s, the average bank's ratio of equity capital to total assets was 15 per cent.[20] But explicit capital numbers fail to capture the full ownership stake of bank owners as they emerged from the Depression. The efforts of the 1930s policymakers to limit competition among financial institutions created substantial franchise value. A bank charter, in and of itself, was worth a great deal, and throughout much of the post-war period, even as explicit capital levels fell, bank owners still had an incentive to protect their bank charters.[21] Many banks were, in fact, passed from father to son for generations almost as a birthright. In this sense, franchise value, although much more nebulous, may have been almost as important as explicit capital. The value of the bank charter was always there; it could be reduced but not eliminated by poor management. Therefore, as long as bank charters were valuable themselves, bank owners always had something else to lose in a failure. Beginning in the 1970s and continuing through the 1980s, however, bank and S&L managers found that the laws and regulations meant to protect them from competition were losing their power. New competitive threats arose from multiple non-depository sources, and in many cases, banks and S&Ls found they were unable to respond. As a result, the franchise value enjoyed by bank owners has been substantially eroded.

Limits on deposit interest rates were designed to keep depositories' costs of funds low, for example. With a few adjustments, interest rate ceilings seemed to work until the late 1970s when advancing technology combined with a volatile economic environment to give relatively small depositors a real alternative.[22] Although money-market mutual funds were introduced in 1972, they grew only slowly until 1978. Then rising rates of inflation and rising market interest rates encouraged growing numbers of long-time bank and S&L depositors to seek alternatives to the 5 to $5\frac{1}{4}$ per cent they could earn on passbook savings accounts. At the end of 1978, MMMF assets were $9.5 billion. By the end of 1982, they had grown to $236.3 billion, mostly at the expense of banks and savings and loans.[23] Ironically, MMMFs sold some of this money back to banks and S&Ls in the form of large (above $100 000) certificates of deposit on which there were no interest rate limits. Eliminating deposit interest-rate ceilings allowed banks and S&Ls to retain their customers, but it also led to increased competition and a national market for insured deposits.[24]

The deregulation of deposit interest rates coupled with advancing communications technology significantly changed bank customers' attitudes toward their banks. When all banks offered the same interest rates, depositors emphasized convenience and a local presence. With deregulation, depositors' emphasis shifted toward return, and well-capitalized institutions found themselves competing with institutions hundreds, even thousands, of miles away. Federal guarantees made many depositor/investors indifferent to the financial health of the institutions in which they placed their money. During much of the 1980s, weaker institutions effectively determined interest rates, and net deposit flows were from healthier institutions to weaker banks and S&Ls.[25]

Increased competition did not stop with the liability side of depositories' balance sheets as bank and S&L customers also found attractive alternative sources of credit. Consider thrift institutions, for example. As S&Ls reeled from the effects of rising costs and stagnant returns, they also faced competition from growing numbers of new sources of mortgage money.[26] The growth of the secondary market in home mortgages made such loans attractive investments, and by 1991, more than half of home mortgages were originated outside of traditional banking institutions.[27] General Motors, Ford, General Electric, and Sears are only the better known names among a large number of mortgage finance companies eager and willing to lend to support home ownership.

Commercial banks also found themselves increasingly squeezed out of their traditional markets. First commercial paper provided a way for the country's largest firms to gain direct access to capital markets. Then in the 1980s, non-investment grade bonds (better known as 'junk' bonds) were introduced, providing a means through which mid-sized firms could directly access capital markets.[28] As Milligan (1990, p. 99) observed, 'Through much of the 1980s, bankers watched their bread-and-butter corporate business migrate to the capital markets, where the trend toward securitization made it cheaper for large companies to raise money'. Meanwhile, alternative financing sources also expanded for smaller firms, though at a slower rate. Small business finance companies and supplier-provided financing have increasingly substituted for bank loans.[29]

By the 1980s, increasing competition had reduced market share and squeezed profits. Commercial banks' share of US financial market assets shrank from 51 per cent in 1950 to 31 per cent in 1989.[30] Banks lost ground in every market they serve – from auto loans to inventory loans.

Their profits evaporated as well. For the decade of the 1970s, banks' return on assets averaged 0.77 per cent. By 1989–1990, their ROA had dropped to 0.49 per cent. Similarly, banks' return on equity was 12.1 per cent for the 1970s, but only 7.7 per cent in 1989 and 1990. The insurance deductible in bank charters had been substantially reduced in terms of both explicit (paid-in) and implicit (franchise value) capital. In growing numbers of cases, bank owners had little to lose if their bank failed.[31]

10.2.3 Shifting Regulatory Emphasis

Rounding out the changes experienced by depository institutions during the past 15 years, was a shift in regulatory emphasis. Emerging from the Depression, bank regulators were primarily interested in 'safety and soundness' issues, including chartering restrictions that kept the number of banks in the United States fairly constant from 1935 to 1985.[32] As time progressed, however, policymakers turned their attention to other issues. The first major consumer protection laws were introduced in 1968, and others were added at an accelerating rate through the 1970s. (See Table 10.1) This focus on the social responsibilities of banks has consumed an increasing share of regulators' and bankers' attention and there is every indication that this trend will continue.[33]

Table 10.1 Consumer protection and antidiscrimination laws

Title	*Year Passed*
Truth in lending act	1968
Fair housing act	1968
Fair credit reporting act	1970
Real-estate settlement procedures act	1974
Equal credit opportunity act	1974
Home mortgage disclosure act	1975
Federal trade commission improvement act	1975
Consumer leasing act	1976
Community reinvestment act	1977
Right to financial privacy act	1978
Electronic fund transfer act	1978

Source: Golembe and Holland (1986), pp. 81–92

10.3 WHERE FROM HERE?

The roots of the trends discussed above – reduced depositor discipline, a shrinking equity base, and broader social responsibilities for banks – can all be found in the decades before 1980. But by the late 1970s, these trends combined with several other factors to undermine the stability of traditional depository institutions. The volatile economic climate of the 1970s and advancing telecommunications technology helped create profit opportunities for new financial services providers. Faced with increasing competition, banks' and S&Ls' capital standards were allowed to slip. Policymakers hoped that, given a chance, weakened depositories would recover their financial health.

Some institutions did manage to recover, but the majority simply lost more money. In retrospect, the failure of forbearance seems almost inevitable for several reasons. In the first place, an insolvent institution by definition has more liabilities than assets. That is, the total of the funds on which interest is paid exceeds the value of the assets on which interest is earned. Given this situation, a conservative investment strategy is unlikely to return the bank or S&L to prosperity. As Garcia (1988, pp. 242–3) pointed out, 'It is difficult for [an insolvent] firm, especially one that is not growing, to earn profits and accumulate capital. Achieving these goals requires that the rate of return earned on assets exceed that paid on liabilities by a margin great enough to counterbalance the deficiency in assets.' Increasing the rate of return paid on assets requires accepting greater risk, of course, and greater risks mean a higher level of losses. These problems were only compounded when managers chose to invest in areas where they had relatively little experience.

Most depositors, meanwhile, had little or no interest in curbing risk-taking at depository institutions. Depositors, like other investors, seek the highest possible return for a given level of risk and, for accounts of $100 000 or less, the risk for all insured depositories is the same. The federal government's credibility is substituted for individual institutions' creditworthiness. As a result, healthy institutions pursuing safer lending opportunities were often forced to match deposit rates paid by insolvent competitors desperate for new funds.

So where were the regulators? Whether stricter regulation would have prevented the problems apparent among thrift institutions and banks depends on the type of regulation we are discussing. It is important to distinguish between regulatory supervision – enforcement of capital standards, for example – and regulation of banks' and S&Ls' activities and locations.

With regard to capital regulation, forbearance was a clear mistake, both for S&Ls and to the extent it occurred among banks.[34] But, while stricter capital regulation of both S&Ls and banks during the 1980s probably would have reduced losses to taxpayers, it is unlikely that the number of failures over the past 12 years would have been significantly affected. The fundamental problem among banks and thrifts was (and remains) overcapacity. Increased competition among depositories and from firms outside the industry made many banks and S&Ls redundant. In this sense, the exit of banks and thrifts from the financial market is both expected and desirable, and the lesson policymakers should learn from the S&L fiasco is that facilitating the exit of undercapitalized, unneeded depositories will save taxpayers and the economy in the long run.[35]

It is important at this point to note the distinction between creditor and owner discipline. For well-capitalized firms, these two types of market discipline tend to work in the same direction, although there will always be some tension between them.[36] As a firm approaches insolvency, however, creditors and owners have increasingly divergent incentives. Creditors are interested in conserving the firm's resources and minimizing losses, while owners are more inclined to take gambles in an effort to recoup past losses and recover the firm's financial health.[37] That is why owner discipline, in and of itself, is never enough to control risk-taking. Owner discipline must always be reinforced either by creditor discipline or by regulatory discipline. For financial firms without government guarantees, creditors often insist on higher levels of capital and the power to intervene in the firm's activities if capital falls below a given level. Indeed, creditor/ depositors of uninsured financial institutions are inclined to move their funds elsewhere if they have reason to question the competence of management or the financial strength of the institution. For financial firms with government guarantees, we have traditionally relied on regulatory discipline to close insolvent institutions. Unfortunately, in too many cases during the 1980s, both creditor and regulatory discipline were absent.

The case regarding the deregulation of S&L activities and investments is a bit more complex. A substantial portion of the thrift industry's losses occurred before deregulation. In fact, the thrifts' initial problems were a result of overly strict requirements that S&Ls invest the bulk of their portfolios in 30-year fixed-rate mortgages drawn from a limited geographic area. Allowing S&Ls broader investment powers seemed a reasonable policy response to the problems caused by inadequately diversified, mismatched portfolios. Unfortunately, policymakers did not insist that institutions taking advantage of new powers have adequate capital. When insolvent institutions invested insured deposits in new areas, only the federal government had anything to lose, and the result was increased risk-taking.[38] But deregulation, to the extent it occurred, probably did not destroy significant numbers of S&Ls that would have survived otherwise. Deregulation of insolvent thrifts was a policy mistake because it increased taxpayer losses by keeping zombie institutions in the game longer. In the absence of new S&L powers during the 1980s, the industry probably would have shrunk more quickly.

In short, stricter regulation in and of itself would not have saved us from the failures of the 1980s. The 1930s legislation worked for 40 years because it established a government-sponsored cartel, and for a long time cartel members benefitted from the arrangement. As Huertas (1983, p. 23) observed, however:

> No market is an island, and no cartel can prevent non-members from designing and offering close substitutes at a competitive price. If these substitutes prove attractive to consumers, cartel members may find themselves in a situation where costs are abundant, but customers scarce. If this occurs, the rules of the cartel will not coddle members, but condemn them to extinction as business flows to the unregulated market. If its members are to survive, a cartel must adapt, either by embracing the interlopers or by permitting more open competition. If the cartel does neither, it may spark the very crisis it was intended to prevent.

Gerald Corrigan (1991, p. 4) noted in testimony before Congress, 'The current configuration of the banking and financial system in the United States is entirely too accident prone'. The regulatory system is in need of restructuring. The question is, what should replace the 1930s design?

10.4 WHAT ROLE FOR DEPOSIT INSURANCE?

Just as federal deposit insurance formed the centerpiece of the 1930s legislation, the decision about how to handle federal deposit guarantees is the basic issue facing policymakers attempting to reconfigure the current regulatory structure. A wide range of proposals have been offered that range from eliminating federal guarantees entirely to expanding them to include all bank and S&L deposits. Internally consistent reform proposals recognize the implications of their deposit insurance decision on banks' likely risk-taking profiles and attempt to apply regulatory discipline consistent with the incentives created by insurance choices.

10.4.1 Proposals to Eliminate Federal Deposit Insurance

A relatively small, but growing number, of scholars have called for the elimination of federal deposit guarantees.[39] These students of banking identify the 1930s collapse and virtually all other 'systemic' crises as examples of government failure rather than market failure, and they would resolve the current problems by scrapping the entire 1930s system.[40]

In the absence of federal deposit guarantees, the government's primary role would be to enforce contracts and laws against fraud. It is expected that depositors, or their agents, would monitor the activities of banks with more diligence than have regulators, and uninsured creditors would be unlikely to 'forbear' in dealing with insolvent depositories.[41] Applying the full force of depositor discipline and removing banks' line of credit with tax-payers would also eliminate the need to regulate banks' decisions about where to locate or what financial products or services to offer.[42] In the absence of such restrictions, banks would be better able to adapt to changing market conditions in ways that protect the interests of both bank owners and bank creditors. Advocates of a significantly reduced government role in banking argue that the result would be a greater financial stability, as well as a system that is more responsive to the financial needs of both businesses and consumers.[43]

10.4.2 Proposals to Make Federal Deposit Guarantees Redundant

Proposals to create a system of 'narrow' banks and efforts to introduce a '100 per cent reserve requirement' all represent attempts to make federal deposit insurance redundant. Under such systems, insured deposits, including all transactions accounts, would be fully collateralized with relatively liquid assets.[44] Banks that allowed the market value of their collateral to fall below the value of their insured liabilities would be subject to immediate closure. The deposit insurance system would, thus, be substantially insulated from losses except in cases of fraud. Accordingly, deposit insurance fees could be significantly reduced.

As a rule, proponents of narrow banking would remove branching restrictions and, with collateral requirements in place, would also remove the limits on the products and services banks offer to the extent they fund such activities with uninsured liabilities. Narrow banking proposals differ regarding banks' subsequent organizational structure. Some proposals would require insured and uninsured activities to be conducted through separate subsidiaries. Other plans would not require such corporate separateness as long as bankers made clear to depositors and through record-keeping systems what accounts were protected and which were not. With the exception that all checkable accounts be insured, bank customers would be left to determine how they divided their funds between insured and uninsured accounts.[45] Regulators would focus their attention on overseeing banks' compliance with collateral requirements for their insured deposits, and banks' other activities would be left largely to the supervision of the market-place.[46]

The most important question regarding narrow banking, concerns how bank regulators would react to a failure. Would political decisionmakers have the resolve necessary to pay only insured depositors and allow other customers with deposit-like accounts to suffer losses? Failure to honor the distinctions inherent in the narrow banking system – even once – would undermine the advantages represented by such proposals.

10.4.3 Proposals to Limit Deposit Guarantees

A wide variety of proposals represent attempts to adapt the 1930s system to 1990s realities. Many of these proposals would roll back or strictly limit deposit guarantees in an effort to reintroduce depositor discipline. Other efforts, along similar lines, would impose higher capital requirements or more stringent regulatory oversight. Proponents of these proposals see a continuing role for federal deposit insurance – either because they believe deposit guarantees are necessary for market stability or because they believe elimination of deposit insurance is politically impossible. The authors of some of these changes are interested in deposit insurance reform as a first step toward removing the geographic and powers restrictions from insured banks. Others are interested, primarily, in protecting taxpayers and the general economy from abuses like those experienced during the 1980s with savings and loans.[47]

10.4.3.1 Rolling Back Deposit Guarantees

Many observers have suggested that deposit guarantees – both explicit and implicit – should be rolled back. Some of these proposals would simply require stricter enforcement of the $100 000 limit.[48] Others would roll back explicit guarantees to, say, $50 000 or lower. Some proposals would fully protect the first $50 000, for example, and then some smaller fraction, say 75 per cent, of amounts above $50 000. The Bush administration suggested limits on the number of accounts an individual could protect within a single bank or S&L. Others have suggested limiting the number of accounts an individual could protect within the banking system.

Efforts to roll back either explicit or implicit guarantees raise again the question of whether policymakers would adhere to stated limits in the event of a large bank failure. Although the 1991 banking bill is a step in the direction of limited guarantees, Congress still gave regulators maneuvering room that would allow them to protect all depositors in a given failure.[49]

10.4.3.2 Modified Payouts

Assuming that government decision makers would adhere to any new limits on federal deposit insurance, limiting deposit guarantees raises concerns about the stability of the payment system. One of the problems deposit insurance addressed was illiquidity associated with a bank failure. If the financial assets of a large company are tied up in a bank liquidation proceeding, for example, the payment system could be threatened because of questions about the company's ability to meet its payment obligations. Such concerns have led to calls for 'modified payouts'.

Modified payouts were introduced by the FDIC during the early 1980s. Under its modified payout policy, the FDIC ended its practice of making all depositors whole in purchase and assumption transactions.[50] Instead, depositors with accounts exceeding \$100 000 were given \$100 000 plus a percentage of their remaining funds based on what the FDIC was able to recover when it sold the failed bank. Depositors with more than \$100 000, thus, shared in losses associated with resolving an insolvent bank.

This practice ended, in 1984, with the blanket protection provided to Continental Illinois depositors and creditors, but some analysts have suggested it be revived. In comments to the Treasury Department, for example, the American Bankers Association (1990) advocated a return to modified payouts through their 'final-settlement-payment' case resolution. The ABA suggested that to speed the payout process, the FDIC base its payout rate on average historic losses rather than on expected losses for a particular institution.

10.4.3.3 Prompt Corrective Action

Efforts to impose depositor discipline by limiting deposit guarantees will not be effective if depositors with accounts exceeding the insured limit are given an opportunity to withdraw their funds before their bank is closed.[51] Apparently, just such escapes occurred frequently during the 1980s as weak banks and S&Ls were allowed to stay open long past the point of economic insolvency. In fact, withdrawals by large customers from failing depositories were facilitated by extensive discount window loans from regional Federal Reserve Banks. Because discount window loans are always fully collateralized, the FDIC bore the costs when these institutions were finally closed, either through liquidations or forced mergers.

These considerations led to calls for stricter enforcement of higher capital standards and more timely resolution efforts when a bank's capital fell below specified limits. A proposal for prompt corrective action was spelled out by Benston *et al.* (1989), and this proposal was the basis for requirements written into the 1991 FDICIA.[52]

Briefly, prompt corrective action establishes five 'tranches' or categories of banks. As a bank falls from 'well-' or 'adequately-capitalized' groups (that is, those with capital at or above specified standards) through the 'undercapitalized', 'significantly undercapitalized', and 'critically undercapitalized' tranches, regulatory oversight of the bank's activities become increasingly stringent.[53] If book-value capital falls to two per cent or less, regulators can move to take control of the bank.

Proponents of prompt corrective action hope to accomplish two basic goals. First, by limiting the activities of undercapitalized institutions – including, for example, limits on their growth rates, on dividend payments and salary increases for senior bank officers, and on interest rates that can be paid to attract new deposits – prompt corrective action would protect the deposit insurance fund (and, hence, taxpayers) from the worst abuses of the savings and loan fiasco. Architects of prompt corrective action hope to limit bankers' risk-taking by closely monitoring or prohibiting activities that may be a source of mounting losses, but the ultimate goal of prompt corrective action is to avoid the need for stringent government control of a bank's activities. Advocates hope that depository owners and managers will find the prospect of onerous government controls alarming enough to take steps to avoid falling into the 'undercapitalized' categories. Proponents of prompt corrective action applaud news accounts of bankers' complaints that they must now maintain higher levels of capital than required to avoid inadvertently slipping into a category entailing government 'micromanagement'. Thus, prompt corrective action is designed to reinstate owner discipline through effective capital standards. These higher capital standards are then reinforced by the threat of enhanced and more certain regulatory discipline should equity capital fall below specified limits.[54]

10.4.3.4 Puttable Subordinated Debt

There have also been efforts to identify groups other than depositors or owners who could provide effective market discipline. The most widely discussed proposal in this category are variants of Wall's (1989) suggestion to use puttable subordinated debt as a source of market discipline.

Under these proposals, banks would be required to issue a specified amount of subordinated debt as part of their capital structure.[55] This debt would be uninsured and subordinate to the FDIC's claims in the event of a failure. By requiring that banks structure this debt so that they had to return to the market frequently to replace maturing issues, regulators would gain clear signals about the market's perception of individual banks' future prospects. Difficulty placing new debt would be an indication of serious problems. In the extreme, banks that could not place the required amount of subordinated debt would be closed. Indeed, Wall suggests that subordinated debtholders should be allowed to force closure by putting their debt back to the bank in question. If the bank could not find new investors to purchase this debt in a specified time period, it would be closed.

10.4.4 Proposals to Expand Deposit Guarantees

Finally, there are the proposals that would expand deposit guarantees to cover all deposits. There are two distinct camps favoring expanded guarantees. One group would extend federal deposit insurance to protect all deposits while the other would require that all deposits be insured through private insurance contracts.

White (1991, p. 235) argues, for example, that '100 per cent coverage would be the only way to deal conclusively with depositor runs. The continuation of partial coverage is a continued invitation to runs by nervous depositors, and proposals to cut back the extent of deposit insurance would exacerbate this problem'. White would, thus, extend federal guarantees to protect all depositors.

To compensate for the absence of depositor discipline, White would strengthen regulatory oversight. He would impose higher capital standards, and he would judge compliance with those standards using market-value accounting. White would also employ risk-based insurance premiums, and he would expand the use of subordinated debt in banks' capital structures. Finally, White would insist on prompt closure of undercapitalized institutions. Thus, although White would eliminate any role for depositor discipline in the supervision of banks and thrifts, he would attempt to increase owner discipline by requiring they place more equity capital at risk and by making losses more certain in the event an institution becomes undercapitalized.

Once his system of discipline was in place, White suggests that Congress and the regulators should reexamine the range of allowable activities for depository institutions. According to White (1991, p. 240):

> The basic criterion for the inclusion of an activity within the domain of the insured institution should be the capability of the field force of examiners and supervisors to assess its riskiness (preferably, in a portfolio approach) and to be able to monitor its performance and the institution's capability at managing it successfully.

Finally, White would allow otherwise healthy institutions to open offices throughout the United States.

Ely (1990) and Wallison (1990) agree that insurance coverage should be extended to all deposits, but they would require the protection through private insurance contracts. Ely's proposal of cross-guarantees, on which Wallison's proposal is also based, would have banks and S&Ls establish syndicates through which they would then guarantee other depositories.[56] These private insurance contracts would be subject to federal oversight and approval. With the contracts in place, Ely and Wallison would shift most of current bank regulation to the insurance syndicates. Because these syndicates would be subject to losses in the event of a failure, they should have the necessary incentives to establish responsible capital guidelines and enforcement procedures.

Many advocates of cross guarantees would extend insurance syndicates' regulatory decisions to the activities of banks and S&Ls. Individual syndicates could establish guidelines for the depositories they insure, or they could, theoretically, grant broader powers on a case-by-case basis, depending on the situation facing any individual institution.

10.5 CONCLUSION

The 1930s package combined several elements that, in combination, led to considerable financial stability. Banks and S&Ls also clearly benefitted from the relative economic stability of the 1950s and 1960s. Although we can hope the return to relative price stability is long-lived, other elements of the earlier success are gone forever.

In particular, policymakers will never again be able to protect the markets of individual depository institutions as they did emerging from the Depression. Regardless of what powers are granted, a bank charter will probably never again be as valuable, in and of itself, as charters were in the 1950s and 1960s. There are simply too many nonbank competitors in domestic as well as international markets. Because protecting franchise value as a source of bank capital is no longer possible, we must find another road to controlling risk-taking among depository institutions.

In the end, analysts believe either in market discipline from creditors or they believe in regulatory discipline. Owner discipline can be increased by imposing higher capital standards, but in the end those capital standards must be enforced either by skeptical creditor/depositors or by stricter regulators. The question is: Which group represents the more reliable source of discipline for the next 60 years?

Notes

1. See Bartholomew (1990), pp. 142–3.
2. For 1982 to 1989, see Bartholomew (1990), p. 143. For subsequent years, see Skidmore (1992) and Rehm (1993).
3. Congress delayed and debated for several years before biting the bullet and committing public resources to the savings and loan insurance fund. The lack of financial resources seriously undermined regulators' ability to deal with undercapitalized and insolvent institutions, exacerbating losses. To its credit, when the Bank Insurance Fund appeared on the verge of insolvency, Congress moved more quickly, passing the Federal Deposit Insurance Corporation Improvement Act (FDICIA) in 1991. It should be noted, however, that Congress allowed funding for the Resolution Trust Corporation, the agency charged with cleaning up the S&L mess, to lapse in April 1992, stalling the S&L clean-up process. The analysis herein assumes that the need for any taxpayer infusions is a sign that the system of government oversight has failed and needs repair or replacement.
4. Bartholomew (1990), p. 9. It should be noted that the experience of the 1920s in terms of bank failures was not typical of the years before 1920. Bank suspensions from 1901 to 1920 averaged 89 per year.
5. *Ibid.*
6. Canada, with its nationally branched banking network, did not have any bank closures during the early 1930s despite similar reductions in real output and prices. There is some debate today about whether Canadian banks were actually insolvent or not and about whether their apparent stability came from the market's confidence in their ability to survive in the long term, or from government officials' promises to protect bank customers. Nevertheless, the dramatic difference between Canadian and US banking experience during the early 1930s was not lost on observers in this country.
7. See Burns (1974).
8. See Phillips (1993).
9. Federal deposit guarantees were not a new idea. Proposals for such a system had been introduced frequently over the past 150 years. See Golembe (1960).

10. 'Moral hazard' is an insurance term that refers to the fact that insured individuals are less likely to take care to avoid an insured-against event than uninsured individuals. Thus, insurance may increase the likelihood of a particular event occurring. For example, an individual whose car is insured against theft is less likely to return to see that the car is indeed locked than is an individual without insurance. In the case of banks and S&Ls, insured depositors are likely to exercise less discipline over their bank or S&L than they would in the absence of deposit guarantees. For a recent description of the 1930s literature on and debates about federal deposit insurance, see Flood (1992).
11. Boyd and Rolnick (1989), p. 4.
12. Branching restrictions for national banks were 'liberalized' in the sense that national banks were made subject to state branching laws. The ability of the states to limit interstate branching was reaffirmed, however, at least in part by the rejection of proposals to federally preempt branching restrictions as a solution to the banking crisis.
13. The separation of commercial and investment banking has also been viewed as one means by which policymakers hoped to limit the 'risky' activities of insured banks. That argument would carry more weight if large numbers of banks combining commercial and investment banking had failed during the 1930s. In fact, commercial banks with investment banking interests had a much lower failure rate than the banking industry as a whole during the period (Benston, 1990).
14. Savings and loan associations were not subject to limits on the interest rates they could pay to attract new deposits until 1966.
15. Such restrictions on competition did not always lead to the best deals for consumers of banking services, of course, but protecting consumers was not so high on the 1930s political agenda as it is today.
16. The Federal Savings and Loan Insurance Corporation was created in 1934 to provide S&Ls with deposit insurance similar to that provided banks through the FDIC.
17. Boyd and Rolnick (1989), p. 4. The 1980 Depository Institutions Deregulation and Monetary Control Act increased explicit insurance from $40 000 to $100 000 per account.
18. *Ibid.*
19. Miller (1992), p. 10. When Continental Illinois Bank of Chicago failed in 1984, government officials promised that all creditors would be made whole. The subsequent articulation of a 'too-big-to-fail' policy caused an uproar among owners of smaller institutions, and the FDIC responded by taking steps to protect virtually all depositors in all failed institutions.
20. Miller (1992), p. 6.
21. Bank capital levels have, in fact, been following a downward trend since at least 1840. In 1890, the average bank's equity capital was almost 25 per cent of total assets. For all banks, explicit capital levels hovered around the 6 per cent level from 1971 throughout the 1980s. For the nation's largest banks, explicit capital levels were even lower during this period, ranging from 4.04 per cent to 5.38 per cent during the 1971 to 1989 period. See Department of the Treasury (1991), p. II-4 and Table II-5.

22. Schwartz (1988) has documented the important negative impact of volatile economic conditions, particularly volatile monetary conditions, on the stability of depository institutions in this country and elsewhere. It is no coincidence that the roots of the S&L and banking problems are found in the inflation of the late 1970s.
23. White (1991), p. 69.
24. The process of removing deposit interest rate ceilings was begun in 1980 and basically completed by 1986.
25. An important contributing factor was, of course, forbearance through which undercapitalized institutions were allowed to remain open. We will discuss the impact of inadequate capital more fully below.
26. For a more in-depth discussion of the savings and loan fiasco, see Barth (1991), Kane (1989), or White (1991).
27. Brookes (1991), p. 12.
28. 'Junk' bonds' bad reputation came largely from their use in takeovers and other highly leveraged transactions, not from their role in financing the internal growth of mid-sized firms. In addition, some investors underestimated the risks associated with these instruments. They are not investment-grade securities, and their default rate is closer to that of the bank loans they tended to replace.
29. Becketti and Morris (1992) provide evidence regarding the growing number of substitutes for bank loans and confirm the widely-held perception that small businesses are still most dependent on their banks for debt capital.
30. Miller (1992), p. 9.
31. Commercial bank profitability improved dramatically in 1992, as the industry recorded record profits. It is still unclear whether the banking industry has indeed turned a corner or whether these profits were a temporary phenomenon caused by an especially steep yield curve. At any rate, they were welcome news for both bank managers and stockholders and federal policymakers.
32. Golembe and Holland (1986), p. 95.
33. This is certainly not to suggest that abuses in banks' relationships with their customers did not or do not occur. It is important to acknowledge the shift in regulatory emphasis, however. As the Depression ended, policymakers' primary goal as far as banks were concerned was to avoid widespread failures. They attempted to protect the profits of banks in ways that often put consumers at a disadvantage. As the worst problems of the Depression have faded from memory, the interests of consumers generally and particular groups of borrowers have become more important to policymakers. This is reflected in the consumer legislation of the 1970s.
34. 'Forbearance' allowed undercapitalized and insolvent depository institutions to continue operating, particularly in cases where the institutions' problems were viewed as arising from macroeconomic conditions 'beyond the control of management'. Forbearance occurred in part because the limited resources (both human and financial) of the deposit insurance funds were overwhelmed by the large number of failures during the 1980s and in part because political decisionmakers were reluctant to have large numbers of banks or thrifts fail on their watch (Kane, 1989).

35. In the sense in which I use the terms, any institution that is undercapitalized for more than a very brief period is, by definition, unneeded. If owners do not foresee enough profit opportunities to find it worthwhile to keep a bank or S&L adequately capitalized, then that is strong evidence that bank or S&L is not needed. Releasing the resources used by chronically undercapitalized institutions will lead to more efficient capital allocation.
36. Creditors tend to be more risk averse than owners, in part because creditors do not typically share in the upside gains associated with successful risk-taking. In addition, creditors generally have a shorter time-horizon (lasting only to the end of their contracts) than owners. An extensive literature exists on this subject. See for example, Jensen and Meckling (1976).
37. After all, at the point of insolvency, when economic net worth is zero, creditors still have the entire value of their investment to lose, while owners have nothing left to lose.
38. Of course, banks and thrifts do not require new powers to increase the risk of their portfolios. They can pursue higher returns by mismatching their assets and liabilities or lowering credit standards. This has led some observers to argue that banks activities should be deregulated even in the absence of deposit insurance reform because a broader base of permitted activities will give depository institutions the opportunity to reduce risk by better diversifying their portfolios. See, for example, O'Driscoll (1988). Pursuing new, unfamiliar activities may create some risk in and of itself, however. Further, the danger highlighted by the savings and loan experience was in allowing undercapitalized and insolvent institutions to pursue new activities using the government's guarantee to fund their efforts. We will return to this issue.
39. See, for example, Dowd (1992), England (1988), or Selgin (1988).
40. The 1930s crisis is viewed as a result of the failures of the Federal Reserve System coupled with the weaknesses inherent in a banking system with severe branching restrictions, for example. For case studies of unregulated banking systems in several countries (Dowd, 1992).
41. England (1988) focuses on the ways in which depositors might protect their interests in unregulated banks.
42. Proponents of unregulated or 'free' banking often find that government restrictions, including branching and product restrictions, have in many cases been responsible for observed failures.
43. My goal herein is to present alternatives, not to provide an analysis of the various proposals' political chances. It is obvious, however, that Congress is unlikely to eliminate federal deposit insurance in the foreseeable future.
44. Proposed collateral requirements vary. Some would allow insured deposits to be backed only with Treasury securities, while others would allow depositories to use any readily marketable asset (for example, securitized loans) as backing for their deposits. For descriptions of different proposals, see for example, Bryan (1991), Litan (1987), Pierce (1991), or Phillips (1993).
45. Requiring that all checkable accounts be insured would reduce concerns about possible payment system problems in the event of a failure.
46. Other regulated markets banks chose to enter would lead to regulation in line with accepted industry norms. Banks choosing to offer insurance, for example, would be subject to regulation of their insurance activities by state insurance commissioners.

47. Cargill and Mayer (1992, p. 97) argue, for example, that limiting deposit insurance coverage is the 'only effective way to deal with the fundamental flaw in the financial reform process'. But although they would remove interstate branching restrictions, they would not introduce broad new powers.
48. The 1991 FDICIA made a move in this direction by requiring that the FDIC liquidate a bank (imposing losses on uninsured depositors) if that represented the least costly resolution method. The FDIC can choose another course only when the Fed and the Treasury agree with the FDIC that liquidation would have serious systemic implications. (Some observers feel that is a lower hurdle than others.)
49. See Miller (1992), pp. 29–32.
50. The two most common resolution methods used in bank failures are liquidations and purchase and assumption agreements. Of these, purchase and assumption agreements (or P&As) are used most often. In a liquidation, the FDIC takes control of the failed bank, sells the assets and pays depositors. In a P&A, the FDIC finds another bank willing to purchase the failed institution. Traditionally, the FDIC only agreed to P&As in which the purchasing bank agreed to take on all the deposit liabilities of the failed institution, thus making all depositors whole.
51. Large depositors fleeing a bank can help force regulators to move in, however, as in the case of Continental Illinois.
52. The FDICIA also limits the Fed's ability to recover interest on its discount window loans when it continues to lend for more than a specified time period.
53. The sifting of banks into different categories or tranches would, of course, be more accurate in the presence of market-value accounting, and proponents of prompt corrective action also generally support the use of market-based accounting procedures. Market-value accounting will not be discussed as a separate proposal in this paper because the more important question is who does what with the more accurate information.
54. For further discussion of the prompt corrective action proposal as it was enacted in FDICIA see Kaufman (1993).
55. Proposals differ on whether or not all banks would be required to issue subordinated debt or only those institutions above a certain size. Still another variation on the theme would tie new powers to the willingness and ability to issue a specified proportion of capital as subordinated debt.
56. Ely has clearly given a lot of careful thought to what pitfalls would exist and how to avoid them. For example, his plan spells out how to avoid the systemic risk that would be created if Bank A insured Bank B while Bank B insured Bank A. Indeed, one of the criticisms of Ely's plan is that it is so detailed it eliminates much of the discovery process normally associated with private contracts.

References

American Bankers Association (1990) 'Federal Deposit Insurance: A Program for Reform', Comment to the Treasury Department (March).

Barth, James R. (1991) *The Great Savings and Loan Debacle* (Washington, DC: American Enterprise Institute).

Barth, James R., Carl D. Hudson and Daniel E. Page (1991) 'The Need to Reform the Federal Deposit Insurance System', *Contemporary Policy Issues* (January) **9**, 24–35.

Bartholomew, Philip (1990) *Reforming Federal Deposit Insurance* (Washington, DC: CBO, September).

Becketti, Sean and Charles Morris (1992) 'Are Bank Loans Still Special?' Federal Reserve Bank of Kansas City *Economic Review* (Third Quarter) **77**, 71–84.

Benston, George J. (1990) *The Separation of Commercial and Investment Banking: The Glass–Steagall Act Revisited and Reconsidered* (New York: Oxford University Press).

Benston, George J., R. Dan Brumbaugh, Jr., Jack M. Guttentag, Richard J. Herring, George G. Kaufman, Robert E. Litan and Kenneth E. Scott (1989) *Blueprint for Restructuring America's Financial Institutions: Report of a Task Force* (Washington: Brookings Institution).

Boyd, John H. and Arthur J. Rolnick (1989) 'A Case for Reforming Federal Deposit Insurance', *1988 Annual Report* (Minneapolis: Federal Reserve Bank of Minneapolis).

Brookes, Warren T. (1991) 'Have We Seen the End of Banks?' *Durell Journal of Money and Banking* (May) **3**, 12–20.

Bryan, Lowell L. (1988) *Breaking up the Bank: Rethinking an Industry under Siege* (Homewood, IL: Dow Jones–Irwin).

Burns, Helen M. (1974) *The American Banking Community and New Deal Banking Reforms 1933–1935* (Westport, CT: Greenwood Press).

Cargill, Thomas F. and Thomas Mayer (1992) 'US Deposit Insurance Reform', *Contemporary Policy Issues*, (July) **10**, 95–103.

Corrigan, E. Gerald (1991) 'Balancing Progressive Change and Caution in Reforming the Financial System', Federal Reserve Bank of New York, *Quarterly Review* (Summer) **16**, 1–12.

Department of the Treasury (1991) *Modernizing the Financial System* (Washington, DC: Treasury Department, February).

Dowd, Kevin (1992) *The Experience of Free Banking* (London: Routledge).

Ely, Bert (1990) *Making Deposit Insurance Safe through 100% Cross-Guarantees* (Washington, DC: National Chamber Foundation).

England, Catherine (1988) 'Agency Costs and Unregulated Banks: Could Depositors Protect Themselves?' in *The Financial Services Revolution: Policy Directions for the Future*, ed. Catherine England and Thomas Huertas, (Boston: Kluwer Academic Publishers) 317–43.

Flood, Mark D. (1992) 'The Great Deposit Insurance Debate', Federal Reserve Bank of St Louis *Review* (July/August) **74**, 51–77.

Garcia, Gillian (1988) 'The FSLIC Is "Broke" in More Ways than One', in *The Financial Services Revolution: Policy Directions for the Future*, ed. Catherine England and Thomas Huertas (Boston: Kluwer Academic Publishers) 235–49.

Golembe, Carter H. (1960) 'The Deposit Insurance Legislation of 1933', *Political Science Quarterly* (June) **76**, 181–200.

Golembe, Carter H. and David S. Holland (1986) *Federal Regulation of Banking, 1986–87* (Washington, DC: Golembe Associates).

Huertas, Thomas F. 'The Regulation of Financial Institutions: A Historical Perspective on Current Issues', in *Financial Services: The Changing Institutions and Government Policy*, ed. George J. Benston (Englewood Cliffs, NJ: Prentice-Hall).

Jensen, Michael C. and William H. Meckling (1976) 'Theory of the Firm: Managerial Behavior, Agency Costs and Ownership Structure', *Journal of Financial Economics* (October) 305–60.

Kane, Edward J. (1985) *The Gathering Crisis in Federal Deposit Insurance* (Cambridge, MA: MIT Press).

Kane, Edward J. (1989) *The S&L Insurance Mess: How Did It Happen?* (Washington, DC: Urban Institute Press).

Kaufman, George G. 'The Current State of Banking Reform', Chapter 8 in this volume.

Litan, Robert E. (1987) *What Should Banks Do?* (Washington, DC: Brookings Institution).

Malburn, W. P. (1934) *What Happened to Our Banks?* (Indianapolis: The Bobbs–Merrill Co.).

Miller, Tom (1992) *A Citizen's Guide to Banking Reform: Building a Fiscal Firewall between Taxpayers and Failing Banks* (Washington, DC: Citizens against Government Waste).

Milligan, Lawrence J. (1990) 'Why America Needs a Banking Crisis', *Institutional Investor* (November) 104–12.

O'Driscoll, Gerald P., Jr. (1988) 'Bank Failures: The Deposit Insurance Connection', *Contemporary Policy Issues* (April) **6**, 1–12.

Pierce, James L. (1991) *The Future of Banking* (New Haven: Yale University Press).

Phillips, Ronnie J. (1993) 'The "Chicago Plan" and New Deal Banking Reform', and Chapter 5, this volume.

Rehm, Barbara A. (1993) 'Bank Closings in '92 Fewer, but Costly', *Washington Post* (5 January) D3.

Schwartz, Anna J. (1988) 'Financial Stability and the Federal Safety Net', in *Restructuring Banking and Financial Services in America*, ed. W. S. Haraf and R. M. Kushmeider (Washington, DC: American Enterprise Institute).

Selgin, George (1988) *The Theory of Free Banking: Money Supply under Competitive Note Issue* (Totowa, NJ: Rowman & Littlefield).

Skidmore, Dave (1992) 'Bank, S&L Failures Declined in '91, but Analysts Expect a New Upswing', *Washington Post* (2 January) D13.

Wall, Larry D. (1989) 'A Plan for Reducing Future Deposit Insurance Losses: Puttable Subordinated Debt', Federal Reserve Bank of Atlanta, *Economic Review* (July/August) 2–17.

Wallison, Peter J. (1990) *Back from the Brink: A Practical Plan for Privatizing Deposit Insurance and Strengthening Our Banks and Thrifts* (Washington, DC: American Enterprise Institute).

White, Lawrence J. (1991) *The S&L Debacle: Public Policy Lessons for Bank and Thrift Regulation* (New York: Oxford University Press).

White, Lawrence J. (1992) 'What Should Banks *Really* Do?', *Contemporary Policy Issues* (July) **10**, 104–12.

Comment

LARRY R. MOTE

Catherine England has put together a concise and extremely useful overview of the key issues in the ongoing debate over regulatory restructuring that, for the past decade or so, has been the major preoccupation of many of those attending this conference. By and large, I find the facts of the story to be accurately and fairly represented; the analysis generally on the mark; the conclusions, with few exceptions, to be consistent with the results of more rigorous theoretical and empirical treatises on narrower aspects of the issue; and the description of proposed solutions, if not comprehensive, at least representative of the seemingly infinite number of proposals that have been offered in recent years. Catherine is also to be commended for her restraint in simply listing her own preferred solution as but one of those that have been proposed.

My first comment is one that I suspect the author will agree with. It concerns the impression given by the statements early in the chapter that 'the regulatory structure today was fundamentally established during the Depression, and the system worked for more than 40 years' and several pages later that, 'With occasional adjustments, this package worked extremely well for 40 years'. In conjunction with the author's assertion that serious problems in the 'world of financial markets' first became evident in the early 1980s, that statement suggests that everything was satisfactory between the 1930s and the early 1980s. However, I would suggest that banking regulation worked between 1933 and the early 1980s largely in the sense that communism worked between 1917 and the fall of the Berlin wall. There is abundant evidence elsewhere in the chapter that the author is quite aware of many of the problems that arose in the intervening years. But, perhaps because of a concern for brevity, some serious questions regarding the effectiveness of regulation are left out of the discussion. First of all, much of the undeniable gain in terms of safety and soundness of the banking system after 1933 may not reasonably be credited to the new regulatory regime at all. That fewer banks failed and that those that survived became more conservative in their lending policies was less a result of regulation than of the fact that 9000 of the weakest institutions had been removed from the market between 1930 and 1933 and of the fear of runs that had been instilled in bankers by that trauma. As is widely known, banks' excess reserves swelled to unprecedented levels in the late 1930s, reflecting both weak loan demand and bankers' obsession with maintaining liquidity. It was only as the economy recovered after World War II and bank loan-to-deposit ratios again rose toward their previous highs that the ability of regulation to contain bank risk-taking was put to the test.

The point is well illustrated by the experience with regulation of interest rates on deposits. After little more than a year, the market rates on deposits fell below the new deposit rate ceilings and remained well below them until the early 1950s. When banks did begin to be constrained by the ceilings, the fed raised them and continued to adjust them to changes in market rates until 1966, when its refusal to do so precipitated the first major post-war credit crunch and ended banks' naive reliance on purchased funds as the solution to the liquidity management problem. Once the ceilings became continuously binding, they caused an enormous amount of mischief, including the transfer of billions of dollars from unsophisticated consumers to owners of banks, recurring episodes of credit stringency, the waste of large amounts of resources and ingenuity on regulatory avoidance, and – to me, the ultimate absurdity – circumvention of the regulations by the regulators themselves, who continued to limit explicit interest while averting their gaze from the spectacle of banks bartering electric toasters for deposits. The bottom line was a situation in which regulators spent resources trying to enforce deposit rate ceilings, the regulatees spent resources trying the avoid them and competing in an inefficient manner through merchandise premiums and overexpanded networks of branch offices, consumers were deprived of the usual benefits of competition, and – in case anyone still cared – banks' costs were driven up so that little, if any, of the intended benefits to bank profits remained. As early as the credit crunch of 1966, it was becoming apparent that, given the open market alternatives then available, the ceilings offered little protection to depository institutions. (Of course, that was the year that Congress chose to extend the ceiling to savings and loan associations.) This experience does not justify England's assertion that, 'With a few minor adjustments, the limits on deposit interest rates designed to keep depositories' cost of funds low seemed to work until the late 1970s…' By the late 1970s, regulators had already thrown in the towel.

On the other hand, I think the chapter is quite right in characterizing the 1930s regulatory regime as a 'system of "controlled" competition' that was 'designed to protect the profits of individual depository institutions and thus reduce the number of failures'. However, it is slightly off the mark in suggesting that policymakers were totally preoccupied with 'safety and soundness' issues as late as 1968 when Truth in Lending, the first of a series of consumer protection acts, was enacted. As early as the 1950s, Congress had expressed concerns regarding the growing merger and acquisition movement in banking and its effect on concentration. After several years of hearings, it enacted the Bank Holding Company Act of 1956, followed in a few years by the Bank Merger Act of 1960. By restricting anticompetitive mergers and acquisitions, these acts were intended to protect bank customers from exploitation through the exercise of monopoly power (or at least to limit their exploitation to that sanctioned by deposit rate ceilings). Indeed, consideration of the seemingly irreconcilable conflict between this legislation and that of the 1930s leads to the conclusion that what policymakers have tried to do is to fine tune the degree of competition in the banking industry, avoiding the extremes of both unfettered free competition and unrestrained monopoly, but with a distinct bias toward maintaining supranormal profits in the banking industry as a means of bolstering bank safety. Whether the system ever really worked as intended is another question. As noted above, I do not believe that it did.

England's chapter provides a first-rate description of the process by which depositor discipline was undermined; first, by repeated increases in the insurance limit and, later, by the actions of the bank regulatory agencies in protecting uninsured depositors in the failures of several large banks in the 1980s. She does an equally fine job of describing the weakening of owner discipline by forbearance in the face of the sudden erosion of bank equity by the sharp increases in interest rates in the late 1970s and early 1980s.

So far as solutions are concerned, it is difficult to quarrel with England's categorization of most current reform proposals as being based on a belief either in market discipline or in regulatory discipline, although a few of them combine elements of both. The proposals at the extremes pose the choice in a particularly stark form. For example, Lawrence White's proposal to provide 100 per cent federal insurance coverage for deposits, while using capital requirements, regulation, and risk-based insurance premiums to control risk, goes the furthest toward relying on regulatory discipline at the expense of market discipline. The desirability of such a solution rests heavily on the importance of the adverse economic effects associated with bank runs, which are viewed as something that should be prevented, if not at all costs, certainly at very substantial cost. But, before adopting such an approach, it would be useful to at least review George Kaufman's summary of the evidence on the costs of bank runs, which suggests that runs have been given something of a bad reputation and that, under conditions less severe than those of the 1930s, they can be a constructive means of market discipline.

The approach actually taken by Congress in enacting the Federal Deposit Insurance Corporation Improvement Act of 1991 was to include elements of both market and regulatory discipline, although the latter seem to predominate. To remedy past regulatory failures, the act attempts to circumscribe regulatory discretion within fairly narrow boundaries. Indeed, a careful reading of the act may cause one to wonder just how the regulators can avoid obeying its clear mandate. However, when the perceived need arises, regulators can respond with almost as much energy – though rarely as much originality – as the private sector to avoid enforcing unwanted regulations. For that reason, I think it is premature to celebrate the demise of the too-big-to-fail doctrine or to assume that prompt corrective action will work as intended.

My deep-seated skepticism regarding the effectiveness of regulation is rooted in the dominance of form over substance in bureaucratic behavior. For a quarter century being in the employ of a regulator, it persuades me that the wiser course is to place greater emphasis on market discipline than on regulatory discipline in reforming deposit insurance. Of course, for market discipline to be fully effective may require that we extend the principle of transparency from the securities markets to bank supervision. In contrast, up until now, the reigning principle of bank supervision has been one of opacity.

11 The Changing World of Banking: Setting the Regulatory Agenda

James R. Barth and
R. Dan Brumbaugh, Jr.

11.1 INTRODUCTION

The approach taken in the 1980s, and thus far in the 1990s, to setting the regulatory agenda for banking (a term we will use to include all federally insured depositories) has been relatively narrowly focused on trying to resolve specific problems that have arisen in the deposit-insurance and bank regulatory system. The several changes in federal banking regulation in the 1980s reflect this narrow and reactive approach. These changes were largely made in five separate pieces of federal legislation – the Depository Institutions Deregulation and Monetary Control Act of 1980 (DIDMCA), the Depository Institutions Act of 1982 (Garn–St Germain), the Competitive Equality in Banking Act of 1987 (CEBA), and the Financial Institutions Reform, Recovery and Enforcement Act of 1989 (FIRREA). Finally, in 1991 the Federal Deposit Insurance Corporation Improvement Act (FDICIA) was enacted.

Although each of these laws is complex, all have become known for specific contributions to addressing various banking problems that occurred during the past decade.[1] In 1980, DIDMCA began the process of phasing out deposit rate ceilings, allowing negotiable order of withdrawal (NOW) accounts at all depositories, and permitting savings and loans to make consumer loans and to issue credit cards. The Garn–St Germain Act allowed interstate mergers and mergers between banks and savings and loans and granted savings and loans the right to make commercial loans. CEBA limited the growth of nonbank banks and provided for limited recapitalization of the Federal Savings and Loan Insurance Corporation (FSLIC). FIRREA continued the recapitalization process by directly committing federal tax dollars to the savings and loan clean-up, reorganized the savings and loan regulatory and insurance apparatus, and increased the minimum required lending by savings and loans for housing-related finance. Finally, FDICIA provided back-up funding for the Bank Insurance Fund (BIF) and mandated that the Federal Deposit Insurance Corporation (FDIC) take prompt corrective action against 'critically undercapitalized' depositories. It also provided for risk-based deposit-insurance premiums and operating restrictions for depositories that were not 'well capitalized'.

Each piece of legislation was essentially an *ad hoc* reaction to specific problems that were thought to require immediate attention. Deposit rates were deregulated because of concern about disintermediation at banks when market interest rates rose substantially above regulated interest rates. Asset deregulation at savings and loans was an attempt to reduce their reliance on fixed-rate, long-term lending for home mortgages funded by shorter-term, variable-rate deposits. The subsequent increase in required holding of housing-related assets reflected concern over the excessive risk-taking of non-traditional savings and loans. Requirements for prompt seizure of deeply troubled institutions reflected concern over the high costs of closing institutions that had been left open, often for years, while reporting insolvency.

For the most part, the federal legislation that was enacted and the subsequent regulatory changes, as well as similar changes in state legislation at various times for state-chartered banks, modified the existing deposit-insurance and bank regulatory structure. In the process of modifying the structure, little attempt was made to understand or to care much about whether there were fundamental changes in the overall market for financial services that were affecting or contributing to the problems being addressed by the enacted legislation and changes in regulation. We conclude that after 13 years of upheaval and turmoil among federally insured and regulated depositories, the bank regulatory environment is inconsistent with the evolving financial marketplace.

This chapter approaches the bank regulatory issue by addressing whether, or to what extent, the existing deposit-insurance and regulatory system is consistent with the desired function of the financial system. We begin with a discussion of the goals of regulation and how they facilitate the desired operation of the financial system. We then describe the methods currently employed by the government to regulate banks, as well as other government interventions in the financial system. Because there are many other financial service firms besides banks, we then describe several competitive developments in the market for financial services that have important implications for the performance of banks and their regulation. We focus on the evolution of competition among financial service firms over the past few decades, noting recent developments in particular.

In the final section of the paper we point out some inconsistencies between the goals of regulation and the current methods of regulation, and we discuss several reform options. This analysis has implications not only for changes in US regulatory policy, but also for the policies of the many other countries that are currently assessing changes in their financial systems.

11.2 GOAL OF BANK REGULATION: FROM THE PERSPECTIVE OF SOCIETY

11.2.1 Confidence and Stability in the Financial System

The most frequently stated goal of bank regulation is to maintain confidence and, hence, stability in the financial system.[2] The reason this is so desirable is that a stable financial system facilitates the efficient allocation of scarce economic resources – the primary function of the financial system. The system accomplishes this fundamental goal by essentially fulfilling two functions: providing a reliable payments mechanism to facilitate transactions and providing a reliable credit mechanism to transfer funds between savers and borrowers to facilitate economic growth. Thus, the fundamental goal of bank regulation is to promote the efficient allocation of scarce economic resources by minimizing disruptions in the payments mechanism and in the credit mechanism by which funds are transferred between savers and borrowers.

11.2.2 The Role of the Payments Mechanism and Credit Market

The importance of a well-functioning payments mechanism can be seen by realizing what would exist without it – two-way barter. Transactions would be so cumbersome and costly that they would inhibit economic activity. To the extent that transactions are swift, reliable and low cost, they promote economic efficiency. The importance of the efficient transfer of funds from savers to borrowers can be appreciated by remembering the Great Depression when, as a result of widespread withdrawals from banks, both the payments system and the credit process were disrupted, exacerbating the reduction in real economic activity.

The financial system should also operate so as to provide the most reliable and efficient mechanism to transfer funds from savers to borrowers in several specific respects. All firms in all industries should have access to the system. Projects of all sizes should have access to funding. Funding should be available across all geographic areas. Prices should reflect risk and be based upon timely and accurate information, with the exact allocation of resources determined by the interaction of individuals and firms in the marketplace. These are characteristics of a well-functioning financial system.

11.2.3 Protection of Individual Financial Institutions

The goal of stability in the financial system does not mean that regulation should be designed to ensure the solvency of individual financial institutions. To the contrary, regulation should facilitate the prompt resolution of firms whose performance in a competitive market leads to financial distress. Prompt resolution at minimum cost reallocates more resources more efficiently than if resolution is slower and more costly. In the process, of course, stockholders, bondholders and other creditors suffer fewer losses. In the case of federally insured banks, prompt resolution means that the deposit-insurance agency suffers fewer losses and the taxpayer, who is a contingent creditor if there are insufficient deposit-insurance reserves, faces a lower risk of sharing in those losses. These losses, however, are only part of the total resolution cost, which includes any deadweight losses to society due to incentives that are distorted by a troubled institution's access to mispriced federally insured deposits.

Promotion of competitive financial markets is a desirable goal for both the financial system and bank regulation because the result is in turn more economically efficient financial markets and more economically efficient allocation of scarce resources generally. Thus, a goal of regulation is to promote and to maintain competitive markets and to intervene only to offset market failure and to facilitate the cost-effective exit of deeply troubled or insolvent firms from the marketplace.

11.2.4 Dealing with Financial Market Failures

Financial markets are susceptible to intricate and closely related forms of market failure involving barriers to entry and exit, public-good problems, externalities, agency problems, moral-hazard problems, and adverse-selection problems. We provide a brief overview.[3] The market failure most frequently cited as justification for government intervention in the form of the provision of deposit insurance and the accompanying bank regulation involves the public good qualities of information and externalities that can lead to disruptions in the real economy via disruptions in financial markets.

11.2.5 Public-Good Qualities of Information

Information possesses public-good qualities in the sense that any costly information that is obtained by one person is not reduced if another person gains access to it, and because once an individual acts upon the information it becomes public. Because a private market, without the coercive powers of the government, cannot impose fees on 'free riders' who acquire costly information without paying for it, less information is forthcoming than if free riders were forced to pay for the information. People who possess information and who know that the benefits of the information will dissipate if it becomes public, are less likely to make it public unless they are appropriately compensated. This creates a justification for government intervention: to impose the appropriate fees on free riders, for example, and, thereby, increase the provision of information to a more optimum level.

The public-good analysis implies that too little monitoring of financial institutions will occur in the absence of government intervention to provide monitoring. That is, too little information on the condition of financial institutions will be acquired by depositors. With insufficient information available to depositors, depositors will provide inadequate monitoring and financial institutions may engage in excessive risk-taking. If excessive risk-taking arises in banks, it will generally include illiquid assets whose values are, therefore, difficult for outsiders to discern. The net effect is the increased likelihood of bank failures and bank failure losses.

11.2.6 Negative Externalities and Bank Runs

The second form of market failure most often discussed in the context of banks is the negative externality that exists when runs occur against solvent institutions. Depositors who have imperfect information or lack costly-to-obtain information may run against not only insolvent banks, but also solvent banks with broadly similar portfolios. Depositors may also run against solvent banks because they mistakenly infer insolvency due to widespread economic difficulties that could result in insolvency, but have not. Actions based upon mistakes or inaccurate information could, in the extreme, impair the entire payments mechanism and, in the process, lead to asset sales at distressed prices that impair the intermediation or credit mechanism. Such situations create a justification for deposit insurance to prevent widespread and destructive runs on banks.

11.2.7 Moral Hazard, Agency Problems, and Deposit Insurance

Government regulation itself, however, can cause problems. Although deposit insurance was established primarily to protect against widespread runs, it simultaneously eliminates the incentive of insured depositors to monitor financial institutions and fails to impose discipline on risk-taking by the owners whose losses are limited by corporate liability laws to their equity contribution. This gives rise to the moral-hazard problem that is widely associated with deposit insurance. The owners of depositories have a put option on their institution's assets because of deposit insurance, and, therefore, have an incentive to increase the value of the option by choosing riskier portfolios and lower capital-to-asset ratios.[4] Thus, government intervention to deal with one type of market failure can create another type of market failure.

For adequately-capitalized institutions, the moral-hazard problem is virtually eliminated. As a result, minimum capital requirements have been established by federal law and regulation with the goal of containing the moral-hazard problem. In addition, extensive examination and supervision are designed to detect and prevent excessive risk-taking. In the early 1980s, however, particularly in the case of savings and loans, the required minimum capital level was lowered and the measurement of capital broadened beyond that permitted by generally accepted accounting principles. Even worse, savings and loans were left open and operating for lengthy periods while reporting insolvency. In this regard, the 205 savings and loans that were closed in 1988 had been left open while insolvent for an average of 4.5 years.[5] Similar and more recent examples of forbearance involving depositories exist.[6]

The forbearance developed as the cash reserves of the deposit-insurance funds for savings and loans and banks deteriorated, and regulators were forced to choose between two broad alternative courses of action. On the one hand, they could request additional funds from Congress to cover the cost of resolving failures that were occurring. On the other hand, they could engage in forbearance by – among other things – delaying the resolution of deteriorated and insolvent institutions. Both the savings and loan and bank insurance funds chose the later course, admitting, only after being forced to do so, that their resources were inadequate for resolving the failures being projected at the time. This forbearance is an example of both moral-hazard and agency problems. The depletion of the insurance fund reserves created a moral-hazard problem because the deposit-insurance agencies themselves took risks that they would not have otherwise taken. This represented a principal-agent problem, as well, between the deposit-insurance agencies and taxpayers, whose interest in prompt closures was not adequately protected. The actions of the regulators were clearly inconsistent with the interests of taxpayers.[7]

11.2.8 Barriers to Entry and Exit

By not promptly resolving all deeply troubled depositories, the regulator blockades exit, preventing such institutions from exiting with the least cost, including costs imposed on competitors. The government also controls entry into banking because institutions must be issued charters in order to engage in certain legally defined activities. Markets that are truly competitive have no barriers either to entry or to exit. By erecting barriers to entry and by not expediting exit, bank regulation introduces market imperfections that cannot only affect competition within the banking industry but also the degree and type of competition within the overall financial services industry. The returns and risk associated with banking will be similarly affected.

11.2.9 Innovation, Protection of Individuals, and Allocation of Credit

Another goal of regulation is to promote, or at least not to impede, innovation. Innovation promotes interrelated goals by providing for the more efficient allocation of financial services, which in turn provides for the more efficient allocation of scarce economic resources. All of this contributes to stability in the financial system and facilitates real economic growth.

Still another goal of regulation is the protection of selected individuals. Deposit insurance is considered to be a desirable guarantee for the small deposits of unsophisticated depositors. The guarantee was not designed to provide protection for all depositors or all deposits. Such a large guarantee is not necessary to protect the payments and credit mechanisms. Bank regulation is also designed to protect customers of financial firms against selected risks involving fraud.

Finally, a goal of bank regulation is to allocate credit. The government itself makes loans directly, thus providing an intermediation service between taxpayers and selected borrowers. The government also affects lending by depositories by making loan guarantees available to selected borrowers.[8] More generally, the government may provide broad subsidies through federally chartered and insured depositories for selected products or services. In general, direct loans, loan guarantees, and broad subsidies reduce the cost of borrowing below what the money and capital markets would provide in order to reduce the cost of selected products. These products, called merit goods, are selected because in some fashion the government decides to reduce their cost and, thereby, make them more generally available. The most conspicuous such good is housing finance, for which the government long supported the savings and loan industry, the development of a secondary market in home mortgages, and the provision of tax advantages to both home buyers and lenders.

11.3 METHODS CURRENTLY USED TO REGULATE BANKS

We now review the primary methods currently used to regulate banks in the US. We focus on the method or function of regulation, rather than the institutional regulatory framework. The institutional framework is, after all, of secondary importance. In setting the agenda for possible changes in regulation, it is most important to evaluate whether the methods used currently to regulate banks are consistent with the goals of regulation. If analysis suggests that changes in regulations are needed, the institutional framework should evolve to facilitate those changes.

11.3.1 The Lender of Last Resort and Deposit Insurance

In order to protect against widespread runs at solvent depositories, the Federal Reserve System was established to be the lender of last resort.[9] As described by Meltzer (1986), the role of the Federal Reserve follows principles stated in the nineteenth century by Walter Bagehot (1873). It is to prevent illiquid but solvent banks from being forced to close by making collateralized loans to them when facing heavy deposit withdrawals. If done properly, the lender of last resort can always stop runs. Yet, during the 1930s the Federal Reserve did not provide sufficient liquidity, either through the discount window or open-market operations, and thousands of banks were forced to liquidate their assets simultaneously in depressed markets.[10] Severe losses to depositors occurred and the payment and credit mechanisms ground to a halt.

Deposit insurance also protects against widespread runs and is designed to make certain that the payments mechanism is never disrupted. Deposit insurance is not, in fact, insurance but a guarantee against losses associated with selected deposits. The guarantee is credible because, since CEBA, the full faith and credit of the US government stand explicitly behind it. Taxpayers are the ultimate guarantor. The guarantee is administered by the FDIC, which oversees the BIF and the Savings Association Insurance Fund

(SAIF) for savings and loans. A separate insurance fund, the National Credit Union Share Insurance Fund (NCUSIF), provides federal deposit insurance for credit unions. The FDIC interacts formally and informally with the other bank regulators, including the Federal Reserve, the Office of the Comptroller of the Currency (OCC), the Office of Thrift Supervision (OTS), and the National Credit Union Administration (NCUA).

Deposit insurance creates a need for selected regulation to control moral hazard (as well as closely related principle-agent and adverse-selection problems), which can exacerbate the risk exposure of the deposit-insurance fund as described above.[11] The primary regulatory tools are the establishment of minimum capital requirements, requirements for regular financial reporting, and examination and supervision. Although deposit-insurance premiums are currently designed to rise with selected measures of risk, the band within which they vary is relatively narrow and the risk measures do not capture portfolio risk. Deposit insurance also requires a resolution mechanism in order to prevent costly failures when depositories become critically undercapitalized and subject to seizure by regulators. As a byproduct of the resolution procedure, the deposit insurer must be able to dispose of assets and liabilities of seized depositories. This is generally done without any overall coordination by the agencies themselves. In response to the large number of savings and loan failures, however, the Resolution Trust Corporation (RTC), administered by the FDIC, was created in 1989 to dispose of failed savings and loans turned over to it by the OTS through September 1993.

11.3.2 Restrictions on Bank Ownership, Activities and Geographic Location

Complicated federal and state restrictions on the ownership, activities and geographic location of banks have been imposed by law and regulation for a number of reasons. Ostensibly, they have been imposed for reasons that are consistent with the goals of regulation stated above: primarily to promote confidence and stability in the financial system by increasing safety and soundness. They are often associated with the need to control the moral-hazard problem that arises with deposit insurance. These restrictions, however, are also restrictions on market forces generally associated with competition, and the restrictions in some cases existed before deposit insurance. These restrictions include:

- Chartering of depositories by both federal and state authorities (including limits on who can own or acquire depositories);

- Price and quantity controls;
- Limitations on geographic location (branching and banking); and
- Restriction of activities (both 'intra- and inter-industry'[12] limitations on the financial products and services banks can provide, including the underwriting, sale and distribution of mutual funds, insurance and securities).

These restrictions are consistent with both limiting competition and promoting the stability of existing depositories. These types of restrictions are most effective when there is relatively little innovation in the market for financial services, and when competition exists primarily among depositories ('intra-industry' competition). The development of computer and telecommunication technology and non-depository competition, however, reveals problems with these kinds of restrictions. Non-depository competitors may offer services that are close substitutes for those offered by depositories at lower prices, or even offer new services demanded by customers. Such events may make it appear that the financial system is less stable (for example, by increasing the number of depository failures), when in fact it is instead becoming more efficient through 'inter-industry' competition. The development of 'inter-industry' competition can create the need to reduce some of the restrictions listed above if, as a result, the depository industry displays excess capacity and excessively costly exit as a result of its inability to adapt to a changing financial marketplace.

11.3.3 Antitrust Laws and Regulations

Some laws and regulations are designed to promote competition. Selected antitrust actions involving bank mergers have been taken, over time, by the Justice Department. In particular, there are specific merger guidelines whose general purpose is to prevent mergers between federally insured depositories that would have the effect of reducing or restricting competition.

The merger guidelines, however, can be viewed as a vehicle for anti-competitive and economically inefficient results in some cases. They have been used to prevent or discourage mergers between selected large banks when the relevant geographic and product markets have been narrowly construed to include only parts of a specific state and other depositories as the primary competitors.[13] The relevant geographic and product market may well have been much larger and the relevant competitors may well have been different types of non-depositories. As a result, fewer mergers may have occurred, reducing competitive pressures on other depositories and non-depositories.

11.3.4 State-Chartered Banks

The existence of state-chartered banks significantly complicates the regulatory picture. Historically, much of what state-chartered banks have been able to do has been determined by the states. Federal law effectively granted to the states the power to permit or deny geographic expansion of all banks – national banks and state-chartered banks through branching, and bank holding companies through acquisitions.[14] Tables 11.A1 and 11.A2, in the Appendix, depict the variety of differences in bank regulation of geographic expansion that have developed among the states. As Table 11.A1 shows, 42 states allowed statewide branch banking in 1991, while 12 states limited branch banking in their states. As Table 11.A2 shows, the conditions under which banks may branch across state lines vary greatly, though there has been a movement during the past decade toward permitting branching over wider geographic areas.[15] Sixteen states, however, currently have laws limiting the share of total deposits that any one bank can control within the state.[16]

In addition, as Table 11.A3 shows, state-chartered banks have not been subject to all of the restrictions on activities that apply to national banks – for example, Glass–Steagall Act restrictions, National Bank Act restrictions limiting national banks to banking and activities incidental to banking, and the Bank Holding Company Act restrictions confining bank holding companies to activities 'closely related to banking'. Tables 11.A3 and 11.A4 show the wide variety of activities that have been allowed state-chartered banks. Under widely differing conditions, state-chartered banks have been allowed to engage in securities underwriting and brokerage, real-estate equity participation, development and brokerage, and insurance underwriting and brokerage. We are unaware of any studies that have found an association between wider powers for state-chartered banks and greater bank failures and failure losses, a relationship which some have argued existed between wider powers and savings and loans in the 1980s.

The effect of state-chartered banks on competition has been uneven. On the one hand, limitations on branching within and across state lines limit 'intra-industry' competition. On the other hand, the generally wider array of activities in which state-chartered banks have been able to engage has enhanced 'inter-industry' competition. In doing so it created an incentive for banks regulated solely at the federal level to lobby for access to powers similar to those granted to state-chartered banks. This created a form of competition among state and federal regulators that has had the effect of increasing 'intra-industry' competition. As Table 11.A3 shows, the result has been expanded access for national banks and bank holding companies to activities related to securities underwriting and brokerage and the sale of insurance.

Effective 19 December 1992, however, FDICIA limited state-chartered banks to activities that are permissible for national banks unless granted a specific exemption by the FDIC. At the moment, the full effect of these changes is unclear because of grandfathering clauses and limited exemptions provided by the FDIC to well and adequately capitalized state banks. In effect, FDICIA has transferred more of the authority to determine allowable activities to the federal deposit-insurance agency from the state chartering authorities. Based on the historical differences between the activities allowed national and state-chartered banks, this shift in authority signals a substantial reduction in the influence of state-chartered banks on 'intra and inter-industry' competition.[17]

11.3.5 Merit Goods and the Allocation of Credit

Bank regulation is also used to support the provision of merit goods, with the effect of allocating credit. Housing finance is perhaps the single biggest example. The savings and loan commitment to housing finance was given a boost in 1933 with the Home Owners' Loan Act that gave the newly established Federal Home Loan Bank Board (Bank Board) the power to charter and regulate federal savings and loans, whose charter required a substantial commitment to housing finance. The 1933 Federal Home Loan Bank Act that created the Bank Board also created a twelve-district Federal Home Loan Bank System to provide liquidity for savings and loans. As shown in Table 11.A5, total assets of the Bank System have grown from $75 billion in 1981 to $158 billion in 1991. In 1991, its equity capital-to-total asset ratio was 6.8 per cent and the return-on-equity was 10.5 per cent. The shrinkage in the savings and loan industry, however, has impaired the Bank System and forced it to try to replace lost members with commercial banks and credit unions.

The federal government also established and chartered the Federal National Mortgage Association (Fannie Mae), the Federal Home Loan Mortgage Corporation (Freddie Mac), and the Government National Mortgage Association (Ginnie Mae) to facilitate the development of secondary markets into which home mortgages could be sold. As shown in Table 11.A5, Fannie Mae assets have grown from $62 billion in 1981 to

$519 billion in 1991. Over the same period, the assets of Freddie Mac have grown from $26 billion to $406 billion. In part reflecting their relatively low capital-to-total-asset ratios of 1.0 per cent and 0.6 per cent, respectively, Fannie and Freddie earned returns-on-equity of 27.7 per cent and 23.6 per cent in 1991.[18]

Many similar programs have been established by the federal government. The Student Loan Marketing Association (Sallie Mae) facilitates a secondary market in student loans. The Farm Credit System issues bonds to support agricultural loans, whereas the Small Business Administration (SBA) provides loan guarantees for small businesses.[19]

Still other federal regulations focus on financial issues relating to low-income individuals. The Community Reinvestment Act (CRA) of 1977 establishes certain requirements for federally insured depositories regarding lending in low income communities. FIRREA specifically required funding for housing be provided by the Bank System for low income individuals. More recently, there have been proposals to charter new financial institutions called community development banks to be located in low income communities within larger cities.[20]

Finally, other types of regulation provide protections against specific risks to individuals. They include consumer protection legislation, including protection against discrimination provided by the Equal Credit Opportunity Act (ECOA) of 1974 and the Home Mortgage Disclosure Act (HMDA) of 1975. Disclosure requirements, in general administered by the Securities and Exchange Commission (SEC), are also designed to protect investors by making more and better information available so that investors will incur no more risk than desired.

11.4 EVOLUTION OF THE FINANCIAL SERVICES MARKET: IMPLICATIONS FOR BANKS AND THEIR REGULATION

Whether bank regulation is consistent with the goals of bank regulation depends substantially on the nature of the market for financial products and services.[21] One structure of bank regulation may be appropriate if the market for financial services is characterized by substantial 'intra-industry' competition among banks, but with little 'inter-industry' competition involving nonbank financial firms. The same structure of regulation, however, may be inappropriate if 'inter-industry' competition is substantial and shows signs of dynamic growth. In particular, if the regulatory structure prevents adaptation to the nonbank competition, the result could be the long-term degeneration of the banking industry characterized by excess capacity, falling returns on equity capital, larger numbers of failing institutions, and the possibility of excessively costly exit.

11.4.1 Dramatic Shifts in Market Shares: Declining Shares for Banks

There has, in fact, been a substantial change in the market for financial services in the past several decades that has significantly reduced the importance of depositories as they have traditionally operated. The crux of the change has been a dramatic increase in nonbank competition that has contributed to a substantial shrinkage of the financial assets held by depository institutions as a percentage of total US financial assets held by all financial service firms. As Table 11.1 shows, the share of US financial assets held by US-chartered banks has fallen, from approximately 51 per cent in 1950 to 20 per cent in the third quarter of 1992. Since 1980, the share of US financial assets held by all US-chartered insured depositories (US-chartered banks, savings and loans, savings banks and credit unions) has fallen from approximately 50 per cent to 30 per cent. Although the decline in market share has been sharpest for savings and loans, falling more than 9 percentage points since 1984, US-chartered banks have seen their share fall 11 percentage points since 1980.

With the exception of life insurance companies and real-estate investment trusts (REITs), all other financial service firms shown in the table have gained market share since 1950 and in the 1980s. Only life insurance companies have experienced a substantial decline in their market share, which fell from approximately 21 per cent in 1950 to 11 per cent in 1980, with small fluctuations around that level since then. In contrast to depositories and life insurance companies, mutual funds and money-market mutual funds have increased their collective share of US financial assets from 1 per cent in 1950 to 3 per cent in 1980 to 11 per cent in the third quarter of 1992. The market share for both private pension funds and state and local retirement funds has risen from 4 per cent in 1950 to 17 per cent in 1980 to 24 per cent in the third quarter of 1992. Security brokers' and dealers' share has grown significantly since 1980 – from 1 per cent to 3 per cent in the third quarter of 1992. Although finance companies hold a greater share of assets at 5 per cent today, their market share has grown only slightly since 1980.

As Table 11.1 also shows, total US financial assets held by financial service firms have grown substantially. Total financial assets have more than doubled since 1984, rising to $13.4 trillion (million millions) in the third quarter of 1992. As Tables 11.A6 and 11.A7 show, the total assets of

Table 11.1 Percentage distribution of US financial assets held by all service firms, 1950–92

	1950	*1960*	*1970*	*1980*	*1981*	*1982*	*1983*	*1984*	*1985*	*1986*	*1987*	*1988*	*1989*	*1990*	*1991*	*1992 3rd qtr*
Depository Institutions[1]																
Commercial Banks	51.2	38.2	38.6	36.8	36.3	35.2	34.2	34.0	33.1	31.9	31.2	30.8	30.4	30.0	26.9	26.6
US chartered	50.5	37.5	36.6	31.4	30.6	29.9	29.1	28.9	27.9	25.5	26.5	24.9	23.9	23.8	20.9	20.4
Foreign offices in US	0.4	0.6	0.7	2.5	2.8	2.3	2.0	2.0	2.1	2.6	2.3	2.8	3.4	3.6	3.4	3.6
Domestic affiliates	0.0	0.0	1.1	2.6	2.6	2.7	2.8	3.0	3.1	3.0	3.0	2.9	2.9	2.7	2.2	2.4
Banks in US possessions	0.3	0.1	0.3	0.3	0.3	0.3	0.2	0.1	0.1	0.1	0.1	0.2	0.2	0.2	0.2	0.2
Savings and loans	5.8	11.8	12.8	15.2	14.6	14.2	14.9	15.7	14.8	13.9	14.1	14.2	11.6	10.2	7.2	6.3
Savings banks	7.6	6.9	5.9	4.3	3.9	3.5	3.5	3.3	3.1	2.9	3.0	3.0	2.7	2.4	1.9	1.8
Credit unions	0.3	1.1	1.3	1.7	1.6	1.7	1.8	1.8	1.9	2.0	2.1	2.0	1.9	2.0	1.9	1.9
Contractual Intermediaries																
Life insurance companies	21.3	19.4	15.0	11.5	11.4	11.5	11.5	11.1	11.1	11.0	11.3	11.7	11.8	12.3	11.8	11.8
Other insurance companies	4.0	4.4	3.7	4.3	4.2	4.1	4.1	3.9	4.0	4.2	4.4	4.5	4.6	4.7	4.6	4.6
Private pension funds[2]	2.4	6.4	8.4	11.6	10.9	11.7	12.4	11.5	11.9	11.5	11.4	10.9	11.0	10.4	17.1	16.8
State and local government retirement funds	1.7	3.3	4.5	4.9	5.0	5.3	5.7	5.7	5.7	5.7	5.8	6.3	6.9	6.7	7.0	7.1

Table 11.1 Continued

	1950	*1960*	*1970*	*1980*	*1981*	*1982*	*1983*	*1984*	*1985*	*1986*	*1987*	*1988*	*1989*	*1990*	*1991*	*1992 3rd qtr*
Others																
Finance companies	3.2	4.6	4.8	5.0	5.1	4.8	4.8	4.8	4.9	5.0	5.1	5.1	5.8	7.0	6.2	5.9
Mutual funds	1.1	2.9	3.5	1.5	1.3	1.6	2.0	2.2	3.4	5.1	5.2	5.0	5.2	5.2	6.3	7.5
Security brokers and dealers	1.4	1.1	1.2	1.1	1.4	1.7	1.7	1.9	2.2	2.3	1.6	1.4	2.2	2.4	2.6	3.0
Money-market mutual funds	0.0	0.0	0.0	1.9	4.2	4.5	3.3	3.7	3.4	3.6	3.6	3.5	4.0	4.5	4.2	4.1
REITs[3]	0.0	0.0	0.3	0.1	0.1	0.1	0.1	0.1	0.1	0.1	0.1	0.1	0.1	0.1	0.1	0.1
SCO issuers[4]	0.0	0.0	0.0	0.0	0.0	0.0	0.1	0.2	0.4	0.8	1.2	1.4	1.7	2.0	2.1	2.2
Total assets ($ Billions)	294	597	1340	4032	4455	4916	5503	6232	7141	8185	8840	9667	10 633	11 113	12 795	13 423

Notes:

1. Commercial banks consist of US chartered commercial banks, domestic affiliates, Edge Act corporations, agencies and branches of foreign banks, and banks in US possession. Foreign banking offices in US include Edge Act corporations and offices of foreign banks. IBF's are excluded from domestic banking and treated like branches in foreign countries. Savings and loan associations include all savings and loan associations and federal savings bank insured by the Savings Association Insurance Fund. Savings banks include all federal and mutual savings banks insured by the Bank Insurance Fund
2. Private pension funds include Federal Employees' Retirement Thrift Savings Fund
3. REITs are real-estate investment trusts
4. SCO issuers are securitized credit obligations

commercial banks nearly doubled from 1980 to 1988, growing at an average annual rate of 12 per cent. Since then, the average growth rate has fallen to 5 per cent. As shown in Tables 11.A8 and 11.A9, the total assets of savings and loans actually fell from a high of $1.4 trillion in 1988 to approximately $850 billion in the third quarter of 1992. The overall growth in US financial assets, combined with the declining shares held by federally insured depositories, suggest that depositories are holding a shrinking share of a growing market for financial services. The declining growth rate in bank assets and the absolute decline in savings and loan assets are also consistent with this secular trend. For comparison, Tables 11.A10 through 11.A21 provide balance-sheet data on the other financial service firms listed in Table 11.1. The importance of these changes is not simply that depositories have lost market share, but that regulations may have impaired their ability to adapt to a rapidly changing financial marketplace and, thereby, contributed to their excessively costly exit.[22] The net effect is a less competitive and more inefficient financial system.

11.4.2 Effects of Technology on Competition and Shifting Market Shares

This pattern of shifting shares reflects an increase in 'inter-industry' competition that largely resulted from developments in computer and telecommunications technology. Technology has been increasingly reducing the need for depositories to intermediate between borrowers and lenders by gathering, evaluating and monitoring information on borrowers that was too costly an activity for lenders themselves to perform. Securitization has turned formerly illiquid assets on bank balance sheets like mortgages (fixed and variable rate), automobile loans, credit-card receivables and, increasingly, commercial real-estate loans into securities than can be held by individuals and by many firms like pension funds, mutual funds and insurance companies. Overall, the manifestations of this technological revolution and developments in financial theory are new products, new firms, lower costs of producing financial products and lower prices for products. Not surprisingly, competition has increased, too, with the consequent squeezing of profits and more failures.

Banks are put in particular jeopardy in this process. The traditional bank, as it has developed since the 1930s, transformed liquid deposits (or deposits payable on demand at par) into illiquid loans. By taking the risk of holding illiquid loans in portfolio, banks earned an acceptable return on their owner-contributed equity. It was also this risk borne by banks that led to the instability associated with banks as discussed above. By turning illiquid depository assets into more liquid securities, securitization is undermining the traditional depository function involving the linkage of the two sides of the balance sheet. Securitization, moreover, is not the only 'villain' from the banks' perspective. The increasingly deep market for individual loan sales and the access of more firms to the commercial paper and bond markets, both reflecting the effect of technology on lowering the cost of processing and disseminating information, have had similar effects.

There are a number of other fronts on which the banks seem particularly vulnerable to the effects of technological developments. Banks, unlike insurance companies, pension funds and mutual funds, have a large commitment to 'brick and mortar' in the form of branches and to the employees of the branches. As the provision of financial services becomes more electronic, these branches and employees may become a burden. Since 1986 employment at commercial banks has declined by over 100 000 employees. Electronic provision of financial services also has the effect of increasing the size of the relevant product market for financial services. Limits on geographic location and ownership may inhibit banks' adaptation to an increasingly international market. Efficient electronic provision of financial services could come from a firm that simultaneously provided telephone, television, and financial services. The prohibition of ownership of banks by commercial firms would seem to inhibit banks becoming part of such a service, and banks might suffer competitively as a result. Banks, however, are increasingly attempting to provide more products and services offered by their nonbank competitors, with an emphasis on fee income rather than traditional intermediation income. This may enable them to make better use of their branches and employees.

11.4.3 Changes in Household Holdings of Financial Assets and Liabilities

As the provision of financial services has evolved, so has the way in which individuals and households (including personal trusts and non-profit organizations) hold their financial assets. Information on the balance sheet for individuals in the 1980s is presented in Table 11.A22. Information on the balance sheet for households since 1950 is presented in Table 11.A23. As shown in Table 11.A23, household holdings of corporate equities were halved between 1950 and 1980, falling from 30 per cent to 15 per cent of their total financial assets. The share has remained relatively stable since 1980. Holding of government securities fell from 15 per cent of household assets in 1950 to 4 per cent in 1980, and again has remained stable thereafter. The same pattern has occurred with life insurance reserves. They represented 12 per cent of household assets in 1950, but fell to 3 per cent by 1980 and thereafter. Small time and savings deposits fell from 18 per cent of household assets in 1980 to 14 per cent in the third quarter of 1992. This 4 percentage point decline indicates that not only is the asset side of the banks' balance sheet under attack, but the liability side is also. In 1950, households held 4 per cent of their assets in mortgages but as of the third quarter of 1992 they held 2 per cent of their assets in mortgages.

These changes reveal a dramatic change in the way households, and hence individuals, hold assets. In 1950, 57 per cent of all household financial assets were in corporate equities, US government securities and life insurance reserves. Today, households hold only 22 per cent of their assets in those categories, a drop of 35 percentage points.

The most dramatic increase in holdings occurred in pension fund reserves, which rose from 5 per cent in 1950 to 14 per cent in 1980 to 28 per cent by the third quarter of 1992. Mutual funds grew from 1 per cent of household assets in 1980 to 5 per cent in the third quarter of 1992. Money market mutual funds grew from 1 per cent of household assets in 1980 to 3 per cent in the third quarter of 1992. The net increase in these three categories – pension fund reserves, mutual funds and money market mutual funds, has been 29 percentage points.

The net effect is that households have shifted from direct holdings of stocks and bonds and holdings in depositories and life insurance companies to indirect holdings of stocks and bonds through pension funds and mutual funds. From the perspective of nonbank financial firms and the consumer of financial services, the line of causation creating this change in pattern is relatively clear. First came the technological advances that lowered the cost of gathering, monitoring and processing information. Then came the changes in the provision of financial products that reflected the technological change, for example, the development of mutual funds that allowed a consumer to hold indirectly a diversified portfolio of financial assets in relatively small denominations. Finally, over time consumers have shifted their holdings of financial assets, fueling the growth in non-bank financial service firms.

11.4.4 The Interaction of Competition with Government Regulation

This is, in general, the market's way of adapting to change. The market changes with technological innovation, creating new firms and products. There can be a contrast between the adaptation of firms largely free to adapt to market changes and that of highly regulated firms like banks. Bank regulation was established largely by legislation in the 1930s following the Great Depression, significantly preceding the technological changes that are driving the contemporary provision of financial services. The legislation substantially limited both 'intra- and inter-industry' competition, narrowly specifying the roles of federally insured depositories. Banks that had investment banking operations were forced by law to separate the two functions. Afterward, banks could not underwrite or broker stocks or bonds, and investment banks could not accept household deposits and make commercial loans. Thus, there was a regulatory separation of long and short-term corporate finance. Savings and loans were required to make fixed-rate, long-term home mortgage loans, and were prohibited from making commercial or consumer loans. Life insurance companies' ownership of corporate equities was limited by state law, and they were large holders of corporate debt, a pattern which, as Table 11.A12 shows, persists today.

Remnants of this pattern and distribution of financial services are obviously observable today, despite the changes noted above in allowable activities for state-chartered banks and the competition for regulation that has developed. To some extent the persistent pattern reflects behavior consistent with the economic theory of regulation, which suggests that there will be a demand for the use of the government's power to protect competitors from competition.[23] Competitors in the financial service market have demanded (lobbied for) protection from competitors in the following general sequence of steps. Technical innovation occurred (including intellectual breakthroughs in finance theory). New competitors and products emerged. Observable deterioration in selected competitors occurred. A demand for legislation and regulation to buttress the specialization and protection of competitors arose as a result.

The securities industry has lobbied for continued separation of banks from securities underwriting and brokerage. The insurance industry has lobbied likewise for the separation of banks from insurance underwriting and brokerage. Small banks have lobbied to limit interstate branching to slow big bank movement across state lines. The net effects for banks in limiting branching, allowable products and ownership have been summarized above. Overall, these events have not slowed down market forces but have harmed those firms that could not adapt to the forces.

By far the biggest losers, thus far, have been federally insured depositories, primarily savings and loans but also commercial banks, reflecting the inability of depositories to adapt to the competition because of regulatory constraints – many of which they have lobbied for themselves. The inability to adapt due to regulatory constraints has had many manifestations. The unusually large number of depositories exiting in a relatively short period of time, sometimes at great cost, has captured most of the attention. More fundamental problems remain. As Barth and Brumbaugh (1992) show, the commercial bank mean return-on-equity fell 2.4 percentage points in the period 1980–1991 compared to the 1970s. The standard deviation of the return-on-equity for commercial banks rose 2.6 percentage points. Another measure of risk, the ratio of net charge-offs-to-assets, more than tripled from 0.07 per cent in the 1970s to 0.24 per cent in the 1980–91 period. For savings and loans, the mean return-on-equity became negative in the 1980s and indices of risk soared relative to previous decades. Falling *ex post* returns for commercial banks and savings and loans combined with rising *ex post* measures of risk, suggest further attrition unless the process is reversed.

11.5 RECENT DEVELOPMENTS IN THE FINANCIAL SERVICES MARKET: COMPETITIVE IMPLICATIONS

11.5.1 Commercial Banks

Recent developments in the financial services market suggest that the process is unlikely to be reversed. In general, the reaction of the banks, savings and loans, and credit unions – with the assistance of federal and state legislation and regulation – has been to change the asset and liability mix within relatively narrow limits. Difficulties surfaced for commercial banks in the early 1980s concerning their loans to lesser developed countries. That banks made so many loans in the first place reflected a more serious long-term problem, the declining demand for bank loans from corporations which were increasingly served by the commercial paper market.[24]

As Table 11.A7 shows, commercial and industrial loans as a per cent of total assets fell from 22 per cent in 1981 to 16 per cent in the third quarter of 1992.[25] Over roughly the same period, bank-real estate loans to total assets rose from 14 per cent in 1982 to 25 per cent in the third quarter of 1992. As Table 11.A24 shows, commercial bank holdings of home mortgages as a percentage of real estate mortgage loans held by different lenders was 17 per cent in the third quarter of 1992, for the first time exceeding the holdings of savings and loans, which were 14 per cent. Toward the end of the 1980s, bank holdings of US government securities also rose precipitously, from 12 per cent of total bank assets to 18 per cent. For nearly 20 years beforehand, bank holdings of government securities was relatively stable, having declined slightly from 1970.

One must ask whether the stream of income from these sources is sustainable. Primarily because of action taken by the Federal Reserve to stimulate economic activity following the 1990–1 recession, short-term interest rates fell dramatically and the spread between short-term and long-term interest rates rose to more than 400 basis points by early 1993. In essence, a large portion of the banks' recent profitability has come from borrowing from the insured depositor at a relatively low interest rate and lending to the government at a much higher rate. As the yield curve flattens, this source of profits will diminish.

Whether banks can earn profits from real-estate loans is also uncertain. Carron and Brumbaugh (1991), for savings and loans, and Passmore (1992), more generally, have investigated whether retail depositories can fund home mortgages profitably. Passmore, like Carron and Brumbaugh, found that the cost of collecting retail deposits combined with the regulatory capital requirements for depositories make mortgage lending largely unprofitable. Profitability has also been affected by the dramatic growth of the secondary home mortgage market. As Table 11.A24 shows, 40 per cent of home mortgages are now in mortgage pools. Passmore concluded that it was possible for very efficient savings and loans to fund fixed-rate conforming mortgages profitably but that 'almost all S&Ls and probably most banks and credit unions do not fit this description'. He also concluded that most depository institutions are not efficient enough to make securitized fixed-rate and adjustable-rate mortgages profitably. Commercial real-estate mortgages provide a wider interest-rate spread, but this spread is likely to narrow as more commercial real-estate loans are securitized.[26] This could affect banks significantly because, as Table 11.A24 shows, banks held 45 per cent of all commercial mortgages held by the different real estate lenders in the third quarter of 1992.

Barth, Brumbaugh and Litan (1992) point out that banks became much less liquid in the 1980s, with cash and cash due from other depositories falling from 18 per cent in 1980 to 9 per cent in 1990. This fall in liquidity was offset by an increase in total loans and leases from 55 per cent to 62 per cent. The shift to illiquid assets increased risk as banks sought more revenue. They also point out that the growth of off-balance-sheet items has also been dramatic. The off-balance-sheet items in the banking industry as a whole are approximately four times the volume of balance-sheet items, and they are increasing. Other signs of potential risk-taking showed up on the liability side of the banks' balance sheet, where there was an important shift away from non-interest-bearing demand deposits to deposits that paid interest – demand deposits decreased by 9 percentage points in the 1980s, while time and savings deposits more than doubled to approximately 23 per cent and interest-bearing transaction accounts, which did not exist nationwide in 1980, accounted for approximately 20 per cent of liabilities in 1989.

Some banks have adopted strategies by which they earn greater income in fees than interest income on assets in their portfolios. Some of these banks such as J. P. Morgan, whose ratio of non-interest revenue to total revenue was 63 per cent in 1992 – are among the most profitable banks with the most stable earnings during the past decade of turmoil for banks. Bankers Trust and Citicorp had non-interest revenue to total revenue of 67 per cent and 52 per cent, respectively, in 1992. Although our focus is on the adaptation of banks moving away from traditional assets and, in some cases, toward fee income, a similar type of adaptation is occurring among life insurance companies, which as noted above, have been the other major financial firms losing market share in recent years. As Table 11.A12 shows, in 1950 life insurance reserves accounted for 83 per cent of liabilities for life insurance companies but only 47 per cent in 1980 and 27 per cent in the third quarter of 1992. In 1950, only 9 per cent of life insurance companies liabilities came from pension fund reserves, rising to 39 per cent in 1980 and 62 per cent in the third quarter of 1992. Thus, life insurance companies have become substantial managers of pension fund reserves, increasingly invested in mutual funds and government securities.

As Table 11.A6 shows, banks increased the proportion of government securities in their portfolios from 12 per cent in 1989 to 18 per cent in the third quarter of 1992. This shift contributed to the substantial increase in bank profits that has occurred in 1992 and thus far in 1993. As Table 11.A7 shows, net operating income for banks more than doubled from $14.8 billion in 1991 to $31.5 billion through the third quarter of 1992. These profits have allowed the banking industry to make substantial additions to capital. As Table 11.A7 shows, capital has risen from $181 billion in 1987 to $257 billion in the third quarter of 1992, an increase that raised the aggregate capital-to-asset ratio.

11.5.2 Savings and Loans and Credit Unions

In reaction to the damage caused by their maturity mismatch in the early 1980s, savings and loans substantially reduced their home mortgage portfolios and increased their lending and investment in commercial real estate. As Table 11.A8 shows, mortgages fell from 79 per cent of savings and loans' assets in 1980 to 64 per cent in the third quarter of 1993, having fallen as low as 56 per cent in 1988. The rebound in 1989 reflected FIRREA, which led to the resolution of hundreds of non-traditional troubled savings and loans, and increased minimum required levels of housing finance assets for savings and loans.

As Table 11.A11 shows, credit unions grew substantially in the 1980s, from $68 billion in total assets in 1980 to $202 billion in 1989. From 1990 to the third quarter of 1992, credit unions have grown from $217 billion to $260 billion in total assets. Most of the growth has been channeled into second mortgages on homes, which grew from 7 per cent of assets in 1980 to 20 per cent of assets in the third quarter of 1992. The growth also went into government securities, which grew from 7 per cent in 1980 to 20 per cent in the third quarter of 1992. Credit unions have not experienced problems leading to sufficiently high failure costs to pose difficulties for NCUSIF.

As Passmore (1992) and Carron and Brumbaugh (1991) indicate, the profitability of mortgage lending, except for the most efficient depositories, is substantially threatened by competition and, more specifically, lower mortgage rates resulting from the securitization activities of the government-sponsored enterprises. Credit union holdings of large shares of government securities is subject to the same observation made above about banks' holding large shares of government securities: credit unions cannot earn sustainable income by borrowing from insured shareholders and lending to the government – despite their tax-free status.

The pattern of *ex post* risk and return for savings and loans is similar to the pattern for banks, although the measures of risk rose far more dramatically and measures of return fell equally dramatically.[27] *Ex post* return-on-equity fell from the 1950s through the 1970s when it averaged 11.2 per cent. In the 1980–1991 period, return-on-equity averaged a negative 12.3 per cent. The standard deviation of return-on-equity rose from the 1950s through the 1970s, when it averaged 2.2 per cent. The standard deviation rose to 24.5 per cent in the 1980–91 period. Even if the problems of the savings and loans moderate from the gravity of the 1980s, these indices combined with the nature of competition we have discussed suggest future turmoil.

11.5.3 Summarizing the Trends

In each area into which depositories have expanded their assets, there is substantial competition, with the likelihood that the future income stream may be limited. In residential real estate, mortgage-backed securities have lowered revenues and many low-cost providers compete with depositories. There is significant evidence that only the most efficient depositories will be able to compete profitably in the market. There is an excess supply of commercial real estate with the expected effect on prices and asset quality. There is also a significant number of non-depository commercial real-estate lenders. As a result of these phenomena, there has been a significant movement among big banks toward off-balance sheet items and toward nonbank activities generating fee income, including the significant movement into the managing and selling of mutual funds. There remains substantial competition from securities firms in these areas as well, some of which have formed joint ventures with banks offering mutual fund services.

The desire of banks to shift asset mix, move off balance sheet and seek fee income will likely intensify because demand for business loans from banks will continue to decline. New products will continue to emerge and threaten the commercial and industrial loan business at banks. Banks will also continue to labor under related regulatory disadvantages. Banks, for example, cannot hold junk bonds, which are essentially more liquid commercial and industrial loans. New and old competitors, with a changing menu of products and services, will continue to develop. The demand for small, non-homogeneous business loans continues to be relatively strong, which helps explain the relative strength of small banks. As technology improves, however, one can expect this market to become more contested as well.

There have also been substantial competitive changes in the market affecting the liability side of depositories' balance sheets. The growth of money-market mutual funds has been a conspicuous case in point. As Table 11.A25 shows, money-market mutual fund balances have risen from 1 per cent of M2 in 1980 to 10 per cent in the third quarter of 1992. Before 1980, money-market mutual funds were not even included in M2 because they were so relatively insignificant. Another interesting aspect in the growth of money-market mutual funds, as shown in Table 11.A19, is that they have been increasingly moving funds from banks' time deposits elsewhere, with time deposits as a percentage of their total assets falling 21 percentage points from 1980 to the third quarter of 1992.

The fact that money-market mutual funds are now included in M2 reflects the new reality that the funds are a close substitute for deposits at banks and savings and loans. A still broader measure of money would show the declining importance of depository liabilities compared to other financial service firm liabilities. The expansion of money-market mutual funds represents the unbundling of bank balance sheets, as do the securitization of loans, the growing corporate paper market and the movement to off-balance sheet activities and fee income. From the perspective of setting the agenda for bank regulatory reform, the unbundling signifies a potential reduction in the inherent instability of banks that in part generated the need for regulation in the first place. The existence of money-market mutual funds suggests that the payments system may be less vulnerable to problems in the banking industry than in the past.

This analysis points to a separate issue of importance involving money-market mutual funds and other nonbank financial service firms. The existence of money-like assets available from nonbanks can complicate monetary policy. If the Federal Reserve were to focus on an inappropriate measure of money, then the monetary authorities could mistakenly take inappropriate action.

11.6 REFORM ALTERNATIVES: RESOLVING ASPECTS OF BANK REGULATION INCONSISTENT WITH THE GOALS OF BANK REGULATION

The existing regulatory structure for banks, as well as any suggested agenda for reform, should be judged by how well it corresponds to the goals of regulation. In this respect it should be clear from the preceding analysis that there are many aspects of the regulation of banks that appear inconsistent with the goals of regulation. Many aspects of the regulation appear to be mutually contradictory. There has always been an inconsistency between the anti-competitive restrictions and the promotion of economic efficiency discussed above.

This tension was not particularly harmful as long as 'intra-industry' competition was the major concern and 'inter-industry' competition was relatively minimal. Now, 'inter-industry' competition is intense and growing. As discussed above, the increasing competition combined with restrictions on competition has produced economically inefficient results. This has included a decline in *ex post* return-on-equity for banks and an increase in *ex post* measures of risk, which has resulted in excessively costly exit of depository institutions. These developments motivate the need for reform.

With this background, we offer the following reform alternatives for consideration.

11.6.1 Protect Depositories from Competition

Non-depository financial firms now provide many of the services that banks provide. One reform alternative is to grant monopoly-like powers where possible to banks. This could be combined with new regulatory restrictions on non-depository financial service firms by, for example, prohibiting mutual funds from offering check-writing services. At the moment, the inability of mutual funds to access Fedwire directly provides banks with a competitive advantage in check-writing services. The government could erect additional barriers to discourage or roll back nonbank provision of selected financial services.[28] This approach is similar to the approach taken by many firms and industries. While nonbank financial firms like securities firms and insurance companies have increasingly provided services historically provided by banks, they have simultaneously lobbied to prevent banks from providing their other services. The goal in general is to protect oneself from competition.

This reform alternative, then, has as its goal the very antithesis of many of the goals of regulation, primarily to enhance competition with the attendant benefits for consumers of financial services and the efficient allocation of scarce economic resources. Perhaps the best reason for calling attention to it here is to reinforce the observation that many of the existing bank regulatory practices are inconsistent with the society-wide goals of bank regulation and the efficient provision of financial services. As a result, if this reform alternative were successfully adopted, the policy would increase inefficient allocation of resources, and, if unsuccessful, would maintain policies that still encourage misallocation of resources. This reform alternative is merely an extension of the current policy of attempting to erect barriers to entry and exit in the provision of financial services.

11.6.2 Maintain the Deposit-Insurance System with Required Prompt Corrective Actions and Cost-Effective Closure Mechanisms

Another reform alternative is based on recommendations that evolved from analyses of the failure to close insolvent savings and loans in a timely fashion and the resulting adverse effects on the cost of closure. As described in Barth (1991), savings and loans, closed in 1988, were open while reporting insolvency for an average of more than four years. Barth, Brumbaugh and Litan (1992) and Barth and Brumbaugh (1991) show that similar closing patterns developed with commercial banks and credit unions.

Open but insolvent depositories have a great incentive to take excessive risk in an attempt to return to solvency. This is particularly true of stock-type institutions in contrast to mutual institutions. Excessive risk-taking by insolvent institutions can result in significant returns to stockholders and managers with equity interests if such risk-taking is successful, while losses accrue to the deposit-insurance system or taxpayers if it is unsuccessful. This is one of the manifestations of the moral-hazard problem in federally insured depositories.

One reform proposal is to retain the current deposit-insurance system but to require truly prompt corrective actions against troubled institutions in order to reduce the moral-hazard problem. In general, corrective actions and, ultimately, closure would be triggered by falling capital or net worth. As capital fell relative to assets, supervisory intervention would increase and an institution would be more likely to face limitations on its ability to increase risk. Ultimately, closure would be triggered if capital approached zero. Such an approach was specifically outlined by Benston, *et al.* (1989) based on studies indicating that delay in closure of insolvent savings and loans increased the cost of closure.

In 1991, FDICIA implemented a form of this approach. As described by Brumbaugh and Scott (1992), it differed significantly from what was proposed by Benston, *et al.* Book-value measures of capital were used to trigger increased intervention, rather than market values. As a result, it is unclear to what extent intervention and closure are, actually, what one would call prompt or timely. As institutions near insolvency, existing book-value measures of capital or net worth tend to exceed market-value measures of capital, sometimes substantially. In addition, unlike the Benston, *et al.* proposal, the regulators were granted considerable discretion in the design and implementation of the early intervention and closure mechanism, and consequently given substantial opportunities to engage in forbearance. As Brumbaugh and Scott point out, the law seems designed to provide such opportunities to regulators.

An alternative is to build on FDICIA by basing prompt corrective actions on deterioration in market-value capital and by eliminating regulatory discretion in order to eliminate forbearance. Although this alternative maintains deposit insurance, it does not rule out substantial changes in addition to the closure mechanism. Deposit coverage levels could be maintained at the current or a reduced coverage level. Other regulatory constraints could be changed. Branching and banking restrictions could be eliminated. Limits on allowable activities could be reduced. Ownership beyond bank holding companies could be authorized for nonbank and nonfinancial companies, as is the case with the ownership of savings and loans.

Past experience suggests that this alternative is difficult to implement effectively. There is significant resistance to reducing regulatory constraints, particularly as long as deposit insurance is still provided. Regulatory constraints should be reduced only for healthy institutions in order to minimize moral-hazard problems, but blocking out unhealthy institutions has proved difficult to accomplish in the past. In addition, examination and supervision become more difficult as institutions become more complex and diverse, as they certainly would if regulatory constraints were relaxed as described. Timing prompt corrective actions, particularly seizure, is difficult. Given the significant debate surrounding the wisdom and the ability to implement market-value accounting,[29] it would face substantial opposition and take time to effect. The elimination of discretion is also difficult, and the tendency is strong to reinstate it if prompt corrective actions prove inadequate and losses mount.

Even if all of these difficulties did not exist or posed little impediment, this alternative is essentially a rearguard action, attempting to cope with new and sometimes quickly developing competitive threats through slow and piecemeal legislative and regulatory edicts. Some restrictions on assets and liabilities would undoubtedly survive and potentially prevent movement of financial resources to their most efficient use. As new and unexpected competitive developments occurred in the provision and delivery of financial services, further tinkering would be necessary in order to maintain the level of efficiency that had already been achieved. The possibility of significant deterioration and large losses would remain, though perhaps in a lessened state.

From an economics point of view, this alternative fails to address very convincingly one major issue. Given the goals of financial regulation and the purpose of the financial system, is the deposit-insurance system – even if the changes this alternative includes are desirable and achievable – the kind of system one would design today if one were starting from scratch? Does this alternative essentially represent an attempt to tune an instrument that one would not select if it had not been handed down through several generations? If a different system offers substantial advantages, perhaps one should explore devising a new instrument.

11.6.3 Eliminate Deposit Insurance and Adopt a Form of the Narrow-Bank Proposal

This proposal begins with the elimination of deposit insurance. This does not mean eliminating the protections that deposit insurance was designed to provide: protection for small and unsophisticated depositors, protection of the payments and credit mechanisms, and protection of the taxpayer. Any proposal that entails elimination of deposit insurance must offer an alternative that will ensure those protections, as well as meet the goals of bank regulation.

To prevent runs and to provide individuals with a perfectly liquid asset – one that is payable on demand at par with extremely low user cost – this proposal would create a narrow bank at every depository, along the lines discussed by Litan (1988) and Benston *et al.* (1989).[30] The assets of the narrow bank would be short-term Treasury securities. Under certain circumstances as discussed by Benston *et al*, other assets could be included. The liabilities would be demand deposits only. As a result, the return to the depositor would essentially be limited to the return on short-term Treasury securities minus fees for servicing accounts.

Simultaneously, the proposal would eliminate all other regulatory constraints on depositories except for those that apply to other financial service firms, such as SEC disclosure requirements, consumer protection requirements, and all the requirements that are implicit in avoiding antitrust violations. Thus, this proposal is designed to promote efficiency because the new 'non-narrow' bank, associated with but separated functionally from the 'narrow' bank, becomes a purely private financial service firm with the ability to adapt to competition as do all other financial service firms.

Even the prospect of unleashing this competition by releasing banks from current regulatory constraints on their activities would no doubt unleash a frenzy of lobbying by every conceivable financial service firm. Their goal would be to protect themselves as much as possible from prospective competition. It is all too easy to imagine, how each threatened competitor would agree with other threatened competitors that the resulting competitive blood bath would result in financial instability. Each individual firm going out of business would be cited as a sign of overall financial instability.

As discussed above, swift restructuring or exit of insolvent firms in a competitive market enhances efficiency, an essential ingredient in the stable provision of financial services, which is the goal. If large numbers of banks exited the financial services industry as a result of this proposal, imposing losses on stockholders and some debt holders, what does this mean from that economic perspective? Is there an efficiency loss or gain that can be inferred from such an outcome?

The answer is complicated. It involves, most profoundly, a calculation of the opportunity cost of maintaining the current system that provides financial services in a way inconsistent with the efficient allocation of financial services and, hence, allocation of scarce real resources. To some extent, the losses caused by the attrition of firms would represent part of the opportunity cost of the current system of regulation. The losses would represent amounts that would otherwise have been earned and kept if the provision of financial services had been more efficient in the first place. Thus, the losses that would seem to be attributed to the implementation of the reform proposal would, in fact, represent realized losses that had accrued from past inefficiency.

Opponents of this proposal will also tend to create images of forlorn, formerly insured depositors walking the streets, hopelessly seeking a place to deposit their funds safely. Others will have understandable and genuine concern for formerly insured depositors who under this proposal would have to choose between a risk-free, low-return liquidity account and some level of risk and return associated with a less liquid account. Will this not lead to befuddlement and unnecessary losses for some individuals, perhaps many?

In order for this result to obtain, a number of things would have to occur. For some reason, the market for financial services would have to be unable to provide individuals with appropriate information on the nature of risk and return trade-offs. This would probably take some form of widespread, persistent fraudulent information. It would also entail the inability, ultimately, of financial consumers to understand appropriate information when they were provided with it. Extraordinarily large amounts of non-depository financial products entailing risk and return are provided to currently insured depositors without the equivalent of deposit insurance – all insurance products, mutual funds, equities, real estate, pension and retirement funds (even those covered by the Pension Benefit Guarantee Corporation), stamps, coins, baseball cards, antiques, art and more. To conclude that the absence of deposit insurance will throw massive numbers of people to the financial wolves seems erroneous.

11.6.4 Eliminate Deposit Insurance and Create a Federal Money-Market Mutual Fund

As with the previous proposal, this proposal would eliminate deposit insurance. It would also eliminate all regulatory constraints on depositories except for those that apply to other financial service firms. The difference is that, instead of creating just a narrow bank at former depositories, it would also create a federal government money-market mutual fund. There should be no reason why banks should not be able to offer a competing money-market mutual fund or risk-free account in a narrow bank if they so chose. As with the narrow bank, assets of the government money-market mutual fund would be short-term Treasury securities and liabilities would be demand deposits only. Access to the fund would be through check writing or a debit card issued to anyone who wanted to purchase shares in the fund. The fund would allow for electronic deposit of all government checks such as payroll, social security and welfare checks, a service that could also be provided through the narrow bank.

All non-narrow banks would become purely private financial service firms with the ability to adapt to competition as do other financial service firms. The goals of deposit insurance would also be met. The provision of the money-market mutual fund through the government is also a function for which the government seems particularly efficient, more so than the narrow bank. Basically, the service would be a large-scale electronic debit and credit mechanism requiring a large-scale computer operation and retail outlets at, for example, post offices. This type of service was offered in the past through postal banks; therefore there is a historical precedent for this type of mechanism.

There are other advantages to this approach relative to a narrow bank alone. The proposal provides a vehicle for providing low-income individuals with certain financial services at low cost, and may represent a more efficient alternative to providing them to low-income individuals through banks, proposed community development banks, or through a narrow bank. At the moment, individuals with low incomes have difficulty cashing checks and establishing checking accounts of their own, in part because there are relatively few convenient financial service outlets near their homes. In addition, theft of government checks is a problem. With access to the government money-market mutual fund, these individuals could have checks deposited in their account, and could draw down on the account through the use of checks or a debit card. Electronic transfer of funds to pay bills could also be arranged easily. The government money-market fund would become an efficient, low-cost provider of universal liquidity in the US. In essence, just as the government has provided currency over the years, it would be updating the process by providing the modern-day equivalent of such a payments vehicle.

Finally, it is frequently said that implicit federal deposit insurance exists even for the narrow bank in the sense that if difficulties arose, however remote the possibility, the government would step in to protect depositors. This reform proposal eliminates this prospect because of government provision of a liquidity service in the first place. Individuals would never need to run to currency.

11.7 SUMMARY AND CONCLUSIONS

One approach to setting the regulatory agenda for banks is, first, to examine whether the existing regulatory structure is consistent with the goals of bank regulation. The main role of bank regulation is to maintain confidence and, hence, stability in the financial system because a stable financial system facilitates the efficient allocation of scarce economic resources – the primary function of the financial system. The fundamental goal of bank regulation is to promote the efficient allocation of scarce economic resources by minimizing disruptions in the payments and credit mechanisms. Disruptions can emanate from a number of intricate market failures primarily involving barriers to entry and exit, public-good problems, externalities, agency, moral-hazard and adverse-selection problems.

While the fundamental goal of bank regulation is to minimize the likelihood of disruptions in the payments and credit mechanisms, another goal is to promote competitive financial markets. Regulation itself can raise significant barriers to entry and exit, and create market failures that inhibit competition and the efficient allocation of scarce economic resources. We have pointed out several ways in which limitations on bank ownership, price and quantity controls, limitations on geographic location and restriction of activities can limit competition and, hence, the efficient allocation of scarce economic resources.

These limitations and restrictions were first adopted in legislation in the 1930s, and have evolved, since then, with changes in legislation and regulation that were, essentially, *ad hoc* adaptations to specific problems that appeared to need immediate attention. This was particularly true of the five pieces of federal legislation since 1980. These changes, however, fundamentally ignored the development that could not have been envisioned in the 1930s but exploded dramatically in the 1980s – the revolution in computer and telecommunications technology, which in turn has spurred dramatic competition in the provision and distribution of financial products and services.

We have attempted to show how market-driven forces have created and distributed new financial products and services. We have also attempted to show that federally insured and regulated depositories are finding it difficult to adapt to the competition because of the regulations under which they operate. As a result, depositories are suffering from a long-term decline in profitability, an increase in risk, and costly exit. We have pointed out why current attempts by banks to secure profitability through shifting on-balance-sheet assets, moving to off-balance-sheet assets, and seeking fee-based income are unlikely to overcome the long-term competitive disadvantages imposed by regulatory limitations and restrictions.

Our conclusion in setting an agenda for regulatory reform is that a reform proposal must pass a two-part test. It must meet the fundamental goal of bank regulation by protecting the payments and credit mechanisms from disruption, while at the same time promoting competition. Meeting both of these tests is the only way to maximize the efficient allocation of scarce economic resources. We have described four regulatory reform proposals. The first approach would be to protect depositories from competition by granting monopoly-like powers, where possible, to banks and by attempting to impose regulatory restrictions on non-depository financial service firms. This reform is an extension of the current regulatory policy of attempting to erect barriers to entry and exit in the provision of financial products and services.

Another reform is to maintain the deposit-insurance system and to impose prompt corrective action and closure mechanisms. A form of this approach was adopted in 1991 in FDICIA, although it lacked many of the characteristics that economists have associated with prompt corrective action. FDICIA based corrective action on book-value accounting rather than market-value accounting, and allowed for significant regulatory discretion that in the recent past has led to slow and costly resolution of troubled depositories. Even if these difficulties could be overcome, this approach does not enable healthy banks to adapt to competitive developments in financial markets.

The final two reform proposals would eliminate deposit insurance. The proposals would, nonetheless, provide all the protections that deposit insurance was designed to provide: protection for small and unsophisticated depositors, protection of the payments and credit mechanisms, and protection of the taxpayer. One proposal would adopt a form of the narrow-bank proposal by itself, while the other would combine it with a federal government money market mutual fund. The narrow bank would substitute for deposit insurance by providing individuals with a perfectly liquid asset backed by short-term Treasury securities and, thereby, payable on demand at par with extremely low cost. A federal money-market mutual fund would provide the same protection with no defalcation risk and would eliminate the potential implicit federal deposit insurance that may exist even for the narrow bank.

Simultaneously, the final two reform proposals would eliminate all regulatory constraints on depositories except for those that apply to other financial service firms, such as SEC disclosure requirements, consumer protection requirements and all other requirements that are implicit in avoiding antitrust violations. The 'non-narrow' bank would become a purely private financial service firm with the ability to adapt to competition, as do all other financial service firms.

Appendix

Table 11.A1 Summary of state bank branching laws: state classifications by branching types prevalent 31 December 1991

Statewide branch banking prevalent (42 states)		*Limited branch banking prevalent (12 states)*
Alabama	New Jersey	Arkansas (a)
Alaska	New Mexico	Colorado (a,b)
Arizona	New York (g)	Georgia
California	North Carolina	Guam
Connecticut	Ohio	Illinois
Delaware	Oklahoma (h)	Iowa
District of Columbia	Oregon	Kentucky (c)
Florida	Pennsylvania	Minnesota
Hawaii	Puerto Rico	Montana
Idaho	Rhode Island	Nebraska (d)
Indiana	South Carolina	North Dakota (e)
Kansas	South Dakota	Wyoming (f)
Louisiana	Tennessee	
Maine	Texas	
Maryland	Utah	
Massachusetts	Vermont	
Michigan	Virginia	
Mississippi	Virgin Islands	
Missouri	Washington	
Nevada	West Virginia	
New Hampshire	Wisconsin	

(a) Permitted through mergers, consolidations and acquisitions of a failing bank
(b) Holding companies may also convert subsidiary banks to branches: 60 per cent 1991; 80 per cent July 1992; 100 per cent July 1993 One DeNovo allowed 1 July 1993. Wide-open branching 1997
(c) Countywide facilities plus merger, consolidations statewide
(d) Five branches in home city, unless acquired by merger of failure
(e) Permitted only through mergers and consolidations, with no geographic restrictions
Also, facilities and stations are permitted subject to geographic restrictions and are in essence 'branches'
(f) Permitted only through mergers and consolidations
(g) Prohibited in so-called 'home office' protection communities
(h) Permitted through mergers, consolidations and acquisitions of a failing bank DeNovo branching geographically restricted to within 25 miles of main bank

Source: Congressional Research Service.

Table 11.A2 State interstate banking laws and effective dates: compendium 31 December 1991

Nationwide		*Regional reciprocity required/trigger nationwide*		*Regional reciprocity required*		*States without interstate statutes*
State	*Date enacted*	*State*	*Effective date*	*State*	*Date enacted*	*States*
AK	07/82	IN	07/92	AL	07/87	HI
AZ (a)	10/86	KS	07/92	AR	01/89	MT
CA	01/91	DE	01/88	FL	07/85	
CO	01/91			GA	07/85	
CT (b)	03/90			IA (c)	01/91	
ID	01/88			KS	07/91	
IL				MD	07/85	
KY (d)	07/86			MN	07/86	
LA (e)	07/89			MS	07/88	
ME (f)	01/78			MO	08/86	
MA	07/90			NC	01/85	
MI (f)	10/88			SC	01/86	
NE (d)	01/91			VA	07/85	
NV (a)	07/85			WI	04/86	
NH (f)						
NJ (d,f)	01/88					
NM (a)	01/90					
NY (d,f)	06/82					
ND (d)						
OH (d)	10/88					
OK	05/86					
OR	07/89					

Table 11.A2 Continued

Nationwide		*Regional reciprocity required/trigger nationwide*		*Regional reciprocity required*		*States without interstate statutes*
State	*Date enacted*	*State*	*Effective date*	*State*	*Date enacted*	*States*
PA (f)	08/86					
RI (d,f)	01/88					
SD (d,f)	02/80 (g)					
TN (d)	01/91					
TX (a)	01/87					
UT	01/88					
VT (f)	01/88					
WA (d)	07/87					
WV	01/88					
WY	05/87					

(a) DeNovo entry permittted after specified time period: AZ 30 June 1992; CO 1 July 1993; NV 1 July 1990; NM 1 July 1992; TX 1 Sept 2001
(b) May drop reciprocity after trigger of 1 July 1993
(c) Reciprocity not required
(d) Reciprocity required
(e) After 1 July 1994, out-of-state bhc may open any new bank and aquire a nonestablished state bank if aquirer has established in the State
(f) DeNovo entry permitted
(g) Revised 02/88.

Source: Congressional Research Service.

Table 11.A3 Restrictions on banks' activities or powers

National banks	*Banks in holding companies*	*State-chartered banks*
	Insurance	
National banks in towns of 5000 or less have been permitted to sell insurance	Bank Holding Company Act (BHCA) says that insurance is not permitted as a 'closely related to banking activity' for bank holding companies (bhc's)	Several States permit State-chartered banks to sell or to underwrite insurance or to do both
Comptroller of Currency (OCC) has allowed National banks as incidental powers of banking to: • sell fixed and variable-rate annuities • sell credit life insurance	Federal Reserve Board (FRB) recently permitted a bhc to continue to sell insurance through two State-chartered banks that it was acquiring in Indiana. In another ruling FRB refused to grant Citicorp the same power through a Delaware State-chartered bank	
	Securities	
Glass-Steagall Act (G-S) prohibits National banks from selling, under-writing, or affiliating with securities businesses but allows banks to deal with certain 'bank-eligible' securities, such as Treasury issuances, and to buy and sell on order for bank customers	G-S prohibits banks from affiliating with entities in the securities business. BHCA forbids bhc's and their affiliates or subsidiaries from engaging in businesses other than banking or those so 'closely related as to be a proper incident thereto'	G-S theoretically forbids all banks from engaging in investment banking, directly

Table 11.A3 Continued

National banks	*Banks in holding companies*	*State-chartered banks*
Activites authorized by the Comptroller of the Currency for National banks: • discount brokerage • investment company advice • collective investment fund management (IRA's) • placing securities privately • commercial paper sales • general obligation bond underwriting	FRB has authorized: • sale and underwriting of corporate debt securities • underwriting commercial paper • underwriting municipal revenue bonds • underwriting consumer-related receivables and mortgage-backed securities • providing investment advice • brokering services • underwriting and dealing in money market instruments and • providing foreign exchange advisory and transactional services	The following activities are permited by at least several States to their State-chartered banks: • equity investment • underwriting general obligations and revenue bonds • offering full service and discount brokerage

Table 11.A3 Continued

National banks	*Banks in holding companies*	*State-chartered banks*
	Real Estate	
National Bank Act limits National banks to explicit powers and 'incidental powers as shall be necessary to carry on the business of banking'	BHCA limits bhc's to banking and activities so closely related as to be a proper incident thereto	Various States authorize real-estate development, equity participation, and brokerage activities for State-chartered banks
National banks may lease bank property and hold property that devolves upon them through loan default	FRB has ruled the following activities to be 'closely related' to banking: • leasing personal or real property • community development • real estate and personal property and appraising; and • arranging commercial real estate equity financing	

Source: Congressional Research Service.

Table 11.A4 State authorization of selected expanded activites for state-chartered banks[a] March 1992

Securities brokerage (discount and/or full)	*General securities underwriting*	*Real-estate equity participation*	*Real-estate development*	*Real-estate brokerage*	*Insurance underwriting*	*Insurance brokerage*
Alabama [b]	Arizona [b]	Arizona [b]	Arizona [b]	Alabama [b]	Delaware	Alabama [b]
Arizona [b]	California [c]	Arkansas	Arkansas	Arizona [b]	Massachusetts [d]	California
Arkansas	Connecticut [b]	California	California [d]	California	New Jersey [e]	Delaware
California [c]	Delaware	Colorado	Colorado	Connecticut [b]	North Carolina [d]	Idaho
Connecticut [b]	Florida	Connecticut [e]	Connecticut [e]	Florida	South Dakota	Indiana [g]
Delaware	Iowa [b]	Florida [b]	Delaware	Georgia	Utah [f]	Iowa
Florida [c]	Maine [b]	Georgia	Florida [b]	Idaho		Massachusetts [d]
Georgia	Massachusetts [d]	Iowa	Georgia	Massachusetts [d]		Minnesota
Hawaii [c]	Montana	Kentucky	Kentucky	Minnesota [b]		Nebraska [h]
Idaho [c]	New Jersey [e]	Maine	Maine	Nebraska		New Jersey [e]
Illinois	New York [b]	Massachusetts [d]	Massachusetts [d]	New Jersey [e]		North Carolina
Indiana	North Carolina [d]	Missouri [b]	Michigan	North Carolina [d]		Oregon
Iowa [b]	Rhode Island	Nevada	Minnesota	Rhode Island		South Dakota
Kansas [b]	Tennessee	New Hampshire [b]	Missouri [b]	Utah		Utah [f]
Kentucky	Texas [b]	New Jersey [e]	Nevada	Wisconsin		Virginia
Louisiana		North Carolina [d]	New Hampshire [b]			
Maine		Ohio	New Jersey [e]			

Table 11.A4 Continued

Securities brokerage (discount and/or full)	*General securities underwriting*	*Real-estate equity participation*	*Real-estate development*	*Real-estate brokerage*	*Insurance underwriting*	*Insurance brokerage*
Maryland		Oregon	North Carolina [d]			
Massachusetts [d]		Pennsylvania	Ohio			
Michigan		Rhode Island	Oregon [b]			
Minnesota [b]		South Dakota	Pennsylvania			
Missouri [b]		Tennessee [d]	Rhode Island			
Nebraska		Utah	Tennessee			
Nevada		Virginia	Utah			
New Hampshire [c]		Washington	Washington			
New Jersey [e]						
New Mexico						
New York						
North Carolina [d]						
North Dakota						
Ohio						
Oklahoma						
Pennsylvania						
Rhode Island						

Table 11.A4 Continued

Securities brokerage (discount and/or full)	*General securities underwriting*	*Real-estate equity participation*	*Real-estate development*	*Real-estate brokerage*	*Insurance underwriting*	*Insurance brokerage*
Tennessee						
Texas [b]						
Utah [b]						
Vermont						
Virginia [b]						
Washington [b]						
West Virginia [d]						
Wisconsin						
Tennessee						
Utah						
Washington						

(a) Expanded activities above those permitted national banks and bank holding companies under the bank holding company act. Extent of practice unknown
(b) Through a subsidiary
(c) Laws are silent, but regulatory approval is possible
(d) Possible through equity investment authority
(e) Possible through leeway authority
(f) Grandfathered institutions
(g) Except for life insurance
(h) Only in towns with less than 200 000 population
Source: Congressional Research Service.

Table 11.A5 Government sponsored enterprises devoted to housing

	1981	1982	1983	1984	1985	1986	1987	1988	1989	1990	1991
Total on-balance-sheet assets ($ billions)											
Federal home loan banks	74.7	80.3	72.5	97.0	112.1	131.7	154.2	174.8	180.8	165.7	154.6
Federal national mortgage assoc	61.6	73.0	78.4	87.8	99.1	99.6	103.5	112.3	124.3	133.1	147.1
Federal home loan mortgage corp	6.3	6.0	8.9	13.1	16.3	23.2	25.7	34.4	35.5	40.6	46.9
Total off-balance-sheet assets ($ billions)											
Federal home loan banks	NA	NA	0.5	0.5	0.9	1.7	2.6	2.3	3.8	3.6	3.0
Federal national mortgage assoc	0.7	14.5	25.1	36.2	55.0	97.2	140.0	178.3	228.2	299.8	372.0
Federal home loan mortgage corp	19.9	43.0	58.0	70.9	100.5	169.2	212.6	226.4	272.9	316.4	359.2
Equity capital-to-total on-and off-balance-sheet assets ratios (%)											
Federal home loan banks	NA	NA	10.4	8.7	8.8	8.7	8.7	8.7	7.7	6.9	6.8
Federal national mortgage assoc	1.7	1.1	1.0	0.7	0.7	0.6	0.7	0.8	0.9	0.9	1.0
Federal home loan mortgage corp	1.0	0.6	0.6	0.7	0.7	0.5	0.5	0.6	0.6	0.6	0.6
Return on average assets (%)											
Federal home loan banks	0.8	1.2	1.0	1.0	1.0	1.2	0.9	0.9	1.0	0.9	0.7
Federal national mortgage assoc	(0.3)	(0.1)	0.1	(0.1)	0.0	0.1	0.4	0.5	0.7	0.9	1.0
Federal home loan mortgage corp	0.5	1.0	2.1	2.0	1.3	1.1	1.2	1.1	1.2	1.0	1.2
Return on average equity (%)											
Federal home loan banks	7.9	13.0	9.5	10.1	10.7	12.4	9.7	9.4	11.5	11.9	10.5
Federal national mortgage assoc	(17.6)	(11.0)	5.1	(7.4)	(0.7)	9.6	25.1	24.9	31.1	33.7	27.7
Federal home loan mortgage corp	13.1	21.9	44.5	52.0	52.0	28.5	28.2	28.2	25.0	20.5	23.6

Source: Annual reports; federal home loan banks, federal national mortgage association, federal home loan mortage corporation.

Table 11.A6 Commercial banks' balance sheet

	1950	*1960*	*1970*	*1980*	*1981*	*1982*	*1983*	*1984*	*1985*	*1986*	*1987*	*1988*	*1989*	*1990*	*1991*	*1992 3rd qtr*
Total financial assets ($ billions)	150	230	518	1483	1620	1732	1889	2129	2377	2617	2773	2952	3232	3336	3441	3576
US govt. securities (%)	43	28	15	12	11	12	14	12	11	12	12	12	12	14	17	18
Tax-exempt securities (%)	NA	NA	NA	10	10	9	9	8	10	8	6	5	4	4	3	3
Corporate and foreign bonds	1	0	1	1	1	1	1	1	1	2	3	3	2	3	3	3
Mortgage loans (%)	9	13	14	18	18	17	17	18	18	19	21	23	24	26	26	25
Consumer credit loans (%)	5	9	10	12	11	11	11	12	12	12	12	13	12	12	11	10
Bank loans NEC (%)	19	27	31	31	32	31	30	29	28	28	26	26	25	24	23	22
Open-market paper (%)	0	1	1	1	1	1	1	1	0	0	0	0	0	0	0	0
Other (%)	22	22	28	16	17	18	17	19	19	19	19	18	20	18	18	20
Total liabilities ($ billions)	140	212	487	1411	1562	1673	1829	2021	2252	2485	2658	2860	3119	3220	3330	3456
Domestic checkable dep	69	59	39	22	21	20	20	19	19	21	19	18	16	16	17	17
Small time & sav. dep (%)	26	34	42	34	33	37	41	40	39	39	37	37	37	40	41	40
Large time deposits (%)	0	1	5	19	21	20	15	16	15	13	14	15	14	13	12	10
Fed. funds & security RPs (%)	NA	NA	NA	8	8	8	8	8	8	8	8	8	9	8	7	8
Other (%)	5	6	13	17	18	15	16	17	19	19	21	22	23	23	23	25

Source: Flow of funds accounts, board of governors of the federal reserve system.

Table 11.A7 Selected financial data for commercial banks

	1980	*1981*	*1982*	*1983*	*1984*	*1985*	*1986*
Number of institutions	14 435	14 415	14 453	14 467	14 472	14 393	14 188
Total assets ($ billions)	1856	2029	2194	2342	2508	2731	2941
Capital ($ billions)	108	118	129	140	154	169	182
Net after-tax income ($ millions)	13 974	14 737	14 881	14 932	15 499	17 981	17 412
Net operating income ($ millions)	14 443	15 542	15 475	14 867	15 414	16 182	13 194
Taxes ($ millions)	4657	3873	2980	4017	4721	5643	5304
Real-estate loans to total assets (%)	14.5	14.4	14	14.4	15.4	16.1	17.5
Commercial and industrial loans to total assets (%)	21.1	22.4	23	22.4	22.5	21.2	20.4
Agricultural production loans to total assets (%)	1.7	1.7	1.7	1.7	1.6	1.3	1.1
Loans to individuals to total assets (%)	10.1	9.5	9.1	9.6	10.6	11.3	11.4
Number of problem banks	NA	NA	NA	NA	NA	1098	1457
Assets of problem banks ($ billions)	NA	NA	NA	NA	NA	NA	NA
Resolutions – Commercial & savings banks							
Number	10	10	42	48	79	120	145
Total assets ($ millions)	236	4859	11 632	7037	3274	8337	6830
Estimated present-value cost ($ millions)	NA	NA	NA	NA	NA	850	1732

Table 11.A7 Continued

	1987	*1988*	*1989*	*1990*	*1991*	*1992 3rd qtr*
Number of institutions	13 694	13 120	12 705	12 338	11 927	11 590
Total assets ($ billions)	2999	3131	3299	3389	3510	3481
Capital ($ billions)	181	197	205	219	232	257
Net after-tax income ($ millions)	2806	24 817	15 647	16 626	18 568	24 205
Net operating income ($ millions)	1176	23 722	14 541	15 503	14 823	31 515
Taxes ($ millions)	5424	9991	9658	7885	8404	10 856
Real-estate loans to total assets (%)	20	21.6	23.1	24.5	24.8	24.8
Commercial and industrial loans to total assets (%)	19.7	19.2	18.8	18.2	16.3	15.5
Agricultural production loans to total assets (%)	1	1	0.9	1	1	1.1
Loans to individuals to total assets (%)	11.7	12.1	12.1	11.9	11.4	11
Number of problem banks	1559	1394	1092	1012	997	909
Assets of problem banks ($ billions)	329	305	188	342	528	488
Resolutions – Commercial & savings banks						
Number	203	221	207	169	127	80
Total assets ($ millions)	9198	52 623	29 538	16 265	63 300	22 373
Estimated present-value cost ($ millions)	2017	5530	5998	3767	7400	3499

Source: Congressional Budget Office.

Table 11.A8 Savings and loan associations' balance sheet

	1950	*1960*	*1970*	*1980*	*1981*	*1982*	*1983*	*1984*	*1985*	*1986*	*1987*	*1988*	*1989*	*1990*	*1991*	*1992 3rd qtr*
Total financial assets ($ billions)	17	71	176	623	655	698	819	977	1058	1141	1247	1360	1233	1097	926	850
US Govt. securities (%)	9	7	7	7	8	12	15	15	14	17	19	19	16	16	14	14
Tax-exempt securities (%)	NA	NA	NA	0	0	0	0	0	0	0	0	0	0	0	0	0
Corporate & foreign bonds (%)	NA	NA	NA	1	1	2	3	3	4	4	5	5	4	4	4	4
Mortgages (%)	81	84	85	79	78	69	65	62	62	58	57	56	61	61	63	64
Consumer credit (%)	1	1	1	3	3	3	3	4	4	4	4	4	4	4	4	3
Other loans (to businesses) (%)	NA	NA	NA	NA	0	0	0	1	2	2	2	3	3	2	2	2
Other (%)	NA	NA	NA	NA	10	14	14	14	14	14	13	13	12	14	13	13
Total liabilities ($ billions)	16	66	164	597	638	692	817	979	1062	1143	1233	1342	1224	1097	932	858
Checkable deposits (%)	NA	NA	NA	0	1	2	3	3	3	4	3	4	5	5	6	7
Small time & savings (%)	NA	NA	NA	79	74	73	70	66	62	63	62	58	63	63	65	63
Large time (%)	NA	NA	NA	7	8	9	11	13	12	11	10	10	9	8	8	8
Fed. funds and security RPs (%)	NA	NA	NA	1	2	1	3	5	4	5	7	7	5	4	2	2
Other (%)	NA	NA	NA	13	15	14	13	14	18	17	19	20	18	20	19	20

Source: Flow of funds accounts, board of governors of the federal reserve system.

Table 11.A9 Selected financial data for savings and loan associations

	1980	*1981*	*1982*	*1983*	*1984*	*1985*	*1986*
Number of institutions	3993	3751	3287	3146	3136	3246	3220
Total assets ($ billions)	604	640	686	814	978	1070	1164
Capital ($ billions)	32	27	20	25	27	34	39
Net after-tax income ($ millions)	781	–4631	–4142	1945	1022	3728	131
Net operating income ($ millions)	790	–7114	–8761	46	990	3601	4562
Taxes ($ millions)	407	–1519	–1578	576	764	2087	3141
Home mortgages to total assets (%)	67	65	56	50	45	42	39
Mortgage backed securities to total assets (%)	4	5	9	11	11	10	13
Mortgage assets to total assets (%)	71	70	65	61	56	53	52
Number of tangible insolvent S&Ls	43	112	415	515	695	705	672
Assets of tangible insolvent S&Ls ($ billions)	0	29	220	234	336	335	324
Resolutions–S&Ls							
Number	11	28	63	36	22	30	46
Total assets ($ millions)	1458	13 908	17 662	4631	5080	5601	12 455
Estimated present-value cost ($ millions)	167	759	803	275	743	979	3065

Table 11.A9 Continued

	1987	*1988*	*1989*	*1990*	*1991*	*1992 3rd qtr*
Number of institutions	3147	2949	2597	2342	2064	1954
Total assets ($ billions)	1251	1352	1157	1006	876	816
Capital ($ billions)	34	46	51	50	52	55
Net after-tax income ($ millions)	–7779	–12 057	–3124	–965	2282	4049
Net operating income ($ millions)	2850	907	–3549	–1099	3506	5462
Taxes ($ millions)	2699	1952	–109	331	2370	2223
Home mortgages to total assets (%)	38	39	43	44	47	47
Mortgage backed securities to total assets (%)	16	15	14	15	14	15
Mortgage assets to total assets (%)	53	54	57	59	61	62
Number of tangible insolvent S&Ls	672	508	239	109	33	43
Assets of tangible insolvent S&Ls ($ billions)	336	283	192	89	41	70
Resolutions–S&Ls						
Number	47	205	37	315	232	68
Total assets ($ millions)	10 660	100 660	11 019	108 896	75 947	33 861*
Estimated present-value cost ($ millions)	3704	31 180	4899	38 383	33 833	6684*

Source: Congressional budget office.
* 1992:2nd qtr.

Table 11.A10 Mutual savings banks' balance sheet

	1950	1960	1970	1980	1981	1982	1983	1984	1985	1986	1987	1988	1989	1990	1991	1992 3rd qtr
Total financial assets ($ billions)	22	41	79	170	174	173	193	203	217	237	261	285	284	264	249	244
US government securities (%)	48	17	6	13	14	14	17	17	15	17	18	14	13	13	15	18
Mortgages (%)	37	66	73	59	58	54	51	51	51	50	53	56	59	61	59	57
Consumer credit (%)	0	0	1	3	3	4	3	5	6	5	5	4	3	4	3	3
Other (%)	14	17	19	25	25	28	29	28	28	28	24	26	25	23	23	23
Total liabilities ($ billions)	20	37	73	160	166	165	183	193	204	218	239	263	260	245	228	221
Checkable deposits (%)	NA	NA	NA	2	2	3	4	5	7	10	11	5	5	6	7	8
Small time deposits (%)	NA	NA	NA	85	89	89	84	78	73	65	55	61	62	68	79	83
Large time deposits (%)	NA	NA	NA	3	4	4	6	10	12	14	19	18	19	13	4	NA
Other (%)	NA	NA	NA	10	6	5	6	7	9	12	16	16	14	12	10	9

Source: Flow of funds accounts, board of governors of the federal reserve system.

Table 11.A11 Credit unions' balance sheet

	1950	*1960*	*1970*	*1980*	*1981*	*1982*	*1983*	*1984*	*1985*	*1986*	*1987*	*1988*	*1989*	*1990*	*1991*	*1992 3rd qtr*
Total financial assets ($ billions)	1	5	15	68	71	81	96	111	135	163	178	192	202	217	240	260
US government securities (%)	11	4	5	6	6	7	9	8	10	10	11	11	9	10	13	17
Home mortgages (%)	8	8	5	7	6	5	7	8	9	12	17	20	22	22	21	20
Consumer credit (%)	69	79	84	65	65	58	56	60	54	47	45	46	46	43	39	36
Other (%)	12	10	6	22	22	29	28	23	27	31	27	23	23	25	27	28
Total liabilities ($ billions)	–	–	–	65	68	77	92	106	128	156	170	183	191	205	226	244
Checkable deposits (%)	–	–	–	5	6	7	9	9	10	10	10	11	11	11	12	13
Small time & savings (%)	–	–	–	89	89	89	88	87	87	87	86	86	86	86	84	84
Large time deposits (%)	–	–	–	1	1	1	1	1	1	0	1	1	2	2	1	1
Other (%)	NA	NA	NA	5	5	3	3	3	2	3	2	2	2	2	2	2

Source: Flow of funds accounts, board of governors of the federal reserve system.

Table 11.A12 Life insurance companies' balance sheet

	1950	*1960*	*1970*	*1980*	*1981*	*1982*	*1983*	*1984*	*1985*	*1986*	*1987*	*1988*	*1989*	*1990*	*1991*	*1992 3rd qtr*
Total financial assets ($ billions)	63	116	201	464	508	568	633	697	796	906	1005	1133	1251	1367	1505	1598
Money mkt. fund shares (%)	NA	NA	NA	0	1	1	1	1	1	1	1	1	0	1	2	2
Mutual fund shares (%)	NA	NA	NA	0	0	0	0	0	0	2	1	2	2	2	3	3
Corporate equities (%)	3	4	8	10	9	9	10	9	9	8	8	8	9	7	8	8
US government securities (%)	22	6	2	4	4	6	9	11	13	13	12	12	12	13	16	17
Tax-exempt securities (%)	NA	NA	NA	1	1	2	2	1	1	1	1	1	1	1	1	1
Corporate & foreign bonds (%)	40	42	37	39	37	36	35	35	35	35	39	40	41	41	40	40
Mortgages (%)	26	36	37	28	27	25	24	22	22	21	21	21	20	20	18	16
Open-market paper (%)	NA	NA	NA	2	2	3	3	3	3	3	3	3	3	2	1	2
Other (%)	10	13	16	16	17	18	17	17	16	15	14	13	13	12	12	12
Total liabilities ($ billions)	59	108	188	438	483	540	601	665	759	858	961	1074	1196	1302	1420	1511
Life insurance reserves (%)	83	73	65	47	45	41	39	35	32	31	30	29	29	28	27	27
Pension fund reserves (%)	9	17	22	39	39	45	38	50	53	56	57	58	59	61	62	62
Other (%)	8	10	13	13	16	14	23	15	15	14	13	12	12	11	11	11

Source: Flow of funds accounts, board of governors of the federal reserve system.

Table 11.A13 Other insurance companies' balance sheet

	1950	*1960*	*1970*	*1980*	*1981*	*1982*	*1983*	*1984*	*1985*	*1986*	*1987*	*1988*	*1989*	*1990*	*1991*	*1992 3rd qtr*
Total financial assets ($ billions)	$12	$26	$50	$182	$194	$212	$235	$251	$299	$354	$405	$454	$500	$529	$592	$619
Corporate equities (%)	22	28	26	18	17	18	20	18	19	17	16	16	17	15	19	20
US government securities (%)	45	21	9	10	11	11	12	15	17	18	18	18	19	21	23	24
Tax-exempt securities (%)	NA	NA	NA	44	43	41	37	34	30	29	31	30	27	26	23	22
Corporate & foreign bonds (%)	6	6	17	13	14	12	9	10	11	14	14	14	16	17	16	16
Commercial mortgages (%)	1	1	1	1	1	1	1	1	1	1	1	1	1	1	1	1
Other (%)	26	43	47	14	15	17	21	22	22	21	20	21	20	20	17	17
Total liabilities ($ billions)	$7	$16	$34	$128	$139	$150	$163	$177	$215	$259	$304	$336	$370	$396	$423	$442

Source: Flow of funds accounts, board of governors of the federal reserve system.

Table 11.A14 Private pension funds' balance sheet

	1950	*1960*	*1970*	*1980*	*1981*	*1982*	*1983*	*1984*	*1985*	*1986*	*1987*	*1988*	*1989*	*1990*	*1991*	*1992 3rd qtr*
Total financial assets ($ billions)	7	38	111	470	487	676	811	880	1038	1198	1216	1313	1536	1506	2192	2259
Money mkt. fund shares (%)	NA	NA	NA	1	1	1	1	1	1	1	1	1	1	1	1	1
Mutual fund shares (%)	NA	NA	NA	2	1	1	1	1	2	2	2	2	3	3	3	3
Corporate equities (%)	16	43	61	48	45	45	45	42	45	46	47	48	51	47	43	43
US government securities (%)	30	7	3	11	14	15	16	17	15	15	15	14	13	14	14	14
Tax-exempt securities (%)	NA	NA	NA	NA	NA	0	0	0	0	0	0	0	0	0	0	0
Corporate & foreign bonds (%)	42	41	27	17	17	13	12	13	11	11	11	10	10	10	11	11
Mortgages (%)	2	3	4	1	1	1	1	1	1	1	0	0	0	2	1	1
Open-market paper (%)	NA	NA	NA	4	5	2	2	2	2	1	2	3	2	2	4	4
Other (%)	10	5	6	18	16	21	22	23	24	22	21	21	19	20	22	22

Source: Flow of funds accounts, board of governors of the federal reserve system.

Table 11.A15 State and local government employee retirement funds' balance sheet

	1950	*1960*	*1970*	*1980*	*1981*	*1982*	*1983*	*1984*	*1985*	*1986*	*1987*	*1988*	*1989*	*1990*	*1991*	*1992 3rd qtr*
Total financial assets ($ billions)	5	20	58	198	224	263	311	357	405	469	517	606	735	752	891	949
Corporate equities (%)	1	2	14	22	21	23	29	27	30	32	33	36	41	39	45	46
US government securities (%)	51	31	11	20	23	27	28	31	31	31	33	30	27	29	27	28
Corporate & foreign bonds (%)	12	36	59	48	46	41	34	33	32	30	24	24	25	24	21	19
Mortgages (%)	2	7	12	6	6	5	5	4	4	3	3	3	2	2	2	2
Open-market paper (%)	NA	NA	NA	NA	NA	NA	NA	NA	NA	NA	4	3	3	3	3	3
Other (%)	34	24	5	4	4	4	4	4	4	4	3	3	3	2	2	2

Source: Flow of funds accounts, board of governors of the federal reserve system.

Table 11.A16 Finance companies' balance sheet

	1950	1960	1970	1980	1981	1982	1983	1984	1985	1986	1987	1988	1989	1990	1991	1992 3rd qtr
Total financial assets ($ billions)	9	27	63	243	273	292	327	371	440	531	584	646	719	772	794	789
Mortgages (%)	5	6	9	21	22	23	23	24	24	27	24	25	28	29	28	29
Consumer credit (%)	57	57	52	32	32	32	32	30	30	28	26	24	20	18	16	15
Other loans (to businesses) (%)	27	30	34	37	36	34	35	37	36	33	37	38	38	38	37	37
Other (%)	11	6	4	10	10	10	10	9	10	11	13	13	14	15	19	19
Total liabilities ($ billions)	5	20	57	217	245	262	294	336	405	492	551	602	664	708	729	720
Corporate bonds (%)	33	50	40	42	41	43	42	43	37	38	31	24	26	24	27	24
Bank loans, N.E.C. (%)	50	30	22	11	10	10	9	8	7	7	6	5	5	5	5	5
Open-market paper (%)	14	19	38	28	30	28	30	30	35	37	39	45	45	47	46	47
Other (%)	3	1	0	19	19	19	19	19	21	18	25	26	24	24	22	24

Source: Flow of funds accounts, board of governors of the federal reserve system.

Table 11.A17 Mutual funds' balance sheet

	1950	*1960*	*1970*	*1980*	*1981*	*1982*	*1983*	*1984*	*1985*	*1986*	*1987*	*1988*	*1989*	*1990*	*1991*	*1992 3rd qtr*
Total financial assets ($ billions)	NA	NA	NA	62	60	77	112	137	240	414	460	478	566	602	812	1013
Corporate equities (%)	NA	NA	NA	69	63	64	66	59	47	39	39	39	44	39	43	43
US government securities (%)	NA	NA	NA	3	5	7	5	9	27	30	29	24	21	23	24	21
Tax-exempt securities (%)	NA	NA	NA	7	9	10	12	14	14	16	15	16	17	18	17	16
Corporate & foreign bonds (%)	NA	NA	NA	14	17	13	12	12	8	11	12	14	13	15	12	15
Open-market paper (%)	NA	NA	NA	6	6	4	4	5	2	2	3	4	3	4	3	4
Other (%)	NA	NA	NA	1	1	2	1	2	2	2	1	2	1	1	2	1
Total shares outstanding	NA	NA	NA	62	60	77	112	137	240	414	460	478	566	602	812	1013

Source: Flow of funds accounts, board of governors of the federal reserve system.

Table 11.A18 Security brokers and dealers' balance sheet

	1950	*1960*	*1970*	*1980*	*1981*	*1982*	*1983*	*1984*	*1985*	*1986*	*1987*	*1988*	*1989*	*1990*	*1991*	*1992 3rd qtr*
Total financial assets ($ billions)	4	7	19	45	60	83	91	118	156	185	138	136	237	262	333	405
US government securities (%)	15	15	18	–8	8	14	5	15	5	14	9	–3	36	47	49	52
Tax-exempt securities (%)	NA	NA	NA	6	5	6	7	9	13	9	6	6	3	3	3	2
Corporate bonds (%)	12	7	10	4	6	7	9	12	15	13	14	21	14	11	12	14
Open-market paper (%)	NA	NA	NA	15	19	20	13	15	9	7	10	11	8	7	4	4
Other (%)	NA	NA	NA	83	62	54	66	50	58	58	60	66	40	32	32	27
Total liabilities ($ billions)	3	5	14	39	53	75	80	108	141	164	115	112	213	241	305	377
Security RPs (net) (%)	NA	NA	NA	–22	–1	32	10	24	17	22	–8	–20	30	34	35	39
Security credit from banks (%)	62	60	60	53	50	35	36	32	32	24	30	30	18	15	15	21
Customer credit balances (%)	34	23	33	41	28	24	26	20	25	27	34	37	25	26	29	20
Other (%)	NA	NA	NA	27	23	9	28	25	26	27	43	53	27	26	21	19

Source: Flow of funds accounts, board of governors of the federal reserve system.

Table 11.A19 Money-market mutual funds' balance sheet

	1980	*1981*	*1982*	*1983*	*1984*	*1985*	*1986*	*1987*	*1988*	*1989*	*1990*	*1991*	*1992 3rd qtr*
Total financial assets ($ billions)	76	186	220	179	234	244	292	316	338	428	498	540	553
Time deposits (%)	27	24	19	13	10	7	7	11	10	10	4	6	6
Security RPs (%)	7	8	7	7	10	11	11	12	12	13	12	13	13
Foreign deposits (%)	9	10	11	12	9	8	8	7	9	6	5	4	4
US government securities (%)	11	17	25	20	18	18	15	13	9	8	17	22	24
Tax-exempt securities (%)	2	2	6	9	10	15	22	19	19	16	17	17	17
Open-market paper (%)	41	38	31	37	42	41	36	35	38	44	41	36	34
Other (%)	2	1	1	1	1	2	2	2	3	3	4	3	3
Total shares outstanding	76	186	220	179	234	244	292	316	338	428	498	540	553

Source: Flow of funds accounts, board of governors of the federal reserve system.

0Table 11.A20 Real-estate investment trusts' balance sheet

	1950	*1960*	*1970*	*1980*	*1981*	*1982*	*1983*	*1984*	*1985*	*1986*	*1987*	*1988*	*1989*	*1990*	*1991*	*1992 3rd qtr*
Total financial assets ($ billions)	NA	NA	4	3	3	4	4	6	8	9	11	14	13	13	13	15
Home mortgages (%)	NA	NA	17	12	9	9	6	4	4	4	3	3	3	3	3	3
Commercial mortgages (%)	NA	NA	41	73	50	43	43	34	47	46	42	38	40	38	34	35
Multifamily mortgages (%)	NA	NA	27	39	25	23	26	23	22	21	20	18	19	17	17	18
Other (%)	NA	NA	15	NA	16	26	26	39	27	29	35	42	38	42	46	45
Total liabilities ($ billions)	NA	NA	2	4	4	4	4	5	6	7	9	12	11	12	13	15
Mortgages (%)	NA	NA	27	46	48	49	55	52	44	40	36	27	31	35	37	34
Multifamily residential (%)	NA	NA	9	15	15	17	18	17	15	13	12	9	10	12	12	5
Commercial (%)	NA	NA	18	32	33	34	37	35	30	26	24	19	21	23	25	23
Corporate bonds (%)	NA	NA	29	34	18	17	18	17	25	26	27	20	23	25	23	22
Bank loans n.e.c. (%)	NA	NA	39	0	13	15	11	10	11	13	6	34	26	24	22	26
Other (%)	NA	NA	5	20	23	20	16	21	20	21	31	19	21	16	17	17

Source: Flow of funds accounts, board of governors of the federal reserve system.

Table 11.A21 Issuers of securitized credit obligations' balance sheet

	1950	*1960*	*1970*	*1980*	*1981*	*1982*	*1983*	*1984*	*1985*	*1986*	*1987*	*1988*	*1989*	*1990*	*1991*	*1992 3rd qtr*
Total financial assets ($ billions)	–	–	–	–	–	1	4	14	25	64	103	136	187	232	268	294
Agency securities (%)	–	–	–	–	–	100	100	100	100	100	100	100	73	64	60	58
Consumer credit (%)	–	–	–	–	–	–	–	–	–	–	–	–	26	34	37	38
Loans to business (%)	–	–	–	–	–	–	–	–	–	–	–	–	1	2	3	3

Source: Flow of funds accounts, board of governors of the federal reserve system.

Table 11.A22 Individuals' balance sheet

	1980	*1981*	*1982*	*1983*	*1984*	*1985*	*1986*	*1987*	*1988*	*1989*	*1990*	*1991*	*1992 3rd qtr*
Total financial assets ($ billions)	4700	5010	5604	6353	6973	8118	9086	9547	10 448	11 775	12 043	13 592	13 993
Checkable deposits & curr. (%)	6	7	6	6	6	6	6	6	5	5	5	5	5
Time & savings deposits (%)	27	27	26	26	27	24	23	23	23	21	21	18	17
Money market fund shares (%)	1	3	3	2	3	3	3	3	3	3	4	3	3
Securities (%)	34	32	31	31	30	34	34	33	33	34	33	33	33
US savings bonds (%)	2	1	1	1	1	1	1	1	1	1	1	1	1
Other US Treasury Securities (%)	3	3	3	3	4	3	3	2	3	2	3	2	1
US govt. agency securities (%)	1	1	1	1	1	1	1	1	2	2	3	2	2
Tax exempt securities (%)	2	2	3	3	3	4	3	4	4	4	5	4	4
Corp. & foreign bonds (%)	1	1	1	1	1	1	1	1	1	1	1	1	0
Open-market paper (%)	1	1	1	1	1	2	1	1	2	1	2	1	1
Mutual fund shares (%)	1	1	1	2	2	3	4	4	4	4	4	5	6
Corporate equities (%)	24	21	20	20	18	20	19	17	16	17	15	17	17
Private life insur. reserves (%)	4	4	4	4	3	3	3	3	3	3	3	3	3
Private insured pension res. (%)	4	4	4	5	5	5	5	6	6	6	7	6	7
Private noninsured pen. res. (%)	10	10	12	13	13	13	13	13	13	13	13	16	16
Govt. insurance & pen. res. (%)	6	6	7	7	7	7	7	8	8	8	8	9	9
Miscellaneous finan. assets (%)	7	7	7	6	6	6	6	7	7	6	7	6	6
Total liabilities ($ billions)	2167	2361	2539	2819	3194	3624	4034	4361	4766	5172	5485	5653	5747

Source: Flow of funds accounts, board of governors of the federal reserve system.
Note: Data for earlier years not available.

Table 11.A23 Households, personal trusts and non-profit organizations' balance sheet

	1950	*1960*	*1970*	*1980*	*1981*	*1982*	*1983*	*1984*	*1985*	*1986*	*1987*	*1988*	*1989*	*1990*	*1991*	*1992 3rd qtr*
Total financial assets ($ billions)	447	973	1917	6391	6806	7393	8154	8694	9819	10 804	11 383	12 356	13 804	13 984	15 441	15 806
Checkable deposits & curr. (%)	NA	NA	NA	4	4	4	4	4	4	4	4	4	4	4	4	4
Small time & svgs. deposits (%)	NA	NA	NA	18	17	18	19	19	19	18	18	17	16	16	15	14
Money market fund shares (%)	NA	NA	NA	1	2	3	2	2	2	2	2	2	3	3	3	3
US government securities (%)	15	8	5	4	4	4	4	4	4	4	4	5	5	6	4	4
Corporate and foreign bonds (%)	1	1	2	1	1	1	1	1	1	1	1	1	1	1	1	0
Mortgages (%)	4	3	2	2	2	2	2	1	1	1	1	1	2	2	2	2
Mutual fund shares (%)	NA	NA	NA	1	1	1	1	1	2	3	4	3	4	4	4	5
Corporate equities (%)	30	41	38	17	15	15	16	15	16	16	14	14	15	13	15	15
Life insurance reserves (%)	12	9	7	3	3	3	3	3	3	3	3	3	3	3	3	3
Pension fund reserves (%)	5	9	12	14	15	17	19	20	20	21	22	22	23	24	27	28
Total liabilities (%)	8	23	25	23	23	23	23	24	24	25	26	27	26	28	26	27

Source: Flow of funds accounts, board of governors of the federal reserve system.

Table 11.A24 Percentage distribution of real-estate mortgage loans by lender

	1950			*1960*			*1970*			*1980*			*1985*			*1992 3rd qtr*		
	HM	*MM*	*CM*	*HM*	*MM*	*CM*	*HM*	*MM*	*CM*	*HM*	*MM*	*CM*	*HM*	*MM*	*CM*	*HM*	*MM*	*CM*
Commercial banks (%)	21.0	10.2	18.1	13.6	5.4	20.4	14.4	5.5	27.2	16.8	9.1	31.6	14.3	10.9	37.7	16.8	13.2	45.2
Savings and loans (%)	29.0	2.5	2.5	39.0	10.5	7.5	41.9	22.9	13.4	43.0	26.8	17.7	32.6	34.9	19.6	14.3	19.8	6.9
Savings banks (%)	9.5	29.5	9.3	14.5	18.0	7.7	14.3	13.0	9.2	7.1	11.3	6.4	5.1	6.8	4.2	3.3	5.3	3.2
Credit unions (%)	0.1	0.0	0.0	0.3	0.0	0.0	0.3	0.0	0.0	0.5	0.0	0.0	0.8	0.0	0.0	1.7	0.0	0.0
Life insurance companies (%)	18.8	28.1	29.4	17.5	18.6	30.1	9.1	26.6	30.4	1.9	10.0	31.6	0.8	9.3	26.6	0.4	10.0	29.0
Private pension funds (%)	0.1	0.3	0.2	0.4	1.7	1.0	0.6	2.0	1.4	0.1	0.3	0.7	0.1	0.6	0.8	0.3	0.2	1.7
State and local government retirement funds (%)	0.1	0.3	0.1	0.6	2.2	0.5	1.0	3.3	1.1	0.4	2.7	1.4	0.2	2.8	1.2	0.2	1.4	1.4
Finance companies (%)	0.8	0.4	0.1	1.0	0.8	0.2	2.0	2.0	0.4	2.6	1.5	1.2	3.1	0.9	0.9	7.1	1.3	1.6
REITs (%)	0.0	0.0	0.0	0.0	0.0	0.0	0.2	2.1	2.4	0.0	1.1	0.9	0.0	0.8	0.8	0.0	0.9	0.7
Mortgage pools (%)	0.0	0.0	0.0	0.0	0.0	0.0	1.0	0.1	0.0	11.2	4.2	0.0	24.3	3.3	0.0	40.3	8.4	0.0
Government sponsored enterprises (%)	0.0	0.0	0.0	2.0	0.0	0.0	5.3	0.5	0.0	6.1	4.7	0.0	7.2	4.0	0.0	5.4	5.3	0.0
US government (%)	3.3	0.4	0.1	3.0	4.9	0.1	2.1	5.1	0.5	1.9	7.3	2.2	1.6	4.8	1.7	1.2	9.8	2.5
State and local governments (%)	0.5	0.0	0.0	1.0	0.1	0.0	0.6	3.3	0.2	2.1	7.5	0.7	3.0	10.9	0.9	2.1	14.3	1.5
Households (%)	16.8	28.0	39.2	7.2	37.9	32.1	7.6	13.2	13.5	6.3	10.1	5.3	5.8	5.9	0.6	6.4	7.5	4.5
Total assets ($ billions)	45	9	13	142	21	33	294	60	86	955	142	256	1490	214	480	3023	295	726

HM – Home mortgages.
MM – Multifamily mortgages.
CM – Commercial mortgages.
Source: Flow of funds accounts, board of governors of the federal reserve system.

Table 11.A25 Measures of money

	1950	*1960*	*1970*	*1980*	*1981*	*1982*	*1983*	*1984*	*1985*	*1986*	*1987*	*1988*	*1989*	*1990*	*1991*	*1992 3rd qtr*
M1 ($ billions)	119	144	226	415	442	481	525	552	621	726	752	790	794	825	898	1024
Currency (%)	21	20	22	28	28	28	28	28	27	25	26	27	28	30	30	29
Travelers checks (%)	NA	NA	NA	1	1	1	1	1	1	1	1	1	1	1	1	1
Demand deposits (%)	79	80	78	64	53	50	46	44	43	42	38	37	35	34	32	33
Other checkable deposits (%)	NA	NA	NA	7	18	21	25	27	29	32	34	36	36	36	37	38
M2 ($ billions)	NA	217	428	1633	1797	1965	2196	2364	2567	2811	2910	3069	3223	3328	3440	3504
M1 (%)	NA	66	53	25	25	24	24	23	24	26	26	26	25	25	26	29
Overnight RPs and eurodollars (%)	NA	NA	NA	1	2	5	20	21	23	24	21	19	17	8	3	2
MMMF balances (%)	NA	NA	NA	4	8	9	6	7	7	7	8	8	10	4	10	10
Savings deposits (%)	NA	34	47	25	19	18	14	12	12	13	14	14	13	28	30	34
Small time deposits (%)	NA	NA	NA	45	46	44	36	37	34	30	31	33	35	35	31	25

Source: Flow of funds accounts, board of governors of the federal reserve system.

Notes

1. For analyses of the legislation of the 1980s, see Barth (1991), Barth and Brumbaugh (1990), Benston and Kaufman (1993), Brumbaugh (1988, 1993), Brumbaugh and Scott (1992), Brumbaugh and Litan (199), Carnell (1992), and Kane (1983, 1985, 1986).
2. For additional discussion, see Merton (1992).
3. For additional discussion, see Merton and Bodie (1992) and Stiglitz (1992).
4. For a detailed discussion of the moral-hazard and agency problems as they apply to depositories, see Barth and Brumbaugh (1992) and the references cited therein.
5. See Barth (1991).
6. See Barth, Brumbaugh and Litan (1992).
7. See Kane (1992, 1993) and Romer and Weingast (1992) for a discussion of this issue.
8. According to the Office of Management and Budget, the face value of all federal credit and insurance programs amounted to $6.8 trillion in 1992.
9. For a discussion, see Barth and Keleher (1984) and Kaufman (1988, 1992).
10. See Friedman and Schwartz (1963).
11. See Flannery (1982) and, for an historical perspective, Calomiris (1990 and 1992).
12. We use the terms 'intra- and inter-industry' to distinguish between government restrictions that most directly affect competition among federally insured depositories (intra-industry) and those that most directly effect competition between federally insured depositories and non-depositories (inter-industry). An analysis of relevant product and geographic markets for financial services would obviously result in significant overlap between depositories and non-depositories.
13. As Rhoades (1993) points out, the Federal Reserve uses a statistical measure of concentration that includes only 100 per cent of the deposits of commercial banks and at least 50 per cent of the deposits of thrift institutions.
14. As of December 1991, state-chartered, member banks were 8 per cent of all federally insured banks; state-chartered, non-member banks were 60 per cent of all insured banks; and the remaining 32 per cent of federally insured banks were national banks. For a discussion of these and related issues, see Wells, Jackson and Murphy (1992).
15. In May 1992, moreover, the OTS rewrote regulations to pre-empt state controls over savings and loans' entry into new states. Interstate branching by savings and loans is therefore currently decided solely by the OTS.
16. See Cox and Klinkerman (1993).
17. Selected state authorities first authorized adjustable-rate mortgages for savings and loans, with the Congress prohibiting their use nationwide until after the industry suffered enormously from sharply rising interest rates in the late 1970s.
18. The Federal Housing Enterprises Financial Safety and Soundness Act of 1992 set minimum capital requirements for Fannie Mae and Freddie Mac at 2.50 per cent of on-balance sheet assets, plus 0.45 per cent of outstanding mortgage-backed securities and substantially equivalent instruments, including 50 per cent of commitment to purchase mortgages.

19. For a thorough discussion of federal credit programs, see Bosworth, Carron and Rhyne (1987).
20. See, for example, Minsky, Papadimitriou, Phillips and Wray (1993).
21. For discussions of the changing nature of the financial services market and the effects on depositories, see Barth (1991), Barth and Bartholomew (1992), Barth and Brumbaugh (1992), Barth, Brumbaugh and Litan (1992), Brumbaugh (1988, 1993), Congressional Research Service (1992), Gorton and Pennacchi (1992), Kane (1985), and Litan (1987, 1991).
22. From 1980 through June 1992, more than 4500 federally insured depositories failed with assets of more than $630 billion at a present-value cost of about $150 billion to the deposit-insurance funds and taxpayers. For a discussion of the budgetary implications, and implications for deposit-insurance reform, see Congressional Budget Office (1991).
23. See Peltzman (1965, 1976), Posner (1974), and Stigler (1971).
24. Whereas non-financial commercial paper outstanding as a proportion of banks' commercial and industrial loans outstanding was 10.6 per cent in 1979, it had grown to 21.2 per cent in 1991. For more information on the difficulties facing commercial banks in the past decade, see Barth, Brumbaugh and Litan (1992), Gorton and Pennachi (1992), and Litan (1991).
25. In the Appendix tables for commercial banks and savings and loans, the data are obtained from the Congressional Budget Office and the Flow of Funds Accounts of the Federal Reserve. In some cases there are discrepancies between the two sources of data for a given activity. The discrepancies do not alter the basic patterns we describe.
26. Through early 1993 the RTC itself had securitized $20 billion of commercial mortgages, with more securitization likely to follow.
27. See Barth and Brumbaugh (1992).
28. An example of such a tactic is CEBA, which closed the nonbank bank loophole leaving 168 such institutions currently operating because of a grandfather clause.
29. See, for example, Beaver, Datar and Wolfson (1992).
30. For an excellent description of early developments relating to the narrow bank, see Phillips (1993).

References

Bagehot, Walter (1962) *Lombard Street* (Homewood, IL: Irwin).

Barth, James R. (1991) *The Great Savings and Loan Debacle* (Washington, DC: The American Enterprise Institute).

Barth, James R. and Philip F. Bartholomew (eds) (1992) *Emerging Challenges for the International Financial Services Industry* (Greenwich, CT: JAI Press).

Barth, James R. and R. Dan Brumbaugh, Jr. (1990) 'The Continuing Bungling of the Savings and Loan Crisis: The Rough Road from FIRREA to the Reform of Deposit Insurance', *Stanford Law and Policy Review* (Spring) **2**.

Barth, James R. and R. Dan Brumbraugh (eds) (1992) *The Reform of Federal Deposit Insurance: Disciplining the Government and Protecting Taxpayers* (New York, NY: HarperBusiness).

Barth, James R. and R. Dan Brumbaugh (1992) 'Depository Institution Failures and Failure Costs: The Role of Moral-Hazard and Agency Problems', Conference on Rebuilding Public Confidence through Financial Reform (Columbus, OH: Ohio State University, 29 June).

Barth, James R., R. Dan Brumbaugh, Jr. and Robert E. Litan (1992) *The Future of American Banking*, the Columbia University Seminars Series (Armonk, NY: M. E. Sharpe, Inc).

Barth, James R. and Robert Keleher (1984) 'Financial Crises and the Role of the Lender of Last Resort', *Economic Review* (Federal Reserve Bank of Atlanta).

Beaver, William H., Srikant Datar and Mark A. Wolfson (1992) 'The Role of Market Value Accounting in the Regulation of Insured Depository Institutions', in James R. Barth and R. Dan Brumbaugh, Jr. (eds), *The Reform of Federal Deposit Insurance: Disciplining the Government and Protecting Taxpayers* (New York, NY: HarperBusiness).

Benston, George J. (1989) 'The Federal 'Safety Net' and the Repeal of the Glass–Steagall's Separation of Commercial and Investment Banking', *Journal of Financial Services Research* (September) 2.

Benston, George J., R. Dan Brumbaugh, Jr., Jack M. Guttentag, Richard J. Herring, George G. Kaufman, Robert E. Litan and Kenneth E. Scott (1989) *Blueprint for Restructuring Banking and Financial Institutions: Report of a Task Force* (Washington, DC: Brookings Institution).

Benston, George J. and George G. Kaufman (1993) 'The Intellectual History of the Federal Deposit Insurance Corporation Improvement Act of 1991', Working Paper Series, Center for Financial and Policy Studies (Chicago: Loyola University).

Bosworth, Barry P., Andrew S. Carron and Elizabeth H. Rhyne (1987) *The Economics of Federal Credit Programs* (Washington, DC: Brookings Institution).

Brumbaugh, R. Dan, Jr. (1988) *Thrifts Under Siege: Restoring Order to American Banking* (Cambridge, MA: Ballinger).

Brumbaugh, R. Dan, Jr. (1993) *The Collapse of Federally Insured Depositories: The Savings and Loans as Precursor* (New York: Garland).

Brumbaugh, R. Dan, Jr. and Robert E. Litan (1991) 'Ignoring Economics in Dealing with the Savings and Loan and Commercial Banking Crisis', *Contemporary Policy Issues* (January) IX:1.

Brumbaugh, R. Dan, Jr. and Robert E. Litan (1992) 'A Critique of the Financial Institutions Recovery, Reform and Enforcement Act (FIRREA) of 1989 and the Financial Strength of Commercial Banks', in James R. Barth and R. Dan Brumbaugh, Jr. (eds), *The Reform of Federal Deposit Insurance: Disciplining the Government and Protecting Taxpayers* (New York, NY: HarperBusiness).

Brumbaugh, R. Dan, Jr. and Kenneth E. Scott (1992) 'The Endless Banking Crisis: Prospects for Reform in 1992', *Challenge* (March/April).

Calomiris, Charles W. (1992) 'Getting the Incentives Right in the Current Deposit Insurance System: Successes from the Pre-FDIC Era', in James R. Barth and R. Dan Brumbaugh, Jr. (eds), *The Reform of Federal Deposit Insurance:*

Disciplining the Government and Protecting Taxpayers (New York, NY: HarperBusiness).

Calomiris, Charles W. (1990) 'Is Deposit Insurance Necessary?: A Historical Perspective', *Journal of Economic History* (June).

Carnell, Richard Scott (1992) 'A Partial Antidote to Perverse Incentives: the FDIC Improvement Act of 1991', Conference on Rebuilding Public Confidence through Financial Reform (Columbus, OH: Ohio State University, 29 June).

Carron, Andrew S. and R. Dan Brumbaugh, Jr. (1991) 'The Viability of the Thrift Industry', *Housing Policy Debate* (Federal National Mortgage Association, Summer).

Congressional Budget Office (1991) *Budgetary Treatment of Deposit Insurance: A Framework for Reform* (May).

Cox, Robert B. and Steven Klinkerman (1993) 'Iowa Banks Fight Expansion by Norwest', *American Banker* (11 March).

Flannery, Mark J. (1982) 'Deposit Insurance Creates a Need for Bank Regulation', *Business Review* (Federal Reserve Bank of Philadelphia, January/February).

Friedman, Milton and Anna J. Schwartz (1963) *A Monetary History of the United States, 1867–1960* (Princeton, NJ: Princeton University Press).

Gorton, Gary and George Pennacchi (1992) 'Financial Innovation and the Provision of Liquidity Services', in James R. Barth and R Dan Brumbaugh, Jr. (eds), *The Reform of Federal Deposit Insurance: Disciplining the Government and Protecting Taxpayers* (New York, NY: HarperBusiness).

Kane, Edward J. (1983) 'A Six-Point Program for Deposit Insurance Reform', *Housing Finance Review* (July).

Kane, Edward J. (1985) *The Gathering Crisis in Federal Deposit Insurance* (Cambridge, MA: MIT Press).

Kane, Edward J. 'Confronting Incentive Problems in US Deposit Insurance: The Range of Alternative Solutions', in George G. Kaufman and Roger C. Kormendi (eds), *Deregulation Financial Services, Public Policy in Flux* (Cambridge, MA: Ballinger).

Kane, Edward J. 'The Political Foundations of the Thrift Debacle: The Incentive Incompatibility of Government-Sponsored Deposit Insurance Funds', in James R. Barth and R. Dan Brumbaugh, Jr (eds), *The Reform of Federal Deposit Insurance: Disciplining the Government and Protecting Taxpayers* (New York, NY: HarperBusiness).

Kane, Edward J. (1993) 'Banking Reform as Market-Constrained Political Process', prepared for the 1993 meeting of the American Association for the Advancement of Science (3 February).

Kaufman, George C. (1988) 'The Truth about Bank Runs', in Catherine England and Thomas Huerta (eds), *The Financial Services Revolution: Policy Directions for the Future* (Boston: Kluwer).

Kaufman, George C. (1992) Lender of Last Resort, Too Large to Fail and Deposit Insurance Reform', in James R. Barth and R. Dan Brumbaugh, Jr (eds), *The Reform of Federal Deposit Insurance: Disciplining the Government and Protecting Taxpayers* (New York, NY: HarperBusiness).

Litan, Robert E. (1987) *What Should Banks Do?* (Washington, DC: The Brookings Institution).

Litan, Robert E. (1991) *The Revolution in U.S. Finance* (Washington, DC: The Brookings Institution).

Meltzer, Allan H. 'Financial Failures and Financial Policies', in George G. Kaufman and Roger C. Kormendi (eds), *Deregulating Financial Services: Public Policy in Flux* (Cambridge, MA: Ballinger).

Merton, Robert C. (1992) 'Operation and Regulation in Financial Intermediation: A Functional Perspective', mimeo (September).

Merton, Robert C., and Bodie, Zvi (1992) 'On the Management of Financial Guarantees', *Journal of the Financial Management Association* (Winter) 21:1.

Minsky, Hyman P., Dimitri B. Papadimitriou, Ronnie J. Phillips and L. Randall Wray (1993) 'Community Development Banking', Public Policy Brief, The Jerome Levy Economics Institute of Bard College, no. 3 and Chapter 13, this volume.

Passmore, Wayne (1992) 'Can Retail Depositories Fund Mortgages Profitably?' *Journal of Housing Research*, **3:1**.

Peltzman, Sam (1965) 'Entry in Commercial Banking', *Journal of Law and Economics* (October) **8**.

Peltzman, Sam (1976) 'Toward a More General Theory of Regulation', *Journal of Law and Economics* (August) **19**.

Phillips, Ronnie J. (1993) 'The "Chicago Plan" and New Deal Banking Reform', The Jerome Levy Economics Institute, Working Paper no. 76 (June) and Chapter 5, this volume.

Posner, Richard A. (1974) 'Theories of Economic Regulation', *Bell Journal of Economics and Management Science* (Autumn) **5**.

Rhoades, Stephen A. (1993) 'The Herfindahl–Hirschman Index', *The Federal Reserve Bulletin* (March).

Romer, Thomas and Barry R. Weingast (1992) 'Political Foundations of the Thrift Debacle', James R. Barth and R. Dan Brumbaugh, Jr. (eds), *The Reform of Federal Deposit Insurance: Disciplining the Government and Protecting Taxpayers* (New York, NY: HarperBusiness).

Shadow Financial Regulatory Committee, Statement on an Outline of a Program for Deposit Insurance and Regulatory Reform, 13 February 1989, in George G. Kaufman (ed.), 'Shadow Financial Regulatory Committee Statements Numbers 1–69', *Journal of Financial Services Research*, **6:2**.

Stigler, George J. (1971) 'The Theory of Economic Regulation', *Bell Journal of Economics and Management Science* (Spring).

Stiglitz, Joseph E. (1992) 'S&L Bailout', James R. Barth and R. Dan Brumbaugh, Jr. (eds), *The Reform of Federal Deposit Insurance: Disciplining the Government and Protecting Taxpayers* (New York, NY: HarperBusiness).

Stiglitz, Joseph E. (1993) 'The Role of the State in Financial Markets', mimeo.

Wells, Jean F., William D. Jackson and M. Maureen Murphy (1992) 'Commercial Banking: An Analytical Survey of Its Regulation and Structure', *CRS Report for Congress*, Congressional Research Service, The Library of Congress (Washington, DC, 8 September).

Comment

GARY A. DYMSKI

Discussions of financial reform too often reduce to how much deregulation to allow in banks' geographic, product and ownership markets. But, because of the depth of the US financial intermediation crisis, adequate reform proposals should describe what functions the financial system should perform, as well as what structural modifications should be made. Barth and Brumbaugh have taken the harder, second path.

For the authors, the financial system has two *intrinsic* functions. First, it should provide stable payments and credit mechanisms. Second, it should allocate scarce resources efficiently: that is, lenders should earn the maximum competitive return on their financial assets, while credit should flow to those borrowers best able to use the economy's savings productively.[1] In addition, the government may induce or coerce the financial system into performing *extrinsic* functions. For example, financial intermediaries provide 'merit goods' such as credit or transactions services in low-income areas in response to governmental incentives or directives.[2]

In the authors' view, the crisis in the US banking system has arisen because government interventions designed to achieve the first intrinsic function have gradually undercut banks' performance of the second. Technological change has not only made financial arrangements more efficient, it has created inter-industry competition; this, in turn, has made financial resource allocation more efficient. This sea-change in financial structures has also exposed the hidden costs imposed by regulatory strictures. Much of the inefficiency in resource allocation can be traced to governmental limitations on geographic location, activities, and market entry and exit. Whatever benefits these checks on competition once provided are now exhausted, and barriers to competition should be speedily dismantled. All financial intermediaries should be exposed to no more oversight than the SEC provides for securities firms. The authors believe that efficient credit allocation will result, but concede that the stability of the payments mechanism will be put at risk. They advocate special arrangements for stable transactions services–including narrow banks and a governmental mutual fund which could provide low-cost transactions for low-income households.

These changes would allow banks' transformation into diversified financial services firms. Post-reform, banks will be less involved in intermediation – that is, in information-intensive monitoring of borrowers, since technical change has, in the author's view:

> reduced the need for depositories to intermediate between borrowers and lenders by gathering, evaluating, and monitoring information on borrowers that was too costly an activity for lenders themselves to perform. Securitization, for example, has turned formally illiquid assets on bank balance sheets like mortgages ... into securities ... the manifestations ... are new products, new firms ... and lower prices for products.

I agree with these authors on many points: regulations that squeeze only some market participants are counterproductive; the scope of deposit insurance should be restricted; the lesser role of thrifts and of commercial banks in mortgage and other lending markets has to be acknowledged. I agree that special steps must be taken to insure that low-cost transactions facilities are readily available for all. Nonetheless, my own view differs about what is dysfunctional in the financial system, and how it should be fixed.[3]

My discussion here centers on my most emphatic disagreement. The authors contend that credit-market outcomes will be more efficient, the more banks are integrated into modern financial markets. Banks can no longer turn a profit on many of their traditional intermediation activities; but fortunately, banks are no longer needed as financial intermediaries, because technology-driven innovations insure that credit markets are efficient. I disagree. In my view, the intermediation function remains viable for banking firms, *and* it remains crucial in the US economy. The withdrawal of banks as information-intensive intermediaries has profoundly deleterious consequences for the total – private *and* social – efficiency of credit-market outcomes. This has already been demonstrated in one ongoing experiment: the experience over the past 25 years of lower-income and minority neighborhoods in American cities. Barth and Brumbaugh have ignored an important public-good aspect of credit markets; and this has led them to misassess how financial reforms will affect the financial system's performance of its functions. In their assessment, *competition guarantees an efficient allocation of credit.*

There can be little argument that a stable financial environment and an efficient allocation of resources are goals for any financial system. We might be more specific, and define a socially efficient allocation as one that supports productive investment, and fosters economic opportunity by channeling financial resources to neglected areas and to economically productive units that lack resources.[4] Contrary to Barth and Brumbaugh, fewer constraints on financial competition will not bring about a socially efficient allocation of credit.

In these authors' conception, financial innovations are bringing US society ever closer to the idealized efficient capital markets envisioned in modern finance theory. The information and computer revolutions are reducing the extent of private information about borrowers, in this view; so lenders in credit markets can assess creditworthiness at arms' length – by reading credit reports – much more accurately than in the past. The need for institutions to intermediate between lenders and borrowers is correspondingly greatly reduced, if not eliminated.

If this point is granted, then the real sector generates a fixed set of credit demands for financial markets; the role of intermediaries and of innovative instruments is to segment and redistribute risks and returns. So, worthy borrowers find lenders at the market price of credit; and the system of intermediation allocates a fixed pool of savings. Resources will not find their 'best and highest use' if impediments restrain market prices or market entry and exit. Financial innovation by market participants is then market completion; it allows more efficient arbitrage.

But competition has not eliminated intermediation or credit-market segmentation. This argument misinterprets the character of competition among intermediaries in the past several years. Competition has been fierce. However, it has been limited to portions of the spectrum of borrowers and lenders. The credit market remains split into distinct segments, and increased competition has widened the gap between these segments, not erased it.

Figure 11.C1 describes one crucial disjuncture in credit markets – that between borrowers with direct access to lenders and borrowers who must access credit indirectly through intermediaries. Borrowers separate into these two markets based on their size, reputation, experience and net worth. Lenders can, in principle, easily ascertain all the information they need about borrower creditworthiness at arms' length in direct finance markets; but intermediated markets, by contrast, arise, in the first place, due to intermediaries' role as information specialists.

Innovations in the commercial credit and corporate bond markets have vastly increased the volume of direct finance, causing some banks to lose their largest credit customers. Banks that lost these customers adjusted by opening new borrowing markets (with sometimes disastrous results, as with loans for LDCs and commercial real estate), and by servicing their former credit customers in new ways. This is the shift from an 'intermedi-

	Borrower types (polar extremes):	
	Large size; vast experience; established reputation; substantial net worth and collateral	Small size; little experience and reputation; small net worth and collateral
Credit market access:	Choice of direct finance (commercial paper, bonds) or intermediated credit	Reliant on intermediated credit (loans, lines of credit)
Distribution of information:	Effectively symmetric; lenders know all the need to about borrowers	Asymmetric; assessing creditworthiness involves costly processes
Role of intermediary:	Broker role: backup credit facilities, lines of credit, guarantees	Intermediation role: Creditworthiness assessment, information-intensive monitoring of borrowers
Intermediary's income basis:	Fees	Lending margin

Figure 11.C1 Borrower types and intermediary roles

ation' to a 'broker' role highlighted by Barth and Brumbaugh. To a large extent, bank competition has involved a contest to gain market share – or to regain a market role – in these markets. Borrowers requiring intermediation have not been pursued as assiduously, except in lending areas with

Table 11.C1 Money center versus superregional banks: some comparisons for 1990 and 1991

AGGREGATE FIGURES

BANK GROUP:	Money Center Bks		% Change	Superregionals		% Change
YEAR:	1990	1991	1990–91	1990	1991	1990–91
Total Assets	792.1	798.4	0.80	799.531	828.9	3.67
Total Loans (est.)	446.34	416.69	–6.64	512.70	570.77	11.33
Total Deposits	470.65	466.59	–0.86	600.89	635.05	5.69
Total Tier-1 Capital	40.18	44.60	11.00	40.71	43.57	7.03
Loss Provisions	5.31	6.77	27.41	7.66	9.14	19.25
Net Earnings Total	3.35	2.66	–20.52	3.49	2.58	–26.02

FINANCIAL RATIOS

BANK GROUP:	Money Center Bks		Superregionals	
YEAR:	1990	1991	1990	1991
Loans as % of Assets	56.35	52.19	64.12	68.86
Deposits as % of Assets	59.42	58.44	75.16	76.61
Tier-1 Capital as % of Assets	5.12	5.50	6.16	7.19
Loss Prov's as % of Loans	1.19	1.62	1.49	1.60
Nonperformg Assets as % of Assets	3.90	4.07	2.87	3.13

Table 11.C1 Continued

COMPETITIVE FACTORS						
BANK GROUP:	Money Center Bks		% Change	Super-regionals		% Change
YEAR:	1990	1991	1990 91	1990	1991	1990 91
Net Interest Margin	2.58	2.81	8.93	4.15	4.30	3.50
Net Interest Income	17.52	18.65	6.47	22.01	23.65	7.43
Net Noninterest Income	17.51	18.55	5.95	11.11	12.73	14.65
Noninterest Income as as % of Interest Income	106.66	111.55		54.24	56.98	
Noninterest Expenses ($B)	25.20	26.63	5.68	25.11	27.53	9.63
Noninterest Expenses as % of Assets	3.27	3.43		2.99	3.16	

Notes: Banks are classified as 'money center' or 'super-regional' based on the criteria set forth in the *American Banker* (26 November, 1991). Money center banks are large in assets; oriented toward commercial and industrial loans, many of which are securitized; non-core funded; and international in scope. Super-regional banks have at least $20 billion in assets and full commercial banking presence across state lines. Tier 1 capital consists of the invested value of all true equity claims (primarily common shares). All data are drawn from earning statements published in the *American Banker* in October 1991 and January 1992.

secondary markets, where loans can be booked and sold off (as with mortgage and credit-card debt).

The extent of the shift out of intermediation is exaggerated, however, as is the notion that no money can be made by intermediaries that actually intermediate. The authors' perspective on these issues may stem from their primary focus having been on money-center banks. Table 11.C1 provides balance-sheet data for money-center and super-regional banks for 1990 and 1991. The data clearly shows that money-center banks (such as J. P. Morgan) have, indeed, shifted away from intermediation – loans are growing less important in their asset portfolios, and fee income is larger than interest income. But, this picture is reversed for super-regional banks (such as NationsBank): this group, which was pulling ahead of the money-centers in assets and capital during this period, earns much more of its income from interest income, and has a substantially higher loan-to-asset ratio.

However, even in intermediated credit markets, segmentation has occurred: in this case, it is geographic. Figure 11.C2 characterizes the differences between well-served and underserved geographic areas. Well-served areas, which have extensive branch networks and substantial depository loan volumes, usually have financially secure households and adequate public and commercial infrastructures; and vice versa for most underserved areas.[5]

Intermediated credit flows for geographically fixed assets generate 'spillover' effects. In any market, 'public-good' effects skew market outcomes – and may necessitate public intervention – because prices won't fully capture benefits and costs for buyers and sellers. Barth and Brumbaugh acknowledge that information about bank solvency may have 'public good' effects and, thus, that some public oversight of bank solvency is warranted. But another 'public-good' dimension has been overlooked; when fully considered, it leads to very different conclusions about the nature of credit-market efficiency.[6]

A 'spillover' effect accompanies credit-market flows that finance the sale or upgrade of *geographically fixed assets* – that is, of most homes and smaller businesses. These are invariably intermediated credit flows as shown in Figure 11.C1. Because these assets are immobile, their value when bought or sold depends not only on their own condition, but also on the perceived condition of the surrounding environment. Any buyer or financier of such assets assesses not only the current status of the asset, but the anticipated trajectory of values in the surrounding environment. Its price will be severely discounted if difficulties in reselling it are anticipated.

	Type of geographic segment (polar extremes):	
	Well served: extensive branch network of insured depositories	Underserved: few or no branches of insured depositories
Household characteristics	Stable jobs, incomes; large accumulated financial wealth	Intermittent jobs, unstable incomes; little accumulated financial wealth
Community characteristics:	Well-maintained and adequate public infrastructure, commercial outlets, physically secure	Poorly-maintained and inadequate public infrastructure, few commercial outlets, unsafe
Costs of intermediation	Marginal cost of signal extraction and loan monitoring	Marginal cost of signalling and monitoring plus xed (bricks and mortar) costs
Returns to intermediation:	Private returns plus spillover returns	Private returns only; spillovers are not captured
Character of competition:	Intense competition among insured intermediaries; few informal-sector lenders	Monopoly rents extracted by intermediaries; informal-sector lenders charge exorbitant rates
Credit market outcomes (for the polar cases)	Large cash-flows-based credit flows by insured depositories, resulting in wealth accumulation over time	Large collateral-based credit flows by informal-sector lenders, resulting in wealth reduction over time

Figure 11.C2 Geographic segments in intermediated credit markets

The benefits from financing any geographically fixed asset spill over to the assets surrounding it; but, these social benefits will be *captured* only if other buyers or lenders invest in the community. So, the return any bank can expect from lending in any community depends, in part, on how much lending other banks have done there. If enough lending supports asset values in a community, a qualitative transformation may occur as spillover effects are captured.

A ‘Catch 22’, thus, pertains to lending and other economic activity levels in any given community. The availability of jobs and the value of homes and businesses depends on whether bank credit is available there for residents and firm owners. But the volume of credit on assets in the community depend on the value of homes and businesses.

These spillover effects clearly may set off unstable dynamic trajectories. Over time, economic units in communities receiving lower credit flows will become relatively less creditworthy as the relative value of their properties lags behind values elsewhere. Areas with lower credit flows and declining values, in turn, will appear less attractive to depositories seeking borrowers. So some communities accumulate extensive bank branch networks and credit flows, and, in turn, job and business opportunities, while others languish and fall behind. Units in communities with robust credit flows and active asset resale markets can more readily build up equity than units in stagnating neighborhoods. In some neighborhoods, property titles change hands when households move out; in other neighborhoods, only residents’ names change.

Because of these unstable dynamics, slight initial differences in areas – which may be based on racial perceptions or on unequally distributed bank branches – will eventually rigidify into material differences. If enough lenders decide our area is a bad investment, they will make lending and locational decisions that, in combination with other factors, will bring their prophesy to pass. Unconstrained banking dynamics will tend to produce a checkboard pattern of prosperity and depression.[7]

Unconstrained competition will deepen credit-market segmentation and social inefficiency. If these spillover effects are important, then Barth and Brumbaugh’s core conclusions – that competition will bring about an efficient allocation of scarce financial resources, and that intermediation has become redundant because of technological change – do not hold. The notion of social efficiency used here assumes it is socially optimal for all communities’ residents and businesses to be able to capture spillover benefits from lending; in this way, opportunities for wealth accumulation by households and for expansion by businesses will be maximized.

Competition will not lead to a socially efficient allocation of credit in this sense because the spillover effects discussed above will drive a wedge between the social and private efficiency outcomes. Lenders are subject to a prisoner's dilemma: it is individually rational for any lender to invest in underserved communities *only* if other lenders do; but no others want to be first, so lenders collectively do not lend. Banks react to competitive pressure, and this has been coming from direct finance markets (and from mutual funds, on the liability side), *not* from other institutions committed to outperforming them in intermediation.

A second flaw in Barth and Brumbaugh's argument follows from the presence of spillover effects in lending: the stock of wealth allocated by the financial system is endogenous, not fixed. If spillover effects pervade the credit market, then credit-market participants' wealth (net worth) depends, to a large extent, on the previous pattern of credit commitments. Those who have not built up equity in their homes may simply have been starting from the 'wrong place'.

The third flaw in Barth and Brumbaugh's argument is perhaps the deepest: if the above argument is granted, then the very structure of credit markets is an endogenous social construct, not a pregiven datum. In this event, technically-driven financial innovations cannot be understood as simply performing an 'arbitrage' function for wealthholders' portfolios; rather, these innovations have to be understood as putting forces in motion that not only open some credit channels, but close other channels. Channel-closing would occur if the presence of new roles for bank resources caused these lenders to turn away from some intermediated markets in which they had previously been active.

This last point leads to the conclusion that intermediation is not redundant. Recognizing the tenuous connection between spillover effects and the volume of market participation, it is clear that at least some intermediated credit markets exist only if intermediaries are willing and able to expend the resources to keep them open. If intermediation disappears as an economic activity, then at least some of the intermediaries' borrowers will not be able to borrow.

How important are the spillover effects described here – in how many communities are credit flows so retarded that spillovers are not captured and asset values have atrophied? I have no direct empirical evidence to offer. Spillover effects could be one factor accounting for the significance of individual race and of community racial composition in residential credit flows (Dymski, Veitch and White, 1991; Munnell *et al.*, 1992). Informal empirical 'test' is available. A tour of many inner-city neighborhoods in the US would reveal a world of stunted economic flows.

Businesses in these neighborhoods are, in general, not thriving; many residents are not working; few own their homes; and many more fear for their job security. These communities' residents are often cut off from the mainstream of American life and opportunity. It is clear that lack of access to intermediation is not the only cause of this isolation, as Figure 11.C2 suggests; but it is equally clear that the paucity of intermediation is one key element in this pattern.

The chapter by Barth and Brumbaugh is too brief to address the question of whether the disappearance of intermediation means a reduced set of borrowers. It is instructive to consider the response of James Pierce (1991) to this question, since his approach is close to Barth and Brumbaugh. Pierce agrees that banks now largely duplicate what other players do, except for:

> furnishing loans to businesses too small to use securities markets. Banks have special expertise in assessing and monitoring such projects. One would not want this service to disappear, but it is probably less than 10% of what the banking industry does. Is it really necessary to protect and regulate the other 90% of bank activities to assure provision of this credit? (pp. 81–2).

The answer to his well-posed question is perhaps not the clear-cut negative he anticipates. *For isn't this '10%' of what banks do precisely their unique economic function in today's economy?* And isn't this '10%' concentrated in communities that have been isolated from the rapid currents of financial innovation in deposit and credit instruments?

Intermediation makes and unmakes credit markets, and many still need these markets. If my argument to this point is granted, several consequences follow: competition will not cause lenders to exploit all possible credit opportunities in all communities, because spillover effects will lead to a prisoner's-dilemma standoff; wealth is a function of the level of intermediation; and intermediation is not redundant, because intermediaries make some credit markets which would not otherwise exist. This argument has three implications for the debate on financial restructuring. First, to restore healthy asset markets in communities where lending is too low to capture spillovers, enhanced intermediation is needed. But there are many different types of underserved community, with very different credit needs; see Figure 11.C3. It makes a large difference whether residents typically have stable jobs, and whether the community has significant numbers of corporate offices and/or small businesses. A community whose residents generally have stable jobs, but which is 'red lined', needs con-

	Employment structure:	
Business structure:	Stable jobs for most residents	Few job options for most residents
Many large corporate offices	Credit needs: Consumer and housing-related credit flows to maintain and turn over properties	N/A
Many small businesses	Credit needs: Consumer and housing-related credit flows, plus small business working capital and expansion lending	Credit needs: Small business working capital and expansion lending, entrepreneurship capital; 'emergency' household lending
Few businesses of any kind	N/A	Credit needs: Entrepreneurship capital; 'emergency' household lending

Figure 11.C3 Community resource structures and credit needs

sumer and housing-related credit in sufficient volume to overcome spillover-effect barriers. A community whose adults often can find no jobs has a different set of needs, including emergency lending and 'entrepreneurial' lending.

The second implication of my argument is that restoring intermediation in underserved communities must occur on a sufficiently large scale to capture lending spillovers. This is one element in the successful redevelopment strategy pursued by the South Shore Bank of Chicago. The need for a 'large scale' effort in some communities may extend as well to jobs training and creation, social infrastructure rehabilitation, and so on.

The third implication is that reform proposals for community development banking, and more generally proposals for reforming the community reinvestment responsibilities of lenders, are an intrinsic part of the broader debate on how to restructure the US financial system. The notion of 'trading off' community reinvestment responsibilities for other concessions has already occurred to some participants in the debates over financial restructuring. The point made here is that such a 'trade off' may have deeper consequences, involving the root question with which we began – what functions are expected of the financial system, and specifically what functions are expected of financial intermediaries within that system.

It may be objected that these implications are too strong – that the legitimate intermediation needs of underserved communities will be met by private-market restructuring, so that publicly-mandated restructuring is unneeded. In considering this objection, it *should* be clear, first of all, that some banks – including the largest – are withdrawing from a direct intermediation role in underserved communities. Nationwide, many of the largest banks have been going through excruciating staff and branch reductions. These reductions are often associated with 'herd behavior' overlending in the LDC and commercial real-estate manias. But does the withdrawal of a Citibank mean that no other intermediaries will fill in the lending gap?

Apart from the big banks, there are three other contenders for the role of intermediary to the underserved. First are the smaller ('community') banks. Characteristically, these institutions have remained close to home in lending markets they know well. However, these smaller banks' lending margins have been squeezed by the rising cost of bank funds. A constraint on lending capacity looms for this sector. These banks already operate on slim margins. To increase the cost of financing their lending activity – as would occur if the narrow-banking proposal of Barth and Brumbaugh were adopted – could tip them into insolvency, with the result of decreased intermediation capacity.

The second possibility for serving the underserved is community development banking in some form. While many proposals for community development banks are now being prepared, one should keep in mind that there are less than a handful of these institutions now in operation. In general, the community development bank concept is an intriguing idea that cannot be fully evaluated because of paucity of experience. The analysis of this paper suggests that community development banks should not be designed as 'miniature' in scale if no other provision is made for enhanced lending in underserved communities. Our analysis also suggests that the lending areas authorized for these banks should be responsive to community credit needs (see Figure 11.C3).

The third possibility is to hope that informal-sector lenders (finance companies, mortgage brokers, and so on) motivated by profits will step into the intermediation gap and close it. Our analysis has suggested this is unlikely; the small scale on which these lenders operate would not allow them to capture lending spillovers. Further, as set out in Figure 11.C2, these informal lenders often make credit contracts aimed not at asset accumulation, but instead at asset liquidation. Many informal lenders aim at squeezing margins out of borrowers for a limited time, not at sustaining long-term relationships with these borrowers.[8]

So, it is not realistic to expect the problem of inadequate intermediation in underserved communities to solve itself. Instead, this problem should be addressed in the context of financial restructuring *per se*; for example, deposit insurance could be restricted to intermediaries that make 'socially productive' loans in underserved areas; or such intermediaries could be ceded a reduced deposit-insurance premium.

The reluctance of insured depositories to lend in underserved communities can be attributed to several intertwined factors, including spillover effects, banks' net worth crisis in the wake of the Basle Accords, banks' retrenchment in the wake of a reduced credit-market role, and so on. But this quandary should not be solved by eliminating banks' social responsibility. Rather, this obligation should be broadened to include all financial intermediaries. Many elements must go into restoring the vitality of ignored and underserved communities throughout the US. Financial intermediaries cannot do it single-handedly, but their presence as intermediaries and as socially functional institutions is crucial in any sustainable solution.

Notes

1. For the authors and for me, a 'lender' is a 'surplus unit' (Gurley and Shaw, 1960): a household or firm with more financial resources than it plans to spend in the near term.
2. The terminology 'intrinsic' and 'extrinsic' is mine. An extrinsic function involves an activity that the marketplace would provide much less of without governmental intervention.

3. I recently participated in a Economic Policy Institute working group that has suggested a progressive approach to financial restructuring, monetary policy, and investment policy (Dymski, Epstein and Pollin, 1993). This commentary draws on the ideas developed in that volume.
4. The definition of 'efficient allocation' used in modern equilibrium theory is replaced here with an older conception derived from Schumpeter. In Schumpeter's theory of economic development (1934), credit markets' crucial function is to transfer purchasing power from those who don't need it to entrepreneurs and innovators who do. This financial process parallels and precedes the technical innovation that would spur capitalist growth.
5. There are exceptions, usually involving the presence of a substantial proportion of people of color in the community in question. Note that the same segmentation we have described on the credit market has split the deposit/transactions-service market. Whereas in the past most wealth-holders held demand deposits, now new forms of transactions accounts and new distinctions between transactors (depending on balance levels) have proliferated. Those with higher balances are courted by numerous intermediaries; those with small ones often become unbanked, and must use money-order and check-cashing services, usually at much higher prices.
6. In economic theory, a 'public good' is one whose 'use by one agent does not prevent other agents from using it'; an 'externality' is an 'effect ... created by an economic agent other than the one who is affected and ... not transmitted through prices' (Laffont, 1988: 6, 33).
7. Clearly, while underserved geographic market segments not only receive less credit and have fewer bank branches, it is usually true that their residents have less stable jobs, and their communities' amenities and infrastructures are underdeveloped; see Figure 11.C2. There is not an opportunity here to delve into the 'chicken and egg' question of whether lower credit flows and lesser banking services reflect or generate lower economic growth. But see Dymski and Veitch (1992) for a discussion of the links between development and financial intermediation in six Los Angeles communities.
8. I recently did a comparative analysis (Dymski 1992) of the interrelations between formal and informal-sector credit, income flows and impoverishment in rural Bangladesh and inner-city Los Angeles. This analysis suggested that some of the beneficial aspects of informal-sector credit in Bangladesh could not be replicated in Los Angeles. The principal problem was the lack of any parallel in Los Angeles to the agricultural cycle in rural Bangladesh.

References

American Banker (1991) '1991 Performance of Top US Banking Companies; Performance Study Peer Groups', 26 November, p. 16.

American Banker (1991), 'Footnotes, Definitions, and Methodology', 26 November, p. 16.

American Banker, various issues from October 1991 to January 1992: Stories on Earnings statements of commercial banks.

Dymski, Gary (1992) 'On the Political Economy of Banking and Impoverishment', Working paper (Riverside, CA: University of California Department of Economics, August).

Dymski, Gary, Gerald Epstein and Robert Pollin (1993) *Transforming the US Financial System: An Equitable and Efficient Structure for the 21st Century* (Armonk, NY: M.E. Sharpe).

Dymski, Gary and John Veitch (1992) 'Race and the Financial Dynamics of Urban Growth: L.A. as Fay Wray', in Gerry Riposa and Caroline Dersh (eds), *City of Angels* (Dubuqe, IA: Kendall/Hunt Press) 131–58.

Dymski, Gary A., John Veitch and Michelle White (1991) *Taking it to the Bank: Race, Poverty and Credit in Los Angeles,* (Los Angeles: Western Center on Law and Poverty, November).

Gurley, John, and Edward Shaw (1960) *Money in a Theory of Finance* (Washington, DC: The Brookings Institution).

Laffont, Jean-Jacques (1988) *Fundamentals of Public Economics*, translated by John P. Bonin and Helene Bonin (Cambridge: MIT Press).

Munnell, Alicia H., Lynn E. Browne, James McEneaney and Geoffrey M. B. Tootell (1992) *Mortgage Lending in Boston: Interpreting HMDA Data*, Working Paper No. 92–7. (Boston: Federal Reserve Bank of Boston).

Pierce, James (1991) *The Future of Banking* (New Haven: Yale University Press).

Schumpeter, Joseph A. (1934) *The Theory of Economic Development* (Cambridge: Harvard University Press).

12 Narrow Banks: An Alternative Approach to Banking Reform*

Kenneth Spong

Banks for many years have been regarded as the pillar of stability in our financial system. Over the last decade, however, significant portions of the industry have been at the forefront of each recurring crisis, whether it be energy, agricultural, real estate, commercial or LDC lending. Bank lending helped foster a boom-bust cycle that went well beyond the basic economic fundamentals in each of these areas. These cycles all ended with increased bank failure rates and high loan losses. This result has further led to substantial declines in the bank insurance fund, causing many to question whether banking is headed in the same direction as the thrift industry with its continuing need for taxpayer funds.

These events provide a strong indication that banks may be suffering from something more serious than regional downturns or a run of bad luck. Recent banking problems demonstrate the need for significant and fundamental reform in the banking and financial system – a reform which would extend well beyond the changes incorporated in recent federal banking legislation.

This chapter examines this need for further banking reform and takes a closer look at one alternative – 'narrow banking' – which could dramatically change the structure and operation of the US financial system. The first section of the article discusses the need for fundamental banking reform, as demonstrated by the basic weaknesses inherent in the US financial system and in recent legislative efforts to reform it. The second part provides an overview of narrow banking, while the final section examines some of the more important questions that narrow banking might raise.

12.1 THE NEED FOR BANKING REFORM

Beginning with the 1980s, the US banking system has demonstrated a number of weaknesses, which seem linked in many cases to the structure of federal deposit insurance. Most notable among these weaknesses are: (1) an inability to maintain a safe and stable payments system without significant taxpayer liability, (2) a banking system that doesn't respond quickly or optimally to market forces in allocating credit and other banking services, and (3) a regulatory and legislative framework that is confining banks to a declining and more risky piece of the financial marketplace. While these banking problems have led to several major pieces of banking legislation and many suggestions for further reform, nearly all of the approaches seem to involve significant compromises and would fail to correct the basic flaws in our banking system.

12.1.1 Payments System Concerns

Since the 1930s, the United States has placed much reliance on federal deposit insurance, backed by the 'full faith and credit of the United States Government', in ensuring depositors of the safety of their funds and in protecting the payments system. The possibility of systemic problems and threats to the payments system have further extended this protection to uninsured depositors in large failing institutions. Overall, this deposit insurance system was generally able to accomplish its objectives until the 1980s, when bank and thrift industry problems led to losses in the bank insurance fund and to the substantial deficit and need for taxpayer funding in the thrift insurance fund.

Because of the nature of deposit insurance, most recent and proposed efforts to reduce taxpayer liability for deposit insurance would conceivably sacrifice some of the stability in our payments system. The Federal Deposit Insurance Corporation Improvement Act of 1991, for instance, attempts to protect taxpayers by limiting the protection that uninsured depositors in failing banks can receive. Several other reform ideas would go beyond this and cut back on the existing levels of deposit insurance coverage.

While the motive for such changes is understandable, a number of arguments suggest another approach is needed. First, a safe transactions and clearing system is more critical to the nation's financial welfare than ever before. The volume and complexity of financial transactions have increased greatly across the economy, and these transactions rely on the existence of a widely acceptable stock of money and a smoothly functioning payments mechanism.

Also, the typical depositor is likely to have a strong preference and expectation of safety and certainty in financial transactions, particularly given the payments system technology available today and the level of resources devoted to the banking system and its regulation. Most depositors, moreover, hold checking accounts almost entirely for the services of making and receiving payments and have far less of a concern over the investment aspects of these accounts. Consequently, the likelihood of occasional disruptions to this transactions framework could reduce public confidence in the financial system, keep the level of business activity from reaching its full potential, and divert an inordinate volume of resources toward tracking transactions or using less efficient alternatives.

Another argument for taking a different approach is that depositor discipline and the threat of loss for uninsured depositors may be hard to enforce. Many large depositors, for instance, may have the ability to react more quickly than the regulatory authorities in problem bank situations. They may also be able to find ways to circumvent any deposit insurance changes and thus avoid being exposed to losses. In addition, recent experience with large bank failures in the United States has shown that depositor discipline will likely raise a number of significant concerns. Major deposit disruptions and losses, for instance, could be harmful to a wide variety of bank customers, regional economies and their credit bases, and the reputation of the US banking and payments systems. These arguments, thus, imply that many proposals for reform may not only be inconsistent with the need for a stable payments system, but may face many practical and political difficulties as well.

12.1.2 Response to Market Forces

The need for a banking industry that is responsive to market forces has become quite evident with the lending problems that some banks have had in recent years. Banks have been at the forefront of nearly every lending crisis and have been extremely slow in working their way out of these problems and finding more favorable alternatives. Moreover, deposit insurance has given weak or high risk lenders virtually the same access to funds as the strongest lenders, thus diverting notable portions of bank lending toward less worthy ventures and away from alternatives more consistent with market needs.

The Federal Deposit Insurance Corporation Improvement Act of 1991 takes a few steps to encourage more market discipline and limit access to funding by problem institutions. Overall, however, this legislation appears to give bank regulators greater responsibility for controlling bank risk-taking, while leaving less of a role for bankers and other participants in the marketplace. The act prescribes exceedingly detailed standards and enforcement actions for banks, but no matter how well this framework is conceived, it will never be a substitute for market forces and the proper management of a bank. In addition, this regulation seems likely to impose a substantial cost burden on both problem and sound banks, while turning much bank decision making away from bankers and more into the hands of bank regulators, examiners, and federal lawmakers.

Recent developments, thus, seem incompatible with increasing the responsiveness of the banking system to market forces. Such developments, moreover, may tend to focus too much supervisory intensity on past banking problems and recent political and regulatory sentiments, thus leaving banks vulnerable to the next crisis – a crisis that will undoubtedly generate a call for even more detailed regulations and stronger intervention.

12.1.3 Future Role of Banks

Changes in the financial marketplace appear to be occurring in a direction counter to the traditional intermediary role of commercial banks. Over the last decade, the availability of financial information for individual investors and nonbank lenders has increased dramatically. In addition, substantial declines have occurred in the transaction costs for making many different types of investments. These developments are giving investors a greater ability to bypass traditional financial intermediaries and directly place their funds in the marketplace.

The same factors are further encouraging the creation of new financial instruments and an expansion in certain financial markets. Several examples of this are securitization of mortgages, consumer loans and other financial paper; introduction of derivative financial instruments; rapid growth in stock and money-market mutual funds; and expansion in commercial paper and other securities markets. In particular, the commercial paper market grew from less than $125 billion in obligations to over $560 billion in just a 10-year period.[1]

At the same time these developments were taking place, commercial banks began facing some changes that made them less able to compete. Compared to investors placing their funds directly in the market or through mutual fund alternatives, the use of banks as intermediaries has involved such additional costs as deposit insurance premiums, non-earning reserves, capital standards, corporate taxes and the burden of regulation.[2] In general, these costs appear to be rising with the higher insurance premiums, capital standards, and more extensive regulation brought on by the 1991 federal legislation and recent industry problems.

As a result of these changes, banks have been losing much of their prime corporate customer base to the commercial paper market and other direct sources of credit. Banks, in fact, have gone from once having over 90 per cent of the short-term business credit market to now having about 60 per cent of this market.[3] The added costs of intermediation compared to direct investment are also prompting banks to securitize and sell many of their other top quality assets.

This loss of business is even more notable because banks have not found many good substitutes. More and more, typical bank borrowers have become those with a very limited access to direct market funding, a need for specialized types of financing, and a risk exposure that is difficult to assess according to usual market standards. This shift in lending, thus, appears to be leaving banks with a less stable asset backing for deposits and a more volatile risk structure.

In addition to these lending changes, banks also have had difficulty in maintaining their share of the household savings market. Pension funds and mutual funds – stock, bond and money market – have been capturing a rising portion of this market at the expense of bank deposit products.[4] Money-market mutual funds gained rapidly when banks were constrained by deposit interest ceilings in the 1970s and early 1980s. These and other deposit alternatives, though, have continued to grow by offering investors an efficient and diversified means of access to financial markets. This broader choice of alternatives makes it unlikely that bank deposits will ever regain the importance they once held in the portfolios of bank customers.

The current banking framework and recent reforms are, thus, unlikely to give the public a banking system that is stable, responsive to market forces, and capable of adapting quickly to ongoing changes in the financial marketplace. Nonbank competition and financial innovation are taking away important pieces of the banking business that have previously provided much of its stability. Many of the commonly suggested banking reforms would increase the level of bank regulation, thereby hastening these trends and taking banking further away from the market process. In addition, ideas for reforming deposit insurance would typically place depositors and payments system stability at risk – all at a time when payments system technology should be capable of creating a more efficient and stable transactions framework. This result suggests that a different solution is needed – a solution that will make the banking system more flexible and move it back toward the market process, but still protect the integrity and confidence in our payments system.

12.2 NARROW BANKING AS A SOLUTION TO THE DEPOSIT INSURANCE PROBLEM

12.2.1 Overview of Narrow Banking

Narrow banking is one measure that could be more compatible with monetary stability, market discipline and ongoing financial developments. The term 'narrow banks' refers to banks that would offer deposit accounts and would back these accounts entirely with either marketable securities of extremely low risk or currency and equivalent holdings. Narrow banks would, thus, ensure a safe payments system through the risk-free nature of their balance sheets. The assets backing narrow bank deposits would provide ready funds to meet deposit withdrawals and would make narrow bank deposits the functional equivalent of currency. As a result, depositors could be confident about the safety and availability of their deposits, without putting taxpayers or others at risk.[5]

Narrow banks would receive income from the interest on their securities and from any fees they charge for transaction services. This income should enable them to cover operating costs and make interest payments on deposits.[6] Because of their need for only minimal amounts of capital, narrow banks could operate on low margins and still have a chance to achieve competitive returns on equity. In addition, narrow banks would encounter very little regulatory burden. They would only need to make frequent reports of their assets and deposits, subject to a quick regulatory verification on occasion.

Several different variations of narrow banking have been proposed as a means of reforming the financial system. One suggestion is to establish separate narrow banking entities which would only offer transaction accounts and related services. Any additional activities, such as traditional bank lending, would have to be split off into separate affiliate organizations funded on an uninsured basis. Because of the risk-free nature of narrow banks, these affiliate activities would not put narrow bank depositors at risk. As a consequence, a broader range of activities and a wider ownership structure might be possible for affiliates, compared to current banking limitations. In addition, affiliate activities could be left to the discipline of the uninsured investors and general market forces. These affiliates would, thus, have the freedom to adapt to ongoing financial developments and innovations.

Other narrow banking alternatives include 'deposited currency' and 'collateralized or secured money'. Banks or, in some cases, the federal government would have authority to offer these deposits. This set of alternatives would not require banks to be split into separate transaction and lending entities. Banks would be required to back their transaction accounts with liquid, low-risk securities, much as they do now with many public deposits. They could continue to offer other financial services or a selected group of such services, provided the funding for these activities was on an uninsured basis.[7]

A final alternative would be a variation of narrow banking and 100 per cent reserves. Under this option, narrow banks would hold their securities with the Federal Reserve or would back deposits with Federal Reserve accounts representing a proportionate interest in the System's portfolio of securities. This alternative would allow regulators to monitor, directly, a bank's security holdings.

The following analysis will focus primarily on narrow banks as separate banking entities, since this alternative provides the clearest distinction between transaction services and other financial activities. However, the other narrow banking alternatives would have virtually the same effects with respect to reforming the financial system and achieving the benefits of narrow banking.[8]

12.2.2 Comparative Benefits of Narrow Banking

Compared to recent legislation and other proposals for deposit insurance reform, narrow banking would offer two significant benefits. First, narrow banking would eliminate the fundamental problem in the current banking system – deposits available at par and on demand that are backed with illiquid and risky loans. This traditional bank asset/liability structure violates the basic principles of financial management by failing to provide an asset base with sufficient liquidity and security to support withdrawable deposits.[9]

Because of this structure, the survival and stability of the banking system depends on an extensive governmental support system – a system that seems to expand over time in response to banking crises, financial innovation, and the development of new bank assets and off-balance-sheet activities. Major elements in this safety net now include: (1) deposit insurance to give depositors confidence, (2) discount window lending to compensate for the illiquid assets at banks, and (3) detailed regulation and supervision to control bank activities and risk taking. Narrow banking would correct this unstable structure by requiring banks to match their deposits with assets that are liquid and of inherently low risk. Consequently, depositors could look directly to the narrow bank for safety and would no longer have any real need for deposit insurance and a complex system of governmental protection.[10]

A second, and related, benefit of narrow banking is that it could eliminate much of the need for extensive governmental involvement in bank lending and other policy decisions. The present banking system is a classic case of where governmental oversight has expanded from an important public policy objective – protection of depositors with transaction accounts and, thus, the payments system – to less appropriate objectives – review of private lending decisions and intervention in managerial and bank policymaking functions.

This credit and managerial oversight by public authorities can add its own distortions to the financial system and divert funds away from normal market channels. Deposit insurance contributes further distortions to the credit granting process by giving the weakest bank lenders the same access to funds as the strongest. While the $200 billion cost of the thrift bailout, along with recent losses in the bank insurance fund, provide some indication of the magnitude these distortions can assume, the total losses to the economy have undoubtedly been several times larger. These additional losses arise from the fact that the capital and assets of poorly managed banks and thrifts might have been directed by market forces into other pursuits yielding much higher returns to the overall economy.[11]

Narrow banking could eliminate much of this need for governmental intervention into bank lending and policy decisions. Lending and other risk taking functions would be shifted into uninsured affiliates where they would have no influence on depositor safety. Furthermore, affiliate activities could be subject to market discipline, which should provide more direction in channeling funds to the better lenders, curtailing funding access for others, and allowing banking organizations to adapt to market changes.

12.3 QUESTIONS THAT MIGHT BE RAISED BY NARROW BANKING

Narrow banking would require a significant restructuring of our financial system. Bank insured deposit and transaction activities would no longer be tied directly with credit activities, thus changing many customer relationships. The roles of many financial institutions would also change with the development of new lenders and the removal of competitive barriers between banks and other financial firms. This transformation of the financial system, consequently, raises many specific questions, which must first be addressed before the overall benefits, weaknesses, and implementation concerns of narrow banking can be judged.

12.3.1 Are There Sufficient Low-Risk Assets Available to Support a Narrow Bank Concept?

The feasibility of narrow banking will depend on whether organizations can obtain enough low-risk assets, such as short-term US Government securities, to back their deposits. This might appear to be a rather dramatic leap for many banks, but, somewhat surprisingly, perhaps, recent balance sheet information indicates that many organizations could reasonably make the transition.

To accomplish this, banking organizations must either already hold enough appropriate assets or be able to obtain any additional assets needed. In this regard, US commercial banks had $888 billion in domestic holdings of cash, reserves, balances with other institutions, and securities at mid-year 1992. This compared to domestic transaction deposits of $710 billion. In general, these numbers indicate that many banks may already have a good start toward constructing the type of asset base needed for a narrow banking system.[12]

Several changes, though, might be necessary in the securities held by banks. Since many of these securities now consist of notes, bonds and mortgage-related debt with maturities of several years or longer, a shift toward shorter maturities would be necessary to minimize any interest-rate exposure for narrow banks. Also, a few of the securities held by banks may not have the marketability or nearly riskless credit characteristics that would be desirable for narrow bank assets. Another limitation is that not all of the cash assets and securities should be viewed as freely available for supporting narrow bank deposits. Some might be used to support the operations of uninsured affiliates or to cover deposit runoffs and affiliate funding shortfalls in the transition to narrow banking.

Even with these qualifications, narrow banks and their parent organizations could conceivably make the necessary adjustments with only moderate changes in their operations and in securities markets.[13] Although short-term federal debt – the most plausible asset for narrow banks – barely exceeds the current volume of bank transaction accounts, the US Treasury would, seemingly, have the flexibility to supply additional amounts. This could include more short-term debt issuance or somewhat longer-term debt with a variable rate structure. Moreover, as narrow banks added to the demand for such instruments and banks sought to sell some of their longer-term securities, market conditions would provide support for this shift in US Treasury funding.[14] A transition period for narrow banking could further ease any market adjustments.

Another possible alternative would be to expand narrow banking assets to include a somewhat broader range of federal, state and local government securities and short-term, highly-rated corporate obligations.[15] Taken together, these instruments could amount to as much as $5 trillion, although narrow bank restrictions on asset maturity and marketability would result in a smaller volume of 'appropriate' securities. There are also other possibilities, including derivative investment products structured to have some payment streams of shorter maturity and very little credit risk. Several of these alternative investments, however, could leave narrow banks with a limited exposure to interest-rate or credit risks – risks that would have to be controlled by higher capital standards, closer monitoring of assets, diversification across the assets, and efforts by debt issuers to create safer securities.

12.3.2 What Would Happen to Credit Availability?

Narrow banking would redirect the existing credit functions of depository institutions toward bank credit affiliates and other market lenders. To a significant extent, a shift toward other market lenders is already occurring and seems likely to continue, based on the added costs banks face as regulated intermediaries. Narrow bank lending affiliates could give banking organizations the opportunity to avoid some of these costs and restructure their lending operations under a more efficient and flexible framework. At the same time, though, narrow bank affiliates would have to find sufficient uninsured funding before they could take over the lending roles now performed by the banking system.

To attract funding, narrow bank affiliates would have to meet the same market standards as other lenders for capitalization, asset quality and other relevant performance measures. With the low risk inherent in narrow banks, much of the equity now in the banking system could be directed toward credit affiliates, provided bank stockholders were willing to make this change. If this equity were to be shifted and the lending affiliates were to assume most bank lending operations, the affiliates, as a group, would be near, but still somewhat below, the equity ratios of comparable finance companies or short-term business lenders.[16]

Consequently, lending affiliates would need to take some steps to raise additional capital, reduce loan portfolios, or achieve an asset quality higher than other lenders. In many cases, these pressures are similar to what banks are already beginning to face under risk-based capital standards and 1991 banking legislation. A more flexible lending framework could help narrow bank affiliates attract additional capital, and the affiliates could also use securitization and asset sales or placements to reduce overall capital needs.

Other related considerations include whether lending by smaller banking organizations would be restricted due to a limited access to market funding and whether affiliate lenders would be willing to take on the many different types of loans offered by banks. Smaller organizations would, presumably, lack direct access to major credit markets and, thus, would have to obtain much of their funding from local investors, other lenders, bank customers that previously held time and savings deposits, and any new funding sources that might develop. While these sources could conceivably meet most needs, any shortfalls might require a small bank exemption from narrow banking or a lengthy transition period for these organizations.[17]

The type of lending by affiliates could differ in a number of ways from that of banks because of differences in funding and market pressures. Although banks seem destined to change part of their lending focus, they have traditionally been viewed as filling a number of borrowing needs not met by other market participants and serving as a backup source of liquidity for many borrowers. Market pressures might limit the ability of narrow bank affiliates to fill these roles. However, a strong demand for such services would, presumably, entice some affiliates or other lenders to maintain the capital backing and funding base necessary to serve different customers and provide various forms of credit enhancements.

A final factor that should lessen credit concerns under narrow banking is the decline in any advantages banks may have once had over other lenders. In recent years, the credit-granting abilities of nonbank lenders have increased substantially with the growth of securitization, commercial paper and other securities instruments. In fact, nonbank sources now represent the predominant force in most parts of the credit market, and this seems likely to continue in step with improvements in financial disclosure and the amount of credit reporting available to investors and nonbank lenders.[18]

As a result, nonbank lenders, investors and narrow bank affiliates would seem to be capable of fulfilling most, if not all, of the general credit needs of the economy. In a number of areas, funding could even be expected to improve if narrow bank affiliates were given the freedom to participate more extensively in debt and equity markets. In particular, with increased market discipline, the better lenders and the more creditworthy customers could actually be expected to gain better access to funding under a narrow banking framework.

12.3.3 Would Narrow Banks be Competitive with Other Financial Firms?

The competitiveness of narrow banks is important if they are to be a lasting part of the financial system and discourage other firms from developing new transaction or deposit substitutes. From a financial perspective, narrow banks, if free of major regulatory burdens, should be able to offer their depositors a return competitive with other low-risk investment alternatives.[19] Most of the potential competitors for narrow banks, such as money-market mutual funds and cash management accounts, are structured in much the same manner as narrow banks and would, thus, have few, if any, natural competitive advantages. Moreover, since narrow banks would be free to offer a complete range of payments services to the banking public, they might even have a competitive advantage over these other institutions.[20] Some of these competitors, in fact, could be expected to convert into narrow banks in order to gain access to the payments system.

From a stockholder's standpoint, efficiently operated narrow banks should also be competitive with other investments. Because narrow banks would need only limited amounts of capital to cover fixed assets and protect against fraud and other risks, they could operate with low margins and still achieve competitive returns on equity. Possible synergies between the transaction services at narrow banks and other financial products offered by affiliate companies would further increase the investment value of narrow banks.

A final competitive question is how narrow banking would compare with the current banking system. While some banking analysts have argued that narrow banking would suffer in comparison, this reform could conceivably offer several significant advantages.[21] Narrow banking would finally recognize checking accounts for what they actually are – a service in which balances are maintained to provide the liquidity necessary to carry out transactions. In addition, this reform would put all other banking functions into a separate and more flexible format, thus eliminating many of the restrictions and regulatory burdens banks currently face. Recent evidence further indicates that traditional lending activities at many banks have not been highly profitable and, in some cases, have not even kept up with bank investment portfolio yields when overhead expenses and credit losses are considered.[22] Narrow banks would also have an advantage in offering their depositors complete safety, in contrast to recent legislative provisions which seek to put uninsured bank depositors at greater risk.

A final competitive consideration is that narrow banking may be more consistent with recent and future trends in the financial system. Electronic banking, automated payments and declining transaction costs are putting added emphasis on safety and liquidity in the payments system. With their entire focus on transaction accounts and services, narrow banks might represent the best structure for developing a more efficient and stable payments system. The ongoing shift toward direct investment and nonbank savings products can also be expected to leave banks with a declining role as a financial intermediary, and the narrow bank affiliate format would likely provide more flexibility in adjusting to this environment.

12.3.4 What Would Happen to Financial and Credit Market Stability?

Under the present framework, banks are viewed as a source of liquidity during financial crises and as a support to credit markets. This liquidity and support comes from the protection banks receive under the federal safety net, their access to the discount window, and the various commitments, guarantees, and contingent obligations of banks that back up the financial system.

With a narrow banking system, there has been some concern that key elements of this support would be lost to the detriment of financial stability. A related concern has been that narrow bank lending affiliates would not be immune from the types of problems that have been inherent in the traditional banking system, including depositor panics, liquidity squeezes, and difficulties in resolving failing institutions. According to those holding such concerns, much of the existing regulatory framework would just have to be reestablished for narrow banks and their affiliates, thus eliminating any potential benefits.

A number of sound arguments suggest that these concerns either are not likely to be realized or can be prevented with a much simpler safety net. First, narrow banking would provide the means to create an extremely stable payments system, thus correcting an important historical source of instability in the US economy and in the credit system.

Another important piece of evidence is that the vast majority of credit transactions already take place outside of the banking industry, leaving credit stability largely dependent upon these other, less regulated markets. These same markets, moreover, have shown a high level of stability in past years while dealing with economic fluctuations and credit problems.[23] In a number of ways, this record stands in contrast to the problems that have been encountered in thrifts and banks, which have been under close regulation and the protection of the federal safety net.

Narrow bank lending affiliates would be subject to the same type of forces that have helped stabilize the private credit markets. For instance, lending affiliates of narrow banks would typically need strong capital backing and a longer-term debt structure in order to attract and retain uninsured investors. These changes could conceivably lead to a sounder financial structure for lenders, to more stable and conservative lending policies, and to investors more capable of judging risk exposure and providing a disciplinary influence. Public disclosures would further serve to reinforce these policies.

Market forces, in fact, would give narrow bank credit affiliates and their stockholders and creditors strong incentives to curtail funding of speculative activities. Investors that are fully at risk would be far less likely to fund questionable loans than in the case of bank depositors, who have insurance protection and a much shorter term focus. These same incentives would help credit affiliates resolve in a more orderly and efficient manner any problems that might arise. One indication of how credit problems might be resolved can be found in recent investor workouts associated with corporate takeovers and 'junk' bond financing. These workouts, in nearly every case, have proceeded without the same crisis atmosphere and inefficiency associated with the S&L collapse and subsequent RTC operations. Although painful for some investors, these private resolutions have engendered their own corrective forces, free of governmental intervention and taxpayer exposure.

Since credit markets would continue to fluctuate in response to the economy and a variety of other factors, a final source of credit stability could continue to be the Federal Reserve discount window. Under narrow banking, this 'lender of last resort' function could no longer be provided through traditional banking channels. However, the Federal Reserve could provide liquidity directly to credit affiliates and other uninsured lenders in the event of a systemic credit collapse. Although such temporary assistance might pose a variety of administrative issues, it would keep the discount window consistent with its original purpose of maintaining a stable economy.[24]

12.3.5 How Would Monetary Policy be Affected by Narrow Banking?

Narrow banking raises many monetary policy questions with regard to open-market operations, reserve requirements, and discount window credit. In addition, it could influence the structure and relationship of the monetary aggregates, the behavior of the short-term securities market, and the manner in which money is created and expanded.

These monetary policy questions involve a variety of technical issues that have yet to be considered in a thorough fashion. Some questions, such as the need for reserve requirements and the relationship of the monetary aggregates, involve a number of the same issues and problems posed by the current banking system. Other aspects of narrow banking, including its effect on the securities market and on money and credit expansion, may entail several new considerations. While narrow banking does not appear to have any obvious drawbacks with regard to monetary policy, many of its policy effects will need to be analyzed more carefully before implementation.

12.3.6 What International Banking Issues Would Arise with Narrow Banking?

If the United States were to adopt narrow banking on its own, a number of issues could arise concerning foreign entry into the United States and expansion abroad by domestic organizations. Foreign banks entering this country would need to establish narrow banks and carry out other activities here through uninsured affiliates. This would, thus, give them the same powers as US banks and would allow them to continue, or even expand, their existing operations through the use of affiliates. For US banking organizations with narrow banks, foreign activities would have to be conducted through foreign-chartered banks or affiliates isolated from the narrow bank.

Since much of US banking expansion abroad is through branches, the United States may need to create special international banking charters, much like that of Edge Corporations, and allow these 'banks' to establish branches abroad. Such banks would be separate from narrow banks, thus allowing US organizations to branch and conduct international operations without compromising the safety of narrow bank depositors. While foreign banking activities would be subject to the regulatory restrictions of the foreign country, US authorities might also have a limited oversight role in order to protect the reputation of the US banking system.

12.4 SUMMARY

Recent banking problems have prompted a variety of proposals for reforming deposit insurance and the banking system. Nearly all of these proposals, however, suffer from a common flaw – they would fail to create a banking system that is both stable and free to respond to market forces and financial developments.

Narrow banking offers a possible means for accomplishing these objectives. Narrow banking would create a stable payments system by backing transaction deposits with only those assets that are truly appropriate for this task – marketable securities with virtually no interest rate or credit risk. As a result, narrow banks would essentially be 'fail-safe' institutions and could operate without the inherent weaknesses of the current system. They would not pose a risk to depositors, taxpayers, or federal authorities and, unlike commercial banks, would not require extensive governmental support and intervention. These features of narrow banks would allow market forces to guide everyday banking decisions and the activities of any affiliated firms, thus returning the market to its proper role in allocating financial services.

In many respects, narrow banking mirrors another banking reform that took place in the 1860s – the use of US Government securities to back national bank notes. This earlier reform and the following change to Federal Reserve Notes collateralized largely by US obligations have produced a stable currency and ended any public concern about its acceptability. This success provides strong evidence that narrow banking is a workable system that could stabilize our deposit system and its transactions function.

Narrow banking, much like this earlier reform, appears to involve a dramatic change in the banking system. However, recent financial trends are making narrow banking a less radical change than commonly believed. In addition, most of the other approaches to recent banking problems entail a movement toward greater regulatory and governmental control of our financial system and its credit allocation functions – a response that is unlikely to make banking a vibrant, competitive industry. All of these factors thus suggest that narrow banking deserves careful consideration in efforts to reform the financial system.

Appendix

Possible Bank Industry Balance Sheet Changes in Shifting to a Narrow Banking System

To establish narrow banks, banking organizations in the United States would have to divide their banks into several separate entities. A narrow bank would take over the transaction accounts and much of the liquid assets and securities from its traditional bank predecessor. A credit affiliate would assume responsibility for the bank's loan portfolio and would obtain funding on an uninsured basis from market sources. In addition, an international banking entity might be needed to continue the activities that major US banks now conduct through foreign branches.

A number of changes in these activities could be expected once banking organizations converted to narrow banking. For instance, some shifts in transactions accounts might occur as narrow banks establish rates on deposits and compete with each other to provide the most efficient services. Also, as they begin to face greater market discipline, credit affiliates may pursue a different direction in choosing to hold, sell or securitize loans. In a similar fashion, organizations may alter their lending functions if they receive authority to provide a broader range of debt and equity financing. For simplicity, however, the following analysis will look at the banking industry as it is structured today and how bank assets, liabilities and capital might be apportioned among narrow banks, credit affiliates and international banks.

This analysis looks at the entire banking industry and the aggregate changes that would be involved in shifting to narrow banking. For individual banks, the ease in making this transition will depend on their current balance-sheet structure and overall condition relative to that of the typical bank. While these individual bank considerations would be important in implementing narrow banking, no attempt will be made here to examine the effects on certain banks or particular groups of banks.

In the following analysis, all domestic transaction accounts, cash assets, and reserves held by US banks are assumed to be passed on to the narrow banks, along with a sufficient level of securities to back deposits and enough capital to create a two per cent capital-to-asset ratio.[25] The credit affiliates of narrow banks would receive any remaining, domestically held securities and all of the domestic loans and other assets now held by banks.[26] These credit affiliates would then attempt to replace the deposits and other liabilities supporting bank loans with various sources of market funding. International banking affiliates would hold all of the foreign assets and foreign deposits. Credit affiliates and international banking entities are assumed to divide the remaining bank equity base evenly in proportion to their adjusted asset holdings.

Table 12.A1 reflects the banking assets, liabilities, and capital held by all US banks at mid-year 1992. The hypothetical balance sheets in Table 12.A2 reflect what these organizations would look like as a combined group if all the above steps toward narrow banking were to take place. Because these steps reflect simplified assumptions, Table 12.A2 should be

Table 12.A1 Assets, liabilities and capital in all US commercial banks, mid-year 1992
(All figures are in billions of dollars)

US Commercial Banks			
Cash, reserves, and due from balances		Domestic transaction accounts	710
Domestic	191		
Foreign	84	Other domestic deposits	1626
Securities		Foreign deposits	304
Domestic	697		
Foreign	30	Other liabilities	531
Loans		Total liabilities	3171
Domestic	1759		
Foreign	208	Equity capital	247
Other assets	449		
Total assets	3418		

viewed primarily as a general guide to the types of adjustments that might occur in a transition to narrow banking.

The balance sheets indicate that three factors would be important in implementing narrow banking. First, if banks could retain much of their liquid assets and securities, they would already have much of the backing they would need for transaction accounts under a narrow banking system. A shift toward shorter term securities would likely be necessary, but banks would not need a major expansion in their securities portfolio.[27]

Second, the credit affiliates would have to obtain a vast amount of uninsured funding from market sources. Some of this funding could come directly from the customers that previously held CDs and other savings instruments at commercial banks. The funding could also come indirectly from these depositors as they move their money into commercial paper, mutual funds, and other alternative instruments. Credit affiliates would also have the opportunity to develop new types of debt and equity offerings. Overall, a key factor in these financing efforts would be the ability of credit affiliates to meet the same market standards as other private lenders.

Finally, to meet market standards and secure funding, credit affiliates would have to maintain an equity base similar to other lenders. The figures in Table 12.A2 indicate that the existing capital in banks would give credit

Table 12.A2 Assets, liabilities and capital in all US commercial banks under a narrow banking system mid-year 1992

(In billions of dollars)

Narrow Banks			
Cash, reserves, and due from balances	191	Transaction accounts	710
Securities	519		
Facilities and fixed assets	14	Equity capital	14
Total assets	724		
Domestic Credit Affiliates			
Loans	1759	Liabilities (Commercial paper, uninsured deposits, long-term debt, etc.)	2057
Securities	178		
Other assets	315		
Total assets	2252	Equity capital	195
International Banks			
Foreign holdings of cash and due from balances	84	Foreign deposits	304
Foreign securities	30	Other liabilities	100
Foreign loans	208	Total liabilities	404
Other assets	120		
Total assets	442	Equity capital	38

affiliates an equity capital-to-asset ratio of nearly 8.7 per cent. This assumes that current bank stockholders would be content to invest in credit affiliates in much the same manner as they were with commercial banks. If these affiliates concentrated on lending and did not retain many of the other assets now held by banks, this equity ratio could rise to as much as 10 per cent. In comparison, domestic finance companies and short-term business credit companies have maintained average capital ratios between 8.5 and 13.7 per cent, depending on the definition of capital, the time period, the types of companies included, and the degree of perceived parent company support.[28] At year-end 1990, for instance, the ten largest finance companies not affiliated with banks had equity capital equal to 10.7 per cent of assets.[29]

These capital ratios imply that a simple division of present banking industry portfolios between narrow banks and their credit affiliates could leave the affiliates with capital ratios several percentage points below that of comparable lenders. To narrow this gap, credit affiliates would need to raise additional capital, reduce their holdings of loans and other assets, or achieve an asset quality higher than other lenders.

In summary, present bank balance-sheet figures do not indicate any insurmountable difficulties in moving toward a narrow banking system. The banking industry would appear to be capable of finding an asset base to support narrow bank deposits. Some additional capital and new funding sources could be needed to finance credit affiliates. However, similar changes are likely to occur with or without narrow banking as banks face tighter capital requirements and as investors and savers continue to make greater use of a variety of market investment instruments. The narrow banking format could, in fact, give banking organizations more flexibility in making these adjustments.

Notes

* The views expressed in this chapter are those of the author and do not necessarily reflect those of the Federal Reserve System or the Federal Reserve Bank of Kansas City.

1. The types and variety of borrowers using this market have also expanded rapidly. For more on the growth of this market, see Mitchell A. Post, 'The Evolution of the US Commercial Paper Market since 1980', *Federal Reserve Bulletin 78* (December 1992): 879–91.
2. The FFIEC's 1993 study on regulatory burden lists previous research as showing that regulatory costs alone might represent 6 to 14 per cent of total bank non-interest expenses, or a total of between $7.5 billion and $17 billion for the industry in 1991 (Federal Financial Institutions Examination Council, 'Study on Regulatory Burden', January 1993, pp. 3–4 of the Executive Summary).
3. For these statistics, as well as additional information on the role of banks and changes in financial intermediation, see Gordon H. Sellon, Jr., 'Changes in Financial Intermediation: The Role of Pension and Mutual Funds', *Economic Review* (Federal Reserve Bank of Kansas City), third quarter 1992, pp. 53–70.

4. For a more detailed presentation of the changes in household savings patterns, see Sellon, 'Changes in Financial Intermediation: The Role of Pension and Mutual Funds'.
5. For several examples of narrow banking proposals, see James B. Burnham (1991), 'Deposit Insurance: The Case for the Narrow Bank', *Regulation* (Spring) 14: 35–43; John H. Kareken (1986), 'Federal Bank Regulatory Policy: A Description and Some Observations', *Journal of Business* (January) 59: 3–48; Robert E. Litan (1987), *What Should Banks Do?* (Washington, DC: The Brookings Institution); James L. Pierce (1991), *The Future of Banking* (New Haven: Yale University Press); Alex J. Pollack (1992), 'Collateralized Money: An Idea Whose Time Has Come Again', *Challenge* (September/October) pp. 62–4; and James Tobin (1987), 'The Case for Preserving Regulatory Distinctions', in *Restructuring the Financial System* (a symposium sponsored by the Federal Reserve Bank of Kansas City, pp. 167–83).
   Many narrow banking concepts, such as safe banks and minimizing regulatory intervention, can also be traced back to earlier proposals for 100 per cent reserve banking developed by such individuals as Henry Simons (1948), *Economic Policy for a Free Society* (Chicago: University of Chicago Press) pp. 62–5; and Milton Friedman (1959), *A Program for Monetary Stability* (New York: Fordham University) pp. 65–76. These proposals would have restricted bank assets to cash and Federal Reserve Bank balances, thus providing complete control over the money supply.
6. Because of their limited powers and liquid asset structure, narrow banks would primarily offer transaction accounts and services. Narrow banks could also be allowed to offer savings accounts, but the terms on such accounts would probably not differ much from transaction accounts in a competitive marketplace.
7. Separate narrow banks are suggested in Litan (1987), *What Should Banks Do?* and in Burnham (1991), 'Deposit Insurance: The Case for the Narrow Bank'. The case for a deposited currency or collateralized money is discussed in Tobin (1987), 'The Case for Preserving Regulatory Distinctions', and in Pollack (1992), 'Collateralized Money: An Idea Whose Time Has Come Again'.
8. Narrow banking should, however, be distinguished from core banking proposals, which allow banks to continue most traditional lending activities but with restrictions on the size of individual loans and on deposit interest rates (see Lowell L. Bryan (1988), *Breaking Up the Bank* (Homewood, IL: Business One Irwin). While core banks might be of some benefit in limiting bank risk-taking, they would still not lead to the type of nearly risk-free deposits characteristic of narrow banking proposals.
9. For a more detailed discussion of this issue, see John H. Kareken (1985), 'Ensuring Financial Stability', in *The Search for Financial Stability: The Past Fifty Years* (a conference sponsored by the Federal Reserve Bank of San Francisco pp. 53–77).
   The unstable nature of the current banking structure and its divergence from market principles is obvious in other ways. Financial institutions that operate without a federal safety net have been forced by the market to adopt a much different balance sheet structure than banks. Uninsured lenders, for instance,

must typically maintain longer-term and more stable funding and somewhat higher capital standards. Similarly, those institutions that offer investment accounts with transaction privileges, such as money-market mutual funds, generally confine their asset holdings to low-risk, short-term marketable securities.

10. For this level of safety to be realized, narrow banks and their customers would not only have to refrain from credit transactions, but would also have to be limited in their ability to overdraw any of their accounts during the business day and over longer periods. For a narrow bank, daylight overdrafts would pose a risk to customers and the payments system whenever the overdrafts could exhaust bank capital. In many ways, these payments system issues are similar to those that currently exist in the banking system and might require many of the same steps toward reform. However, the low capital requirements of narrow banks and their 'fail safe' nature could make these reform steps even more urgent.
11. In reference to the federal outlays for recapitalizing the bank and thrift insurance funds, Benjamin Friedman stated, 'In this era of shrunken capital formation, [these outlays are] approximately equal to three entire years' worth of net additions to our stock of productive plant and equipment' ('The Nature and Necessity of Financial Reform', a public policy forum of The Jerome Levy Economics Institute of Bard College, 6 April 1991, p. 7).
12. For greater detail on the current structure of US banks and the type of balance sheet changes that would be required under a narrow banking system, please see the Appendix to this paper.
13. For a similar type of analysis, see Burnham, 'Deposit Insurance: The Case for the Narrow Bank', pp. 41–2; and Litan, *What Should Banks Do?*, pp. 169–73.
14. Because the total volume of federal debt in private hands is now approaching $3 trillion, the US Treasury would have a large base for starting to make these maturity changes.
15. A broader range of securities, particularly with respect to private sector issuers, would help to limit any added preference that narrow banking would give to US Government securities in the marketplace. Unless the list of acceptable securities were greatly expanded, though, the market effects would likely be marginal.
16. The Appendix to this paper provides a more detailed comparison of the lending affiliates of narrow banks and other types of lenders. On a more limited basis, many banking organizations already have experience managing uninsured lending affiliates through the bank holding company structure. This experience includes holding company subsidiaries operating as finance, mortgage, leasing and factoring companies. As uninsured lenders, these companies typically must meet the usual market standards.
17. A small bank exemption is discussed in Burnham, 'Deposit Insurance: The Case for the Narrow Bank', p. 38; and in Litan, *What Should Banks Do?*, p. 182.
18. The information that bank lenders presently gain from knowing a customer's deposit history need not be lost under a narrow banking system. Narrow banks, for instance, would be free to disclose such information to their lending affiliates or to other lenders.

19. For narrow banks to be free of major regulatory burdens, their capital requirements and degree of regulation would have to fully reflect their low level of risk and they would have to receive a competitive return on any reserves they were required to hold.
20. Although many of the banking organizations establishing narrow banks might maintain more of an office structure and have higher fixed costs than money-market funds or other potential competitors, the added expenditures, if wisely invested, should help attract customers or generate more fees.
21. For articles discussing the advantages of the existing banking structure, see Randall J. Pozdena (1991), 'The False Hope of the Narrow Bank', *FRBSF Weekly Letter* (Federal Reserve Bank of San Francisco, 8 November); and Bert Ely (1991), 'The Narrow Bank: A Flawed Response to the Failings of Federal Deposit Insurance', *Regulation* (Spring) 14, pp. 44–52.
22. For a comparison of the net earnings on bank lending and investment activities, see Bruce W. Morgan (1991), 'Financial Services after the Decline of Deposit Banking', *Banking Policy Report* (21 October) 10, 1, pp. 12–5. For additional information on the net returns to various banking activities, see *Functional Cost Analysis, National Average Report – Commercial Banks*, Federal Reserve System, 1988.
23. An important factor in this record is that credit markets have grown to where they now serve a wide variety of borrowers and investors, thus providing many opportunities for diversification, additional liquidity and products for specialized needs.
24. On an operational level, discount window lending might also be needed if narrow banks maintained required reserves or clearing balances with the Federal Reserve and had to replenish these accounts after large, end-of-day clearing activities.
25. This capital level is based primarily on the need to finance the facilities and fixed assets that narrow banks might require in their operations. From a supervisory standpoint, narrow banks would only need to maintain enough capital to discourage fraudulent activities and to cover any minimal levels of risk in their asset portfolios.
26. Credit affiliates would also need to hold some cash assets in order to conduct their operations. However, for most credit affiliates, these assets would only need to be of a marginal amount based on the typical holdings of most nonbank lenders today.
27. The level of securities held by banks has increased over the last few years in response to declines in loan demand and changes in regulatory policy. Securities holdings in prior years, though, would have also provided much or all of the deposit backing needed for narrow banks.
28. For more information on the capital ratios of other lenders, see *Federal Reserve Bulletin* 78 (November 1992), Table 1.51, p. A34; 'Recent Trends in Commercial Bank Profitability: A Staff Study', Federal Reserve Bank of New York (1986), p. 278; 'Modernizing the Financial System', Department of the Treasury, February 1991, pp. 12–3; *American Banker*, 1 December 1991, p. 8; and 'Finance Companies, Bank Competition, and Niche Markets', *Quarterly Review* (Federal Reserve Bank of New York), Summer 1992, p. 36.

29. The ten largest finance companies owned by banking organizations had capital ratios similar to those of the finance companies not affiliated with banks. Thus, banking organizations appear to have had some success in meeting market standards in their nonbank operations.

References

American Banker (1991) (8 December) 8.

Bryan, Lowell L. (1988) *Breaking Up the Bank* (Homewood, IL: Business One Irwin).

Burnham, James B. (1991) 'Deposit Insurance: The Case for the Narrow Bank', *Regulation* (Spring) **14**, 35–43.

Department of the Treasury (1991) 'Modernizing the Financial System', (February) 12–13.

Ely, Bert (1991) 'The Narrow Bank: A Flawed Response to the Failings of Federal Deposit Insurance', *Regulation* (Spring) **14**, 44–52.

Federal Financial Institutions Examination Council (1993) 'Study on Regulatory Burden', *Executive Summary* (January) 3–4.

Federal Reserve Bank of New York (1986) 'Recent Trends in Commercial Bank Profitability: A Staff Study', 278.

Federal Reserve Bulletin (1992) (November) **78**, Table 1.51, A34.

Friedman, Benjamin (1991) 'The Nature and Necessity of Financial Reform', public policy forum of the Jerome Levy Economics Institute (6 April) 7.

Friedman, Milton (1959) *A Program for Monetary Stability* (New York: Fordham University) 65–76.

Functional Cost Analysis, National Average Report - Commercial Banks (1988) (Washington, DC: Federal Reserve System).

Kareken, John H. (1986) 'Federal Bank Regulatory Policy: A Description and Some Observations', *Journal of Business* (January) **59**, 3–48.

Kareken, John H. (1985) 'Ensuring Financial Stability', *The Search for Financial Stability: The Past Fifty Years* (Federal Reserve of San Francisco) 53–77.

Litan, Robert E. (1987) *What Should Banks Do?* (Washington, DC: The Brookings Institution) 169–82.

Morgan, Bruce W. (1991) 'Financial Services After the Decline of Deposit Banking', *Banking Policy Report* (21 October) **10**:1, 12–15.

Pierce, James L. (1991) *The Future of Banking* (New Haven: Yale University Press).

Pollack, Alex J. (1992) 'Collateralized Money: An Idea Whose Time Has Come Again', *Challenge* (September/October) 62–4.

Post, Mitchell A. (1992) 'The Evolution of the US Commercial Paper Market Since 1980', *Federal Reserve Bulletin* (December) **78**, 879–91.

Pozdena, Randall J. (1991) 'The False Hope of the Narrow Bank', Federal Reserve Bank of San Francisco Weekly letter (Federal Reserve Bank of San Francisco, 8 November).

Quarterly Review (1992) 'Finance Companies, Bank Competition, and Niche Markets', (Federal Reserve Bank of New York, Summer) 36.

Sellon, Gordon H., Jr. (1992) 'Changes in Financial Intermediation: The Role of Pension and Mutual Funds', *Economic Review* (Federal Reserve Bank of Kansas City, Third Quarter) 53–70.

Simons, Henry (1948) *Economic Policy for a Free Society* (Chicago: University of Chicago Press) 62–5.

Tobin, James (1987) 'The Case for Preserving Regulatory Distinctions', *Restructuring the Financial System* (Federal Reserve Bank of Kansas City) 167–83.

13 Community Development Banks

Hyman P. Minsky, Dimitri B. Papadimitriou, Ronnie J. Phillips and L. Randall Wray

13.1 INTRODUCTION

The Clinton/Gore proposal for the creation of a network of 100 Community Development Banks (CDBs) to revitalize communities is bold and crucial for the success of the US economy. Banks are essential institutions in any community and the establishment of a bank is often a prerequisite to the investment process. For this reason, the creation of banks in the communities lacking such institutions is vital to the welfare of the country.

The vitality of the American economy depends upon the continual creation of new and initially small firms. It, therefore, is in the public interest to foster the creation of new entrants into industry, trade and finance. It follows that it is in the public interest to have a set of strong independent profit seeking banking institutions which specialize in the financing of smaller businesses.

When market forces fail to provide a service that is needed and potentially profitable, then it is an appropriate role for government to help create the market. Community Development Banks fall into such a category. They do not require a government subsidy, and after start up costs, the banks are expected to be profitable.

The primary perspective of this chapter is that the main function of the financial structure is to advance thc capital development of the economy, that is, to increase the real productive capacity and wealth producing ability of the economy. The second perspective is that capital development is encouraged by provision of a broad range of financial services to various segments of the US economy, including consumers, small and large businesses, retailers, developers and all levels of government. A third perspective is that the existing financial structure is particularly weak in servicing small, new and start up businesses, and in servicing certain consumer groups. The fourth perspective is that this problem has become more acute because of a decrease in the number of independent financing alternatives and the rise in the size distribution of financing sources which have increased the financial system's bias towards larger transactions.

13.2 RATIONALE FOR COMMUNITY DEVELOPMENT BANKS

The greatest danger to the community bank concept may be a lack of clarity in the concept. The primary goals of the CDBs are to deliver credit, payment, and savings opportunities to communities not well served by banks and to provide financing throughout a designated area for businesses too small to attract the interest of the investment banking and normal commercial banking communities.

The community service aspect of the banks involve the payment mechanism and the savings facility. These aspects require none of the 'underwriting and judgement' skills of the banker who takes risks. An assumption underlying the lack of credit facilities assertion is that there are 'bankable risks' and feasible 'equity investments' in distressed communities and in less stressed communities that involve too small an amount for the established banking community.

There are six identifiable banking functions:

(1) Payments system: check clearing and cashing, credit and debit cards;
(2) Secure outlets for savings and transaction balances;
(3) Household financing: housing, consumer debts and student loans;
(4) Commercial banking services: loans, payroll services and advice;
(5) Investment banking services: determination of appropriate liability structure for the assets of a firm, and placing these liabilities;
(6) Asset management and advice for households.

The argument for Community Development Banks is that one or more of the above functions is not being adequately performed by existing institutions for well defined segments of the population: the low-income, African-Americans, hispanics, the inner cities and entrepreneurs who seek modest financing for small businesses. Furthermore, this unsatisfactory situation has been aggravated by a variety of problems that financial institutions of all kinds have faced over the past years.

The 1980s and 1990s have seen a decline in the number of independent financing outlets for businesses and a shift in the size distribution of banks and savings and loan institutions in favor of larger banks. Small, family-owned enterprises have seen a recent tightening of terms on which credit is available from factoring companies. Previously terms were given so that invoices could be paid by a certain date of the month and a discount received. This discount (when available it averaged 8 per cent) has been eliminated in the past two years by many of the factoring companies. Though the factoring companies are often subsidiaries of a financial holding company, the commercial loan departments frequently refuse to provide loans for the business credit previously provided by the factoring companies. Banks now find it increasing unprofitable to serve many parts of the population and in particular the smallest enterprises which were never well served by the banking community. Our proposal would increase the supply of short-term credit to small businesses.

One aim of the CDBs should be to seek out projects which promise to be profitable but which will not be financed because of the small size of the project, the riskiness of the project, or the 'inexperience' of the prospective management. The CDB will be successful as the projects it finances are profitable. The aim of the CDBs is to be profitable. Government seed money may be involved, but the government's investment in the CDBs system should be viewed as a profit-making investment. This means that if the Congress mandates subsidized financing by these banks, the Congress should budget the expected cost of the mandated spending as a subsidy to the endeavor.

Capital development of the country, in general, and of depressed regions, in particular, requires a broad range of financial services in order to raise effective demand and revitalize the regional and national economies. In other words, 'capital development' is the primary concern, but this does not mean solely provision of investment finance. The whole community needs financial reform; this includes provision of financial services to all segments of the economy, including consumers, small and large business, retailers, developers, and all levels of government. The CDB proposal will address most of these (it will ignore finance of big business and of federal and state government).

13.3 ASSESSMENT OF COMMUNITY DEVELOPMENT BANK EXPERIENCE

The existing models of CDBs provide a useful starting point for a nationwide strategy. Community Development Banks have been successful when they are able to attract deposits from outside the community, while using the funds for residential mortgage loans. The most successful Community Development Bank, and the oldest, is the Shorebank Corporation, a holding company which includes: a bank, a real-estate development corporation, a small venture-capital firm, and The Neighborhood Institute which offers low-income housing development, remedial education, vocational training and the like. On the asset side, its greatest success has been residential mortgages, typically made on the condition that the structures be renovated and improved. The loan–loss ratio at South Shore is around 0.20 per cent, less than half the ratio at many commercial banks of similar size. The key to its success is residential housing and, as Ron Grzywinski of Shorebank recognized, 'the principle small business of South Shore was quite simply housing'. The Southern Development Corporation uses a subsidiary called the Good Faith Fund which offers loans from $500 to a few thousand dollars to low-income people trying to start a business. The activities in small business loans, have been less successful, as have attempts to provide low-cost checking and savings deposits for the community residents.

On the liability side, the most important innovation has been 'Development Deposits', funds attracted from outside the community from institutions and individuals who share the goals of the Corporation. Presently, development deposits account for almost half of the deposit base at Shorebank. Some depositors accept below-market rates to subsidize Shorebank's work, but generally these deposits offer market rates of interest. Home rehabilitation Certificates of Deposit *CDs*, which typically pay 200 basis points below the market interest rates, make up 4.1 per cent of South Shore's deposits. Thus, the banks are subsidized to some extent by philanthropists and socially conscious people who are willing to accept a lower rate of return on their money in exchange for doing something that they consider an important contribution to society. This asset/liability structure, which also carries federal deposit insurance, has been the key to the success of the Corporation.

Shorebank's one big weakness is that although it pays for itself, it is not profitable enough to convince other entrepreneurs with capital to imitate its success: its returns to its owners have been lower than average for banks its size.

13.4 POTENTIAL PROBLEMS WITH A NATIONWIDE STRATEGY

The strengths of existing Community Development Banks may turn out to be weaknesses, if followed as a national strategy. Attracting funds from the outside is important for particular CDBs, but to establish a nationwide group of banks and then expect them to compete to try to attract funds from the 'socially conscious' public will be self-defeating. It is not a viable long-run strategy to promote as a national policy the transfer, for example, of the 'socially conscious' funds of New York City to rural Alabama (or vice versa). A national policy should encourage *local* markets for the CDB liabilities just as it encourages *local* markets for the CDB assets. This will help to ensure that local consumers receive the broad range of financial services needed to encourage capital development of the community. The banks of a nation-wide system of CDBs cannot rely on *local* short-term loans as a primary asset while the primary liabilities are external funds.

A key aspect of South Shore bank is that its neighborhood was still perhaps two-thirds middle and working class, only one-third low-income when the bank came into existence. CDB managers do not claim that their model would work in the very worst ghettos. A strategy based on existing models would therefore neglect those at the very bottom of the economic ladder, who presumably need the most help. Reliance on external funds ignores the necessary provision of bank services to local consumers. This is why we believe that a CDB should be restricted to providing financial services in the community.

The shopping habits of Americans have changed in recent decades and in virtually all towns and cities in the US, the downtown areas have faced the problem of competition from shopping malls. Creating small businesses within a community does not guarantee that the shopping habits will change and people will decide to shop locally. Though many lament this change in shopping habits, for the time being it is a fact that CDBs in and of themselves can not be the sole agents of change. However, this does not mean that CDBs do not have a role to play in providing transactions services for local residents even when they shop at suburban malls.

Another important factor is that the existing CDBs, because they are unique in their communities, face little competition for their core business. When they do face competition, they often do well, especially in residential loans. Shorebank discovered that its creation of the rehabilitation loan generated a demand from consumers for other banks to also provide rehabilitation loans. This is an example of the market working to the benefit of both business and consumer. However, in a nationwide system, existing banks under pressure of competition can be expected to respond and provide competition for the CDBs. Any weakening of the prohibitions on interstate banking will likely intensify this effect.

The CDBs are not intended to be welfare programs, but to provide services to the community's residents and must, therefore, meet the long-run market tests of profitability. Aside from the service aspect, community development banks will improve the well being of our citizens by increasing opportunities: directly for potential entrepreneurs and for potential employees. The basic assumption underlying the Community Development Bank is that all areas of the country need banks that are clearly oriented towards the small deal: the household that has a small net worth, small Individual Retirement Account (IRA) and a small transactions account, and those businesses that need financing measured in thousands rather than millions or billions of dollars.

13.5 A PROPOSAL FOR A NATIONWIDE SYSTEM OF COMMUNITY DEVELOPMENT BANKS

Our proposal deviates from existing examples of CDB-type banks, and from other proposals, by emphasizing the need for the development of an equitable payments system for the bottom quintile of the population which is generally denied access to checking accounts or credit cards. More stress should be placed on this payments function of banking. Others have argued that commercial banks should be required to provide 'life-line accounts'. We believe that this represents an unnecessary cost that commercial banks can ill afford at the present time. However, by the same token, we recognize that it is important to bring the bottom quintile of the population into the banking system without burdening them with the costs associated with a 'fee for services' payment mechanism. The current credit card system is an example of a fee for services system, but it forces those who cannot get credit cards (mainly those with low income) to bear the burden of the vendor's discount to subsidize the purchasers who do have credit cards: in general, there is no discount for payment by cash. The current checking component of the payments system is too expensive for commercial banks to provide small accounts needed by those with low income, thus cannot serve as the basis of a universal payments system available to all. For this reason, we believe the CDB system can be designed such that a profitable payments system is incorporated within the package of services provided to the community.

We would expect that a fully funded and mature CDB would provide many of the six functions of banking described above. However, these functions may be implemented in phases. The payment system, secure outlets for savings, short-term commercial loans, mortgage loans and student loans should be included in the initial phase. Investment-type banking services, and asset management and advice for households could be added later. If the demonstration project (which begins with 100 CDBs) proves successful, we anticipate the creation of a nation-wide system of CDBs that could provide all six banking functions in selected communities.

The CDB should rely to a great extent on local markets for its liabilities – this is the other side of the coin to the concern with provision of small commercial loans. First, reliance on external sources of funds conflicts with the goal of bringing the populations of the depressed areas into the banking system. Second, there is some evidence that reliance on external, brokered money may have contributed to the thrift crisis (brokered money is volatile, and it allowed some thrifts to grow too quickly). Instead, a maximum limit (say, 10 per cent) should be set for external funds. This will help to ensure that local consumers receive the broad range of financial services needed to encourage capital development of the community. *The depressed areas* **are** *great sources of funds, but these have been flowing into megabanks that use them elsewhere.* Both the assets and the liabilities of the CDBs should be regionally restricted. Thus, CDBs should be permitted to hold no more than, say, 10 per cent of their assets in the form of liabilities that originate outside the community. These would probably consist primarily of federal government bonds. Local government obligations would also form part of the CDB's portfolio. This will help to provide a source of funding to the local community.

13.5.1 Creation of a Federal Bank for Community Development Banks

The funding, regulation and supervision of CDBs can be carried out most effectively by the creation of a federal bank for CDBs. The Federal Bank for Community Development Banks (FBCDB) will be the clearing bank, central bank, correspondent bank, link with financial markets and supervising authority for the Community Development Banks. It will provide up to 50 per cent of the equity for the Community Development Banks, and as an investor will have access to the books of these banks. This FBCDB will also have oversight responsibilities for the development of the professional staff of the CDBs. There are a great number of trained bankers who are at liberty because of the fate of their bank. Although the community bank will be able to draw on this pool of talents, the clientele and the purposes of the community bank will be special.

The Federal Bank for Community Development Banks will be where the community banks hold their reserves and their operating deposits: The Federal Bank will be the correspondent bank for the Community Development Banks. The 'checks' that the CDB makes available to the holders of savings deposits may well be negotiable orders of withdrawal drawn on the Federal Bank.

As the Community Development Banks develop a mortgage business, the Federal Bank would be the agency that securitizes these instruments.

The Federal Bank will be responsible for establishing and maintaining underwriting standards for the Community Development Banks. It will have a training responsibility for the CDBs and be the link by which the mortgages initiated by the community banks enter financial markets. Its oversight functions will exist by the right of its position as an owner.

The Federal Bank for Community Development Banks will be started with an initial investment of $1 billion by the US Congress which could be augmented to $5 billion as, and if, the system warrants. It will report to the Congress. Its Directors and its Chief Executive Officer will be nominated by the President and confirmed by the Senate. It will have an initial ability to borrow up to twice the federal government investment in the market. The bank should be profitable once the start up period is over. For clearing purposes, this bank will become a member of the Federal Reserve System. The FBCDB will match up to $10 million of private investment in each CDB. Because the FBCDB is a major investor in each CDB, it will have representation on each board and as a co-investor will automatically have the right to inspect the books of the CDBs. Finally, if necessary, the FBCDB will have access to the Fed's discount window to obtain reserves required in check clearing between the CDB system and the commercial bank system. In short, the FBCDB will combine the functions of a central bank, a correspondent bank and an investor for the CDBs.

13.5.2 The Payment System and Secure Outlets for Savings

Every payment system involves the use of resources, and therefore there are costs involved in operating the payment system. These costs have to be borne by some sector of the economy. Access to a payments system may require an ability to pay for the services used. The payment system has evolved into a three-part structure: deposits subject to check, debit and credit cards and currency and coin. The deposit-subject-to-check payment system is expensive and relatively inefficient. To realize how inefficient our check payments system is all that has to be done is to trace the flow of bills and payments through the banking system and note the number of records that are needed by the flow of payments and orders. The costs of operating the checking system have been borne in a variety of ways. Non-par clearing, where one depositing or cashing a check received less than the face value of the check that was either deposited or cashed, was a common practice for non-local checks prior to the great depression. In recent years the costs of the checking system were borne by the difference between the interest paid on deposits and the interest earned on bank assets, where access to the system without explicit service charges depended upon the size of the deposit balance. In addition, the Federal Reserve operates a check clearing service which in effect subsidizes the checking system. Over the years, the checking system's penetration grew, especially after the Savings and Loan Associations and the other varieties of savings banks began to have deposits that were subject to check, although coverage and access was never universal.

Commercial banks are restricting access to checking accounts by setting higher minimum balances, requiring a minimum customer relation, and leveling explicit charges for account activity. The result is that larger segments of the population are now outside the check-using system than hitherto, and this trend of diminishing coverage by the check system can be expected to continue.

In contrast to the now increasingly overt costs of a checking account, the costs of the credit–debit card systems are carried by an annual fee and are covert to the user vendor's discount. (The payments aspect of the credit card should be distinguished from the credit aspect.) Furthermore, of the three payment systems only the credit–debit card system is capable of being fully electronic: with a 'smart' cash register the 'paper' that is signed never leaves the place of origin unless a charge is challenged. There is little doubt that an electronic plus plastic payments system will be of increasing importance in the total payments system. The losses that banks and other issuers of credit cards have taken in the current recession has led to a restriction of access to the credit–debit card payments mechanism.

For many communities, the only available banking services are those that are performed by the currency exchanges. These exchanges are a 'fee for services bank' which exchanges check-book money for currency and provides payment services (money orders) in exchange for currency, charging a 2–4 per cent fee for its services. In some jurisdictions the currency exchanges are allowed to receive welfare and social-security checks. The currency exchanges show that the fee schedule for making the exchange between currency and checking forms of money can make the institution profitable. The situation was aptly described by President Clinton in a speech at the Rainbow Coalition National Convention on 15 June 1992:

> One community leader in Los Angeles told me that in that vast place we know as the inner city, there were 177 check cashing stands in the

neighborhood where the riots began and only thirty-three banks. In the Washington, DC, area, there are fifty major banks but only two have branches in Anacostia and neither of them has a lending office.

The currency exchange business should be one facet of the Community Development Banks. A recognition by the government that it is the payer's responsibility to pay its debts in a money form that the recipient can use implies that the government needs to absorb the charges levied upon recipients of its checks for the exchange of checks for currency. A payment by the government of 1 per cent of the face value to all converters of government checks into currency for those who are otherwise excluded from the check system may be in order.

If the now existing currency exchanges were licensed to accept savings accounts, and if they were required to hold only short-term government securities as assets for these accounts, they would be a savings equivalent of a narrow bank. Because their assets would be restricted to short-term government bonds, these narrow banks could carry a 100 per cent Federal Government guarantee on their deposits regardless of the size of any deposit, without any fee to the institution for this insurance.

These 'narrow banks for savings' would solve the problem of the non-par exchanges for some of the recipients of government checks. The deposit of Government checks into these accounts could well be an electronic transfer. Savings deposits which accept automatic deposits and allow a limited number of withdrawals per month without explicit charges would become a feasible way of offsetting the lack of elementary household banking services in poor neighborhoods. In addition, the savings facility might allow a limited number of free negotiable orders of withdrawal to be written against these deposits, the rest would carry a service charge.

In order to protect against interest-rate risk, a 2.5 per cent equity against such deposits may be required, even though if a vast majority of the assets are short-term government securities both interest-rate and default risk are minimal. The interest rate that these banks pay on their liabilities will be keyed to the interest rate earned on the portfolio: a $\frac{1}{2}$ to $\frac{3}{4}$ of 1 per cent differential would make the savings facility profitable.

If such narrow banking facilities spread beyond the community development banks, government endorsed insurance of deposits that finance a variety of assets could be phased out. The check cashing and savings facility dimensions of the Community Development Banks cover the service functions to poorer households which these banks are designed to perform. The NOW accounts would eliminate the relatively substantial payments system costs incurred by the poorest members of the community; it would bring them into the banking system, and it would be the first point of contact with a population in which we wish to encourage thrift.

13.5.3 Financing Housing and Consumer Debt

The Community Development Bank will act as a mortgage originator within its community. It will not engage in construction loans through this department. The mortgages will be on homes and minor community-level commercial property. In many cases, mortgage loans will include provisions for rehabilitation of property. Those mortgages that are carried will be funded by long-term certificates of deposit through the commercial bank, but as the banks develop it should be possible to securitize such mortgages by way of facilities that the Federal Bank for Community Development Banks will develop.

The consumer debt facilities which are available in prosperous communities were generally not available in the communities where the development banks will function. The Community Development Banks will be able to make credit cards available to those who have built up a savings account. The CDBs may provide students loans and other loans for investment in human capital.

13.5.4 Commercial Banking Services

The CDBs will provide commercial loan services for their clients. These loans will be financed by demand deposits, certificates of deposit, and other types of deposits that will carry the ordinary deposit insurance. The development and solicitation of business, the structuring of loans and the supervision of credits are three essential aspects of commercial banking. The bank's staff for commercial banking consists of business development and loan officers. In smaller banks these two functions may be combined. In small banks the top management is likely to be the key business development agent.

The business development officers of a bank are just what the name indicates, they are the salesmen of the bank's services to businessmen. Like all salesmen they work a territory. A community, even if it is under banked, has going businesses. The calling program of the business development officers of a Community Development Bank will necessarily include the existing businesses in its neighborhood, whose needs will be explored. The question of how the bank can serve the existing businesses, not perhaps as the sole bank but as a supplement to existing banking connections, will be on the 'agenda' of the business development officer.

Being devoted to the community in which the businesses they are financing function, the Community Development Banks will, over time, develop a better awareness of the potential successes and failures in their community than is available to the branch officers of the larger traditional bank which at best will have a peripheral interest in the community.

The structure of a financing agreement is what is finalized in the contract in which a bank's customer promises to pay money at future dates in exchange for being financed 'now'. The structuring of loans begins with a 'pro forma' in which the business sketches what it will do with the funds and how the funds to repay the loan will accrue to the business. The function of the loan office is to apply a quizzical and skeptical eye to the presentation. In all these negotiations the ability of the loan applicant to perform is one question on the table. Loan officers not only structure the loans, they often need to intervene to put an adequate structure in place to administer the enterprise.

Successful loan negotiations lead to an agreement on a scenario (program) for the borrowing firm, which yields the schedule of payments on the loan along with an understanding as to what will happen if various codicils of the contract are not fulfilled.

Supervision is the post-loan relation between a bank and its borrowing client. The relation between a business and its bank is not a one-shot affair. In a successful relationship, new credits are being negotiated even as maturing credits are paid down. The business development and loan officer's relation with a bank client includes follow-ups which are designed to assure the bank that the business is developing in such a way that the codicils are being satisfied and the payments on the debts will be forthcoming.

The success or failure of the Community Development Bank concept will ride on how well the solicitation, structuring and supervision functions are carried out.

Given the character of banking, a system of committees within the lending institution which approves and reviews credits is important. As banking is a highly-leveraged business, it is vital that those whose equity investment in the bank is at stake be represented on these committees. The development of a cadre of business development and loan officers is vital to the success of the Community Development Bank concept.

13.5.5 Investment Banking Services

As was indicated in the discussion about commercial banking, Community Development Banks will quite naturally find that there are investment banking activities which their clients require: in particular, a successful business may require a faster growth in its equity than is allowed by the growth of equity through retained earnings. The restrictions of the Glass–Steagall Act would not apply to these banks, for there is no feasible alternative to a Community Development Bank for raising the size of equity infusions that are contemplated. The dollar value of each underwriting that a CDB will undertake will fall below the usual minimum for underwritings by investment bankers.

Investment banking activities consist of underwriting and taking positions in the equity and bond liabilities of clients. The position-taking may well be by way of a venture-capital fund in which the bank joins with other investors. Although Community Development Banks will often be centered in a poor neighborhood of a city, there are local firms, both service and manufacturing, whose principles both know the community and have investable funds. Even the poorest of our city neighborhoods is not a community that is universally impoverished.

One aspect of the investment subsidiary of the Community Development Bank will be the development of the special knowledge needed for the businesses it works with to qualify for the various aids to small businesses that are part of the Small Business Administration and other Federal State and local agencies.

The existence of underwriting and investment bank activities within the Bank for Community Development Banks implies that the Bank will be involved in the governing of some of the businesses which it serves.

The Federal Bank for Community Development Banks, described earlier, may well take positions in the equity and long-term debt issues that CDBs underwrite. This may be done directly, or by way of venture-capital funds which it sponsors that may well be able to raise money on capital markets. The Federal Bank for Community Development Banks may well create mutual funds whose assets are liabilities of either the companies underwritten by the Community banks or the venture-capital funds that Community Development Banks sponsor.

The investment banking activities of the Community Development Banks and the Bank for the Community Development Banks are natural outgrowths of the banking activities of these institutions. As the business development and loan officers of the community banks 'work their street', they identify and develop not only clients for the loan and the underwriting of the bank, they also develop knowledge of those in the community who are able to invest in other businesses. The essential postulate of the community development banking approach is that the poorer and underbanked parts of our economy are not a 100 per cent economic wasteland:

that there are human, entrepreneurial and financial resources that can be developed.

13.5.6 Asset Management Advice and Special Accounts

The advice that lower-income and wealth persons get about investment alternatives is very poor. The CDBs might develop a department that advises and sells instruments for the portfolios of its clients. There is, however, a potential conflict of interest if a CDB were to give advice and sell its own liabilities to its customers, a matter which will fall under the supervisory responsibility of the FBCDB.

13.5.7 Structure of a Community Development Bank

A CDB will be organized as a bank holding company under a special act of Congress. The holding company will have a variety of structures. Examples are:

(a) A narrow bank which includes a fee for service check-cashing operations and a pass-book savings facility. This narrow bank would be able to make credit or debit cards available to its clients. The payments on credit card balances may well be automatically debited from the pass-book savings account and forwarded electronically to the card processor;

(b) A commercial bank which will also do mortgage financing. This commercial bank will do ordinary commercial bank business for clients in its neighborhood. Its funding would be by means of business checking accounts, household checking accounts and certificates of deposit;

(c) An investment bank is a key subsidiary of a CDB. Its main function will be to intermediate in a process which furnishes equity and longer-term debt funding to both existing businesses as well as new businesses in its community. One function of the business development and loan officers is to discover the potential entrepreneurial resources in the community that require financing. Another will be to know the Federal, State and Local agencies and laws that aim to advance business development and to expedite and facilitate their use;

(d) A trust bank which would not only act as a Trustee for various activities but would also operate a financial advise facility.

13.5.8 Chartering and Financing of CDBs

The US Congress will define the chartering process and the activities of CDBs in legislation that will also authorize the Federal Bank for Community Development Banks. These banks will be a special category of Federally chartered banks that will have powers and responsibilities beyond those granted to either national or state banks. The chartering process needs to be simple. Entry should be relatively easy and not costly. The acceptance of rather close supervision and guidance by the Federal Bank for Community Development Banks will be a prerequisite for chartering. The financial parameters for a Community Development Bank may well run from a minimum private equity investment of $1 million and a maximum total equity investment of $10 million. The Federal Bank for Development Banks may well be authorized or instructed to match the initial private investment, up to a maximum of $5 million per CDB.

These limits are set because of the prudential rule that no single financing relation should involve more than 10 per cent of a banks capital and surplus. These parameters make the maximum financing relation at the smallest of these institutions $200 000, and the maximum at the largest $1 million.

If we use an 8.5 per cent capital to asset ratio, the total footings of the CDBs will run from $24 million to $120 million. However as the 'narrow bank' facility can operate at a 40 to 1 ratio, a CDB that specializes in savings and payment facilities could have as much as $400 million in total assets.

13.6 THE CDB ROLE IN THE US ECONOMY

The Clinton/Gore proposal for Community Development Banks called for some 100 such banks over 4 years. Even if each of these banks has assets of $100 million by 1998, they would total only $10 billion. A set of financial institutions that add up to $10 billion is not very impressive in an American economy that will have a Gross Domestic Product much in excess of $8000 billion by the time these institutions can make a significant contribution to the prosperity of their area.

These institutions are not to be envisaged as a significant counter-cyclical force, nor as a major factor in the growth of the economy. They are to be envisaged as a set of institutions that cover a gap in the ongoing institutional structure. They may well provide part of the institutional setting in which a climate of opportunity replaces stagnation for many segments of the population.

14 Finance and its Reform: Beyond Laissez-Faire

Gerard Caprio, Jr. and Lawrence H. Summers

14.1 INTRODUCTION

The reform of financial systems is an area of economics which has seen broad swings in economic thought. For much of this century, with notable exceptions such as Schumpeter, orthodox thought was that money and finance did not matter or were not all that important in the development process. However, by the mid-1970s, the orthodoxy held that financial repression had to be stopped at all costs, and this liberalization in the financial sector led the way for the more general acceptance of the view that reliance on the free market should be complete. Likewise, in the early 1980s the pendulum swung back to the left in the approach to financial systems a bit earlier than it did in other areas of economics. Based partially on evidence, especially from Latin America, that overly rapid reform had real costs, and partially on an increased appreciation of market failure in finance, it was accepted in the financial sector that blind adherence to free market principles was not quite appropriate.[1] And a counter-counter revolution is in sight, with some swing back towards the view that the market makes a mess of it but the government makes it even worse.

The status of this debate is of direct relevance for developing countries and transitional socialist economies (TSEs), where financial crises – overt and hidden – are rife and authorities are confronting basic decisions about the role of government in the financial sector.[2] Some policy makers and advisers in particular appear to be embracing 'the market' without a clear appreciation of its limitations in the area of finance. Moreover, in addition to the well-known episodes of bank failures in the United States in the 1980s (and ongoing concerns in the 1990s), other industrial-country governments, including those from Scandinavia to Japan, are experiencing concerns about – and large actual and potential losses in – banking. Indeed, latest unofficial estimates place non-performing loans (NPLs) for the Japanese banking system at 42–58 trillion yen ($336–464 billion); if half of these NPLs result in losses, the cost would be roughly equal to estimates of actual losses in the S&L debacle ($150 to 225 billion) in the United States and *a fortiori* would represent a larger fraction of GNP.[3]

Developing countries also offer lessons on financial reform for other countries. In some, banking systems that were restructured just a few years ago are in difficulty again. And in several developing countries, as in the industrialized world, banking systems liberalized with little attention to their initial conditions encountered subsequent financial distress. Given the generality of financial sector crises, then, it is opportune to reflect on how finance functions and on what should be the government's role in the process.

This chapter presents a few thoughts on finance that are relevant for policy makers regardless of their position concerning government's role in finance. The next section reviews some recent empirical evidence that lends support to the belief that market-oriented financial systems function better than those with heavy government intervention. But no study shows that the best intervention is no intervention, nor that the optimal rate of adjustment to a state of less intervention is instantaneous. Section 14.2 argues that, because of implicit or explicit government guarantees, coupled with externalities generated by the payments system, the financial system – and, in particular, those institutions called banks – are special. We suggest that, unless a convincing way can be found to remove these guarantees, bank management must resume its role as the main line of defence against unsafe and unsound banking, not least because of the difficulties inherent in external bank supervision. Therefore, incentives (influenced by the value of bank charters) should be increased to encourage management to reassume this role. Section 14.3 notes that there may be case for speed limits regarding some aspects of financial sector reform, and section 14.4 treats special problems where financial systems are either rudimentary – as in the very low income countries – or virtually nonexistent, as in the TSEs. Both situations call for a creative role for government, focusing on what governments can do best, and not expecting that the market can solve all problems satisfactorily.

We should note that prescriptions to increase the safety and soundness of financial systems should be offered with some modesty, as it is difficult to select any country that has succeeded. Our preferred solution,[4] which relies on increasing the franchise value of bank licenses, means less competition and perhaps less innovation, so the gains from safety and soundness must be weighed against possible losses in terms of a narrower menu of assets or poorer service. Authorities in each country must weigh these factors against the costs of inaction, or of some other way of lessening the riskiness inherent in many banking systems today. And careful analysis of any changes to financial system regulation is important, especially as it takes some time for changes in the rules of the game to affect the internal incentive systems within financial institutions.

14.2 IS IT REAL?

A first question, given the disparate views on its significance, concerns whether or not finance matters. To some, financial markets are chaotic casinos, whereas many economists regard it as dogma that a more efficient financial system insures a more efficient allocation of resources, funneling capital from low to high-value projects. Is there any evidence that this is actually the case? The first type of such evidence shows that financial development yields more growth. By itself, this evidence is unconvincing because any notion of how financial deepening operates could be expected to go along with growth. And it would not be implausible if a more sophisticated financial system developed in anticipation of future growth. So the attempt of this explanation to disentangle causality from timing evidence seems to be inherently limited.[5] A more interesting attempt by King and Levine (1992), finds that, in a broad cross sectional study, countries with a greater proportion of credit intermediated by commercial banks (in contrast especially to central banks in countries with large directed credit programs) grow faster, as do those with a greater share of credit being extended to the private sector. Moreover, this study finds significant links between bank intermediated credit, credit to the private sector, and economy-wide measures of efficiency. Perhaps most interesting of all, it finds that financial sector development had a more robust link to growth than did other policies.

Although this cross-section approach finds some relationship between the development of the financial sector and growth, it does not show that complete *laissez faire* is necessary to achieve adequate financial sector development. Indeed, King and Levine (1992) find evidence from a cross-section of 90 countries over the 1974–89 period that only severe interest-rate repression has a significant impact on growth (where countries are grouped on the horizontal axis in terms of their relative growth rates) – see Figure 14.1. This evidence is consistent with a study by Gelb (1989), which found that although interest rates and growth are positively associated, most of the relationship relates to reverse causation – higher growth raising efficiency and then interest rates. Direct causation from interest rates to growth was thought to represent more efficient intermediation of funds by the formal financial sector. Also, Reynoso

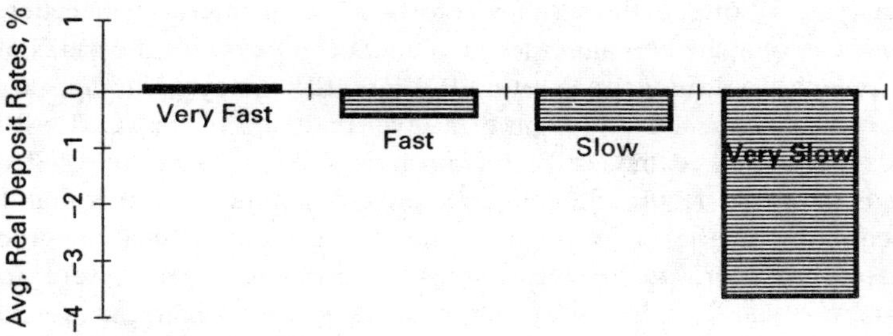

Source: King and Levine (1992).

Figure 14.1 Interest rates and growth: 1974–89

(1989) presented some evidence suggesting that the relationship between saving and real interest rates may be an inverted parabola, with saving increasing most significantly when rates rise from sharply negative rates to near zero.

Thus, empirical evidence appears to be consistent with a policy of ending severe interest-rate repression but while still maintaining some control of or intervention regarding rates, on the condition that no more than mild repression is allowed. In other words, while severe repression is disastrous for financial intermediation and economic growth, slight repression may be preferred to very high real rates, especially when the latter result from competition between banks with negative net worth. For example, Stiglitz (1993) has suggested on several occasions that demand deposit rates be limited to no more than treasury bill rates, especially where the latter are market-determined. This link would indirectly reduce (wasteful) competition among banks for funds to make high-risk loans in the hopes of restoring their net worth to positive levels, as occurred in the US S&L crisis. Where rates are administered, this rule would serve as a useful yardstick for officials.

Another type of evidence for the importance of finance looks at changes in flows of credit following the onset of financial reforms, in particular those that give banks greater discretion over their lending and interest-rate decisions. In Ecuador and Indonesia, Schiantarelli *et al.* (1992) show that credit flows changed significantly following the onset of financial reforms, with evidence that credit flowed to more efficient firms in both cases, even after adjusting for variables such as the age, size and export orientation of firms.[6] Moreover, in Indonesia there was a significant lessening of the extent to which small firms were credit constrained in their investment decisions following the 1983/8 reforms. These micro-level efficiency gains were matched by increases in (some) economy-wide measures of the incremental output–capital ratio (IOCR).[7] Efficiency gains appear less clear-cut in Korea, both in the firm-level data and in the IOCRs. Small firms there also became less credit constrained by the end of the 1980s, but this is likely the result of a deliberate government policy rather than from a reduction in the government's role in the credit allocation process. Again, however, where clear signs of efficiency gains were found (Indonesia and Ecuador), they were associated with a decrease in – not an elimination of – government intervention. So, while the combination of cross-section and country-specific evidence linking less-repressed financial regimes to increased efficiency is convincing, it by no means argues for an end to all interventions, but rather signals an appropriate direction for many countries.

14.3 COMPETITION IN FINANCE

Is too much competition possible in finance? Leaving aside the problem of transition, would the optimum *optimorum* be a freely and fully competitive banking system in which the financial services had the character of perfect competition as idealized in economics textbooks? Several reasons have been offered for being skeptical of that goal. First, the significant externalities related to information issues in finance all point to problems if the market is left to its own devices. Second, some aspects of finance might be welfare-neutral or even welfare-reducing, as when productive activities are interrupted for the purpose of speeding up the clearing of financial markets.[8]

But perhaps the most important reason for being skeptical of a free market as the standard in finance is, what can be called, the deposit insurance conundrum. Many countries have explicit deposit insurance; many countries do not. But in no country is it convincing that the government would be willing to let large financial institutions collapse without taking some kind of action.[9] Indeed, US authorities were not able to allow the Chrysler Motor Company to close, so it is difficult to believe that G.M., with its large financing company, or American Express, much less Citibank, would be permitted to fail. Also, US monetary authorities injected a great deal of liquidity at the time of the 1987 stock market crash, with estimates up to $10 billion in the days immediately afterwards, and an even larger sum before it. It is argued that heavy moral suasion was applied to encourage banks to support brokerage houses, and it is noteworthy that although 58 houses closed in the month after the crash, no large brokerage firms went under.[10]

Many economists think that the case for deposit insurance is clear – their grandmothers should have it but the rich should not. However, there are actually two reasons for having deposit insurance – not only to protect the small saver but to insure the stability of the payments system by preventing rapid withdrawal of 'hot' money. In the modern era, institutional funds can be withdrawn from a bank well before depositors can even queue up outside the bank's doors. The attempt to limit deposit insurance by concentrating on small savings alone, therefore, is not good strategy, as it only encourages large depositors to be more nervous or to spread their large sums into smaller accounts.

Some type of deposit insurance will need to be provided, but is this a function of the private sector or the government? The argument to let the market take care of it is, at least on the surface, persuasive. Without government-provided insurance, depositors would be more inclined to try to monitor their own institutions, and banks would be encouraged to form co-insurance groups or other coalitions, such as the clearing-house system in several US states in the nineteenth century.[11] However, notwithstanding the successes during this period, these systems encountered problems when banks were encouraged or compelled by legal limitations to concentrate their risks. Large numbers of geographically separated, undiversified banks are difficult for banks themselves – or their supervisors – to monitor.

To be sure, banks can be made safer and easier to monitor in many countries by allowing or encouraging them to diversify. The US banking system has been more prone to crises and failures, compared with its Canadian counterpart, largely because of the US ban on interstate branching, which only began to erode in the 1980s, but has yet to be abandoned. Thus, Canadian supervisors have both fewer and more diversified institutions to monitor. Many developing countries' financial systems are more similar to that of the United States: their banks are undiversified due to a combination of small economic size and the concentrated structure of individual economies, in conjunction with capital controls which prevent banks from holding any significant proportion of assets overseas. Consequently, without an abandonment of controls on capital flows (which in many countries is conceived of as the last stage in the reform process), and an easing of branching restrictions among countries, many developing-country banks will necessarily be riskier than their industrial-country counterparts.

Authorities have to be concerned about making banks safer because, ultimately, they will be held accountable when (sufficiently large) banks fail. The counter-argument, that depositors can monitor banks effectively, is not convincing. Empirical studies of the stock market performance of US banks in the 1980s find little evidence that stock prices were able to anticipate the downgrading of banks to problem status.[12] In some cases, the market appears to have gotten the direction of change generally right but the magnitude of price decline was not statistically significant. Moreover, for those banks that Simons and Cross found did experience stock price declines (12 of their sample for which the market at least got the direction of change right, even if statistically insignificant), little negative commentary was discovered in the financial press about these banks. But perhaps most damaging was their finding that insiders – managers and directors – were more often buying shares immediately before the downgrading![13] So there can be little credibility to the assumption that depositors will be able to monitor banks effectively. Governments will, therefore, be impelled to provide explicit or implicit deposit insurance; even a government which wanted to renounce this role could not, given that so many other governments are providing this insurance.

What does this mean? The basic economics invoked here are clear enough – a bank with few assets has a strong incentive to take risks. These risks enable it to compete for deposits more effectively and if it does not win, it is the taxpayers who lose. Even banks that are not inclined to take advantage of deposit insurance will be encouraged to do so in order to compete for deposits. A few bad apples, therefore, create strong pressure toward involvement in risk taking by bidding away deposits. So bank failures will likely continue to be a part of the developing-country financial landscape, barring major changes. Supervision is one part of the solution to this problem; any part of the world without supervision proves that this is true. But supervision faces chronic problems in many countries, typically being starved of resources and subject to severe pay constraints. Moreover, both political and economic forces lean towards supervisors keeping silent about problem banks until net worth is already negative. And the above evidence on stock market anticipations of bank failures also does not give solace to those who believe that supervisors will be able to serve as the main defense against failure. So while better supervision is needed in many countries – both developed and developing – we argue that it is unrealistic to expect government supervision to be the main line of defense.

A second solution is often dubbed 'narrow banking', meaning that banks can be made safe by being required to invest solely in short-term riskless securities, such as treasury bills. Only safe banks would be 'backed' by the government, while all other financial institutions could offer a variety of financial products – even, perhaps, demandable, fixed-rate deposits – but would not be allowed to call themselves banks and would not have government guarantees.[14] Proponents of this solution point to the success of money-market mutual funds, and assume that narrow banks will behave similarly, while critics say that there is insufficient supply of riskless assets (T-bills) to back the potential demand for riskless deposits. But both views neglect changes in the price of riskless assets; in particular, these prices will rise in a narrow banking world if society values such assets so highly. This will occur to the delight of government debt offices but will also lead narrow banks – and the less supervised non-banks – to want to hold some less secure paper.[15] Indeed, one possible result would be that nonbanks would offer deposit accounts backed by higher-yielding assets, which could be subject to default. Thus, while this solution has much to recommend it, authorities may be reluctant to try an untested model, and it will only prove effective if nonbanks, *regardless of size*, are allowed to fail.

Another possibility is to raise capital requirements to high levels; but the difficulty is, first, that it is hard to get international agreement on capital requirements and, second – and relatedly – that capital requirements appropriate for small, low-income countries may be inappropriate for more diversified, higher-income neighbors. Yet, if one country were to raise capital requirements above that of others – without a commensurate increase in expected profits – then that country's banking system would move offshore.[16]

A better solution to the deposit insurance conundrum relates to bank profitability and capital. Successful banking institutions require some cushion of profitability and capital, a cushion that could be driven out by turning the financial industry into one characterized by wide-open entry. As is true for nuclear power plants, *free* entry is not sensible in banking, as unfavorable chain reactions – bank runs – are possible, and the adverse fallout can be severe, in terms of the damage done when payments systems are destroyed and barter returns.[17] One of the reasons why the United States had a financial crisis in the 1980s, rather than in the 1950s, is not entirely macroeconomic, as the 1950s was a decade marked by recessions and sluggish growth. At least in part, it is that over time, technological change and regulatory arbitrage led to reductions in barriers to entry in the deposit-taking and lending business, eroding bank profits and forcing banks to accept or vigorously solicit riskier business. In other words, the franchise value of a bank license was sharply reduced. When that franchise value was eroded, bankers stood to lose less by going bankrupt; with no franchise value there was no reputation to protect and no reason to avoid going bankrupt. And the S&L problem was worse than that in the commercial banking sector, largely because more severe restrictions on asset and liability choices of the former group led to a greater erosion of franchise value; a government guarantee coupled with low franchise value can be expected to attract all sorts of gamblers to an industry.[18]

So, a solution to this conundrum should include some way by which the franchise value of bank licenses is enhanced. Entry limits are one way: authorities should be prepared to restrict entry in order to allow higher bank profits and a build up of capital, in this way leading to an excess demand for bank licenses. Indeed, as Calomiris (1992) has described, it was by restricting entry and allowing for accumulations of profits (bank charter value) that American banks grew and promoted economic development in the early 1800s. When bank licenses have a significant value, bank management will be more likely to set up internal controls and oversight systems that will help to preserve their franchise. Then, bank managers will be the first line of defense, with supervisors there to assist, working with managers in ferreting out unsafe and unsound banking practices. Supervisors will, of course, be needed to assure that required capital and provisions needed are actually there, especially since, even with a high franchise value, some entrepreneurs with very short-term horizons could still be attracted to banking; a bank license in the wrong hands could indeed become a license to steal. Note that this solution has some similarities with that of raising capital requirements, in that owners would have a larger present investment or expected future profits at stake, either of which would encourage safe and sound banking. Also, higher capital requirements would drive banks out of existence and would result in a higher spread between borrowing and lending interest rates.[19] But the franchise value solution does not rely on getting international agreement. Rather than driving banking offshore, greater franchise value would create an excess demand for bank licenses in the country where a bank franchise is truly valuable. Depositors might try to move abroad if insufficient competition led to low deposit rates, but bankers will quickly deduce that deposits are more mobile than loans, given information problems, and price their products accordingly.

In the United States, some may argue that this solution is not feasible: nonbanks have already 'won over' the better risks (blue-chip clients), and financial sector firms can get around any barriers set up to make banking more profitable. However, this view neglects the use of regulations in the United States to reduce the franchise value of bank licenses, in particular by limiting interstate branching. A complete end to these barriers would lead to rapid consolidation of US banking and, likely, boost the value of surviving banks. Truly national banks – certainly fewer than the 12 000–13 000 at present – would be well-placed to compete with non-banks, especially if the current drive to widen the ability of banks to engage in securities-related business continues to be expanded. With stronger national banks, there is little reason to believe that the US bank failure rate would differ significantly from the far lower rate in Canada or Germany.[20]

In developing countries and TSEs, financial engineering is far less advanced, and bank supervision skills are far less developed. Thus, keeping entry limited and, thereby, promoting the franchise value of bank licenses may be the best hope of fostering the spread of safe and sound banking to these countries. But paying attention to franchise value (or bank capital) alone will be insufficient in small, highly specialized economies, as the franchise value (or capital requirements) of banks needed to ensure safe and sound banking might be quite high. In these cases, authorities will need to encourage safe international diversification of banks, as well. Indeed, one could envisage a menu of choices on entry and portfolio limits. When confronted with the choice between allowing pockets of wealth to accumulate at home or permitting the investment of domestic savings abroad, eventually politicians may converge more to the former solution.[21] Authorities will then have to struggle with the tradeoff between too little competition and innovation and potentially unsafe banking practices.

14.4 CONSTRAINTS ON REFORM: POSSIBLE SPEED LIMITS

Should that deregulation which is desirable happen as quickly as possible? The above qualifications notwithstanding, the direction that is appropriate in most countries of the world is clear. Many countries have excessive and/or inappropriate financial sector regulations that are aimed at meeting a variety of goals, such as that of providing cheap credit to the government and to preferred sectors or individuals. Yet contrary to simple minded economics, it seems that for both macroeconomic and microeconomic reasons one should move forward with some caution. First, some of the seeming successes, Malaysia and Korea, moved quite gradually in their reform efforts, in part because they enjoyed the luxury of favorable macro circumstances.[22] Second, financial reforms affect incentives, and it likely takes some time for the ramifications of these changes to filter through to affect internal bank incentive systems. Banking systems that have been designed to respond to government directives will not instantaneously adjust to commercial methods, even if injected with fresh capital and told that all restrictions are off. Third, financial repression, whatever its other aspects, is a way of collecting government revenue, directly, when the banking system has to hold government bonds and, indirectly, when interference with their intermediation reduces interest rates and, therefore, makes it possible for government bonds to remain more attractive than they otherwise could.

One of the lessons learned, after a decade of experience with structural adjustment programs, is that fiscal stability is essential to the broad consequences of reform and that it is often true that bad taxes are better than no taxes. Where the fiscal situation is difficult, it is appropriate to undertake reform more gradually than would otherwise be done. Just as there is a dynamic within the government, whereby many are worried about the budget deficit, but more concerned about their favorite government program, there are similar tendencies among many economists who specialize in certain sectors. Financial specialists want financial repression reduced or eliminated; trade-oriented economists want tariffs reduced; human-resource experts want more total spending; and infrastructure advisers want more infrastructure. So, in the end, nobody is left to focus on the problem of the budget deficit. This orientation is understandable: after all, governments are not known for achieving budgetary savings in the absence of strong pressures, and sector specialists may respond by pressing for more than they reasonably hope to obtain. Bargaining strategies aside, the most sensible course of action would then appear to be to set out a reform program over a period of years, putting pressure on the budget but giving time for realistic budgetary realignments. In the context of financial reform, a government that is funding itself by the forced allocation of bonds to commercial banks might be weaned of this habit over a fixed time horizon.

Another reason for gradualism in the financial sector is that reform in this area cannot, prudently, run too far ahead of those in the real sector. Abrupt reform, such as immediate interest-rate deregulation or bank recapitalization, should be linked explicitly to real sector changes. Complete interest-rate deregulation is unwise when basic macro stability is wanting, as the danger of high and fluctuating rates can impair the stability of otherwise viable firms.[23] As Stiglitz notes, if the government is guaranteeing deposits, then, it is difficult to justify deposit rates above the riskless rate on short-term T-bills. Bank recapitalization, another 'sexy' step in financial reform, is often wasteful where steps are not taken to assure that good money will not be thrown after bad. These steps not only can be expected to entail replacing bank management and installing an effective incentive system and risk evaluation and control processes, but also in many cases ensuring that factors external to the bank are corrected, as well. This may mean removing legal restrictions that limit portfolio diversification or, as in many TSEs, restructuring enterprises.

It should be clear, however, that the case for gradualism does not mean inaction. Governments can move rapidly to eliminate the grossest form of credit subsidies and restore interest rates to levels, at least, close to inflation rates. In fact, Malaysian authorities removed much of the subsidy element for directed credit early in the reform process. Many financial sector reforms are long gestating, can be started at little cost immediately, and are *sine qua nons* for private-sector development. Training of commercial and central bankers, creation or upgrading of accounting and auditing standards (and professions), and legal and judicial reform all help financial markets function by improving methods for contract monitoring and enforcement and will speed the development of markets. In most of these areas, there are significant externalities, so that, without government involvement, less investment will be forthcoming; foreign assistance and expertise also can help to speed up the process, either by providing advisory services or funds conditional on the achievement of certain reforms, especially those where domestic interests are a barrier.

14.5 SPECIAL CASES?

At least two areas stand out where there appears to be a special case for 'extra-market' action. The first set concerns bank regulation and the role for government intervention in the poorest economies, those classified as low-income developing countries. The above discussion of franchise value is, particularly, relevant here: if many industrial countries, including Japan and the United States, have difficulties in managing a banking system, the problems in this area must be very real. In very poor countries, the ability to supervise financial institutions will be even more limited than in the industrial world, and risks may be more pronounced, especially if the country's productive structure is relatively undiversified and capital controls limit diversification. And without substantial foreign assistance, there is, usually, only quite limited bank supervision. In this environment, allowing the market to create its own financial institutions through free entry entails great risk. Instead, governments can intervene and restrict the supply of bank licenses and attempt to ensure that only reputable persons enter into banking. The creation of monopoly rents will both encourage the internal control over banking, without which it will self destruct, and also stimulate the creation of pockets of wealth which can be used to advance real sector development.[24] Indeed, some small, low-income countries already have just a few banks that make high pre-tax profits, but then the government taxes them away, so the banks have little franchise value to preserve.

An even greater difficulty for poor countries concerns government intervention in pricing and allocating credit and in encouraging the spread of the banking habit, especially to rural areas where the cost of delivering banking services is high. As several authors have noted, the grounds for intervention often are unclear, and the record in many countries inspires little confidence.[25] For both the industrial and agricultural sectors, the scarcity of medium and long-term finance in many low-income countries is not disputed, but the popular solutions – set up an institution that will only intermediate medium and long-term funds or require existing banks to lend long some part of their resources – have routinely failed. These solutions are based on the notion that such finance is not provided because of information imperfections. Unless public-sector banks are better at collecting funds or borrowers more prone to pay back when loans are subsidized – in both cases usually far from the truth – neither the information asymmetries nor enforcement problems can be corrected by these direct interventions. Thus, Calomiris, Hubbard and Stock (1986) find that defaults on US government credit in agriculture were double those on private loans, while forced term lending is regularly cited as a factor behind a retrenchment in intermediation.

Rather than information problems, other culprits – macro instability and government failure to honor its own commitments – often appear when term finance is moribund. Also, where the legal system reduces to creditors the value of collateral, short-term contracts are a way of maintaining control over borrowers, as noted by Gertler and Rose (1992). Judicial and legal reform, clarifying property rights, and possibly subsidizing the development of information capital are areas in which governments could better contribute to alleviating the shortage of term finance. The former areas would help improve the returns to intermediation once banks and other financial firms had established themselves, while the latter would contribute to a reduction in the fixed costs of establishing a financial institution.[26] Even a postponing of tax liabilities, perhaps by allowing little or no taxation (or an investment tax credit) during the initial years of a firm's life, could help improve borrower net worth and, thereby, increase access to credit. Once initial banking relationships are established (after perhaps 2 years or so), this form of subsidy could be ended. But this is a last resort intervention, as it may lead to abuses and could prove unnecessary. Banks and informal lenders have shown themselves to be willing to invest in acquiring information where they can exploit the profits to be made from lending (Aleem, 1990). Term finance can also be encouraged by fostering the development of short-term money markets, whereby governments, usually through their central banks, can encourage the development of the trading skills necessary to the growth of longer-term markets.[27]

In rural areas, the spread of the banking habit and the encouragement of finance to agriculture also has been an especially popular area of government involvement. As Akerlof (1970) and Calomiris (1992) note, agriculture is particularly fragile because of the concentration of risk and high fixed costs of establishing financial intermediaries in rural areas. As with lending to small and medium enterprises, governments have little direct ability to solve information problems, but may be able to intervene if high costs are keeping out financial institutions. Often, these high costs result from unclear property rights or other barriers to land sales; governments can help, especially by improving the enabling environment in these areas, as is relevant not only in low-income developing economies but in reforming socialist states (Calomiris, 1992). Where lending is restricted because of monitoring problems, increased reliance on peer monitoring may well prove fruitful, as in the case of Grameen Bank (Stiglitz, 1990). Since society at large benefits from the spread of the financial sector, some subsidization of these institutions appears warranted.

Unfortunately, governments often see greater benefits than appear to exist both from directing credit and from encouraging the spread of banking, and, especially, tend to pass of the costs to the commercial banks. They also get excessively involved in the credit process, leading commercial banks to cease to assess credit risk or monitor the loans, as the risk is viewed as ultimately born by the government. And ruling that banks must have a certain number of branches in rural areas or grant credit on preferred terms is costless to authorities in the short run, which is why they tend to do too much of what appears to be a socially beneficial act. In the process, bank franchise value is eroded and the banks ultimately respond to this new, and perverse, incentive environment. Thus, the challenge for governments is to keep interventions modest and not force the financial institutions to absorb the costs. For directed credit schemes, keeping programs relatively small and broad-based, like those in Malaysia, which also allowed banks to cover their average cost of funds plus a generous markup, appears to offer the best chance of succeeding both in directing credit to targeted groups and in avoiding large losses. The absence of a large subsidy element, in particular, figured prominently in explaining the success of the Malaysian schemes.[28] Interestingly, Japan's reliance on directed credit was much less than many have thought, with only 5 per cent of total credit in the 1950s accounted for by 'policy-based' loans (JDB, 1993). And any subsidy was quite small; first, because real interest rates were maintained in the neighborhood of zero and, second, and more importantly, because effective monitoring and control systems ensured a virtually 100 per cent repayment record, many times the rate in some developing countries today.

Other actions to help producers hedge risks, such as by fostering commodity futures markets or allowing residents to hedge in international commodity futures markets, would also contribute to the development and soundness of domestic credit markets. Where borrowers are unable to hedge themselves, specialized agriculture banks, that have been encouraged by many governments, concentrate risk further, which may account for the poor results seen in these institutions during the 1980s, when many commodity prices were weak. If government authorities wish to encourage rural finance, they should prefer to sponsor diversified institutions – recognizing the diversity of rural economic activities in most developing countries, as well as the need for loan diversification in financial institutions – and promote the use of hedging devices.

What of the special problems of transitional socialist economies (TSEs)? In some sense they are like low-income countries in having undeveloped accounting and enforcement systems, with poor or noisy information channels. However, the problems of pre-existing loan losses are much more formidable. TSEs also make no pretense about having either skilled bank supervisors or skilled bankers. Since these economies will have to function for some time with virtually no bank supervision and will be in environments fraught with risk, a radical solution – endowing bank licenses with a high franchise value, legislating quite high capital adequacy requirements, or moving to a narrow banking system – offers the best chance of successful reform. The polar extreme – completely free banking – makes sense *only* when the government is prepared to allow depositors of all institutions to bear losses; otherwise, 'free' banking will be expensive for the budget. Since government resolve often weakens when losses get large, this extreme solution is dangerous.

Another extreme is to ban all debt since the environment is so risky (McKinnon, 1991). This solution pays too little attention to the need to finance the new private sector and neglects the point here that banking can be made safe when bankers have adequate incentive to police themselves. Our preferred solution, promoting franchise value, may be close to McKinnon's in practice: with, initially, only a few licenses being granted to competent bankers, in all likelihood there will be a relative scarcity of debt finance compared with a free banking model, as he is encouraging. We would argue, however, that more profitable banking would lead to a healthier and less expensive banking sector, once the costs of financial crises are considered, yet would still allow for some debt-based financing.

Financial institutions in TSEs are faced with the challenge of financing the emerging private sector while assisting with the restructuring and/or closing of state enterprises, often in an environment of unstable average and relative prices and fluctuating macro policies. An additional complication is that, for most of the TSEs, the government presently owns much of the financial sector and cannot just walk away from the institutions.[29] One approach – close down all public sector banks and hope that private banks arise – will not be tolerated. Most countries, instead, will likely gravitate towards a combination of trying to reform existing state banks while encouraging entry, in particular, from foreign banks or joint ventures.

Even with entry, however, some government involvement is essential during the transition period. If all TSE banks were miraculously transformed into world-class commercial institutions, they would likely stop lending to all but a handful of private clients because of the riskiness of the environment. So while it may be useful to allow banks on their own to grant loans only on a commercial basis to small state-sector companies, no government – certainly no banking system – will long withstand the closure of a large portion of its industrial base. There is, therefore, no choice but to have credit decisions for large state enterprises made by a government body, either in conjunction with a state bank or through the budget. To ensure that this temporary solution does not become permanent, a limit on the proportion of total credit extended in such a non-commercial fashion could be established and then lowered over a period of years.[30] The government will likely become the caretaker of at least one institution to which many of the bad loans may be transferred, whether in a new fund or an existing bank. Since governments routinely are poor at collecting debts, any efforts in this direction should be contracted out to private firms.

14.6 CONCLUDING THOUGHTS

The common thread to this chapter is the notion that while market-oriented financial systems demonstrably appear to do a better job than ones with extensive government involvement, the assumption that perfect competition will solve all problems in finance is dangerous. Finance is different from steel or autos because of the externalities associated with the payments system, the importance of information problems, and the implicit or explicit government guarantees associated with deposits. We have argued here that, while many governments need to reduce their intervention in the financial system, these differences imply that perfect *laissez faire* competition may well not be the ideal. While governments should recognize this point – few allow anyone to enter banking – public pronouncements and the recommendations of many observers are, usually, to recommend a move to more competition. This view only makes sense under the assumption of no government guarantee, but in fact most governments do provide deposit guarantees, and only differ in the degree of explicitness of the scheme.

Informed views of what finance is about, combined with a look at how reforming economies have fared, also suggest that gradual reform is to be preferred. Deregulation of credit markets and interest rates is likely to be counterproductive as long as macro conditions are unstable and banks are both unsophisticated and have weak balance sheets. As has been clear in other settings, deregulating when banks are bust and bankers unskilled leads to gambling; the resulting losses and the increased volatility of financial markets can set back, rather than advance, the move to more market-oriented systems. However, faster progress can and should be attempted in the areas of institutional development, as noted above.

Governments that have a choice should not attempt to move from a severely repressed financial system to a lightly regulated one overnight. To be sure, some governments have little choice: TSEs are beginning a wide-ranging reform process effectively with no financial system, and need to move quickly. Still, complete *laissez faire* would be disastrous there, as would attempting to move rapidly to the types of systems in force in industrialized economies today, where banks freely make their lending decisions largely apart from the political system. While some new private banks can be licensed to deal with the new private sector, the transformation of the existing state banks will require at least a five–ten year commitment. Lastly, in all countries, governments must remain focused on doing what they do best: providing an enabling environment for the private financial and nonfinancial sectors. While market failure clearly can exist, governments should be rationed in their ability to use this argument as a justification for intervention.

Notes

The authors wish to thank Yoon Je Cho, Ian Giddy, Ross Levine, Millard Long, Donald Mathieson, Anthony Saunders, Andrew Sheng, and Samuel Talley for comments. The findings, interpretations and conclusions are the authors' own, and should not be attributed to the World Bank, its Board of Directors, its management, or any of its member countries, nor do they necessarily reflect the views or policy of the US Treasury.

1. Seminal articles are Akerlof (1970) and Stiglitz and Weiss (1981).
2. See World Bank (1989) for a description of financial distress indeveloping countries, and Caprio and Levine (1992) on the task of financial reform in TSEs.
3. Cargill and Mayer (1992) provide present value estimates of the insolvency and thrift bailout costs for US S&Ls, which represented as much as 4 per cent of GDP in 1991. See *Oxford Analytica* (4 June 1992) for a discussion of official and unofficial estimates of non-performing bank loans in Japan. The larger figure cited in the text for NPLs would be about 14 per cent of the 1992 GDP, and so the assumption in the text (that half of NPLs become actual losses) would put a 'guesstimate' of potential losses at 7 per cent of GDP.
4. It is useful to add that there is little consensus on reform strategies in this area, and that our proposed solution is not a policy of the World Bank or its Board.
5. Jung (1986) tries to disentangle whether finance causes growth or vice versa, and finds not surprisingly that the causality goes both ways.
6. That efficiency gains are possible is plausible. Even in the United States the magnitude of market imperfections that exist is impressive. Somehow the rich appear to have different investment opportunities than those that economists discuss; they scoff at either the five per cent return available on Treasury bills or the eight per cent adjusted real return available historically on stocks. Instead, these investors looking at yields in all sorts of sectors do not look at those with less than a 20 per cent expected return. And many Wall Street houses make substantial profits on arbitrage opportunities. One would assume that unarbitraged profit opportunities are present to a much greater extent in less developed countries. In a microeconomic sense, therefore, liberalization can make a significant contribution to growth.
7. Over a short period of time the IOCR is an unreliable guide to efficiency, and often is quite sensitive to how investment data are deflated.
8. See Summers and Summers (1989) for an elaboration.
9. The Argentine government currently is trying to convince its populace that it will let any bank fail, and has allowed some small provincial banks to close, with depositors taking a loss. However, this new policy has not yet been tested on a large bank.
10. Garcia (1989) provides these data and a view of Fed policy at the time of the crash.
11. See Calomiris (1992, 1993) and other references provided there.
12. See Simons and Cross (1991).
13. A Machiavellian cynic might say that the evidence on insiders probably reflects deliberate buying high to cover their tracks for still larger sales further in advance of the bank's demise.
14. This recommendation dates back to Simons (1948), in the best Chicago tradition, and is closely related to the recommendation for only allowing Islamic

banks, which are in theory checkable money-market funds. See Litan (1987) for an updated view.

15. With the decline of interest rates in the United States in 1991–3, there has been a move away from CDs and safer instruments in search of higher yields – even the junk bond market has enjoyed a resurgence. A move to narrow banking could reinforce this switch.
16. It might be argued that offering deposit insurance would tend to raise franchise value and thereby limit the offshore movement of domestic banks. However, this effect is only true *ceteris paribus*, and can be easily lessened by giving out too many bank licenses.
17. And supervising banking may be as difficult as regulating a nuclear power plant: at least – or at least insofar as scientists are aware – nuclear particles do not have an incentive to misrepresent themselves to regulators!
18. Weisbrod, Lee and Rojas-Suarez (1992) argue that the franchise value of bank licenses has declined in the United States and Japan.
19. With higher capital levels, banks would need larger interest spreads to show the same return on equity, *ceteris paribus*. So, in moving from lower to higher capital requirements, one would expect to see exit from banking until the risk-adjusted return attained its previous alignment with that in other industries.
20. It must be emphasized that reliance on this solution will only work within limits: if entry is restricted so tightly that substantial monopoly profits appear, nonbanks will attempt even more to offer products similar to those offered by banks. But within limits we think that it is feasible to have profitable banks and nonbanks operating side-by-side. Securitized finance or the issuance of paper directly to investors has enjoyed several booms (the 1920 and the 1980s most notably) but usually retrenches during the contractionary phases as investors are reminded of the risks they face. Also, investors confronted with the choice of bank deposits, bills, bonds and stocks, often choose to diversify among all of the above instruments. If nonbanks encroach sufficiently on banking, authorities will be faced with either extending guarantees to these activities or allowing banks into new forms of finance.
21. Just as local US banks often ended up financing money-losing ventures when they ventured outside their markets, and industrial-country banks lost sizeable amounts in foreign markets, developing-country banks also could lose money by investing abroad. But they could as well invest in global mutual funds and thereby enjoy a stable return uncorrelated with that in their own market. In this sense they would become less risky institutions. The main point is that in countries with 20 per cent to 50 per cent of GDP accounted for by one product, swings in the terms of trade will routinely wipe out all but the exceptionally well capitalized, or highly profitable, banks.
22. And when macro circumstances seemed poor, Malaysian authorities put reform efforts on hold and reasserted control of interest rates until borrower (and bank) net worth improved (Zainal *et al.*, 1992).
23. Gertler and Rose (1992) make this point clearly. See also Caprio, Atiyas and Hanson (1992) for additional preconditions for successful interest-rate deregulation.

24. Governments could license a few foreign banks and depend on the concern for the bank's own reputation to encourage them to monitor themselves and to bear the costs of imprudent lending. It is argued that Uruguayan authorities have relied successfully on this effect.
25. See Besley (1992) and Calomiris (1992) for a review of the arguments for intervention.
26. The subsidy could be paid to both banks and borrowers, in effect buying down the interest rate on initial loans for new borrowers, but of course would have to take account of budget pressures, as noted above. Caprio, Atiyas and Hanson (1992) and Gertler and Rose (1992) make this argument. Calomiris (1992) notes the importance of fixed costs in setting up banks in rural areas, but the argument holds wherever information is scarce.
27. Meek (1991) lucidly explains this point in the cases of Malaysia and Indonesia.
28. More subsidized credit was available directly from the budget (Zainal *et al.*, 1992).
29. Caprio and Levine (1992) elaborate on this argument.
30. The government also is the owner of state enterprises, many of which are transforming themselves into financial intermediaries through the accumulation (involuntarily on the creditor side) of interfirm credits. In Romania and Russia, these arrears have reached 80 per cent to 100 per cent of GDP. As owner of the responsible firms, the government must limit these credits if inflation is to be controlled. Caprio and Levine (1992) elaborate on this problem.

References

Akerlof, George (1970) 'The Market for Lemons: Quality Uncertainty and the Market Mechanism', *Quarterly Journal of Economics* (August) **84**.

Aleem, Irfan (1990) 'Imperfect Information, Screening, and the Costs of Informal Lending: A Study of a Rural Credit Market in Pakistan', *World Bank Economic Review* (September).

Besley, Timothy (1992) 'How Do Market Failures Justify Interventions in Rural Credit Markets', mimeo, Woodrow Wilson School, Princeton University (August).

Calomiris, Charles W. (1992) 'Getting the Incentives Right in the Current Deposit-Insurance System: Successes from the Pre-FDIC Era', in James R. Barth and R. Dan Brumbaugh, Jr. (eds), *The Reform of Federal Deposit Insurance: Disciplining the Government and Protecting Taxpayers* (New York, NY: HarperBusiness).

Calomiris, Charles W. (1993) 'Agricultural Credit Markets', in Avishay Braverman, Karen Brooks and Csaba Csaki (eds), *The Agricultural Transition in Central and Eastern Europe and the Former USSR*, A World Bank Symposium.

Calomiris, Charles W, Charles Himmelberg, Charles M. Kahn and Dimitri Vittas (1992) 'Evaluating Industrial Credit Programs in Japan: A research Proposal', mimeo, The World Bank.

Calomiris, Charles W, R. Glenn Hubbard and James H. Stock (1986) *Growing in Debt* (Cambridge, MA: NBER).

Caprio, Gerard Jr., Izak Atiyas and James Hanson (eds) (1992) *Financial Reform: Theory and Experience*, draft manuscript, The World Bank.

Caprio, Gerard Jr., and Ross Levine (1992) 'Reforming Finance in Transitional Socialist Economies: Avoiding the Path from Shell Money to Shell Games', Policy Research Working Paper 898, submitted to *World Bank Research Observer*.

Cargill, Thomas F. and Thomas Mayer (1992) 'US Deposit Insurance Reform', *Contemporary Policy Issues* (July) 10, 95–103.

Cone, Kenneth R. (1982) *Regulation of Depository Institutions*, unpublished dissertation, Stanford University.

Garcia, Gillian (1989) 'Lessons from the Crash of '87: Systemic Issues', *Bank Structure and Competition*, Federal Reserve Bank of Chicago.

Gelb, A. (1989) 'Financial Policies, Growth, and Efficiency', Policy Planning and Research Working Paper, WPS 202, World Bank, (June).

Gertler, M. and A. Rose (1992) 'Finance, Growth and Public Policy', Policy Research Working Paper, WPS 814, World Bank, (August).

Japan Development Bank (1993) 'Policy Based Finance: The Experience of Postwar Japan', draft.

Jung, Woo S. (1986) 'Financial Development and Economic Growth: International Evidence', *Economic Development and Cultural Change* (June) 333–46.

King, Robert and Ross Levine (1992) 'Financial Intermediaries and Economic Development', in Colin Mayer and Xavier Vives (eds), *Financial Intermediation in the Construction of Europe* (Cambridge: Cambridge University Press).

Litan, Robert E. (1987) *What Banks Should Do* (Washington, DC: The Brookings Institution).

Meek, Paul (1991) 'Central Bank Liquidity Management and the Money Market', in Gerard Caprio and Patrick Honohan (eds), *Monetary Policy Instruments for Developing Countries* (Washington, DC: The World Bank).

McKinnon, Ronald I. (1991) *The Order of Economic Liberalization: Financial Control in the Transition to a Market Economy* (Baltimore: Johns Hopkins University Press).

Reynoso, Alejandro (1989) 'Financial Repression, Financial Liberalization, and the Interest Rate Elasticity of Savings in Developing Countries', unpublished doctoral dissertation, MIT.

Schiantarelli, Fabio, Izak Atiyas, Gerard Caprio and John Harris (1992) 'Credit Where It Is Due? A Summary of Empirical Evidence', in Gerard Caprio *et al.*, *Financial Reform: Theory and Experience*, manuscript, The World Bank.

Simons, Henry C. (1948) *Economic Policy for a Free Society*, (Chicago, IL: University of Chicago Press).

Simons, Katerina, and Stephen Cross (1991) 'Do Capital Markets Predict Problems in Large Commercial Banks?', *New England Economic Review* (May/June).

Stiglitz, Joseph E. (1993) 'The Role of the State in Financial Markets', mimeo, Stanford University (January).

Stiglitz, Joseph E. (1990) 'Peer Monitoring and Credit Markets', *World Bank Economic Review* (September).

Stiglitz, Joseph E. and Andrew Weiss (1981) 'Credit Rationing in Markets with Imperfect Information', *American Economic Review* (June).

Summers, L.H. and V.P. Summers (1989) 'When Financial Markets Work Too Well: A Cautious Case for A Securities Tax', *Regulatory Reform of Stock and Futures Markets: A Special Issue of the Journal of Financial Service Research* (Boston: Kluwer Academic Publishers).

Weisbrod, Steven R., Howard Lee and Liliana Rojas-Suarez (1992) 'Bank Risk and the Declining Franchise Value of the Banking Systems in the United States and Japan', IMF Working Paper WP/92/45 (June).

World Bank (1989) *World Development Report*.

Zainal, Aznam Yusof, Awang Adek Hussin, Ismail Alowi, Lim Chee Sing and Sukhdave Singh (1992) 'Financial Reform in Malaysia', *Financial Reform: Theory and Experience*, draft manuscript, The World Bank.

Comment

DONALD J. MATHIESON[1]

The authors have provided us with an interesting chapter that stimulated my thinking on a number of policy issues. They successfully identify the key problem concerning developing countries, in general, and TSEs, in particular, that are undertaking financial reforms – namely, how to obtain the efficiency gains of such reforms without experiencing the adverse consequences that can arise as a result of excessive risk-taking because of the extensive implicit and/or explicit guarantees that the government will ensure the soundness of the financial system. Historical experience in developing countries has shown, time and time again, that the authorities will not allow large financial institutions to fail without taking steps to protect depositors (and often other creditors and even shareholders). The authors argue that the moral hazard problems created by these guarantees cannot be cured by enhanced supervision; they require that steps be taken to increase the franchise value of banks, primarily by limiting entry into the financial system.

In many respects, the authors' proposals are similar to the financial policies followed in many industrial countries from the 1930s to the 1970s. Limit entry, limit competition and, thereby, allow wide enough spreads between lending and deposit interest rates for banks to earn good profits and build up strong capital positions.

In evaluating the ability of the authors' proposals to reduce the cost of banking system bailouts, however, it is useful to keep in mind why the structures of most developing countries make it likely that, even with good financial policies, the authorities will be confronted with the need to support their financial systems more frequently than in the industrial countries. In particular, three structural characteristics of developing countries influence (1) the frequency of financial system bailouts, (2) the types of financing used to support these bailouts, and (3) the likely success of measures such as those contained in the Caprio and Summers' proposals to limit the cost of such bailouts.

First, many developing countries have inflexible financial systems with pervasive regulations governing entry, interest-rate ceiling, credit allocations, and so forth. In addition, financial institutions often hold highly undiversified portfolios. Financial institutions may hold claims on a broad range of domestic firms, but these firms may all be focused on the production of a rather narrow set of export commodities. Even in those countries which have adapted relatively flexible financial policies, banks are unlikely to hold highly diversified portfolios, especially if capital controls still limit the acquisition of external assets.

Developing countries are also typically subjected to larger (in comparison to their GDPs) domestic and external shocks than industrial countries. Moreover, given the often concentrated nature of their domestic industries, a large term of trade shock often means that a large proportion of the nonbank producers will be insolvent. While moral hazard problems can lead to a gradual erosion of capital positions of the banking system, large macroeconomic shocks often lead to an abrupt change in capital positions.

When developing countries are confronted with large external or domestic shocks and they decide to bailout the banking system, they essentially have to use the domestic fiscal and central banks systems to 'finance' this bailout. Since their creditworthiness deteriorates with large adverse shocks, they cannot finance the bailout by borrowing on open international capital markets (such as the Resolution Trust Corporation (RTC) has done) but rather must, typically, take the bad assets of the banking system onto the books of the Central Bank through an exchange of assets (somewhat like combining the balance sheets of the Federal Reserve and the RTC), and then, over time, take these assets off the books of the Central Bank either through fiscal transfers or an inflation tax.

Given the situation, many developing countries are eager to increase the efficiency and flexibility of their financial systems, but they also want to reduce, or at least not increase, the cost of supporting their financial systems. At the risk of some over simplification, two alternative strategies have been proposed for designing financial reforms in developing countries that would, at the same time, limit the cost of supporting the cost of the financial system. One approach would focus on limiting the insurance offered to the financial system, and essentially would force the nonfinancial sector to immediately absorb the losses incurred by the financial system. This could include such proposals as narrow banking (with fixed par value obligations but allowing for only a limited set of safe investment choices) or, alternatively, non-par value banking (for example, a mutual fund approach) that would involve households holding claims on the assets of banks rather than a fixed par value obligation of banks. The problem with this approach is whether there is a political consensus in most developing countries to let the nonbank sector incur these losses immediately rather than absorbing them, over time, through the fiscal accounts.

A second approach is to increase the capacity of the financial system to absorb shocks. This forces the owners of the financial institutions to be the primary absorbers of large external shocks. This could be accomplished by limiting entry and, thereby, enhancing the franchise value of banks, such as proposed by Caprio and Summers. It must be recognized that this approach is equivalent to an implicit tax-subsidy scheme. Limited entry will allow banks to set a wider spread between lending and deposit interest rates. This larger spread could, alternatively, be generated by a tax on the interest income of depositors and a surcharge on the interest paid by borrowers with the proceeds being given as a subsidy to the banks. Another alternative would be to use high capital requirements for banks together with better supervision. Yet another approach would be to allow for international diversification of the banks' assets. The objective of such diversification would be to separate the banks' income stream from domestic production or terms of trade shocks.

There are, however, a number of problems associated with implementing these cost-minimizing reforms. Implicitly, these proposals take most developing countries as closed financial systems with few linkages with external financial markets. However, there is a growing body of empirical evidence that suggests that these linkages have been much stronger than we thought, and have been growing as a result of the diminished effectiveness of capital controls. These linkages reflect the willingness and the growing ability of some residents of developing countries (typically the well-to-do and businessmen engaged in international transactions) to move funds when there are large differences between domestic and external financial market conditions.

What does this imply for the authors' proposed measures to promote safe and sound banking by limiting entry into the domestic financial system? First, the proposal is primarily aimed at dealing with the moral hazard problem, not so much with the macroeconomic shocks problem. In addition, to the extent that this scheme raises the domestic cost of borrowing and/or reduces returns on domestic deposits, then those residents that have alternative external sources of funds (possibly by repatriating past capital flight) or can acquire higher yielding external claims will move the location of their financial activities. While such a shift of financial activities reduces the cost of future bailouts by shrinking the real size of the domestic financial system, it also reduces the resources that the domestic financial system can make available to borrowers. Moreover, the more the franchise value of domestic banks is enhanced, and there may need to be a large increase in bank capital positions if one wants to confront large macroeconomic shocks, the greater will be the incentives for shifting financial activities offshore.

Note

1. I would like to issue the usual disclaimer that the views I am presenting are not those of the International Monetary Fund.

Index